2000

SUBCONTRACT
MANAGEMENT
MANUAL

MARY ANN P. WANGEMANN

2000

SUBCONTRACT
MANAGEMENT
MANUAL

Harcourt Brace Professional Publishing

A Division of

Harcourt Brace & Company

SAN DIEGO   NEW YORK   CHICAGO   LONDON

To my parents, Robert and Lorraine Pater, for teaching me to go after my dreams; my husband, Michael Wangemann, for supporting me as I chase my dreams; and my daughter, Lorraine Wangemann, whom I encourage to dream.

The publisher has not sought nor obtained approval of this publication from any other organization, profit or nonprofit, and is solely responsible for its contents.

Printed in the United States of America

ISBN: 0-15-606970-9

99   00   01   02   EBA   4   3   2   1

Contents

Preface

Subcontract Management Manual describes the processes and techniques you can use to select, develop, operate, manage, and close out subcontracts that support either commercial or federal business. The book is designed to be used by:

- Prime contractors working with subcontractors on commercial business

- Subcontractors working for prime contractors on commercial business

- Prime contractors and subcontractors working to support a government contract.

Contracting Environment

Subcontracting is inherent in the way we operate our businesses every day, because any individual, small business, small and disadvantaged business, or large business can either subcontract work to another company or perform as a subcontractor.

As companies strive to become more competitive, many are streamlining their operations and offering only their own core products and services. By focusing on these core competencies, companies can perfect the design and delivery of a few products and services, thereby providing value to their customers while securing and growing marketshare. At the same time, however, customer needs are becoming more integrated and complex, making it difficult for one company to provide by itself all the products or services required on a contract.

By subcontracting, this one company (or prime contractor) can effectively and profitably resolve this dilemma. The subcontracting relationship enables a prime contractor to provide varied products and services effectively and efficiently and improve its competitive position as it pursues new contracts or performs on existing contracts. That is, a subcontracting relationship allows the prime contractor to stay focused on providing its core products and services and to expand its marketshare by working with other companies to provide non-core competency products and services. Subcontracting also allows the prime contractor to share some of the risk associated with contract performance.

Subcontracting benefits the subcontractor as well. A subcontractor can broaden its customer base to include customers requiring a complex, integrated solution. This market is typically off-limits to companies that by themselves may offer only a small piece of the solution, because customers are looking for contractors that can provide the entire solution. By working with prime contractors that have established customer relationships and that are willing to share the risk and reward associated with contracts, companies that subcontract can offer their products and services (their core competencies) to a wider market.

About *Subcontract Management Manual*

Subcontract Management Manual presents effective, practical techniques for all phases of subcontract management in four parts. Part I, "Defining the Market," provides an overview of subcontract basics and explains a strategic planning process that a prime contractor or a subcontractor can use to define its role for a particular contracting opportunity. Part I also discusses the marketing efforts a prime contractor or a subcontractor can conduct to select a contracting program and a subcontractor. Part II, "Proposing the Solution," provides a description of the proposal development process and discusses after-proposal submission activities. Part III, "Performing the Contract," reviews the tasks required to start up a subcontract, subcontract performance and management issues, and the process for making changes to a subcontract. The final Part, "Developing and Administering the Solution," covers how a subcontract is developed and negotiated, how to administer the subcontract, and business ethics.

Each chapter contains four sections:

- The Process section covers the steps the prime contractor and the subcontractor must accomplish during a particular stage of the procurement.
- The Prime Contractor Considerations section discusses elements relevant to prime contractors.
- The Subcontractor Considerations section discusses elements relevant to subcontractors.
- The Government Considerations section discusses elements that the prime contractor and the subcontractor must consider when conducting business with the federal government.

Contractors and subcontractors can use *Subcontract Management Manual* as a reference throughout the subcontracting process. Specific examples show how to accomplish each of the tasks required. In addition, the accompanying CD-ROM contains checklists, forms, and contracts that will save you time at each step.

It is important, however, to review the samples provided in this book and then tailor them to meet the specific requirements of the particular contract and relationship: Every subcontract is different, and each subcontract should be developed according to the requirements of the prime contract and the relationship established between the prime contractor and the subcontractor.

Working with the Federal Government

Federal government contracting occurs between the government and a prime contractor. Although the steps involved in obtaining federal government business and commercial business are essentially the same, the government–prime contractor relationship is governed by federal government rules and regulations. *Subcontracting* occurs between two commercial companies. The subcontract relationship can be in support of either commercial business or federal government business. That is, there is no such thing as a federal government subcontract.

The government does not work directly with subcontractors; the government uses prime contractors as intermediaries. Subcontracts are always commercial relationships between two companies and are governed by the Uniform Commercial Code. It is true that in subcontracts that support federal government business, the prime contractor will "flow down" contracting clauses from the prime contract between itself and the government to the subcontract between itself and its commercial subcontractor, making the subcontractor subject to federal regulations. However, the federal government would hold the prime contractor accountable if the subcontractor failed to perform according to the contract.

In essence, government contracts typically require products and services that are beyond the scope of a single company. *Subcontract Management Manual* describes the subcontract formation. For companies pursuing prime contracts with the federal government, another work—*Federal Government Contractor's Manual*—describes in more detail how to effectively develop and perform as the prime contractor. Although both books cover the specific federal government process, either can be easily applied to the commercial business process.

Acknowledgments

This book has been accomplished with the continuing support of my agent, Richard Shulman; publisher, Sidney Bernstein, Esq.; director of sales and marketing, Andrew O'Donnell; acquisitions editor, Rachel de la Vega; and editor, Pat Gonzalez. The people at Harcourt Brace have been enthusiastic and helpful throughout each stage of the book development. My dear friend, Pam Murray, used her expertise as an indexer to make this book more useful to the reader. The love and support given to me from my father, Robert Pater, and sister, Lorie Pater, allow me to keep balance in my life. And none of this would have been possible without the love and encouragement that I receive from my husband, Michael Wangemann, and joy that I receive from our daughter, Lorraine Wangemann. My heartfelt thanks to each of you.

About the Author

During 13 years with EDS, Ms. Wangemann has worked in or managed every aspect of procurement and contract performance: marketing, proposal development, business management, contracts administration, technical and management solution development and delivery, contract start-up and shutdown, and strategic planning.

She holds a bachelor of psychology degree and certificate in business administration from the University of Maryland Baltimore County, a master's degree in information systems and business administration from the Johns Hopkins University, and a certificate in contracts administration from the University of Virginia.

She is an adjunct professor with the University of Virginia and teaches courses on marketing, contracting, performance, subcontract management, contract changes, career development, and federal procurement. Her classes are available on the Internet. She conducts seminars and guest lectures on procurement and contract topics for various graduate schools and Fortune 500 companies. She was a speaker at the 1998 National Government Electronics Industry Association and the 1999 National Contract Management Association (NCMA) National Education Seminar.

Ms. Wangemann was awarded the National Contract Management Association's 1996 National Education Award and 1997 Distinguished Service Award. In addition, she was recently named Outstanding Woman of the Year for Loudoun County in the field of business and professional development. Her writing has been featured in *Contract Management* magazine and in the book titled *Contract Changes*. Her book *1999 Federal Government Contractor's Manual*, is published by Harcourt Brace Professional Publishing. Her latest book, *State and Local Government Contractor's Manual*, is forthcoming from Harcourt Brace.

Ms. Wangemann lives in Ashburn, Virginia, with her husband, Michael Wangemann, and their 3-year-old daughter, Lorraine. You may reach the author with any comments or questions at wangemann@erols.com.

About the Computer Disc

The disc provided with *Subcontract Management Manual* contains sample forms, contracts, and checklists to help you cover all the phases of the contract process, from marketing to proposal development, and the specific tasks required for awarding and managing a subcontract.

Subject to the conditions in the license agreement and the limited warranty, which is displayed onscreen when the disc is installed and is reproduced at the end of the book, you may duplicate the files on this disc, modify them as necessary, and create your own customized versions. Installing the disc contents and/or using the disc in any way indicates that you accept the terms of the license agreement.

The data disc is intended to be used in conjunction with your word processing software. There are versions of each document in WordPerfect® 6.0 and Microsoft Word® 6.0, both for Windows™. If you do not own either of these programs, your word processing package may be able to convert the documents into a usable format. Check your owner's manual for information on the conversion of documents.

Installing the Templates

If you are using Windows 95 or above, select the Control Panel from the Start menu. Then choose Add/Remove Programs and select Install. To install the files on the disc using Windows 3.1, choose File, Run from the Windows Program Manager and type D:/INSTALL in the command line or type D:/INSTALL at the DOS prompt. You will be asked a series of questions. Read each question carefully and answer as indicated.

First, the installation program will ask you to specify which drive you want to install to. You will then be instructed to specify the complete path where you would like the files installed. The installation program will suggest a directory for you, but you can name the directory anything you like. If the directory does not exist, the program will create it for you.

You can choose to install the files for Word or WordPerfect. The program will automatically install the files in Word or WordPerfect subdirectories.

Opening the Files

Open your word processing program. If you are using Microsoft Word or WordPerfect 6.0, choose Open from the File menu. Select the subdirectory that contains the loaded files to list the names of the files. Highlight the name of the file you want to open and click OK or press ENTER. You can also open a document from the File Manager (in Windows 3.1) or in the Explorer (in Windows 95 or above) by highlighting the name of the file you want to use and double-clicking your left mouse button.

Refer to the Disc Contents on page xiv to find the filename of the document you want to use. The Disc Contents is also available on your disc in a file called "Contents." You can open this file and view it on your screen or print a hard copy to use for reference.

Word Processing Tips

Wherever possible, the text of the documents has been formatted as tables so that you can modify the text without altering the format of the documents. To maneuver within a table, press TAB to move to the next cell, and SHIFT + TAB to move backward one cell. If you want to move to a tab stop within a cell, press CTRL + TAB. For additional tips on working within tables, consult your word processor's manual. It might be helpful to turn on the invisible table lines in Microsoft Word while modifying the document. This can be done by selecting Gridlines from the Table menu. In WordPerfect, select Reveal Codes from the View menu to reveal all formatting codes at the bottom of the screen; this will help you to determine the shape of the table.

Microsoft Word and WordPerfect are equipped with search capabilities to help you locate specific words or phrases within a document. The Find option listed under the Edit menu performs a search in both Microsoft Word and in WordPerfect 6.0.

Important: When you are finished using a file you will be asked to save it. If you have modified the file, you may want to save the modified file under a different name rather than the name of the original file. (Your word processing program will prompt you for a file name.) This will enable you to reuse the original file without your modifications. If you want to replace the original file with your modified file, save but do not change the name of the file.

Print Troubleshooting

If you are having difficulty printing your document, the following suggestions may correct the problem:

Microsoft Word

- Select Print from the Microsoft Word File menu. Then choose the Printer function.
- Ensure that the correct printer is selected.
- From this window, choose Options.
- In the media box, make sure that the paper size is correct and that the proper paper tray is selected.
- Check your network connections if applicable.
- If you still have trouble printing successfully, it may be because your printer does not recognize the font Times New Roman. At this point, you should change the font of the document to your default font by selecting the document (CTRL + A) and then choosing Font from the Format menu and highlighting the name of the font you normally use. Changing the font of the document may require additional adjustments to the document format, such as margins, tab stops, and table cell height and width. Select Page Layout from the View menu to view the appearance of the pages before you try to print again.

WordPerfect

- Select Print from the WordPerfect 6.0 File menu. Then choose Select.
- Make sure the correct printer is selected.
- From this menu, press Setup.
- Ensure the correct paper size and paper source are selected.
- You may be having difficulty because your printer does not recognize the selected font. You can correct this problem by changing the base font of the document to your default font. From the Edit menu choose Select All (or press CTRL+A). The entire text of the document should be highlighted. Then choose Font from the Layout menu and highlight the font you normally use. Changing the font of the document may require additional adjustments to the document format, such as margins, tab stops, and table cell height and width. Select Two Page from the View menu to view the appearance of the pages before you try to print again.

Disc Contents

Filename   Document

MA-26   SOW Evaluation

MA-27   Types of Contracts

MA-28   Uses for Marketing Information

MA-29   Where to Find Subcontractors

Part 2: Proposing the Solution

PS-01   BAFO Information

PS-02   BAFO Preparation Steps

PS-03   Clarification Report (CR)/Deficiency Report (DR) Form

PS-04   Contract Volume Requirements

PS-05   CPSR Components

PS-06   CPSR Tracking Sheet

PS-07   Discussion Preparation Steps

PS-08   Documenting Risks

PS-09   Government RFP Sections

PS-10   Government Source Selection Hierarchy

PS-11   Live Test Demonstration Sample Agenda

PS-12   Management Solution Development

PS-13   Methods to Minimize Protests

PS-14   Negotiation Issues

PS-15   Negotiation Objectives

PS-16   Negotiation Strategy Items Checklist

PS-17   Parts of a Solicitation Package

PS-18   Price Proposal Milestones

PS-19   Proposal Cover Letter

PS-20   Proposal Kickoff Meeting

PS-21   Proposal Tracking Sheet

PS-22   Proposal Milestones

Filename	Document
PS-23	Proposal Tasks
PS-24	Proposal Tools
PS-25	RFP Considerations
PS-26	RFP Cover Letter
PS-27	Sample Agenda for First Meeting
PS-28	Sample Compliance Matrix
PS-29	Sample Job Description
PS-30	Sample Letter Proposal
PS-31	Sample Negotiation Summary
PS-32	Sample Proposal Outline
PS-33	Sample Source Selection Plan
PS-34	Sample Subcontract
PS-35	Sample Team Analysis
PS-36	Sample Training Section
PS-37	Section Strategy and Outline
PS-38	SEI Evaluation Process
PS-39	Site Survey Information
PS-40	Site Survey Milestones
PS-41	Solicitation Process
PS-42	Source Selection Plan
PS-43	Source Selection Plan Criteria
PS-44	Tasks to Complete the Technical and Management Proposal Sections
PS-45	Technical Solution Development
PS-46	Terms and Conditions Summary
PS-47	Work Functions for Prime Contractor and Subcontractor
PS-48	Writers' Information Packet
PS-49	Writing Proposal Sections

Filename   Document

Part 3: Performing the Contract

Contractor Resources on the Web

The following are some Web sites that you can use to access a variety of information regarding contracts, subcontracts, and government agencies.

For information on shutdowns caused by hardware and software Y2K issues:
http://millennia.bcs.com/Hlthsmry.htm
http://www.new.com/News/Item/0,4,15832,00.html

For information on Y2K remediation efforts:
http://www.pirkle-websites.com/solcomp.html
http://www.year2000.com/archive/Nfchaabouni.html

For information on Y2K insurance:
http://www.y2k.com/insuranc.html

To find the Department of Defense's (DOD) report titled "100 Companies Receiving the Largest Dollar Volume of Prime Contract Awards":
http://web1.whs.osd.mil/diorcat.html

For copies of the new consolidated GSA IT Schedule solicitation:
http://pub.fss.gsa.gov/adp/index.html

For an outline of the 12 acquisition goals of the DOD:
http://www.acq.osd.mil/ar/#otherhot

DOD's Acquisition Revolution homepage:
http://www.acq.osd.mil/ar/

For government standard forms:
http://www.gsa.gov/forms

For information on the North American Industry Classification System:
http://www.census.gov/epcd/www/naics

For acquisition reform information:
http://www.acq-ref.navy.mil

Government Printing Office home page, which provides ordering information for any government publication:
http://www.gpo.gov

For the *Commerce Business Daily's* listing of government contracting opportunities:
http://www.CBDNet.gpo.gov

For the GSA's multiple award schedule information:
http://pub.fss.gsa.gov/adp/index.html

For U.S. government health related information sources:
http://www.library.tmc.edu

Internet guide to the U.S. government:
http://www.unclesam.com

U.S. Code:
http://www.law.house.gov

Phonebooks and locators for U.S. government information:
http://usgovinfo.minigco.com

For miscellaneous government documents:
http://tbwa.volcano.org

Designed to give state and local government officials easy access to federal data:
http://www.statelocal.gov

For electronic government information products:
http://www.access.gpo.gov/su_docs/aces/aaces001.html –

For Army performance measurement information:
http://www.armyec.sra.com/knowbase/interim

GSA links to various procurement regulations:
http://www.gsa.gov/regions/4k/legal/legal25a.htm

For Procurement Executives' Association Guide to a Balanced Scorecard Performance Management Methodology:
http://www.statebuy.inter.net/bsc.htm

SBA applications:
http://www.sba.gov/sdb/forms.html

For information on the Convention of Contracts for the International Sale of Goods (CISG):
http://www.jura.unifreiburg.de/ipr1/cisg
http://www.un.or.at/uncitral

For information on CISG cases:
http://www.cisg.law.pace.edu

For information on Defense Information Technology Contracting Organization contracting opportunities:
http://www.ditco.disa.mil/dcop/Public/ASP/dcop.asp

Veterans Affairs budget:
http://www.va.gov/osdbu/forecast.htm

Government Agency Web Sites

Agency for International Development
http://www.info.usaid.gov/

Air Force
http://www.af.mil/

Armed Services Board of Contract Appeals
http://www.law.gwu.edu

Army
http://www.army.mil/

Census Department
http://www.census.gov/

Central Intelligence Agency
http://www.odci.gov/cia/ciahome.html

Commerce Department
http://www.doc.gov

Congress
http://www.access.gpo.gov/congress/index.html

Department of Agriculture
http://www.usda.gov

Department of Defense
http://www.defenselink.mil

Department of Energy
http://198.124.130.244

Department of Education
http://www.ed.gov

Department of Housing and Urban Development
http://www.hud.index.html.gov/

Department of the Interior
http://www.doi.gov

Department of Justice
http://www.doj.gov

Department of Labor
http://www.dol.gov

Department of State
http://www.state.gov

Department of Transportation
http://www.dot.gov

Environmental Protection Agency
http://www.epa.gov

Federal Communication Commission
http://www.fcc.gov

Federal Trade Commission
http://www.ftc.gov

Framework for global electronic commerce
http://www.ecommerce.gov/

General Accounting Office
http://www.gao.gov

General Services Administration
http://www.gsa.gov

Government EC-EDI standards
http://www.edi.it.si.disa.mil/edi-link.htm

Government Printing Office
http://www.gpo.gov

GPO databases
http://www.gpo.gov/su_docs/aces/aaces002.html

Health and Human Services
http://www.os.dhhs.gov/

House of Representatives
http://www.house.gov/

House of Representatives current floor activities
http://majoritywhip.house.gov/current/now.htm

Law Library
http://law.house.gov

Library of Congress
http://leweb.loc.gov

Marine Corps
http://www.usmc.mil/

National Guard
http://www.ngb.dtic.mil/

National Performance Review
http://www.npr.gov

Navy
http://www.navy.mil/

Office of Management and Budget
http://www.whitehouse.gov/WH/EOP/omb

Patent and Trademark Office
http://www.uspto.gov

Reserves
http://www.raweb.osd.mil

Security and Exchange Commission
http://www.sec.gov

Small Business Administration
http://www.sbaonline.sba.gov

Social Security Administration
http://www.ssa.gov

Supreme Court
http://www.fedworld.gov/supcourt/index.htm

Thomas Legislative information
http://thomas.loc.gov *or*
http://hypatia.gsfc.nasa.gov/NASA_homepage.html

Treasury Department
http://www.ustreas.gov

U.S. Postal Service
http://www.usps.gov/

U.S. Senate
http://www.senate.gov/

Veterans' Affairs
http://www.va.gov

White House
http://www.whitehouse.gov/

Acronyms Used in Contracting

Following is a list of acronyms commonly used in contracting.

ACO administrative contracting officer

B&P bid and proposal

BAFO best and final offer

BPAs GSA's blanket purchase agreements

CAGE commercial and government entity code

CAS Cost Accounting Standards

CASB Cost Accounting Standards Board

CBD *Commerce Business Daily*

CBI computer-based instruction

CBT computer-based training

CCB Configuration Control Board

CCR Central Contractor Registration

CDRLs contract data requirements lists

CISG Convention of Contracts for the International Sale of Goods

CLIN contract line item number

CO contracting officer

CONUS continental United States

COR contracting officer's representative

COTR contracting officer's technical representative

COTS commercial-off-the-shelf

CPM Critical Path Method

CPSR Contractor Purchasing System Review

CR clarification report

DAC Defense Acquisition Circular

DCAA Defense Contract Audit Agency

DCMO Defense Contract Management Office

DFAR Defense Federal Acquisition Regulation

DID data item description

DISA Defense Information Services Agency

DMC defense megacenter

DOD Department of Defense

DPA delegation of procurement authority

DPRO Defense Plant Representative Office

DR deficiency report

DUNS DOD Universal Numbering System

EAR Export Administration Regulation

EC/EDI electronic commerce/electronic data interchange

ECP engineering change proposals

ELOA executive letter of agreement

FACNET Federal Acquisition Computer Network

FAFO first and final offer

FAR Federal Acquisition Regulation

FARA Federal Acquisition Reform Act, also known as the Clinger-Cohen Act

FASA Federal Acquisition Streamlining Act

FOIA Freedom of Information Act

G&A general and administrative

GAO Government Accounting Office

GFE government furnished equipment

GFP government furnished property

GILS Government Information Locator System

GPO Government Printing Office

GPRA Government Performance Results Act

GSA General Services Administration

GSBCA General Services Board of Contract Appeals

GWACs Government Wide Access Contracts

ID/IQ indefinite delivery/indefinite quantity

IFB invitation for bid

IFN items for negotiation

ITAR International Traffic in Arms Regulations

IG inspector general

LTD live test demonstration

MTBF mean time between failure

NAFTA North American Free Trade Agreements Act

NCMA National Contract Management Association

NTE not to exceed

OCONUS outside the continental United States

ODCs other direct costs

OFPP Office of Federal Procurement Policy

PCO procuring contract officers

PERT Program Evaluation and Review Technique

PM program manager

PRAG Performance Risk Assessment Group

RFI request for information

RFP request for proposal

ROI return on investment

SADBOs Small and Disadvantaged Business Officers

SB small business

SBA Small Business Administration

SDB small, disadvantaged business

SEI Software Engineering Institute

SIC standard industry codes

SLA service level agreement

SOW statement of work

SSA Source Selection Authority

SSEB Source Selection Evaluation Board

SSP source selection plan

TCO terminating contracting officer

TDY temporary duty

UCC Uniform Commercial Code

VECPs Value Engineering Change Proposals

WBS work breakdown structure

PART 1

DEFINING THE MARKET

1 SUBCONTRACT BASICS

What Is a Subcontract?

A *subcontract* is first and foremost a contract between two parties that abides by all the rules applicable to contract law and interpretation. A *subcontract*, according to *Black's Law Dictionary*, is "a contract subordinate to another contract, made or intended to be made between the contracting parties, on one part, or some of them, and a third party." The Federal Acquisition Regulation (FAR) states a *subcontract* "means any contract…entered into by a subcontractor to furnish supplies or services for performance of a prime contract or subcontract. It includes, but is not limited to, purchase orders and changes and modifications to purchase orders."

It is interesting that the FAR provides a subcontract definition because the government *cannot* enter into a subcontract relationship with a company; the government is limited to only entering into prime contract relationships. In a prime contract relationship, the government can only take on the role of the buyer. The prime contractor can, and often does, enter into subcontract relationships in order to provide the required support to its government customer. Although the government does not formally enter into subcontracts, it does have the right to influence them, as we shall see later in this chapter.

A commercial company, however, may participate either as a buyer, a prime contractor, or a subcontractor on different programs. Although a commercial company can operate in all three capacities, when it acts as a buyer, the company does not have the same power as the government does to influence its subcontract relationships between a subcontractor and another company acting as a prime contractor.

Who Can Subcontract?

Any entity that has a product or service that is needed by another entity can subcontract. Examples of such entities include large companies, medium companies, small companies, small disadvantaged businesses, or individuals. Although the federal government cannot subcontract per se, one governmental agency can enter into a service level agreement with another agency to provide products or services.

Even though this is similar to a subcontract relationship, it is considered within the same overall organizational structure (the U.S. government) and does not constitute a subcontract.

Buyer–Seller Relationship

Because of the nature of subcontracting and the fact that a subcontract is part of a larger contractual picture, the buyer–seller relationship needs to be discussed. The two parties in a prime contract are the buyer or customer that needs the products and services and the seller that provides those products and services. The buyer can be either a commercial entity or the government. The seller is a commercial entity, which can be a large company, a medium company, a small business, a small disadvantaged business, or an individual. In a subcontract relationship, another tier of buyer–seller relationship exists that must be considered. There is still a buyer or customer and a seller, but in a subcontracting relationship the seller is known as the *prime contractor*. The contractual document that represents this relationship is the *prime contract*. The prime contractor becomes the buyer in need of products and services (to support its customer) and the subcontractor is the seller that will provide those products and services. The contractual document that represents this relationship is the subcontract. Table 1 provides a summary of the buyer–seller relationships.

Privity of Contract

An important aspect of levels of relationship has to do with contract privity. *Privity of contract* according to *Black's Law Dictionary* is "that connection or relationship which exists between two or more contracting parties." This means that in a prime contract, the prime contractor and the customer are the two parties to the contract. There are duties and obligations imposed on both of the parties in the contract and remedies that one party can use if the other party does not comply with the contract. In a subcontract, the prime contractor and the subcontractor are the two parties to the subcontract. Similarly, they have duties and obligations imposed on them in the subcontract and remedies that one party can use if the other party does not comply with the subcontract.

How does privity of contract affect daily transactions? In the prime-contract relationship, the prime contractor is responsible for fulfilling all the product or service requirements stated in the con-

Table 1. Summary Table of Buyer-Seller Relationships

Buyer	Who Can Be	Seller	Who Can Be	Contractual Document
Customer	Federal government, large business, medium business, small business, small and disadvantaged business, or individual	Prime contractor	Large business, medium business, small business, small and disadvantaged business, or individual	Prime contract
Prime Contractor	Large business, medium business, small business, small and disadvantaged business, or individual	Subcontractor	Large business, medium business, small business, small and disadvantaged business, or individual	Subcontract

tract. The prime contractor may use a subcontractor to help fulfill the requirements, however, the prime contractor is ultimately responsible for completing the work for the customer because privity of contract exists between the prime contractor and the customer. The prime contract gives the customer contractual remedies that it can use if the prime contractor does not fulfill its responsibilities. Similarly, in a subcontract relationship, the subcontractor is ultimately responsible for completing the work stated in the subcontract for the prime contractor because privity of contract exists between the prime contractor and the subcontractor. The subcontract gives the prime contractor contractual remedies that it can use if the subcontractor does not fulfill its responsibilities. For example, a subcontractor fails to provide a required product. The prime contractor is now responsible for finding a suitable replacement for the subcontractor's product. If the prime contractor does not find a suitable replacement, the customer could exercise its contractual remedies against the prime contractor but not the subcontractor. There is no privity of contract between the customer and the subcontractor because they are not parties to the same contract. There is privity of contract between the prime contractor and the subcontractor so the prime contractor could exercise its contractual remedies against the subcontractor that are available in the subcontract.

Benefits Derived from Privity of Contract

Privity of contract affords several benefits:

- *Single point of contact*—Privity of contract allows the customer to have the prime contractor as a single point of contact to solve prime-contract issues. The prime contractor can use many subcontractors to do the work, but the customer does not have to work with any of them directly because the prime contractor is ultimately responsible to the customer for completing the requirements of the prime contract. The same principle applies to the prime contractor. It has a single point of contact for each subcontractor it works with even if each subcontractor may have additional subcontractors to help it perform its contractual obligations.

- *Contractual remedies*—Well-constructed contracts have significant contractual remedies available to one of the parties in the event that the other party fails to perform according to the contract.

- *Accountability and control*—The relationship that is established by privity of contract provides accountability and control between the two parties because they are both involved in the contract and must abide by it.

When Do Problems Occur?

Privity of contract plays an important role in subcontracting: It defines who has responsibility to accomplish the contractual requirements. Problems can occur because of privity of contract. Some of these problems include:

- *Subcontractor acts on direction directly from customer.* For example, a subcontractor is working on site directly with the customer and the prime contractor does not have a representative at the customer location. The subcontractor is working closely with the customer and begins to take direction directly from the customer. Some of the customer's requests are different from the requirements in the subcontract between the prime contractor and the subcontractor. To further complicate the situation, the direction could represent a change from what is currently required in the prime contract between the prime contractor and the customer. In this situation, if the subcontractor is doing something that is not stated in the prime contract, the subcontractor is jeopardizing the prime contractor's contract because the customer could terminate the prime contract for default. Similarly, the prime contractor is not obligated to pay the subcontractor an additional sum for this new work, because the work being done is not covered in the subcontract.

- *Subcontract does not reflect changes in the prime contract.* Another possible change problem occurs when the prime contractor modifies the prime contract because of a change requested by the customer but fails to negotiate the change with the subcontractor that needs to do the work. In this situation, the prime contractor is obligated to provide the change to the customer, but the subcontractor is not obligated to provide the changed work until the change is negotiated between the prime contractor and the subcontractor.

Are Subcontracts Necessary?

Although privity of contract is important with regard to subcontracts, subcontracts are not always necessary between two parties. Basically, a subcontract is required between a buyer and seller when both or either of the parties have much to lose if the relationship breaks down. Therefore the two parties need to determine the level of relationship to see if a subcontract is required. The five levels of relationship are discussed in the following section.

Levels of Relationship

One-Time Purchases

The first level of relationship between a buyer and seller is a one-time purchase. For example, when a buyer walks into a store and buys a printer cartridge and uses a credit card to pay for the purchase, a subcontract is not necessary. There is some level of requirement on both parties—the buyer expects to get a printer cartridge that works and the seller expects the credit card payment to be valid—but other than these basic expectations, no further risks are assumed by either party. A subcontract is not needed for one-time purchases.

Purchase Orders

The next level of relationship between a buyer and seller is a purchase order. Continuing with the previous example, the buyer needs 100 printer cartridges and wants to negotiate a lower price per cartridge because the quantity of cartridges that he needs to purchase. In this case, the buyer and seller would enter into an agreement, which could be an oral agreement or one that is minimally documented. If a document is used, it would only need to state the names of the buyer and the seller, the type of cartridge being procured, and the negotiated price per item. Because of the slightly higher level of commitment between the two parties in this scenario—the buyer promises to buy 100 printer cartridges from the seller and the seller promises a lower per unit price—the buyer would typically issue a purchase order that briefly states the terms of the arrangement and, upon receipt, the seller would furnish the cartridges at the price agreed upon. In this example, the buyer and seller could either enter into a subcontract or just use the purchase order as the defining agreement.

Supplier

The next level of relationship between the buyer and the seller is the supplier relationship. Continuing with the same example, except that now the buyer wants to be able to buy thousands of printer cartridges over the next three years for its contract with the federal government. In this situation, the buyer needs the seller to guarantee that a certain printer cartridge will be available over the next three years and provide a fixed-price for the same period of time. Additionally, the buyer may need the seller to deliver the product to the customer and arrange for replacement cartridges if any are defective. Finally, the buyer will pay the seller 30 days after the government has received the cartridge and accepted it. Many of the buyer's terms are the same ones that the government is imposing on the buyer that, in this case, is also the prime contractor. Both the buyer and seller have much to gain and lose in this relationship. The buyer gains a dependable seller that delivers a quality product at a lower price. The seller gains a guarantee to sell thousands of printer cartridges without having to further compete for the business. On the loss side, the buyer could be terminated for default on the prime contract if the seller doesn't comply with all the new requirements imposed by the prime contract. The seller could lose a contract that it could have showcased to lure other prime contractors to buy its cartridges to support their federal business. When the risks and rewards become this significant, the two parties need to document the relationship in a subcontract. A subcontract would include all the flow-down terms and conditions that the prime contractor negotiated with the government as well as any other requirements between the buyer and the seller.

Teaming Partnerships

The next level of relationship is teaming partnerships. The buyer from the previous example wants to obtain a significant discount on printer cartridges. The buyer tries negotiating with the seller, but the seller, in essence a middle-person, cannot cut his price that significantly because he would take a loss on every product purchased. The buyer needs to find a new seller to arrive at these really low costs. The buyer goes to a manufacturer of printer cartridges. For the seller (the manufacturer) to even consider working directly with a company that is not in its pre-defined supplier network, the benefit the seller gains must be great. Luckily, the buyer needs millions of printer cartridges. But in order for the manufacturer to give the buyer the quantity discounts needed, the buyer must be willing to negotiate some of the terms and conditions. The seller requires the buyer to buy cartridges in 10,000 lots, warehouse the cartridges, and ship the product to the end customer. This level or relationship, often known as a *teaming-partner relationship*, requires a subcontract. Because of the numerous requirements, terms, and conditions that must be adhered to between the two parties, a subcontract is needed to clarify the roles and responsibilities.

Strategic Alliances

The last level of relationship is a strategic alliance. This time the buyer is a printer manufacturer. In order for the buyer to be competitive in the printer business, she must come up with a discriminator that differentiates her product from all the other printers. In order to do this, the buyer decides to offer lifetime printer cartridge replacements. The printer manufacturer does not manufacture printer cartridges so in order to offer such a deal, the buyer must enter into a strategic alliance with a printer cartridge manufacturer. This relationship is risky from both sides: The buyer could lose a great deal of money and customers if she promises lifetime printer cartridge replacements and cannot, for whatever reason, supply them. The seller could really increase its marketshare if the printer is adopted as a standard throughout an industry or the government. In this case a strategic alliance exists because both parties are highly interdependent. Strategic alliances are documented in subcontracts.

When Is a Subcontract Needed?

As the level of relationship increases between two parties (i.e., as the parties go from one time purchases to strategic alliances), the level of responsibility and commitment increases (Figure 1). As they increase, both parties will need a subcontract to protect individual rights in the relationship.

Subcontracts help to protect both parties from unnecessary risk because they:

- Are negotiated up front so that both parties can agree on the terms.
- Contain a statement of work that the seller must provide.
- Contain a price for the products or services.
- Contain relevant terms and conditions surrounding the relationship.
- Are enforceable in a court of law.
- May contain provisions that make a party whole as a result of a problem in the relationship.

Following are some of the factors used in deciding whether a subcontract is necessary:

Figure 1. When Subcontracts Are Necessary

Strategic Alliance
Teaming Partnerships
Suppliers
Purchase Orders
One-Time Purchaser

As the level of relationship increases between parties, there is more a need for a subcontract.

- Frequency of purchase
- Quantity of purchase
- Dollar value of purchase
- Prime contract requirements
- Customer requirements
- Degree of risk
- Level of integration required between two companies
- Goals of the relationship
- Commercial or unique products or services
- Degree of control needed by the prime contractor

Governing Laws

Different laws govern the various contract and subcontract relationships. The Uniform Commercial Code (UCC) governs any prime contract or subcontracts between two domestic commercial entities. The FAR governs any prime contract between the U.S. government and a domestic or foreign commercial entity. It also influences any resulting subcontracts stemming from that prime contract relationship.

In the international arena, the United Nations has provided the Convention of Contracts for International Sale of Goods (CISG) to provide direction and guidance for contracts between two foreign commercial entities or a foreign commercial entity and a foreign government. The United States also has the Department of Commerce's Export Acquisition Regulation (EAR) for dual-use commodities that have civilian and military applications. The EAR governs what is being exported, where it is being exported to, who is requesting the export, and what the export will be used for. The International Trade in Regulation (ITAR) stipulates requirements imposed on companies involved in exporting defense articles. See Table 2 for a summary of the governing laws.

Doing Business with the Federal Government

When conducting business with the U.S. federal government, either as a prime contractor or as a subcontractor supporting a prime contract, contractors must know the principles and doctrines that apply.

Table 2. Summary of Governing Laws

Governing Law	Contractual Relationship	Products/Services Procured
Uniform Commercial Code (UCC)	Prime contract or subcontract between two U.S. commercial entities	Commercial products and services Developmental items
Federal Acquisition Regulation (FAR)	Prime contract between the U.S. government and a U.S. commercial entity	Commercial products and services Developmental items
United Nations' Convention of Contracts for the International Sale of Goods (CISG)	Mediation and settlement of issues on prime contracts or subcontracts between a U.S. or foreign commercial entity and a foreign commercial or government entity	Commercial products and services
Export Administration Regulation (EAR)	U.S. commercial entity and foreign commercial or government entity	Dual use items (commercial or defense use) Commercial products and services Developmental items
International Traffic in Arms Regulation (ITAR)	U.S. commercial entity and a foreign commercial or government entity	Items covered by EAR Release of technology or software

Fairness among Competitors

The overriding principle in government contracting is the drive toward fairness among companies competing for federal business. The government cares about ensuring that every company, large or small, has a chance at some government business. The government enacted legislation and established the Small Business Administration (SBA) to help small businesses secure government contracts. The government has established competition advocates within agencies to ensure that, to the maximum extent possible, companies have an equal opportunity at meeting a particular requirement. In addition, the government establishes rules, such as the procurement integrity, which is designed to ensure that no one company has an unfair advantage over another. The procurement integrity bans activities such as offering or requesting job offers, offering or providing source selection information, or offering or accepting bribes in return for favorable contract evaluation.

Regulations Benefit the Government

As discussed earlier, the FAR is the governing body of regulations for federal procurement. The FAR was written and is updated by the Office of Federal Procurement Policy (OFPP) with some industry input on the process. The government contracting officer (CO) is responsible for selecting the FAR clauses that will appear in the contract. The CO is also responsible for interpretation of the FAR. If there is a dispute during contract performance, the agency that is responsible for the contract decides the protest or it is referred to the Government Accounting Office (GAO). The point is that even though the contractor has input into various stages of the FAR regulation implementation, the FAR is a document that is written by the government, to protect the government, and is enforced by the government.

In contrast, the UCC is written to protect both parties in a commercial transaction. This distinction becomes important in subcontracting to a prime contractor for a federal procurement. The prime contract is governed by the FAR; the subcontract is governed by the UCC. The prime contractor attempts to mitigate some of its risk by passing on FAR requirements to its subcontractors using flow-down clauses. In this way, the prime contractor tries to negotiate with the subcontractor to live by some of the same rules and FAR requirements that it has to in the prime contract.

Doctrine of Strict Conformance

The government operates its contracts under a doctrine of *strict conformance,* which means that the contractor is obligated to provide exactly what is in the contract. When the government issues a request for proposal (RFP) and all of its amendments, and the contractor responds with a proposal and all of its updates, and the final deal is negotiated, the contract baseline is established. The prime contractor can only deliver and the government can only order the products and services at the prices listed in the contract baseline. If the government wants to order something that is not in the baseline, the government must procure the item from another source or work with the prime contractor to add the product to the contract baseline using the contract modification process. If the contractor wants to deliver something that is not in the contract baseline, it must first secure government approval through a contract deviation or waiver.

A *contract deviation* occurs when a product or service about to be provided is different from what is currently on the contract. For example, if the contract calls for a 5 foot cable and it is unavailable from the manufacturer and the contractor needs to provide instead a 10 foot cable, the contractor must first obtain the government's approval on a deviation document stating that the contractor is deviating from the contract by providing a 10 foot rather than a 5 foot cable. A *waiver* occurs when the contractor must provide a product or service that does not exactly meet all of the contractual requirements (Figure 2). For example, the prime contractor states that the person proposed as project manager must have a master's degree. The original project manager had a masters degree but is being replaced by a person who does not have a masters degree but does have several years of contract experience. The contractor would request the government to waive the masters degree requirement so that the contractor could provide a person that has contract experience and a bachelor's degree but no master's degree.

Contractors should realize that the government does not just agree to these benefits of contract waivers and deviations. In the interest of fair competition, the government usually negotiates a lower price or improved terms and conditions for the products or services provided under a deviation or waiver. In this manner, the government

---

Figure 2. Sample Waiver

Contract Number _____

Date _____

[Name of Seller] requests [Name of Buyer] to grant a waiver allowing [Name of Employee] to work on the contract in the key position of project manager. [Name of Employee] has ten years of experience, has worked on the contract for three years, and is fully capable of assuming the position of project manager. However, [Name of Employee] does not have the required masters degree required by the government's job description. Therefore, [Name of Buyer] requests that [Name of Employee] be allowed to perform the project manager function and in return [Name of Buyer] will charge the [Name of Seller] the contract rate for a Junior Project Manager rather than the Project Manager rate.

Signature of Seller Representative _____ Date _____

Signature of Buyer Representative _____ Date _____

---

hopes to avoid any perception of one government contractor receiving an unfair advantage over another government contractor.

The doctrine of strict conformance is relevant to subcontracting efforts within the federal government marketplace because a subcontractor must provide only the products or services that are stated in the subcontract baseline. The subcontract baseline is established between the prime contractor and the subcontractor and contains those subcontractor products and services that the prime contractor intends to use to fulfill the prime contract.

Mistakes Can Lead to Fines, Suspension, Debarment or Imprisonment

The government deals with more prime contractors than any individual company ever will. As a result, the government is concerned about fairness in competition and equality among contractors. The government is also spending taxpayers' money and takes its fiscal responsibility very seriously. Because of these two prevailing objectives, the government wants to ensure it conducts all of its procurements in a manner that is fair to all competitors and that results in providing the products and services that represent the best overall value to the government.

Similarly, millions of companies are competing to do business with the federal government. The government could not possibly know if all of its contractor partners conduct business in an ethical and appropriate manner. Because the government cannot be sure whether the contractor made a legitimate human error or was out to defraud the government, it takes a rather conservative view when it comes to a contractor mistake. Basically, the government assumes the worse and the contractor must defend its actions otherwise.

Depending on the severity of the offense, a mistake could lead to:

- A fine levied against a company or individual
- A stop payment action on a contract
- Suspension from government business for a company in whole or in part for a period of time
- Debarment from government business forever
- Imprisonment for individuals

Because a prime contractor can be held liable for the mistakes committed by its subcontractors, the prime contractor must ensure it adequately protects itself in the subcontract against such actions. In addition, constant contract monitoring is imperative in subcontracting efforts that support government prime contracts.

Doctrine of Sovereign Immunity

Another way that the government protects itself is through the doctrine of sovereign immunity. The doctrine of sovereign immunity states that if the government is acting in its *sovereign capacity* (i.e., the government is doing what the government is supposed to do), it cannot be held liable for its actions unless the government consents to the suit. The Federal Tort Claims Act of 1946 took away some of the government's ability to rely on sovereign immunity when the government was involved in a tort and established the conditions under which outside parties could bring suit against the government.

False Statements Equal Criminal Conduct

If you make a false statement to the government, it is perceived by the government as criminal conduct subject to fines and/or time spent in jail. The closest example to anyone working in the federal government marketplace is the statement at the bottom of the time card that basically states that you can be fined up to $10,000 and/or up to five years in prison if you lie on a time card.

Long Arm of the Government

Contractors must also remember that the government has a much farther reach into how a prime contractor interacts with a subcontractor than a typical commercial customer would have. Even though privity of contract exists, establishing relationships between the government and the prime contractor and the prime contractor and the subcontractor, the government through its regulatory ability can influence how the prime contractor/subcontractor relationship operates. Following are examples of how the government could influence a prime contractor-contractor relationship:

- *Competition*—The government has procedures in place to ensure that a prime contractor is selected using competitive methods unless extenuating circumstances, such as national defense, exist. The government takes this responsibility seriously because it is held accountable to the taxpayers, who ultimately fund government programs. The government imposes this responsibility and accountability on prime contractors when it comes to selecting subcontractors. The government wants to ensure that the prime contractors select the subcontractors that represent the best overall value for the government and the taxpayers. Therefore, the government requires prime contractors to use competitive practices to select its subcontractors for federal programs.

- *Source selection*—The government wants to ensure that the prime contractor selects the subcontractor that represents the best overall value to the government. Therefore, it requires prime contractors to document its source selection plan, follow it, and justify its decisions at every step of the process (technical evaluation, terms and conditions consideration, and cost/price analyses).

- *Contractor purchasing system review requirements*—The government requires large companies to conduct a formal solicitation, competition, and evaluation process when selecting subcontractors with which to work. This process must be documented, submitted to the Defense Contract Audit Agency, and adhered to with every new contract or modification. The government will conduct post-award reviews to determine if the purchases that were made over a period of time adhered to the process outlined.

- *Subcontracting plan*—The government also requires the prime contractor to submit a subcontracting plan that identifies the subcontractors, the work that they will perform, and how much contract revenue they can expect to receive. The government reserves the right to approve or reject this plan.

- *Fee decisions*—The government determines how much, if any, of a fee that a prime contractor earns on an award or incentive fee contract. If the government does not like the work that the subcontractor is doing it could minimize the amount of fee that a contract earns in these types of contracts.

- *Termination*—The government also retains the right to terminate a contract in whole or in part for either its own convenience or, in the case of a poor contract performance, default. If a subcontractor is not performing well, the prime contractor could find part or all of its prime contract terminated.

2   Develop and Implement the Strategic Plan

Why Should Prime Contractors and Subcontractors Plan?

A company develops plans because it needs to outline the steps it needs to take to get from where it is today to where it wants to be in the future. The planning process helps a company grow the business because it offers a structured approach for defining and analyzing the variables that can affect the company's success. Once these variables are defined, the company can take appropriate action. Although a company cannot identify every variable that could affect corporate success, identifying and responding to some contingencies will help prepare a company to respond to unexpected changes in the marketplace.

Plans are particularly important in prime contract and subcontract relationships because more than one organization is involved in meeting a particular goal or objective. A prime contractor may develop a strategic plan to determine the overall direction it wishes to take with a particular customer. The prime contractor then may engage a subcontractor's assistance in defining a plan for how the proposal will be written. The prime contractor also may work with the customer after contract award to develop a plan for how the contract will run on a daily basis. Finally, a prime contractor may enlist the help of a subcontractor to develop a plan for how to execute a particular task order. A subcontractor may decide to develop a plan when it conducts its analysis of whether it should pursue a piece of business as a prime contractor or a subcontractor.

When Does a Company Develop a Plan?

A company can use plans at any point during the procurement cycle to accomplish the required tasks. For example, the company may develop plans to pursue marketing activities, or to prepare a proposal, or to start up a contract. The company should develop plans at these and other critical junctures because it usually has much riding on winning an individual proposal effort. It is important for a planning team to meet its objectives by carefully analyzing the variables that can help or hinder its success.

A list of types of plans that a company can develop to support subcontract management include:

- Strategic
- Marketing
- Sales
- Proposal development
- Live test demonstration
- Best and final offer
- Contract start up
- Subcontract management
- Contract operations
- Transition
- Task order
- Contract shut down

A company may develop plans briefly in four to five hours or it may require extensive research and analysis and take a few months to develop. The plan should be developed early enough so that the contract team has time to perform the steps of the plan before the plan's goal must be met. For example, if the plan's goal is to generate $5 million in revenue in the year 2002 from a contract not yet won, the team would need to develop and implement the plan in late 2000 or early 2001 to meet the plan's goal.

What Format Should Be Used?

Although multiple formats can be used to develop a plan, the process presented here is a generic one. It can be used no matter what type of planning a company wishes to accomplish. For example, a company will use the same steps for developing a plan for a live test demonstration as it will for developing a plan for proposal preparation. The company must develop the plan's purpose and identify internal or external influences that will help or hinder the plan's. The contractor must make assumptions about the environment and establish objectives. It has to define programs and supporting projects to meet the plan's objectives. Finally, the company must prepare schedules, resource requirements, and financial implications for each project.

Although a contractor will need to develop plans at various points in the procurement process, the various plans feed into one other. For example, many of the assumptions made about the competition in the marketing plan affect strategies in other plans, such as the proposal development plan. Similarly, the solution developed as a result of the proposal development plan will be key in the account start-up plan. Also, resources targeted in the proposal development plan may be the same resources targeted in the live test demonstration plan. The bottom line is that it is important to conduct a planning process at each stage of the procurement and then to integrate those plans with all the other plans. This will allow a contract team to identify problem areas, such as over utilized resources, and to develop contingencies.

How Much Effort Should This Take?

The magnitude of the planning effort will be commensurate with the corporate resources available, the task to be accomplished, and the size of the procurement effort. One person could develop plans with input from outside industry experts. Or to ensure a more integrated planning effort, representatives from various parts of the company could develop plans for the procurement effort. Items that the company should consider in deciding how much effort planning should take include:

- How much risk is there to the organization if the purpose is not met?
- How much revenue could the organization make if the plan was properly executed and met its objectives?
- What other projects would be affected while resources were being used to develop the plan?
- Are there other organizations, such as internal support groups, customers, or subcontractors, that should be involved in the planning process?
- Does this project or program represent a significant or strategic opportunity for the organization?

Planning Process

Steps of the Planning Process

No matter what planning process the company chooses to use, the following steps are critical to any planning effort:

1. Select the appropriate planning team members.

2. Gather initial data for the plan.

3. Develop and document the plan's components, which include purpose, external conditions, internal conditions, opportunities, assumptions, objectives, policies, programs, projects, schedules, organization, and financials.

4. Communicate the plan to the people responsible for implementing the plan.

5. Implement the plan.

6. Develop and use feedback mechanisms to update the plan.

7. Establish a review mechanism to evaluate the plan's success.

Select Appropriate Planning Team Members

The following sections explore each of the previous steps in detail.

Having the appropriate people develop the plan is critical to the plan's success. The people who are selected for the team must be willing to work as a team to develop the plan. They should either be knowledgeable about how to develop the plan or how to meet the plan's purpose. The planning team may consist of functional area experts, visionaries, a facilitator, a notetaker, support personnel, and internal support members for the duration of the planning effort. Or the team may find it prudent to bring in the talent only when it is required at each stage of the process. Following is a brief description of the types of people necessary to develop the plan:

Functional area experts   Functional area experts represent the line and staff organizations and provide some operational reality. They can include representatives from various departments, such as production, contracts, sales, management, finance, and engineering, or experts in the fields germane to the plan's purpose. For example, when developing a subcontract management plan, the company may want to include people from the purchasing and subcontracts departments to help identify sources for various products and services.

Visionaries   Visionaries help spur the planning team to break out of its standard thought process and to be creative. Visionaries ask "Why?" or "Why not?" They can be found in almost every type of organization and are usually the people who are particularly good at seeing the big picture. Innovative approaches or slight twists on previously failed approaches may be the difference between meeting or not meeting the plan's purpose. Visionaries are needed when the program that the company is working on is large, complex, and highly integrated, because they can assist the team in identifying the types of products and services required to make the solution work as intended.

Facilitator   A facilitator keeps the planning team on schedule and creates an effective group environment. The facilitator ensures that one person does not dominate the conversation, that all participants have an equal chance at being heard, and that the plan gets developed in a timely manner by ensuring that the team does not stray into conversations not germane to the plan's development.

Notetaker   An evolving plan must have continual review and feedback from its originators to ensure that the plan adequately reflects the group's intention. Instrumental in this process is a notetaker who captures the group's ideas during each planning session. Additionally, this person is responsible for producing and distributing the various drafts of the plan to all members so that they can review the plan and note comments on the document. The notetaker can then either incorporate the comments directly into the plan for the next release or submit the comments to the team to review and discuss during its next planning session.

Support personnel   These people help the planning proceed smoothly. Support personnel are not typically in the planning sessions unless they are presenting a report. Examples of support personnel include:

Research analysts—Research analysts gather information needed to make decisions. By having non-team members gather the information, the team can remain focused on its objective and not get sidetracked with additional responsibilities. Researcher analysts join the planning session only when they have to present data.

Cost analysts—Cost analysts are adept at running what-if scenarios, and cost analyses can help the process run smoother by showing the team how much each alternative will cost to implement. Analysts who can quickly provide costs for each alternative help the team to not waste time on cost-prohibitive alternatives.

Scheduler—A scheduler can work with a program planning software package to develop milestone charts and critical path networks. This person works to quickly identify overcommitted resources or resource shortages.

Purchasing—Purchasing representatives can help the team identify products, services, sources, and prices from outside suppliers to help the company meet the plan's purpose.

These functions may be handled by one person or shared among team members. For example, team members could take turns at being the notetaker for each planning session. The key is to keep the size of the planning team as small as necessary to get the job done.

Internal support team members Sometimes it makes sense to include members from other internal support organizations who will be responsible for implementing the contract or project after it is obtained. These internal support team members can include people from the engineering, marketing, sales, production, technical support, and finance departments.

Gather Data for the Plan

Before the team can adequately determine the plan's purpose, it must conduct initial research to determine the options available and to ascertain where the company can achieve the greatest return on investment. The team should collect data before developing a plan for numerous reasons. First, data collection can help determine which obstacles must be overcome to make the plan successful. By knowing these obstacles ahead of time, the team can develop contingency plans, address the obstacles, and allow for a successful implementation process. Additionally, the team can decide before spending a lot of corporate resources whether obstacles to the plan present too great a threat to its success and alter the plan or not pursue the contract. An example of this type of decision making is when a company decides whether it wants to pursue a program as a prime contractor or a subcontractor. Before making this decision, the company must decide if it has sufficient resources or if it can siphon additional resources from other programs to fund the contracting process. The company must also consider the affect fewer resources will have on the programs it takes funds from. After this analysis, the company can decide whether it should be a subcontractor or a prime contractor.

The plan's purpose also determines the kinds of information needed. If a subcontractor team is trying to work with a brand new prime contractor, it may want to collect data on the current or future need for its product or service, programs that the prime contractor is pursuing, budgets and preferences, competitors, and the affect of future, planned, and new technology.

Different data would be necessary for preparing a proposal. In this case, the prime contractor team and the subcontractor team would need to know the customer's schedule and requirements, the competitor's strengths and weaknesses, the internal and external resources available, and proposal logistics.

The planning team should decide what information would be useful to evaluate and determine its approach. The team should collect data from several different sources to discover new perspectives and to ensure accuracy. Data does not support or that negatively affects the plan's purpose is just as important as data that supports the plan's purpose. This is true for a number of reasons:

- The data can help determine the obstacles that must be overcome to make the plan successful.

- By knowing the obstacles ahead of time, the team can develop a contingency plan to address these obstacles and obtain a successful implementation.

- The team can decide up front and *before* corporate resources are spent whether the obstacles present too great a threat to the plan's success and alter the plan's purpose or not pursue the contract.

A word of caution: A team can become immobile if it refuses to make any decisions until all information is collected. Although much of the information gathered is objective, the analysis is subjective. The team must try to be as realistic as possible with the data obtained and not wait until "perfect, complete, and accurate" information is available to begin the planning process. If the team waits until all of the information is in, chances are that some of the information has changed and that the data will need to be reassessed—which will take more time. For this reason, the team should determine the data necessary to provide several different perspectives on the market. Then, if two or more sources yield the same results, the team consider the data to be validated. Conflicting data will require more research.

Finally, data gathering occurs throughout the planning process. The data gathered during the early stages should be monitored throughout the planning process to ensure that market conditions have not changed. The team will also use the data gathered during the feedback process to continually improve the plan and operational approach.

Where to Get the Data

After the team determines what data it needs, the team must figure out where to get the data. Much information is available in the public domain. In addition, the government makes a lot of data available to contractors. These sources include:

- *Trade journals*—Industry and government magazines that deal specifically with an industry.
- *Marketing intelligence*—Information gained from customer visits and marketing meetings.
- *Congress*—Assesses the effect of new regulations, and the appropriations committee actions can significantly affect the program's success.
- *Commerce Business Daily (CBD)*—Publishes many government solicitations.
- *Agency's public relations department*—Basic information about an agency and its plans are available in the agency's public relations department.
- *Agency-published program documents*—Many planning documents are created during the procurement process, some of which are made available to contractors.
- *Customer documents available*—Library documents, agency budgets, acquisition plans.
- *Freedom of Information Act (FOIA) process*—Allows a company to query an agency for previously collected information.
- *Bidders conferences, presentations by government personnel, and customer site visits*—These resources provide a lot of operational detail about the customer's environment.
- *Industry seminars/conferences*—Provide information about potential teaming partners and competitors.
- *Internal corporate library*—If available, allows a proposal team member to review previous proposals to determine applicability.
- *Market research agencies*—There are companies that conduct research on programs or competitors for a fee.
- *Small Business Administration (SBA)*—Has seminars, industry experts, and detailed information on how to develop a marketing plan and where a small company can go for assistance.

- *Internet*—Allows people to quickly scan for information on an industry, or to browse a company's homepage.

Types of Data

Types of data that the team will have to gather fall into three basic areas: product offerings, customers' environments, and the competition.

Understand your product offering   The first step in gathering data is to determine the company's product and service offerings. Typically, a company starts off with a basic product. The company eventually adds complementary products to the product line. It then offers services to help provide the necessary customer support once the products are purchased. The company modifies products and services as new customer requirements, internal considerations, and competitive requirements emerge. Sometimes it drops some products and services because the company can no longer produce it competitively or because it can obtain higher profit margins with an alternative product strategy.

The team must review and understand the company's current products and service offerings at the initial planning stages so that the team can determine what it has to work with. The easiest course is to use the existing products and services in the planning process. However, research may indicate that the company most modify its current products and services in order to meet the customer requirements or the challenges of the competitive environment. This additional research is discussed below.

Understand your customer's environment   It doesn't matter how good of a product or service the company has if it doesn't have a customer base. For this reason, the planning team must consider the next leg of the planning process: the customer environment. An analysis of the customer's environment allows the company to answer the following questions:

- Who are our current competitors?
- How does the customer use our product or service?
- What would make out product or service more useful to the customer?
- Why isn't the customer using the product or service today?
- What budget does the customer have for this product or service?

Once the company understands the customer's environment, the company can then make some realistic assumptions about its own product line, marketing strategy, research and development, and product implementation.

Understand your competition   The final step in this data gathering process is understanding the competition. In today's environment of mergers, acquisitions, and bankruptcies, it is hard to keep track of who is in the market, who has teamed together, and who's out of the market all together. Couple this with the teaming agreements and strategic alliances that are formed between two companies pursuing a certain market, and the team will quickly find that understanding the competition can be a full-time job because the competitive makeup is changing so frequently.

However, understanding who are the dominant players and, more importantly, why they are the dominant players, can yield great benefits in determining the company's strategy. Companies are constantly looking for new and efficient ways to offer their products and services without sacrificing and, hopefully, enlarging marketshare. By capitalizing on the trials and errors of some of the company's competitors, the company can see how certain strategies could be implemented as well as the strengths and weaknesses of implementing them. This industry watching allows the company to gain the benefit of seeing how new strategies would work without the risk associated with actually trying the strategy. Then the company can select the best parts of several competitor strategies to develop its own, and hopefully less risky, strategy. Therefore, it is imperative that the company keep track of the changes that occur in the marketplace in regards to how products and services are being offered so that the company can update or modify its own strategy if necessary.

Develop the Plan

Once the team members have been selected and information has been gathered to create the plan, the team can begin developing the plan. Developing a plan involves several steps:

1. Define the purpose.
2. Analyze the external conditions.
3. Analyze the internal conditions.
4. Identify opportunities.
5. Develop assumptions.

6. Develop objectives.

7. Establish policies.

8. Identify programs and projects.

9. Develop priorities and schedules.

10. Define the organization.

Define the Purpose

The purpose of the plan is its reason for being. In order to develop a purpose, the team must first analyze where the company is today, where it wants to be in the future, and how the plan will take it there. Determining where the greatest return on investment potential exists requires careful research and analysis of the data gathered in the previous step. The team must clearly define the purpose and ensure that everyone on the planning team understands what needs to be accomplished to fulfill the purpose. For example, a company's purpose for a plan could be to develop a marketing plan for a specific deal, to develop a proposal, to conduct a live test demonstration, or to start up an account.

Analyze the External Conditions

The external conditions are those items present outside of the company that will help or hinder the company from meeting its purpose. The team must carefully review outside influences to determine if the plan is achievable. The team should spend a considerable amount of effort obtaining the kinds of data that will provide realism to the plan.

For example, understanding the customer and the competition is useful for planning the procurement process. By focusing on what the customer wants and what the competition is prepared to offer, a company can better determine its own internal priorities for a particular deal. When two companies are working together in a subcontractor relationship, each company must review what is happening in the other company when making decisions that will affect their relationship. For example, reorganizations or mergers may shift priorities with regard to outside projects.

Analyze the Internal Conditions

Internal conditions are those items inherent within the organization that will help or hinder the team in meeting its objectives. The kinds of questions that the team must answer when reviewing internal conditions include:

- What other programs are going on concurrently that will affect the resources needed for this effort?
- Is this plan's purpose in tandem with the organization's overall goals and objectives?
- Can the program requirements be supported if the company wins the contract?
- What are the strengths the company possesses for this program?
- Is the company positioned to meet the plan objectives?

Identify Opportunities

Opportunities are options that the company can explore that will allow it to meet the plan's purpose. Opportunities allow team members to use creative and unique approaches, but opportunities may also require the team to use routine approaches. Working with other companies may give the team opportunities that were not available if the company were to work by itself.

Depending on the plan's purpose, the team may have few or multiple opportunities to consider. For example, when developing a live test demonstration, the team will have few opportunities or alternate ways to approach the demonstration if the customer prescribes step-by-step instructions. On the other hand, if the team is developing a marketing plan, it can pursue numerous opportunities to obtain business with a customer and to meet the plan's goals.

Once the team has identified opportunities, it should determine which opportunities it would like to explore. To do that, the team should first clearly describe each opportunity. Then a team member should be assigned to explore the reasonableness of implementing each opportunity. Some of the questions this person should ask include: How might the opportunity be accomplished? What is the potential cost of implementing the opportunity? What kind of rewards might the company obtain through successful implementation? Once the analysis is conducted on all the opportunities the team wishes to explore, the team can make a business decision as to which opportunities it wants to implement.

Develop Assumptions

Because planning attempts to predict future events, and no one can predict the future, the planning team must have some way of baselining where it is today and what anticipated events will drive future outcomes. Analyzing internal and external conditions will help the team baseline where it is today. Assumptions will help the team define what anticipated events will drive future outcomes. An assumption may include the Consumer Price Index, rate of inflation, or raise percentages. The team develops assumptions by predicting events based on current facts, trends, and historical data. For example, two companies are working together on a sales plan. They need to develop assumptions about the type of commission structure that will be available for salespeople from either company selling the products and services of the program. The team must agree on assumptions, and all the assumptions must be documented as part of the planning process. The team should use the assumptions as the basis for all the plan's components and the assumptions should be clear and quantifiable. As time goes on, these assumptions will either be validated or proven wrong. This is why the team should carefully review and modify its assumptions when conditions change.

Develop Objectives

At this point in the planning process, the team has identified most components relevant to pursuing the plan's purpose. The team has determined and assessed external factors, internal factors, opportunities, and assumptions. Now the team is ready to develop objectives. *Objectives* outline the strategy that the team will take to meet its purpose. Objectives are quantifiable with measurable standards of performance and may be adjusted as the team implements the plan.

Examples of objectives include the following:

- Obtain $600,000 in contract revenue within three years with a new prime contractor.
- Obtain study contracts with five new customers over the next two years.

Establish Policies

Companies develop policies as their guiding principles for conducting business on a daily basis. Company policies deal with hiring practices, compensation, education programs, and so on. If a company is dealing with the federal government, either as a prime contractor or a subcontractor, it must have corporate policies for complying with federal regulations. Examples of corporate policies that must be in place to support federal business include:

- Providing equal employment opportunity
- Providing a drug-free workplace
- Developing and implementing cost accounting standards required for labor accounting
- Disclosing indirect rates to DCAA or other federal audit agencies

Identify Programs and Projects

After ensuring that corporate and federal compliance policies are underway, the planning team must identify programs and projects required for implementing a plan. *Programs* are groups of related projects. The team may not have to group projects into programs, but grouping is useful if many projects are required to accomplish an objective, or if the projects naturally fall into distinct functional areas. An example of a marketing program would include the following projects: attend bidders conference, respond to draft documents, conduct marketing visits, and prepare a position paper outlining the solution approach.

Projects are the specific tasks that need to be accomplished to meet a particular objective. Once the team determines which projects are necessary for achieving a particular objective, the team can assign resources and determine if achieving a particular objective is cost effective.

Develop Priorities and Schedules

After the company has determined which projects to pursue to win new business, its next step is to establish priorities and schedules. The schedule's aggressiveness will be driven by the number of people available to implement the plan, customer-driven deadlines, and the procurement size. Priority should be given to those projects that must be completed before the start of other projects, or to those critical projects that must be completed to ensure the plan's success.

Automated products that can assist in the scheduling process are available. Such products require the user to determine a project's tasks and subtasks, beginning and end dates, milestones, resources required to complete the project, and the interdependencies between the tasks required to complete the project.

Define the Organization

Once the team has defined the programs and projects and decided which projects it is willing to pursue, the next step is to establish the organizational structure that can support these projects. In order to do this the team will need to answer questions such as the following: Is a separate task group needed to accomplish one of the plan's projects or program? Can employees from different divisions in the company staff all the identified projects? Does the existing team need contracted personnel or temporary employees to meet its schedule? The answers to these questions and others determine if the organization can handle project implementation in its current state, or whether it must be restructured or enhanced to accomplish the objectives.

Determine the Method to Achieve Your Plan

Once the company has developed its plan, then it must determine the methods necessary to meet its plan's objectives. The company can use a variety of methods to win a contract or to establish or enhance itself in the marketplace. It can work alone as the prime contractor, it can subcontract out portions of the work to another company, or it can work as a subcontractor for another prime contractor. Each of these options is discussed in the following section.

Do It Alone

The company may decide to pursue a particular contract alone (i.e., without the assistance of any prime contractor or subcontractors). The do-it-alone approach is useful if the company has all the resources available internally to respond to and to meet the customer's requirements. These resources include employees with the appropriate skills, raw materials, production capabilities, and appropriate products. Employees with the appropriate skills are required on a proposal effort and to manage the contract after award. Such employees must be available at the time stipulated by the customer, and those time frames may shift if the customer has a schedule change. The company must assess product availability in terms of the amount of time it will take to produce a product from scratch, or the time it will take to make an existing product conform to the customer's specifications. Once the company determines that it can develop the product within the designated time frame, it must assess whether it can produce and deliver the product quantities the customer requires in the short time frame typically allowed on a contract.

The company must consider the availability of all the resources necessary to fulfill the contract requirements in relation to the company's other business objectives. The company may have employees with the appropriate skill sets and adequate production capabilities, however, if the same resources are required in other areas of the business and cannot be spared because the other business areas could suffer irreparably, then the company cannot work on the contract alone. On the other hand, the company may be able to work on one of the many small contracts (e.g., study, training, consulting, or professional services contracts) with values of $1 million or less. Smaller contracts may make it financially feasible for the company to work alone.

If the company decides to pursue a customer contract on its own, the company must accomplish all of the marketing activities, proposal development, and contract performance. The benefit to this approach is that the company has complete control and decision-making power over all aspects of the procurement. The company can determine how many resources to apply to the effort, how much risk it is willing to take in pricing the contract, and how it will ultimately satisfy the customer's requirements without consulting other partners. Although this approach allows maximum control, it also places all contract risk on the company. All pre-contract costs must be borne by the company. If the company does not meet the contract's requirements, the company is liable for all contractual remedies. The good news is that working alone allows the company to reap all the financial and reputation benefits associated with successful contract performance.

Work as a Subcontractor

Working as a subcontractor for another company, particularly a large company, offers an excellent opportunity for the subcontractor to meet its own objective of getting into new business without many of the risks associated with doing it alone. Large contractors typically have a lot of experience in each aspect of the procurement cycle and can be an invaluable resource to a company trying to break into the new companies or market areas. Often, the subcontracting company benefits from the significant resources available within the larger company. For example, a large company primarily handles the costs associated with marketing, proposal development, and solution demonstrations. The subcontractor's responsibility may be limited to writing a few proposal sections or assisting with marketing initiatives. The bottom line is that with minimal up-front investment, a subcontracting company can work with another company to win customer business.

The disadvantage of working as a subcontractor for another company is that the prime contractor basically makes all decisions. The subcontracting company can negotiate with the other company to determine a mutually agreeable level of risk, but if the subcontractor does not want to comply with the prime contractor's decisions, the prime contractor may find another subcontractor to do the work. Additionally, because the work is not done by just one company, the revenues from the contract do not solely belong to one company. The prime contractor and subcontractor must agree to a revenue-sharing scheme. Finally, the prime contractor ultimately controls the program. Therefore, the subcontractor may need to change the way it offers its products or services based on the prime contractor's decision, or risk losing its place on the team.

Finding a company with which to bid can be a challenge for a subcontracting company. If the subcontracting company wishes to pursue this route, there are several things it can do to enhance its chances of locating a large company with which to do business. The subcontracting company can begin by establishing itself as a reputable contractor on its existing contracts. Nothing speaks louder than a stellar track record of solid performance. The subcontractor's contract performance may be in federal contracts or commercial business. Next, the subcontracting company should understand its own capabilities and be able to clearly articulate them to a potential prime company. Often, a subcontracting company becomes enamored with the thought of becoming a contracting partner, but it cannot define the specifics of its own offering. Finally, the subcontracting company must understand the marketplace and know which customers have money for the goods and services the company offers. By targeting specific customers and prime contractors, the subcontracting company can channel its resources to those opportunities that represent the biggest potential market.

Recent contract announcements in the *Washington Post* or the *Wall Street Journal* are a potential avenue for subcontracting companies. Likewise, the company can review the classified employment section to determine what skills the winning contractor requires. A subcontracting company with a niche product offering can work with the prime contractor of an existing contract to add its product to the prime contract's offering. Finally, marketing directly to the customer may generate a need for the subcontracting company's product. In this situation, the customer may assist the subcontracting company in determining an appropriate contract vehicle through which to sell its products.

Subcontract Work to Other Companies

Another way to pursue business is to be the prime contractor and subcontract work to other companies. If a company has established credibility, is a recognized industry expert, or brings a unique value-added contribution to a particular deal, it may be possible for the company to prime the deal (i.e., get selected as the prime contractor). In this situation, other companies would subcontract to the company in pursuit of a piece of business. Although the company would assume much of the risk as the prime contractor, some of that risk could be shared with the subcontractors. In order for this approach to work, the prime contractor will need to find subcontractors that are willing to be on the team. The degree to which the prime contractor's team is perceived as a viable contract contender dictates how quickly other companies are willing to join the team. As prime contractor, the company makes most of the decisions and relies on the strengths of other companies to complement its own.

Communicate the Plan to the People Responsible for Implementing the Plan

Once the team develops the plan and determines the best method to implement the plan, the team must communicate it to the people responsible for implementing the plan. Although the people who must implement the plan need to know what they are supposed to do, it is also helpful if the whole organization knows what the company is trying to accomplish. This is useful because other personnel may have ideas, contacts, or additional information that the planning team did not consider but that would be useful in implementing the plan. If the company is working with another company to implement the plan, the company should make sure key members of the other company communicate the plan to the individuals responsible for implementing the plan.

Communication can occur in several ways. The team can distribute the plan to all personnel or make a formal presentation. Some companies provide a synopsis of each part of the plan in their corporate newsletters or via electronic mail. Although it is important that the team present the plan to all personnel, it is equally important that the plan be presented in a manner conducive to its implementation. For example, a plan that requires a lot of organizational change or new ways to conduct business will need to be presented carefully because its unveiling may be met with skepticism and fear by the people responsible for implementing it. Many books are available on the market today that specifically discuss how a company can implement change within its organization. It would be worthwhile for the team to review techniques for introducing change before presenting the plan. Peter Senge's book, *Fifth Discipline*, and his follow-up book,

Fifth Discipline Fieldbook, offer techniques for building a work environment that is conducive to change.

Implement the Plan

Once the team has developed and communicated the plan, it can begin to implement the plan. The team begins by assigning resources and managing tasks. It must also review projects and schedules to ensure they are on track. If a plan involves multiple organizations, the team should hold status meetings to ensure that the plan is being properly implemented.

Evaluate the Plan's Success

A plan that is developed and sits on the shelf without being used is worthless. Once all the effort has been expended to develop and implement the plan, periodic reviews of the plan should be conducted to evaluate its success. Determining if the plan is meeting its purpose, or if changes should be made, helps the company to be realistic in its approach to obtain new federal business. To evaluate a plan's success the team must assess the following:

- *Projects*—Are they on track? Are they helping to meet the plan's objectives? Do other projects need to be added to meet the objectives? Does it still make sense to complete each project or has the purpose of the project been overcome by events?

- *Objectives*—Are the objectives helping to meet the plan's purpose? Do other objectives need to be added to meet the purpose? Are the objective's realistic? Does the team need to raise or lower expectations based on the information discovered from implementing the plan?

Update the Plan

The company may need to update the plan. Updating the plan involves periodic reviews, perhaps quarterly, to determine if any of the data used to develop the plan have significantly changed. Specific areas that the company should address include the role of technology, competition, assumptions, customer environment, and significant industry shifts that affect the goods and services the company offers. Periodic reviews may necessitate changes in the following sections of the plan: environment, assumptions, objectives, projects, financials, schedules, and priorities. Most importantly, the plan must be evaluated to determine if it is still on target.

This planning process can be used throughout the procurement process and provides a good way to analyze the variables that can help or hinder the success of a company reaching its goals.

Prime Contractor Considerations

Why Subcontract?

This chapter covers developing and implementing a strategic plan and sets the stage for the prime contractor and subcontractor relationship. Such a relationship is usually started because a prime contractor decides, based on its internal planning and analysis, that it wants to go after certain business and cannot do it alone. Or a subcontractor decides, based on its internal planning and analysis, that it wants to pursue new business opportunities but needs to work with a prime contractor. The next two sections discuss prime contractor and subcontractor considerations and explore some of the facets of this analysis that eventually brings two companies together to work in a prime contractor–subcontractor relationship.

When a prime contractor is determining if it should subcontract some of its work, it explores a lot of data. Some factors that a prime contractor should consider when deciding whether to subcontract include:

- Capability analysis
- Competitive position
- Cost-effective solution
- Contract risk/reward
- Customer preference
- Quantity discounts
- Final analysis

Capability Analysis

A company needs to assess its internal capabilities to determine if subcontracting is a necessary alternative. The company may not have the capabilities needed to conduct a program by itself. Sometimes the company may have the needed capabilities, but the skill level required by the customer is greater than the company possesses. For example, a customer requires 25 logisticians and a company has only ten. Another scenario is that the company has 25 logisticians but because of when the program will occur, the company will not be able to fulfill the customer's requirements and meet the company's existing customers' requirements. If any of these situations existed, the company should seriously consider a subcontractor relationship so that it can bid on a contract.

Competitive Position

Another analysis that the company should complete when decide whether it should work with a subcontractor is whether or not the subcontractor adds anything to the company's competitive position. If the prospective subcontractor has an existing business relationship with the customer that the customer perceives as positive, then the subcontractor could bring competitive strength to the company's team. In such a case, the subcontractor would also have a wealth of customer knowledge that it can share with the team to help win the contract. Typically, a subcontractor that is positioned well and can help improve a team's competitive position will have many teams clamoring to get the subcontractor to work with them. When this is the case, the desirable subcontractor may play off one team against another to secure the best terms and conditions or it will enter into subcontract relationships with all the teams knowing that at least one will win and the subcontractor will have the business. If this is the case, the company will need to conduct further analysis to determine if the subcontractor's improved terms and conditions or the fact that the subcontractor's talents are no longer a discriminator because it is on every team outweigh the benefit it brings to the team.

Cost-Effective Solution

Sometimes the company will select a subcontractor because it can provide a more cost-effective solution to some of the contract requirements than the company can. For example, a contract has numerous requirements for training. The company cannot handle the requirements internally unless it pulls people from existing contracts that are generating revenue, which it cannot do. The company decides to bring in a subcontractor to share the training requirements because the company was able to negotiate a rate with the subcontractor that is less expensive than using internal people and still secure a handsome profit for the work performed. Because the company was able to work with a subcontractor, it could work on the contract without sacrificing profit potential on that contract or the other contracts it was working on.

Contract Risk/Reward

A subcontractor, by taking on some of the terms and conditions that the prime contractor must meet, shares some of the contract risk. As compensation for sharing the risk, the prime contractor shares some of the contract reward or profit with the subcontractor. Contract risk/reward is an important analysis for a prime contractor to conduct because some customers' contract terms and conditions could render a program not worthy of bidding on by a prime contractor. If a subcontractor is willing to accept the terms and conditions that the prime contractor cannot meet, then the prime contractor can bid the program because it knows if the subcontractor does not perform the prime contractor has contractual remedies built into the subcontract.

Customer Preference

Sometimes a prime contractor chooses a subcontractor because the customer either directly or indirectly states a preference for a particular company. Sometimes, the customer hints strongly about including certain subcontractors on the team because of their expertise, product line, or technical talent. Other times, a customer prefers a subcontractor because of the customer's existing environment. For example, the customer may have a lot of the subcontractor's products currently installed or the customer has worked with the subcontractor in the past. In such situations, the subcontractor may have a stronger say in the subcontract relationship than normally expected because the subcontractor has the inside track with the customer.

Quantity Discounts

Another strategy that companies often employ is to work with one subcontractor on multiple contracts so as to secure quantity discounts. The prime contractor usually can negotiate a low price with a subcontractor by offering it increased sales. This strategy also works well if the company needs to buy the subcontractor's products and services for internal use, because it helps to solidify the relationship.

Final Analysis

Finally, a prime contractor must review all of the factors to determine if working with a subcontractor is the right business decision. Often times it is. However, remember that a subcontractor relationship could cause a winning team to lose the contract if the prime contractor does not conduct the analysis properly. For example, poor analysis could cause the contractor to miss a subcontractor's poor-performance track record, to miscalculate the subcontractor's discount, or to misunderstand the customer's subcontractor. Any of these situations could cause the prime contractor to lose the contract.

Subcontractor Considerations

Some companies find subcontractor relationships attractive because they allow companies to work on contracts that the companies may not have been able to work on. For example, if a company is small or if it provides a product that the government or a commercial entity would not typically release an entire contract for, working with another company allows the first company to work on larger programs and sell greater quantities. Other benefits to the subcontractor include the following:

- Cost-competitive solution
- Contract risk/reward
- Program requirements
- Learning opportunity
- Capitalizing on an existing relationship
- Competing on multiple contracts simultaneously

Cost-Competitive Solution

When a company works alone, it is responsible for providing all components of a solution. A small company, or a company providing only one small piece of the overall solution, may not have the leverage to provide a cost-competitive solution like a large company or companies that provide the bulk of the solution internally. In such cases, working with another company would allow the small company to provide greater quantities and work on contracts that it normally could not work on. Likewise, a large company may use subcontracting as a way of trying out new business lines without fully committing its resources.

Contract Risk/Reward

By subcontracting, a company shares the reward that it receives on the contract but it also mitigates some of its risk by sharing it with the prime contractor. The amount of risk and reward (or profit) a company gets by subcontracting is depends on what each side negotiates.

Program Requirements

A subcontractor may not be able to meet all of the program requirements, but it may be able to provide a cost-effective solution. Often times, a small company cannot take on the risk and exposure of meeting all of the contractual obligations; if it did accept the risk and could not meet the contract requirements, the company could go out of business. Subcontracting gives companies the ability provide a piece of the solution without having to meet all the requirements, terms, and conditions imposed by the customer contract.

Learning Opportunity

Subcontracting gives the subcontractor the ability to learn the details of the business in a relatively risk-free environment. By working with other companies, the subcontractor can learn new ways to do business from each new subcontracting opportunity. Because the subcontractor only needs to worry about the requirements, terms, and conditions in the subcontract, the subcontractor can take the time and observe the company with which it is working.

Capitalizing on an Existing Relationship

Subcontracting allows a well-performing subcontractor to capitalize on its existing relationships to grow its business. For example, a subcontractor works for a prime contractor on a commercial contract. The contract is up for recompete. The subcontractor is courted by other contractors interested in the business. By entering into nonexclusive relationships with each of them, the subcontractor improves its chances of winning the recompete work with a minimum amount of additional effort. This situation can also be triggered by the customer. The customer could tell a prime contractor to work with a particular subcontractor if the contractor wants to secure the business. This is known as a *directed subcontract*. Technically, the federal government cannot offer directed subcontracts; however, sometimes prime contractors get very strong "feelings" from the government about working with a particular subcontractor. The government can direct a subcontract if there is a national crisis or emergency or if there is a compelling business reason to do so.

Competing on Multiple Contracts Simultaneously

Depending on the subcontracts, a company may be able to sell its product through multiple contracts at one time. Obviously, spreading a company's resources too thin doesn't do either party any good. However, through careful planning and management, a company can increase its chances at business because it has increased its number of contracts being pursued.

Government Considerations

Subcontracting makes the government marketplace attractive to companies that would not or would be unable to pursue a prime contract with the government on their own. By limiting its exposure and risk, which are usually found in large programs, subcontractors can enjoy the challenge, exposure, and sales typically associated with large complex programs without assuming the high risk associated with these programs. Subcontracting, however, is not risk free. Prime contractors try to flow down many of the prime contract terms and conditions to the subcontractor, however, these terms and conditions must be negotiated between the prime contractor and subcontractor.

Complexity in Government Programs

Government programs, as well as commercial programs, can be highly complex. Program complexity can be driven by the number of requirements, the degree of integration required between components, the number of disparate types of companies that must work together to complete the project, or the amount of risk that the prime contractor must assume in completing the work. Additionally, a company may have difficulty navigating through the government's business regulations if it the company doesn't have a mentor to help it through the first couple of programs.

Requirement to Help Small Businesses

The government spends approximately $105 billion annually on contracting opportunities, but a small company that does not understand the government process may have difficulty obtaining these contract dollars. The government, unlike commercial entities, must have its acquisition programs meet goals that go beyond mere purchasing. For example, the government has socioeconomic goals to ensure that the U.S. economy prospers and grows. The Small Business Administration (SBA) was designed to help small companies thrive and prosper in the U.S. To that end, the SBA uses many initiatives to help small businesses and small, disadvantaged businesses obtain government contracts.

Assistance Available to Companies Pursuing Government Business

If a company decides to pursue federal government business, it may choose to work through the SBA or the Mentor-Protégé program or by using the General Services Administration's multiple award schedule.

SBA

The government established the SBA to help small businesses obtain, maintain, and retain government business. To that end, the SBA offers seminars, literature, Web sites, local offices, skilled expertise, one-on-one business advice, and an automated phone system to help small business owners start a business and move into the government marketplace. In addition to the headquarters office in Washington, D.C. and their regional offices located throughout the United States, the SBA has personnel who work to identify programs as small business set-asides and who work to enact legislation that helps small businesses obtain and keep federal business. They also assist in matching complementary companies to encourage them to work on programs that would offer mutual gain.

Industry Classification

The government helps small business by defining Standard Industry Classification (SIC) codes that stipulate the qualifications of a small business so that small businesses can receive benefits. The government defines small businesses according to a business' industry, revenue, and number of employees. Each industry has a different threshold for what constitutes a small business. For example, the revenue criterion is a lot higher for construction contracts than for consulting contracts because the government assumes that construction contracts cost more to operate and, therefore, it pays more for them. A $10 million construction contract may represent one program, whereas $10 million in consulting contracts may represent 50 or more separate programs.

8(a) Program

Another initiative that the SBA has is the small and disadvantaged business program. The program is commonly called the *8(a) program* because that is the citation of the part of law that enacted the program. For a company to qualify under the 8(a) program, the company must meet the thresholds for revenue and number of employees for its industry. In addition, the company must have at least 51 percent of the business owned and operated by a person from an origin that is considered a minority within the United States. Finally, the company has to enroll and be accepted as part of the 8(a) program.

Set-Aside Programs

The reason that it is important for a company to determine if it is a small business (SB) or if it qualifies as a small and disadvantaged business (SDB) is that the company can then compete on programs reserved for SBs and SDBs. Such programs are called *small business set-asides*. There are also SDB set-asides and only SDBs can compete on them. By limiting the competition and excluding large companies, the government hopes to encourage small businesses to pursue business opportunities within the federal marketplace.

New Business Relationships

Another benefit of set-aside programs is that they help small companies establish new business relationships with other SBs, SDBs, and large companies. A SB or a SDB can work with a large company on a set-aside program because the only requirement for the program is that the SB or SDB perform at least 51 percent of the work to be performed on the contract. So a SDB can be the prime contractor on a program and subcontract 49 percent or less of the work to a SB or large company to help meet program requirements.

SB and SDB Agency Goals

The SBA helps small companies by setting goals for government agencies on how much business they must give to small businesses. An agency then sets goals for each prime contractor on how much of the agency's contract must be completed by a subcontractor that is a small business. As more and more small businesses are established, the SBA increases its goals for agencies. This initiative helps SBs and SDBs because the government must actively seek smaller companies in order to meet their regulations.

Prime Contractor Requirement

Large prime contractors need SBs and SDBs in order to meet the program requirements of certain contracts. As the economy moves toward entrepreneurs and start-up companies, the SBA is requiring that a greater percentage of business be given to SB/SDBs through prime contracts. When a large company works with a small company, the small company helps the large company meet its government-imposed socioeconomic goals. This partnership, in turn, allows the government to meet its socioeconomic objective of keeping people employed through small companies. Most governmental contracts require prime contractors to state how close they can come to meeting an agency's SB/SDB goal. The prime contractors must certify that they will subcontract a certain percentage of the work available on the contract to SB/SDB companies.

SADBOs

The SBA has small-business liaisons called *small and disadvantaged business officers* (SADBOs) who work within agencies and continually try to find new program requirements that could be completed by small businesses and small, disadvantaged businesses. In addition, the liaisons question government procurement officials about why each piece of business is not a SB or a SDB set-aside. The officials must also justify why a small company could not perform the program requirements.

Program Requirements

Once the government decides that a particular program requirement can be performed by a SB or SDB, that requirement remains as a set-aside, even if a new contract for the same work must be obtained. For example, a government agency needed data communication lines installed and the SBA determined that there were SBs or SDBs that could do this work. The program requirement would be released in an RFP that allowed only SBs or SDBs to compete for the program. If after the contract work is over the agency decides it needs more data communication line installed, its RFP would have to be released as an SB or SDB set-aside program because it was once classified as such.

Mentor-Protégé Program

The Department of Defense (DOD) offers a program to help small companies gain the skills required to manage federal contracts. The Mentor-Protégé program teams a large government contractor with a small business that is trying to become a federal contractor. The large company works with the small company on programs and the large company teaches the small company the federal procurement process. The small company gains expertise and assistance in getting started; the large company gains credit toward its subcontracting plan for its participation in the program.

To qualify as a mentor, a company must:

- Be currently eligible to receive government contracts.
- Have been awarded at least $100 million in DOD contracts in the last fiscal year.
- Possess a demonstrated ability to assist protégé development.
- Have Secretary of Defense approval.
- Be performing under an active subcontracting plan.

The protégé must meet the following requirements:

- Be a small and disadvantaged business as defined by the SBA.
- Be eligible for government contracts.

If a company is interested in participating in the Mentor-Protégé program, it should review the *Policy and Procedures for the DOD Pilot Mentor-Protégé Program* (DAC 91-10) issued as part of the Department of Defense FAR Supplement dated February 1996. Once DOD matches the mentor to a protégé, the two companies must enter into a mentor-protégé agreement, which must include the following information:

- Name, address, and telephone number of the contacts at both firms
- Applicable SIC code and protégé certification that it does not exceed the size or dollar standard
- Development program for the protégé
- A program participation term, which can range from a few months up to five years initially with the option to renew for four years
- Procedures for terminating the agreement
- Any additional terms and conditions

GSA Schedule Contract

A less risky approach than running an entire program on its own is for a company to secure a General Services Administration (GSA) schedule through which the company can sell its products and services to anyone within the government. GSA schedules are increasing in popularity because once they are established, they are easy to use and a cost-effective alternative to agency specific procurements. If the company is interested in competing on a GSA multiple award schedule contract, the GSA's Web page (www.gsa.gov) will provide more information.

The Federal Acquisition Reform Act (FARA) has raised the threshold for small acquisitions to $5 million for commercial items and has included a commercial services definition. These two changes and the recent changes in the GSA program make it possible for small companies to put their commercial products and services on a GSA schedule contract. GSA schedule contracts allow all government agencies the opportunity to buy a small company's products and services, and the GSA provides advertising for small businesses on its Web page. The advertising is paid for by the 1 percent industrial funding fee that the GSA collects on every delivery order issued under the schedule. An agency wishing to procure goods and services using the GSA schedule contracts can conduct a quick comparison among three or more companies that are on the schedule and award the contract. To stay competitive, a company can always reduce its GSA price if it really wants to acquire a certain business. Although the GSA merged many of their schedules in 1998, making the Small Business Administration (SBA) worry that small businesses and small, disadvantaged business may be adversely affected, the GSA's administrator, David Barram, stated in a letter to the SBA's administrator, Aida Alvarez, that the GSA "is committed to continuing its efforts to increase small business participation" in the multiple award schedule program. To that end, GSA is currently revising the ordering procedures for information technology professional services to allow agencies to only consider small businesses if they choose when acquiring these services. For additional information, visit the GSA's Web site (pub.fss.gsa.gov/adp/index.html).

Easy-to-Use Small Purchase Ordering Procedures

Small purchase ordering procedures allow contractors to compete for work using their computer and the Internet. Small purchase ordering procedures allow the government to pay for products or services by using credit cards, thereby simplifying the whole financial transaction. Currently, the simplified acquisition procedures may be used for all acquisitions under the small-acquisition threshold that is currently set at $100,000. The only exception is orders placed under an established contract for products and services obtained from a required-sources supply. If the product or service is required for support of humanitarian or peace-keeping missions, the threshold is raised to $200,000. FAR Part 13 explains methods available to COs for small purchases. As the government raises its threshold on small purchases, it will become significantly easier for a company to work on a contract alone. With these electronic systems, full-scale proposals, which can be costly for small companies, will not be required.

3 MARKETING

This chapter presents an overview of the steps a company takes during the marketing phase. The company takes these steps after it has made the strategic decision to enter a particular industry marketplace based on the result of the planning efforts described in Chapter 2. Chapter 3 lists the specific tasks that companies undertake during the marketing phase. These activities will be scaled up or down depending on the size of the contracting program and the role that the company plays on a program, (i.e., subcontractor or prime contractor). Also, many of these tasks—such as analyzing companies to determine which are potential teaming partners, subcontractors, or competitors—can be done for multiple programs, and the results can be applied to a specific deal.

Marketing Process

Analyze Strategic Plan Results

As a result of the company's strategic planning efforts described in Chapter 2, the company now has an overall understanding of its product offering, customers' environments, competitive environment, objectives, programs, projects, schedules, and resources. Now the company must determine how to leverage that information to select one or more programs to pursue.

Identify Which Customers Can Help Meet the Goals of the Strategic Plan

The first step in selling to a customer is to determine which company product or service should be targeted to which customer. A prime contractor needs to determine which customers it should pursue; a subcontractor needs to determine which prime contractor team(s) it should secure a position on. Although the customer does not require a company to develop a marketing plan, the customer does expect the company to analyze contracting opportunities and pursue those for which the company believes it is qualified. When the company is identifying customers that can help it meet its strategic plan, the company should consider the customer's need, the customer's budget, the time frame, the cost of sale, and the competitive environment.

Develop a Marketing Plan for a Particular Program

The process of developing a marketing plan can follow the same process that was outlined for developing a strategic plan. This process is a good way for a company to evaluate market conditions, competition, the needs of the customer, and the company's strengths and weaknesses to determine where its marketing efforts should be directed. As part of the marketing plan, the company develops specific strategies for pursuing a contract program within a customer organization.

Assign a Program Manager and Salesperson to Pursue the Program

Both prime contractors and subcontractors assign program managers and salespeople to pursue the program. The prime contractor's program manager begins developing solutions by defining the acquisition strategy and by determining potential subcontractors. The subcontractor program manager begins meeting with prime contractors to secure the best opportunity. The salespeople from both organizations gather marketing information for the marketing plan and try to determine how the two companies might work together. The program manager and salespeople from each company work together to identify the internal team members, analyze and shape the RFP, and work to secure a positive bid decision.

Gather Marketing Information

One step in the planning process is to gather marketing information for the various components of the plan. The previous chapter discussed what information is needed. This chapter discusses some of the tools needed to get the information and other ways that the data are used besides in developing the strategic and marketing plans.

Tools

Some of the tools that a company can use to obtain the information include:

- An on-line database or database service that makes the research function easier is helpful in quickly determining marketing statistics or trend data.
- An automated system or method that provides facts about the company's current contracts can help in preparing customer briefings or in answering customer queries.

- A database or method of tracking customer contacts will help ensure that the customer receives a consistent message from the company by allowing the company to determine which salespeople are talking to which customers. It will also ensure that one customer does not get bombarded by sales calls.
- Any industry information service (e.g., Gartner Group or Datapro) that provides monthly analyses of available products and services and the pros and cons of each will help in the competition analysis area.
- Agencies with their own informational bulletin board system that allow contractors to access information using a modem and a PC.
- The Internet, which provides a deluge of information on marketing trends, company profiles, technology applications, and so on.
- George Washington University, the University of Virginia, and other schools have excellent seminars available to assist companies in getting into the federal or commercial marketplaces.
- Professional organizations, such as National Contract Management Association (NCMA) or Management Concepts, Inc., conduct lectures, develop federal procurement guidebooks, and provide excellent networking opportunities for companies pursuing federal business. In addition, NCMA sponsors national education seminars that bring industry and government experts together to discuss current procurement trends. Industry specific organizations, such as the Electronic Industries Association and the Aerospace Industries Association, are useful in providing lists of companies within the industry and contact points.
- Agencies with their own competition advocates who are responsible for ensuring that adequate competition exists for each program. Competition advocates can provide information on how to conduct business within a particular agency if the company decides to pursue federal business.

In addition, a company can find out about customer requirements directly by:

- Conducting a site survey to see the location at which the work will be performed and to interview the end-user customer.
- Attending briefings that the customer conducts to share its strategy and direction for a program.

- Conducting the shaping process that is described below.

The result of all this information gathering is to determine:

- Customer's existing environment
- Customer's preference
- The best way to package the company's products and services
- An initial assessment of the competition

Uses for Marketing Information

Once the company has collected all of the information it needs, it uses the data in a variety of ways. Some of the uses are outlined below.

- *Marketing plan*—The information can be used to develop the following sections of the marketing plan: internal conditions, external conditions, assumptions, objectives, and programs/projects.
- *Bid decision*—The information can be used as a basis for deciding whether to bid or not bid on a program.
- *Competition files*—Data collected on competitors become the company's competition files, which are used across multiple program efforts.
- *Vendor files*—Data collected on vendors can be used to determine potential teaming partners and subcontractors on current or future programs.
- *Marketing strategy*—The information that is collected and analyzed is used to develop the corporate marketing strategy, which includes advertising, trade booths, corporate capabilities statement, position papers, marketing meetings, and industry briefings.
- *Customer files*—Information collected on a commercial company or an agency helps the company understand the customer better for current or future programs.
- *Technology files*—Information collected on technology that is applicable to the industry can help the company determine which technologies it should employ to win new business.
- *Proposal*— The information can help the company write a proposal that demonstrates its understanding of the customer environment, highlights the company's strengths that are impor-

tant to the customer, and allows the company to discriminate itself from the competition.

Get on the Bidders List

In order for a company to be considered for a customer's new business opportunity, the company must learn about the opportunity. To do that, the company must secure a position on the customer's bidders list. Governmental customers have standard forms for achieving a place on their bidders list (which are described below in the section titled Government Considerations). Commercial customers, however, usually prefer to keep information about their upcoming plans a secret so as to not give away any of their competitive advantage. Therefore, it is more difficult to get on a commercial customer's bidders list. Following are some ways that the company can use to help secure a position on a commercial customer's bidders list:

- Meet regularly with current customers to determine if they have any upcoming requirements.
- Help customers obtain business in their industries and in turn they may help the company obtain business in its industry.
- Read industry journals to learn of companies' strategic directions and to determine if the company can help them obtain their goals. Then schedule a meeting with a company to talk about how your products and services might be incorporated into its strategic direction.
- Meet with subcontractors to determine if they are aware of new opportunities that they could work on with the company.
- Network with people at various levels of organizations to discover what is going with a particular customer.
- Attend trade shows to learn what a company is offering and how it is permeating the marketplace, then convince them that your company can play a part.
- Do a really great job on current contracts. Existing customers often provide valuable marketing for you when you are outstanding.

Analyze the Requirement

After the company has analyzed the information and determined its position, the company then reviews the program requirements to determine if the company has the capability to bid. The prime contractor reviews the requirements in the customer's request for proposal (RFP). The subcontractor reviews the prime contractor's requirements in the prime contractor's RFP, which is usually similar to the customer's RFP. The requirements of commercial companies and federal agencies may vary in how they inform companies about their requirements.

Commercial Environment

This section discusses the commercial approach to informing companies about proposal requirements, and the government's approaches are discussed in the section titled Government Environment. When reviewing the section titled Government RFP, note the types of information that a governmental customer would include in a requirements document that a commercial customer may include but not present it in the same standard format.

A commercial customer is not governed by the Federal Acquisition Regulation (FAR) and is not required to conduct a solicitation or a fair and equal competition. A commercial customer could just call up the company that it wants to work with, tell it the requirements, and obtain a price. The whole transaction could be oral with a handshake to "solidify" the relationship. Unfortunately, with the risks associated with non-performance, this approach is seldom used.

What typically happens is that a commercial company will document its requirements in a RFP or solicitation document. This document will include the company's technical requirements, terms and conditions, and any other data it cares to share with the competitors. Then the competing companies prepare and submit their proposals. The customer can use whatever evaluation criteria it chooses to select the winner. The relationship is then formally documented in the prime contract, which states the terms the two parties agreed on. Due to the degree of flexibility and autonomy that commercial companies have, seldom will two RFPs look the same unless they are issued by the same customer for similar products and services.

One difference to remember between competing in the commercial environment versus the federal environment is that the federal environment has more restrictions. A commercial company is not obligated to allow any company to bid on its program. It can select whomever it wishes to work with using whatever evaluation criteria it decides. The federal government must either accept proposals from all companies wishing to bid on the program or it must establish non-biased criteria for the number of companies it will allow to bid on the program so that it can conduct an efficient competition.

Shape the RFP

Shaping the RFP is an industry colloquialism used to describe the process of a prospective contractor suggesting changes to the customer's draft RFP requirements. As discussed below, shaping helps the competing companies and the customer. The shaping process can include position papers, marketing meetings, draft document responses, and bidders conference suggestions.

Benefits of Shaping for the Competing Companies

Shaping is useful to a company because it gives the company a better chance at winning by attempting to make the requirements more favorable to its own solution. Shaping can help a company gain a competitive advantage by suggesting changes to the requirements that help distinguish its solution from the competitors' solutions. By suggesting that the customer add certain requirements to the solicitation document or modify existing requirements, the company may have an opportunity to introduce its latest technology and, perhaps, gain a competitive advantage. A commercial company can make whatever changes it deems necessary to the RFP document. The governmental customer must document the change and explain how the change helps the government meet its requirements more effectively. If the changes do not excessively limit competition, the government may decide to accept the suggested changes.

Shaping can also help the company render a positive bid decision on a procurement. If the draft RFP language has terms and conditions that would prevent the company's management team from pursuing the piece of business, the company could suggest language changes that, if accepted, would allow the company to compete for the procurement. Examples of terms that might preclude a company from competing include the date by which products must be commercially available or extensive downtime credits awarded to the customer if the contractor's products fail to work as specified.

Shaping is extremely useful in the subcontracting process for a number of reasons. In order for the shaping process to begin, the customer must give out some information about the program. This information can either take the form of a draft RFP document, a bidders conference, or a one-on-one discussions with selected prime contractors. Once the prime contractor has this information, it has an idea of what the customer is looking for so it can begin discussions with potential subcontractors to work on the business. Likewise, subcontractors can begin to learn which prime contractors are competing for the program so the subcontractors can start marketing their products and services to the prime contractors with whom they would like to work.

If the contract is with the federal government, a large prime contractor will have to run competitions to select a subcontractor. The competition process is time consuming but required for the prime contractor to pass a Contractor Purchasing System Review, during which the government determines if the prime contractor selected the subcontractor that represented the best overall value to the government. Small companies have the competition process requirement waived. The shaping process helps companies competing for federal business by giving them a head start in completing the formalized subcontracting requirements.

Benefits of Shaping for the Customer

Besides maximizing competition, the customer encourages companies to shape the procurement because the process allows the customer to understand specific company concerns and to fix problems early on to avoid or limit issues arising later in the procurement cycle. The customer needs to know the company's concerns because if there are clauses that make a program too risky for one company, chances are the clauses are too risky for other companies as well. This situation would not affect a commercial customer because it can begin negotiations if only one company submits a proposal. However, if a government customer does not get enough proposals, it may be forced to redesign the solicitation and recompete the program. As such, shaping the proposal helps the customer receive more responsive proposals from companies by eliminating problematic requirements. The shaping process also helps to clarify potentially problematic terms, conditions, and specifications before any significant amount of contractor work has commenced.

Another reason that the customer encourages companies to shape the procurement is so that the companies can teach the customer about the industry and help it to determine the products and services available in the commercial market. In addition, the customer can tap company expertise to determine if there is a new, better, or more effective way to meet the customer's requirements. This allows the customer time to analyze solutions immediately instead of spending time collecting data on what is available in the marketplace.

Methods of Shaping the RFP

Position Papers/Marketing Meetings

One way that a company shapes an RFP is by presenting its opinions in a position paper that it sends to the customer or delivers during a marketing meeting with the customer's decision maker. Position papers are an effective way to suggest changes to the customer's RFP. Position papers should clearly present the issue, explain the company's position, explain the benefits of a proposed change, and suggest alternative language for rewriting the requirement. The customer is under no obligation to change the requirement, but if the company presents a good case, the customer may change its requirement.

Companies can issue position papers and/or conduct marketing meetings with both commercial customers and government customers. Marketing meetings can be conducted at the customer location and may include a site visit and discussions with the actual users or they may be conducted at the contractor location to illustrate the company's capabilities and facilities. Governmental customers typically limits these types of discussions to the period before the release of an actual RFP so that there is no violation, or perceived violation, of the Procurement Integrity Act. The Procurement Integrity Act prohibits any job offers, bribes, or source selection information from being offered or secured during a federal procurement.

The company must remember several key items and make many decisions when it prepares a position paper or marketing meeting. The issues are outlined in the following paragraphs.

Determine who should submit or present the team's position. It may make sense for the prime contractor to submit the position paper or conduct the marketing meeting outlining the team's position. However, the prospective subcontractor may be better suited to do this if the issue falls within its area of expertise.

Determine to whom the paper should be submitted or presented. To answer this question, the company should answer the following question: "Who has the authority to make a decision on the issue being raised?" If it is a technical item, the company should submit the paper to the program manager. If the issue stems from a contractual requirement, the contracts person should receive the paper.

Provide information in a precise, accurate, easy to understand manner. Break complex topics into easy to understand steps and keep explanations as simple as possible. By taking these precautions, the message has a much better chance of being understood, explained to others, and acted upon.

Remember that information will circulate. Present as much information as necessary to state the company's position, but remember that documents could end up in anyone's hands. Therefore, don't give away too much of the company's competitive edge.

Make specific recommendations. Present specific recommendations, including specific RFP language changes, when stating a position to the government. This way the customer can accept, reject, or modify the ideas presented based on the stated language and it does not have to spend time developing language that may or may not solve the problem being raised.

Raise an issue that can be resolved. This only applies to governmental contractors. Some requirements may seem totally erroneous to the company but because of FAR stipulations, the government is required to include them. Make sure the problem can be solved within the constraints imposed by the federal procurement process before submitting a change.

Company Response to Draft RFPs, RFIs, and RFCs

For large procurements that require a diverse mix of products and services, the customer may issue several draft documents before it releases the actual RFP. For task order, labor, or commercial-off-the-shelf item procurements, the customer may not issue any draft documents because it has already done its market research and knows what is available commercially. Draft documents allow the contracting community a chance to see what is being requested and the customer to solicit feedback from the community about alternative approaches to meet its requirements.

The customer dictates whether the information that a company provides in the draft process review is shared with the rest of the interested companies. A governmental customer provides a document listing the questions asked by each company and the government's answer to each company. Because governmental customers release the questions and answers, the company must decided whether or not the question its question would give its competitors an advantage. A commercial customer can either share questions and answers with the other companies or work with each company independently and not share the information with all the companies.

The company must remember several key items when preparing a draft document response. These issues are outlined in the following paragraphs:

The customer may or may not issue the entire RFP. Although the company must use all of the sections when making its bid decision, the customer may choose to issue only the technical statement of work or selected portions of the RFP.

The RFP is not contractually binding. The customer's draft document and a company's response to it are not contractually binding. This means that the customer's final RFP requirements can change quite substantially from the draft requirements.

Draft RFP allows companies to get started. Up until the draft document stage, the company has had limited insight into the required solution. The draft document is the first time the company can see the solution as a whole. Armed with this information, the company can start lining up teaming partners, devising a solution, and preparing a program approach.

If interested, respond to the RFP. If the company is genuinely interested in the procurement, it should take the time to review and comment on the draft document. This is important because it lets the customer know that the company is interested in the procurement. The company's response is also important because if it fails to conduct a detailed analysis of the draft RFP then, the customer may be less willing to make requirement changes later.

Try to get rid of onerous terms and conditions. If the draft RFP contains clauses that represent significant risk for the company or that require a product that only one company can provide (thereby limiting competition), the company can suggest less restrictive alternative language to the customer. Often, the customer will evaluate the position offered and, if the problem is affecting more than one company, will change the requirement.

Draft documents represent the unadulterated version. Draft documents primarily come straight from the customer user community and, therefore, they represent the actual user requirements for the program. After this point, competing companies will suggest alternate language that will modify the original requirements. For this reason, the company should review the draft documents in detail to understand exactly what the customer is looking for in its solution.

Draft document provide an opportunity to suggest new ways of approaching the problem. If the company has a new, better, and more efficient way to approach the customer's problem, it should suggest the alternate approaches in the draft stage. When the customer moves into the final RFP stage, the customer is too far along in the approval cycle to consider other approaches. Many customers will not even entertain alternate solution proposals after the draft stage.

When the company receives a draft document, it should take several steps to ensure an adequate review of the document. These steps include the following:

1. Create a team by selecting company members and subcontractors who have expertise in each of the major areas of the RFP (e.g., contracts, technical, management, maintenance, business, user assistance, or training).

2. Ask the team members to review the whole draft document so they understand all the requirements affecting their particular functional area.

3. Divide the RFP into sections based on the individual areas of expertise of the team members, and ask the members to review the sections by answering the following questions:

   — Does it make good business sense to pursue the contract?

   — Are there any requirements that prevent the company from bidding on this procurement?

   — What risks will the company face if it bids on this procurement?

   — Can the company make a profit off the contract?

4. Have the team review the draft document and suggest that each subject expert write his or her comments, questions, and areas of concern.

5. Bring the team together and discuss the members' comments from each section.

6. Conduct a management review to determine which comments should be included in the company's response to the proposal.

7. Arrange the document in a format that is easy for the customer to understand the requested changes. To do this, the company restates the requirement and cites the paragraph number, states the company's interpretation of the requirement, states the

reasons why the stated method may not be the best method, suggests alternatives, recommends a change, and substantiates the recommendation.

Bidders Conferences

Besides preparing position papers, attending marketing meetings, and responding to draft solicitations to shape an RFP, companies also should use bidders conferences to shape an RFP. Bidders conferences are customer-sponsored meetings designed to bring together all the companies interested in a customer's procurement for a general question-and-answer session. Bidders conferences give the customer the opportunity to solicit input from the contractor community face-to-face. The conferences are good for companies because they can determine which other companies might be interested in a teaming relationship and which are potential competitors. Following are several key items that a company should remember when attending a bidders conference:

Competitors   The company should be careful about how much of its solution its divulges at the bidders conference because many of the other attendees will be competitors.

Not contractually binding   Items presented or statements made at the bidders conference are not contractually binding. Therefore, companies still must wait until the actual RFP comes out to know the final customer requirements.

Sign-in sheet   The company can use the sign-in sheet as resource because it will have the names of other companies that are interested in the procurement. The sheet also guarantees the company a spot on the customer's bidders mailing list for the RFP. The company will remain on the bidders mailing list until the company asks for its name to be removed or until the time of proposal submission. Usually, the customer sends amendments after proposal submission only to companies that turned in proposals.

One or multiple bidders conferences   The customer may choose to have a bidders conference before it releases its RFP, after it releases the RFP, or before and after it releases the RFP. If the company is interested in the procurement, it should send one or more representatives to each conference.

Format   Bidders conferences typically follow a standard format. The format for the conferences includes a brief customer description, an overall strategy for the procurement, a discussion on specific problem areas in the RFP, and an opportunity for companies to ask questions.

No matter what shaping method the company uses, the only one way that it will know whether the customer accepted its suggestions for changes to the RFP is by reviewing the final RFP (or an RFP amendment if the RFP has already been released).

Develop a Budget

A bid and proposal (B&P) budget is a key factor in the company's bid decision. The company has to decide how much a program costs to pursue and if the potential revenue justifies the expense. Bid and proposal money is the most sought after money in an organization, particularly in the government division of a company. This is because it represents the budget allotted for work to be done on a government proposal effort. It covers costs for all activities—from pre-RFP marketing to contract award. The source of B&P money depends on whether the pursued contract is commercial or governmental.

Commercial vs. Government Budgets

On commercial contracts, a company can charge back to the customer the full amount of money needed to win the bid through a higher price. A company pursuing commercial business can determine its own rates and may change those rates for each program it works on. Similarly, commercial companies can charge whatever price they want to win business. Because the financial information is confidential, one customer would probably not find out what a company charged another customer for similar work.

On government contracts, financial information is allowed to circulate among government customers. Additionally, only a certain portion of the budget a company used to win federal business is allowable to be charged back to the government customer through its rate structure. Any additional money that the company needs to pursue the program is taken directly out of its profit. The government determines what percentage of a company's federal government business base it will consider allowable. The dollar pool that is equivalent to the percentage allowed by the government is the company's total bid and proposal pool. The company can charge back that amount to the government in the form of overhead and general and administrative (G&A) rates, provided the company disclosed this practice to DCAA. The company applies the overhead and G&A rates to all labor and material costs, and the company must use these same rates on every deal that the company pursues during the applicable period of time. The company can determine how to allocate these dollars across upcoming programs for the year. When proposal efforts exceed the budget because of poor planning or program slippage by the government, the company must decide to either continue bidding on all its desired programs and pay for the difference between budgeted and actual B&P expenses out of profit, or to not bid on other government programs.

B&P Costs

A company develops a B&P budget for a proposal effort early on in the process, usually before the RFP is released. The budget normally includes costs for the following:

- Labor, including writers, editors, technical staff, management team, volume coordinators, production supervisor, and review team members
- Proposal space, office supplies, and equipment, such as PCs, printers, and plotters
- Proposal production tasks, such as graphics, word processing, and duplication
- Temporary living expenses for writers coming from other locations to work on the proposal, visits to the customer site, and visits to vendor sites

How Is the B&P Budget Determined?

To determine what costs go into a B&P budget, the company's program manager, sales manager, and proposal manager first need to determine the likely schedule of events for the procurement effort. The proposal team then estimates the resources required for each stage of the procurement process. The B&P budget is then submitted to upper management, who may modify the budget. The approved budget and actual expenses incurred against the budget are managed by the proposal team's business manager. Frequently, upper management will request a B&P status report to determine if the proposal team is progressing according to schedule and if the funds are being spent in direct proportion to the amount of work accomplished. If the team goes over budget, or if the program gets delayed, the company may decide to review its bid decision to determine if it still makes sense to pursue the program.

Understand the Competition

The purpose of a competition analysis is for a company to gain a competitive advantage by analyzing specific teams competing for the same government program. The information from this analysis helps the company determine strategies for winning and a proposed price. The company should also examine conditions within the customer environment and industry to determine if they present an opportunity for the company or its competitors to exploit. Figure 2 presents a sample checklist that a company can use to compare its team's attributes against the competition's attibutes.

Approach

A company may not have the time, inclination, or resources to analyze every competitor on a program, which the company does not need to do. The key is to select two or three competitors that represent the greatest competitive threat to the company and focus only on them. The company should address several areas when analyzing the competition:

**Figure 1. Sample Checklist for Comparing
a Team's Attributes to the Competitor's Attributes**

Attribute	Our Team	Competitor's Team
Demonstrated technical capability		
Price		
Value		
Previous relationship with customer		
Demonstrated management capability		
Subcontractor's reputation		
Marketshare in customer base		
Industry reputation		
Compliance with terms and conditions		
Customer support		
Degree of risk in offer		
Customer ties		

- Determine what companies the competitor will team with.
  - What types of relationships does the competitor have with other companies?
  - Does the competitor have ownership/partnership/marketing ties with other companies?
  - Does the customer have any preference toward the competitor's team?
  - What subcontractor is the competitor using for each component of the solution?
- Explore what products the competitor will propose.
  - Has the competitor competed for any similar deals recently? If it has, what was its product offering?
  - What is the competitor touting in its advertising, at conferences, and in its marketing literature?
  - Does any section of the RFP seem to favor one company?
- Determine how the competitor will position itself.
  - What win themes is it likely to use?
  - Will it emphasize low cost or technical advancements?
  - What are its strengths and weaknesses?
- Analyze how the competitor will price its offering.
  - What are its contract revenues?
  - What has its recent success record been?
  - Has it decided to back out of other deals lately?
  - What are its overhead and G&A rates?
  - How will it price program management?
  - How has it priced programs in the past?
  - What are its labor rates?
  - Where does it plan on running the program?
  - Does it manufacture the products it offers?
  - How will it price training and other support services? Can it develop the capability internally or does it hire subcontractors?
  - What other contracts is it currently bidding?

- Determine the key players in the customer organization.

  —What are their preferences?

  —What companies have they worked with before?

  —Are any of the former key customer players now working for the competitor?

  —How do members of the customer evaluation board feel about the competitors?

  —How will the customer evaluate the proposals (i.e., what is most important to it)?

- What significant events are occurring within the customer organization that may affect this procurement?

  —Any procurement scandals?

  —Does the company or agency have small business (SB) or small and disadvantaged business (SDB) goals that it must meet? Are there other legislative goals?

  —Is this a best-value procurement?

- What does the company look like to the competition?

  —What does the competition think the company will do in terms of a bidding strategy?

  —What weaknesses does the company have that the competition will try to exploit?

  —How can the company mitigate those weaknesses?

The goal of the competitive analysis is to determine the company's competitive position in relationship to the other companies bidding on the program. This will help the company determine if its product or service has captured a certain market niche or if its solution is no different from that of the competitors. The analysis will also help the company analyze the features, benefits, and discriminators of its solution, which the company will want to emphasize in the proposal. Finally, this analysis will help the company decide how to package its product/service offering. The company's decisions as to which products and services to offer, at what price, and what features to include (such as documentation, warranty, maintenance, training, or user support.) will ultimately either win or lose the program for the company.

Make an Initial Bid Decision

A milestone in the marketing process is the initial bid decision. The purpose of the bid decision process is to gather information germane to a particular program, evaluate the information, and decide to either bid or not bid the program. Both prime contractors and sub-contractors make bid decisions. The company makes this decision by assessing the company's internal capabilities, market conditions, customer understanding, and win probability. The company can make its bid decision at any point during a procurement effort. The company needs to make a careful and thoughtful decision, because if the company decides to not bid a program after it completed significant B&P efforts, the company suffers a loss. Some companies re-evaluate their decisions periodically as changes occur in the status of the five items mentioned below.

Areas of Analysis Required for a Bid Decision

Before the company spends a lot of resources to win a program, it must decide whether the potential success warrants the expenditure. The company must analyze the following areas in order to make a bid decision: customer program, internal capabilities, market conditions, customer understanding, win probability, team attributes, and competitor's attributes.

Customer Program

The customer program components that are critical in making a bid decision include:

- Technical statement of work
- Terms and conditions that will be imposed on the company
- Areas of potential risk to the company
- Regulations that must be adhered to by the company
- Estimated time frames for the procurement
- Past contractor performance expectations
- Contract performance requirements

Internal Capabilities

The internal capabilities that a company should consider when making a bid decision include:

- Technical capability
- Corporate resource availability
- Personnel availability for proposal development
- Personnel availability for contract performance
- Funds availability
- Potential revenue if the company wins
- Past performance
- Risk-mitigation plan
- Company's make or buy decision results

Market Conditions

The market conditions are those items outside of the company that may affect the company's success on a customer program, including:

- Raw material availability
- Labor availability, if required to hire externally
- Pricing strategy
- Economic trends

Customer Understanding

The company must understand the customer environment in order to succeed. To understand the customer to a degree that will ensure success, the company must become knowledgeable of the following:

- Past performance with the customer
- Customer's degree of satisfaction with current contractor
- Customer's decision makers
- Customer's program objectives
- Pending legislation and budget considerations

Win Probability

The probability of the company winning the program is based on two components: the attributes of the company's team and the attributes of the competitors' teams. Components that the company should consider in each of these areas include:

- Team attributes
  - —Customer-perceived strengths
  - —Customer-perceived weaknesses
  - —Strategy for highlighting strengths
  - —Strategy for mitigating weaknesses
  - —Strategy for minimizing competitors' strengths
  - —Strategy for highlighting competitors' weaknesses
  - —Pricing strategies
  - —Strategy for minimizing risk areas
  - —Market position
  - —Past performance
  - —Subcontractors' or prime company's actual strengths and weaknesses
- Competitor's attributes
  - —Customer-perceived strengths
  - —Customer-perceived weaknesses
  - —Pricing strategies
  - —Market position
  - —Past performance

By comparing the attributes of the company's team against the attributes of the competitors' teams, the company can estimate its win probability. This win probability is tempered with the company's analysis of internal capabilities, market conditions, and customer understanding.

Work Completed Before Making a Bid Decision

Besides the analyses listed above, the company should finish other work before making the bid decision. Other work could include:

- Receiving letters of intent to bid from the major subcontractors or from the prime company.
- Estimating potential revenue if the company wins the program.
- Analyzing risks and determining how to mitigate them.
- Developing a high-level technical approach for how to solve the customer's problem.

- Developing a high-level management approach for how the contract will operate after award.
- Developing high-level pricing strategies.
- Identifying the proposal management team.
- Determining key personnel to be used on the contract.
- Developing the proposal schedule.
- Developing the bid and proposal budget.

Figure 3 presents a sample team analysis that can be used to define the strengths, weaknesses, and customer benefits of each team member. The form also can be used to compare the company's team against its competitors.

Implications of the Bid Decision Process

After the company completes the analyses and tasks described in the previous sections, it can make the bid decision. The number and types of people who determine whether or not the company should bid a customer program depends on the size of the company. For example, if a company is small and is owned by one person, the bid decision is made by one individual. If the company is a large corporation, many people may be involved in the decision. Regardless of the number of people involved in the bid decision, the company must consider the following implications of its decision with regard to the rest of its business base: technical abilities, financial security, contractual obligations, personnel resources, operational capabilities, engineering abilities, and marketing approach.

Complexity of the Bid Decision Process

The company must consider many components when making a bid decision. Even though a lot of work is involved in making the decision, the important thing for the company to remember is that the more analysis that it does up front to determine exactly what the company is committing to, the better position it will be in to respond to changes in the procurement. Anyone can slap a bid together and send it to the customer to evaluate. However, companies that follow this practice may encounter problems with the contract if they win. For example, they may default on the contract or lose substantial money because they did not take the time to analyze the deal up front. The savvy bidder understands that a well-organized bid based on solid analysis presents the company in the best possible light and yields the greatest return on investment potential.

Figure 3. Sample Team Analysis

Prime Contractor

Strengths	Weaknesses	Customer Benefits
1. _____	1. _____	1. _____
2. _____	2. _____	2. _____
3. _____	3. _____	3. _____
4. _____	4. _____	4. _____
5. _____	5. _____	5. _____

Subcontractor 1

Strengths	Weaknesses	Customer Benefits
1. _____	1. _____	1. _____
2. _____	2. _____	2. _____
3. _____	3. _____	3. _____
4. _____	4. _____	4. _____
5. _____	5. _____	5. _____

Subcontractor 2

Strengths	Weaknesses	Customer Benefits
1. _____	1. _____	1. _____
2. _____	2. _____	2. _____
3. _____	3. _____	3. _____
4. _____	4. _____	4. _____
5. _____	5. _____	5. _____

Subcontractor 3

Strengths	Weaknesses	Customer Benefits
1. _____	1. _____	1. _____
2. _____	2. _____	2. _____
3. _____	3. _____	3. _____
4. _____	4. _____	4. _____
5. _____	5. _____	5. _____

Prime Contractor Considerations

In addition to all the tasks described above, the company has additional responsibilities to complete during the marketing phase if it will act as the prime contractor on the program.

Identify Components for Customer Solution

The company must identify all the pieces of the customer solution before it can begin writing a proposal. These pieces are all stated in the RFP, so the contractor should not have difficulty identifying them. Early identification and solution development may give the company a competitive edge. Solutions for customers could include locating or developing any of the following:

- Product
- Service
- Training
- Maintenance
- User support
- Installation
- Design
- Manufacture
- Research
- Studies

Conduct Make-or-Buy Analysis

As the company identifies individual solution components, it also needs to conduct a make-or-buy analysis for each component. For each solution component, the company decides whether it wants to provide the component using internal or external resources. If the company is not a manufacturer, or if a manufacturer cannot provide the component in the required time frame, the company must find sources available to meet the customer's requirements. When deciding whether to make or buy a component, the company should review its:

- Internal capabilities
- Personnel's skills
- Program timing

- Competitive position
- Cost to produce or provide

When the company has completed this analysis, it should know which components it will provide and which components it will subcontract out to other companies.

Identify Types of Relationships

The company's next step is to determine the level of relationship it requires with the provider of each product or service. The types of relationships the company may have include one-time purchases, purchase orders, suppliers, teaming partnerships, and strategic alliances, which were discussed in Chapter 1.

Identify Potential Suppliers for Each Component

Once the company decides which components it will subcontract out to other companies, it must find companies that can and are willing to work on the program. In addition, these companies must be willing to offer their products or services at a price at which the company can ultimately win the program. The company may begin looking for subcontractors by looking in the following areas:

- Purchasing department
- Marketing department
- Industry magazines
- Professional organizations
- Supplier files
- Other program efforts within the company

Contact Suppliers to Determine Level of Interest

Once the company has a list of potential companies, it should review the list to determine if it should remove some of the companies. The company should remove those companies that have poor past performance, have not been able to sign on as a subcontractor on other programs, or those that the customer has indicated it would not like to work with. Once the company conducts an initial downswing, it must contact the companies to determine if they are interested in bidding on the customer program. The company can either write to, telephone, e-mail, or conduct a preliminary meeting with each company to determine its level of interest in working jointly on the program. Once the two companies begin meeting, typically, they will require each other to sign a non-disclosure agreement. This agreement states in essence that each party is prohibited from sharing information gained through the relationship in pursuit of a particular business opportunity to anyone not directly involved in the relationship. Non-disclosure agreements help keep the discussions between the two parties confidential so that neither company's competitive position is jeopardized.

Subcontractor Considerations

A company interested in a subcontract relationship also has some special considerations during the marketing phase of a program before it can decide to make a bid.

Determine the Prime Contractors to Target

The subcontractor that does the preliminary work outlined in this section has a better chance at establishing a relationship with the prime contractor that has the best chance at winning the program. Of course, at this point, determining which prime contractor has the best winning potential is speculative at best. However, by determining which prime contractors are competing, understanding the customer environment, analyzing the competitive picture, and making some educated business decisions, a potential supplier can reasonably predict the companies that have a pretty good chance at winning the contract. Methods that a subcontractor can use to determine the prime contractors to target include:

- Building on existing prime contractor relationships
- Building on existing customer relationships

Build on Existing Prime Contractor Relationships

By surveying its current prime contractor relationships, the subcontractor may yield information about the prime contractors considering a new program. Additionally, if the prime contractor with whom the subcontractor is currently working with considers bidding, the subcontractor can discuss its interest in a subcontract relationship. If the prime contractor is not considering bidding, it may be able to direct the subcontractor toward prime contractors that will bid.

Build on Existing Customer Relationships

In commercial business in particular, the customer can suggest to bidding companies some of the subcontractors the customer wants working on the program. When a subcontractor has existing business with the customer and performs well, the customer is more likely to direct the prime contractor to use the subcontractor. The subcontractor should talk with existing customers to determine which prime contractor would have the best shot at winning the program.

Prepare for Meetings with Prime Contractors

Once the subcontractor knows which prime contractors to target, it should meet with the prime contractors directly. Before meeting with them, the subcontracting company should conduct background research on the selected companies to determine their business objectives. This research makes it easier for the company to determine how it fits into each prime contractor's team. To conduct this research, the subcontracting company may review the Dunn and Bradstreet report, each company's annual report, or interview subject matter experts. Next, the subcontracting company should contact the companies to meet their representatives for a particular program and offer to send a capabilities summary statement. During a follow-up phone call, the company should decide with each company's representative if it is worth meeting to explore ways the two companies can work together.

Because subcontracting companies solicit large companies all the time to investigate subcontractor relationships, the subcontracting company must differentiate itself from other solicitors. To do this, the company must understand how it fits into the prime contractor's team before meeting with the prime company. In the initial meeting the subcontracting company must be able to present specific, related contract experience and particular RFP requirements that it can meet. This information helps the prime contractor make a decision. Many subcontracting companies meet with large companies unprepared. The subcontractors basically present their wares hoping that the prime contractor will take the time to figure out the subcontracting company's niche. Most large companies do not have the time or the inclination to do this. Large programs tend to be self-contained within a large company. A program manager on one procurement is busy with his or her own program and seldom knows what other programs require in terms of subcontracting support.

When meeting with a prospective prime contractor, the subcontractor should remember that the prime contractor needs a complete solution for its customer's requirements while the subcontractor wants to sell as much of its products and services as possible. Both companies need to realize that the task at hand is to work creatively to determine a strategy for meeting mutual needs. What each side hopes to get out of the program should be decided early on so that the two companies can decide whether a mutually satisfying business relationship can exist between the two companies.

By targeting a specific program, meeting with a prospective prime contractor, presenting the ways it can help the prime company meet its objectives, and providing success stories and references, the subcontracting company can differentiate itself from its competition and has a good chance at becoming a subcontractor with the prime company. Figure 4 presents sample agenda items for a first meeting between a prime contractor and a potential subcontractor.

Government Considerations

This section covers some of the specific concerns the company should address if it decides to work in the federal government arena including:

- Deciding how to sell to the federal government
- Changes in the government environment
- Government procurement methods
- Government requirements for competition
- Assistance provided by the government
- Government RFP structure

Determine How to Sell to the Federal Government

If the company decides it wants to sell its products and services to the federal government, it must conduct a careful analysis to determine how it wants to compete in the marketplace. The company can either sell directly to the government as a prime contractor or work through prime contractors as a subcontractor. Chapter 2 discussed all the assistance that the federal government provides to companies if they decide to work as prime contractors on a program. In addition, the company can go through the steps listed in this chapter if it would rather work as a subcontractor to a prime contractor on federal business.

Figure 4. Sample Agenda for First Meeting

- Introductions
- Seller presents a high-level overview of its products and services
- Seller explains its understanding of prime contractor's programs and initiatives
- Buyer agrees with seller's understanding of the program requirements, or clarifies any misunderstanding, or provides redirection
- Seller provides statement that it can meet the requirements of a particular program (This means that the seller reviewed the requirements before the meeting.)
- Seller presents detailed description of how it can add to the competitive position of the buyer by providing:
  - Marketing information
  - Customer information
  - Past contract successes
  - Strategic partnerships
  - Unique contributions
  - Competitive information
- Seller should tailor the rest of the meeting based on the results of the above discussion
- Seller should be equipped to provide the following, if needed:
  - Brief company history
  - Relevant statistics (e.g., number of employees or revenue)
  - Contact information for references
  - Any previous experience with the prime contractor
- Seller presents next steps for buyer and seller

Changes in the Government Environment

As part of the decision-making process, the company should understand that there are several shifts evolving in the government business marketplace. Some of those shifts are covered in this section.

Integrated Program Approach to Buying Supplier Products

The government is minimizing its reliance on large system integration type programs in which it pays an integrator to act as a middleman in the procurement process and moving to establishing a contract link directly with the supplier. The large Department of Defense integration contracts still exist, but more frequently the government is going directly to the supplier to buy goods and services.

Big Programs Awarded to Multiple Task-Order Contracts

Another shift from awarding a big program to a prime contractor is awarding task order contracts to multiple prime contractors. In task order contracts, the contractors basically win the right to compete on future task orders. As a government requirement emerges, the government issues a task-order statement of work to all of the winning contractors to bid on. The prime contractor that represents the best overall value to the government wins that task order.

Agency-Centric to Government-Centric Buying Methods

The government used to buy products and services to meet an agency's requirement. The problem with this approach was that it was too cumbersome. For example, a typical scenario would be that the federal government would put out multiple procurements for similar computers for divisions of a single agency. This meant that a lot of money was wasted in duplication of effort. Instead of using the money to buy the computers, the money was wasted on the numerous procurement processes (e.g, dollars were spent on contract award, management, and administration of each similar procurement). Another problem was that the government's price was driven by whatever deal it could strike that day with the contractor, so prices varied widely on the similar contract vehicles. Additionally, if one agency saw that their requirement was very similar to a program already in place, it was difficult to get the scope of that program broadened to include the new requirements so yet another procurement would have to be run.

The government is now taking a much more holistic view of its procurement process. It is trying to enter into specific relationships with vendors for 1 to 5 years. Under such contracts, prices would be fixed across all government agencies and anyone within the federal government could buy the products and services offered by these vendors. The government is allowing contractors to change their products more frequently as technology dictates without going through a significant contract modification process. This approach expedites the procurement process and gets suppliers' products and services out to the government customers quicker than before. An example of a government-centric contract vehicle is the General Services Administration (GSA) Schedule.

GSA Schedules and Government-Wide Programs Now Popular

As discussed in the previous chapter, GSA schedules are gaining popularity because of their low administrative costs, the government's access to many suppliers, and similar prices available to all government customers. Other agencies also are embarking on these types of programs, known as government wide programs or Government Wide Access Contracts (GWACs). The popularity of GWACs has been attributed to their flexibility and the savings realized by agencies for not having to conduct separate solicitations to obtain commercial goods and services. Governmental agencies can access a multitude of contractors, product offerings, and prices by using the automated tools provided by the GSA to help them procure the items they need. GWACs allow governmental agencies to select a contractor that has previously gone through a competition to provide products and services at competitive prices and with standard terms and conditions. A GWAC reduces a governmental agency's responsibility to develop a request for proposal, conduct a solicitation, conduct a thorough evaluation, and deal with potential protest issues before it obtains the goods and services it needs to meet its program objectives. By using a GWAC, a government agency can select three or more companies, send them a statement of work, receive their prices, and make an award decision.

Similarly, with the lifting of the maximum ordering limit on GSA's blanket purchase agreements (BPAs), many agencies are discovering that government-wide programs are the best way to streamline their procurement processes, quickly obtain necessary goods and services, and save precious budget dollars—a good overall combination.

The GSA schedule became popular with the contractor community once the GSA relaxed many of its requirements for commercial products and allowed contractors to provide services through the schedule. Many contractors are going through the process of obtaining a GSA schedule. A GSA schedule contract allows a company to establish a product/service price list from which any governmental agency can buy the company's products. The company reduces its proposal costs because it only needs to put its GSA schedule proposal together once; if the company is awarded a contract, any agency can then buy the company's products and services. For more information on how to obtain a GSA schedule, visit the GSA's web site (pub.fss.gsa.gov/adp/index.html). Once the company has a GSA schedule contract, governmental agencies can set up blanket purchase agreements with the company to further simplify the ordering process. Governmental agencies could also use government-wide BPAs to purchase products.

Easier Than Ever with EC/EDI

Electronic commerce (EC) and electronic data interchange (EDI) are still gaining momentum. Small and large companies can take advantage of the benefits afforded by conducting all their business electronically with the government. Although the government developed the Federal Acquisition Computer Network (FACNET), more and more agencies are using the Internet to make their own solicitations. Governmental agencies are developing Web pages so they can issue solicitations, respond to a company's questions, provide complete contract clauses, and allow companies to register for the agencies' bidders list on-line. By using the Internet, agencies are reducing solicitation time, providing quick responses to a company's questions, and minimizing their own staff's time in conducting the solicitations. Agencies have also reduced costs because they no longer mail solicitations, which eliminates printing and postage costs.

Companies are also embracing the use of the Internet and FACNET. Most companies can already access the Internet and don't have to pay a third-party value-added network (VAN) provider an additional cost to learn of government opportunities, which is required to use FACNET. In addition, governmental Web pages tend to be accurate sources for data because government personnel frequently update the Web pages and provide prospective contractors a wealth of agency information in one area. Previously, the contractor had to uncover needed information by tapping multiple channels. Agency Web pages provide a one-stop-shopping approach to agency data collection.

Procurement Methods

The government may choose either sealed bid or competitive procurement as the procurement method. The government selects the method based on the procurement conditions.

Sealed bid The government conducts sealed bid procurements when the procuring agency determines that the award will be made on the basis of price and that it will not hold discussions with the bidders. In this procurement method the following occurs:

1. The government issues an invitation for bid (IFB) outlining the goods and services to be purchased and the terms and conditions by which those items must be offered.

2. Companies review the IFB and determine if they can be cost competitive. If they can be cost competitive, contractors respond with their price for the work solicited.

3. At a designated time, the agency opens all the bids in a public forum.

4. The company with the lowest cost wins the bid provided the agency deems it is a responsible contractor (FAR 6.4).

Competitive proposals   The government conducts a competitive negotiation if it determines that factors other than price must be considered as part of the evaluation process and that discussions may be required. In this procurement method the following occurs:

1. The government issues a request for proposal (RFP).

2. Each company reviews the RFP to decide whether or not to bid on the program. If the answer is yes, the company responds with a proposal.

3. If required, each company participates in post-submission activities, such as a live test demonstration (LTD), an audit, discussions, and a best and final offer (BAFO) submission.

4. The government makes an award decision based on factors described in RFP Section M, Evaluation Criteria (FAR 6.5).

This book focuses on competitive proposals.

Requirement for Competition

Three main types of competition are used in federal contracting: full and open competition, sole source acquisition, and set-asides.

Full and open competition means that any source (individual or company) may compete. Typically, full competition requires the government to evaluate at least two offers submitted by two different companies before making the award decision.

Sole source acquisition means that an agency contracted with a source after soliciting and negotiating with only one source.

The government does not use sole source acquisitions as much since the Competition in Contracting Act was passed, because it can receive better pricing and terms through the competitive process. The government may use sole source acquisitions, however, in extreme situations, such as:

- Only one source can satisfy the requirements

- Unusual and compelling urgency

- National defense

- Other specialized circumstances (FAR 6.302)

Set-asides allow the government to use the procurement process to meet socioeconomic objectives by limiting the types of companies allowed to bid on an otherwise competitive bid. The government may require that the team comprise the following types of companies:

- *Small businesses*—Small companies are those that meet the government's requirements for revenue and size within a particular industry. The government established standard industry codes (SIC) that categorize the type(s) of work a company performs. If a company applies to the Small Business Administration (SBA) and meets the qualifications, it can be classified as a small business for that particular SIC code and be allowed to compete for small business set-asides within that industry classification.

  Due to the North American Free Trade Agreements Act (NAFTA) and the need for common industry definitions for Canada, Mexico, and the United States, the U.S. Census Bureau is issuing the North American Industry Classification System Manual. Once this classification system is implemented, it will replace the standard industrial code system. Additional information can be found at www.census. gov/epcd/www/naics.

- *Small and disadvantaged businesses*—Small and disadvantaged businesses are those companies that employees a person who has a minority status, runs the company, and owns at least 51 percent of the company. Small and disadvantaged businesses do not have to be a part of the SBA's 8A program. However, if SDB want to be part of that program, they must be pre-qualified by the SBA for 8A participation and then they are eligible for contract awards that are 8A program set-asides.

Assistance Provided by the Government

Agency Bidders List

Before a company can begin shaping a procurement, it must know what procurements are available and obtain basic information on each one. The company can accomplish these goals by securing a position on the customer's bidders list. Once the company identifies the products or services it would like to sell to an agency, it can request to be placed on the agency's bidders list. The SBA, the *U.S. Government Purchasing and Sales Directory*, the *Commerce Business Daily*, and the General Services Administration have information about how to contact the agencies to secure a position on the bidders list. The most expeditious route is for the company to fill out a Standard Form 149 (SF149) for each agency detailing the company's strengths. The company can obtain a copy of the SF149 on the Internet (www.gsa.gov/forms). Once the company is on an agency's bidders list, it should respond to every solicitation that it receives to remain on the list. Although the company may not be able to respond with a proposal to every solicitation, the company should send a simple letter informing the agency that it is not interested in the particular solicitation and with a request to be considered for future opportunities to stay on the active bidders list.

With the preponderance of Internet usage, many agencies are putting their draft solicitation documents on their homepage. This way companies can secure a copy of the draft RFP document just by signing on to the agency's homepage and downloading the RFP without having to get on the agency's bidders list.

After getting on the bidders list or reviewing the customer's homepage, the company can get information about upcoming procurements for the products and services it provides. This information, coupled with the company's own research and customer visits, allows the company to begin shaping the RFP. The company can use several methods to shape an RFP, including position papers/marketing meetings; responding to government draft RFPs, RFIs, and RFCs; and attending bidders conferences.

Bidders' List

When the government issues draft documents, the company does not have to wait until the actual RFP comes out to begin work on the program. The company may obtain a copy of the draft RFP by getting on the agency's bidders' list. To get on the list, the company must

contact the contracting officer and request to be placed on the bidders' list. When the actual RFP comes out, the contractor compares
the company's solution for the draft specifications to the actual RFP
specifications. To ensure that the company receives an RFP, it should
get on an agency's bidder's list. Another option, available with most
agencies, is to download the draft RFP from the agency's Web page.

Requirement for Central Contractor Registration

If the market that the company intends to pursue is the Department
of Defense (DOD), the company must ensure that it is registered in
the Central Contractor Registration (CCR) database. Companies must
be registered in the CCR in order to be eligible for contract solicitation awards with the DOD. Though the registration is submitted
only once, it is confirmed for accuracy annually. All businesses, large
and small, are required to register. The registration allows the contracting officers to transmit the Commercial and Government Entity
(CAGE) code or the DOD Universal Numbering System (DUNS)
number to the payment office. The government cannot pay contractors for work performed if they are not registered with the CCR.

Government RFPs

Most government agencies use a similar format for creating RFPs.
Most RFPs include 13 sections labeled A–M and each section includes standard topics. The term *standard* means that most government agencies label their RFP sections in the same manner, and the
same type of information is found in a section no matter which
agency releases the RFP. RFPs have standard sections because RFPs
follow the uniform contract format listed in the FAR.

Contracting officers (COs) are trying to streamline the procurement process. They are still providing similar types of information to
offerors, however, some COs are changing the uniform contract
format. Such changes make it more difficult for offerors because they
are used to looking in a particular place of the RFP to locate the terms
or conditions related to a particular topic. Now, they must scan the
entire RFP document to locate the information.

RFP Sections

A typical RFP includes the following sections: cover letter, cover
sheet, list of supplies or services, statement of work, directions for
packaging and marking, inspection and acceptance, delivery and
performance, contract administration data, special contract clauses,

FAR clauses, list of attachments, representations and certifications, proposal preparation requirements, and evaluation criteria.

Cover letter The cover letter to the RFP contains several pieces of useful information. Normally, it includes an overview of the procuring agency, a program overview, the proposal due date, the due date for submitting questions to the CO, the contract type(s) used on the procurement, and a brief description of the products and services procured.

Section A: Cover Sheet SF33 Section A consists of Standard Form 33, which is a cover sheet that provides the following information:

- Contract number/Solicitation number
- Type of solicitation—RFP, draft RFP, RFI, etc.
- Number of proposal copies required
- Date, time, and location for proposal delivery
- Name of CO responsible for the solicitation
- List of sections that are provided in the solicitation (draft documents may only contain some of the sections)

In addition, either the government or the company will fill out, at a later date, sections of the cover sheet, which include:

- Length of time the offer is valid
- Discount amount the company will offer for prompt payment
- Checkoff box to acknowledge amendments
- Name of contact person if information is needed
- Name and address of offeror
- Name and title of person authorized to sign the offeror's contract
- Information about where the contract will be administered
- Accounting and appropriation information

Section B: Supplies/Services and Prices Section B is the "menu" for the contract. It lists the supplies and services the government wishes to buy. Section B, when completed, becomes part of the company's price proposal to the government, detailing the solution components and prices for each contract year. Section B will vary depending on the program's particular requirements. Examples of the types of items that a company may be required to provide on a government contract include:

- Manufactured products
- Research and development items
- Hardware, including warranties, spares and repair parts, and documentation
- Software, including warranties and maintenance, software licenses, and documentation
- Program management, including planning, reporting, technical support, data management, security management, training, and field assistance
- Labor, which is supplied from the prime contractor and subcontractors
- Travel
- Other direct costs (ODCs), which include cost items that are required to perform the work and are not covered under another cost category
- Training, including management courses, user training, instructor training, course maintenance, revisions, reviews, and specialized training courses
- Maintenance
- Documentation
- Technical data
- Contract Data Requirements Lists (CDRLs), which are status reports, test descriptions, security plans, or other contract deliverables

Section C: Statement of Work Section C describes the requirements that the company must be prepared to meet during contract performance. Requirements listed in Section C are typically mandatory and the company must propose a product or service that meets the requirements. Sometimes, the government will have optional requirements that allow a company to propose or not to propose the requirements. If the company proposes an optional feature, it will be assessed extra technical evaluation points for the added expense the company may incur by adding the feature to its solution. Companies must understand that all mandatory requirements must be addressed in the contractor solution in order for it to be compliant. Types of requirements found in Section C include product requirements, maintenance requirements, technology requirements, product parameters, environmental requirements, standards compliance, integration with existing government furnished equipment, communication requirements, and maintainability parameters. Because of the market research that is now mandatory because of the FARA enactment, specifications contained in Section C can closely resemble, if not match, the product specifications available in the commercial marketplace.

In addition, Section C may require the company to perform certain management tasks, such as:

- Program planning
- Configuration management
- Information system security planning
- Management reporting
- CDRLs
- Training
- Maintenance
- User support

Section D: Packaging and Marking Section D provides all the requirements the company must meet to mark and ship its products to the government site(s). Types of packaging and marking requirements include:

- Commercial packaging requirements
- Responsible party (the company or the government) for all damage, deterioration, or losses incurred during shipment, handling, and installation
- Warranty start date and duration
- The company's point of contact if supplies are defective
- Replacement and return procedures

Section E: Inspection and Acceptance Section E describes the inspection procedures and acceptance criteria the government plans to use on the contract. The FAR gives the CO the right to inspect products or services to assess the company's performance. Likewise, the government can develop the acceptance criteria that the company's product or service must meet before the government accepts it. *The government must accept the product before the contractor can invoice for products or services rendered.* The following paragraphs describe three types of government acceptance clauses for products:

1. The RFP and resulting contract may state that products must be 99 percent operational for 90 days after delivery. This means

that if the product is functional for 88 days, and nonfunctional for days 89 and 90, the 90-day clock begins again. The contractor cannot invoice the government until the product is 99 percent operational for 90 continuing days, and the government has accepted the product.

2. Acceptance also may be based on the timeliness and quality of CDRLs or deliverables. For example, the government does not have to accept a contractor's deliverable; the government could require the contractor to make modifications before it will accept the deliverable.

3. Another acceptance technique the government can use is qualification testing. In qualification testing, the government may require that each product be tested immediately after contract award to ensure that it still meets the requirements. Once the government tests and approves all products during qualification testing, it will then conduct a simple visual inspection at the time of delivery and then sign the acceptance document. Once the contractor receives the signed acceptance document, it can invoice the government.

Many government agencies use the standard form DD250 as the acceptance document. The contractor prepares the DD250 and submits it with a list of products and services delivered. The authorized government representative at the receiving site signs the document. The DD250 is then included with the company's invoice, which is sent to the government's payment office.

Section F: Delivery and Performance   The government uses Section F to stipulate how delivery and contract performance will occur after contract award. Many different types of information can be included here, such as a delivery order process, a task order process, whether products are to be delivered in the continental United States (CONUS) or outside the continental United States (OCONUS), the terms of the contract, late/early delivery implications, special delivery requirements, and the CDRL review process.

Section G: Contract Administration Data   Contract administration data, which appears in Section G, includes any information that explains how the government and the contractor will work on a daily basis after contract award. This section may include requirements for invoicing, payment, subcontracting reports, and quality assurance evaluator requirements.

Section H: Special Contract Clause   The government uses Section H to cover any contract clauses that are germane to a particular contract. Types of clauses that may be included here are travel regulations, downtime credits, warranty issues, maintenance requirements, training and documentation requirements, software/technical data rights, qualifications for waiver, compliance to standards certification, and engineering change proposals (ECP) requirements. Again, because of the FARA, these clauses should closely mirror what is available commercially.

Section I: FAR Clauses   The program manager and CO determine the contract type that is appropriate for a program. Once this is done, the CO reviews the FAR to determine the types of contract clauses that apply to the selected contract type. These clauses are listed in Section I of the RFP. Only titles of the FAR clauses are listed in both the RFP and the final contract, but the clauses are incorporated in their entirety in the resulting contract and performance.

Section J: List of Attachments   The government uses Section J to provide any additional information the contractor may need. These attachments may include any type of information, such as a list of sites or standards, contractor personnel requirements, a list of CDRLs or contract deliverables, the site plan, or engineering drawings.

Section K: Representations and Certifications   Section K includes all the representations and certifications that a prime contractor must make on behalf of its team. These representations and certifications may include Procurement Integrity, Buy American Act, Equal Employment Opportunity Employer, Drug-Free Workplace, Taxpayer Identification, Debarment Status, List of Authorized Negotiators, and Affirmative Action.

Section L: Proposal Preparation Requirements   The government uses Section L to communicate to a company how it expects to see the proposal formatted. In Section L, the government usually includes:

- Number, title, and sections required in each proposal volume
- Description of how updates will be handled
- Page limitations
- Type size, margin width, paper size, and paper color
- Description of how questions will be handled
- Any other related procurement issues

- Solicitation provisions, such as solicitation amendments, late submissions, and proposal withdrawals or modifications

The most important thing to remember about Section L is that it represents what the government expects to see in the company's final proposal. Often, companies do not use the government's outline because it "makes more sense to do it differently." Not following the outline only frustrates government evaluators who must spend time trying to find where the company "hid" the section they need to review. It is not in a company's best interest to frustrate evaluators. Similarly, the more detailed that the government makes Section L requirements, the more likely that companies will turn in consistent proposals and, thus, the government will have an easier time evaluating the proposals.

Section M: Evaluation Criteria   The government uses Section M to communicate to the companies what solution components are most important during contract performance and the relative ranking of those components. This helps a company determine where the bulk of its time should be spent in solution development. The evaluation criteria are a subset of the source selection plan developed by the source selection authority during the procurement development process. The following is a list of potential criteria for judging the proposal:

- Company's understanding of the requirements
- Results of a live test demonstration (LTD), if required
- Technical content
- Adequacy of the program management solution
- Corporate experience
- Price
- Personnel experience

There should be a direct relationship between Sections L and M. The company should understand how every part of the proposal it is developing is going to be evaluated. Confusion typically results when the government asks an offeror to provide data in the Section L requirements and does not mention how the data is going to be evaluated in Section M.

These are the sections of a government RFP. The government may require a company to submit additional forms with its proposal submission, and most of those forms will be included with the RFP. Forms that are not included in the RFP can be located at the Government Printing Office (GPO) Web site (www.gpo.gov). The most current copy of the forms required can be printed from the Web site. If the forms are not available at the GPO Web site, the company should contact the contracting officer. *Failure to submit the correct forms in a timely manner will result in a delay in contract award.*

PART II

Proposing the Solution

4 Proposal Development

The first step to a successful prime contractor–subcontractor relationship is to develop a proposal that accurately reflects the work that each party will do to support a customer. Chapter 4 discusses how a proposal team is established (including selecting external and internal team members); how the proposal team develops a technical, management, business, and contractual solution; and how those solutions are documented in a proposal to the customer. Before providing the details, a discussion of the two main types of contract types (product and labor), solicited proposals versus unsolicited proposals, and some of the characteristics of a proposal effort is necessary.

Product Contracts vs. Labor Contracts

The two main types of contracts are product contracts and labor contracts. When a customer needs products, a company must provide adequate descriptions in its proposal of the products it will provide and how those products meet the customer's requirements. The customer may require proof, such as testing or user documentation, to demonstrate that the company's products meet the requirements. In such cases, the bulk of the company's proposal tends to be product descriptions, explanations of how its products meet the customer's requirements, and proof that the products will work in the customer's environment.

Sometimes the customer needs to supplement its own staff with contracted resources. The customer may or may not know exactly how many people it needs or the length of time for which it needs them. Or, the customer may know what projects need to be accomplished but is unsure of how long these projects should take. Under these situations, the customer tends to rely on labor contracts. In proposals for labor contracts, the company needs to provide the hourly rate for each labor category prescribed by the customer for each year of the contract. The bulk of the technical volume in a labor contract is to describe how the company will do the work or it may simply be a compilation of the resumes of the people who will work on the contract. The customer may still require proof, such as interviews or a review of each person's resume before they begin work on the contract, to determine if the proposed people meet the customer's requirements.

Solicited vs. Unsolicited Proposals

An inaccurate assumption made in the field is that the customer can only solicit contractors to perform work or provide products by releasing a request for proposal (RFP). However, prime contractors, with or without subcontractors, can submit unsolicited proposals to customers. A company creates an unsolicited proposal without the benefit of a RFP requirements document so it is more difficult for the proposal team to understand exactly the customer's requirements. However, unsolicited proposals are presented and evaluated without going through an active competition. This means that the customer could accept the proposal as is, or with modifications, and the actual requirement is never competed in the open market. Both commercial and government customers can accept unsolicited proposal, however, it is a little more difficult getting an unsolicited proposal accepted by the government due to the tight regulatory and competition requirements.

Characteristics of a Proposal Effort

Proposals Have Finite and Short-Term Objectives

Proposal efforts have a specific task that must be accomplished (i.e., to complete a compliant, responsive, and timely proposal). The amount of time typically available to complete the proposal is anywhere from 30 to 90 days. The amount of work to be accomplished and the short amount of time available do not provide team members the opportunity to grow into their positions. Candidates must be able to join the team, assimilate what needs to be done, and complete the work quickly.

Proposals Are Made Up of Quickly Assembled Teams That Work Together for a Short Period of Time

Proposal teams are put together quickly, and sometimes the team members have not worked together before. Often, a company working as a prime contractor will request support from its subcontractors to help on the proposal. When selecting team members, the company should select people who are knowledgeable in their fields, can handle diverse personalities, and who work as a team to get a project done under tight deadlines. The company and team members should remember that a proposal effort is fully staffed for only a short period of time. Bid and proposal (B&P) costs skyrocket when many people are on the proposal effort for a long time. The company must consider tasks to be accomplished, budget considerations, and the potential of losing critical personnel resources to other projects when determining how long people should remain on a proposal effort. If the company has many proposal efforts or short-term projects, it can rotate people between projects to contain costs.

Critical Decisions Are Made Quickly

The company must make decisions throughout the proposal process. Examples include selecting the vendors, proposing products, and finalizing the terms and conditions of the proposal. Additionally, these decisions must not be made in a vacuum; the company must consider business, technical, and contractual implications. Often, these decisions are critical because they affect many sections of the proposal. Selected people must be able to quickly analyze a situation, make a good decision, and be able to deal in an evolving work environment.

Proposal Efforts May Have a Critical Shortage of Resources

The company probably will not have all the resources it would like to have for a proposal effort. Resource availability, budget constraints, or tight deadlines may explain a critical shortage of resources. People selected for the team must be able to work under less than optimum conditions and be willing to branch into areas outside of their expertise to complete the job.

The Proposal Process Is Highly Interdependent

Proposal tasks progress at a rapid pace, and tasks are highly interdependent. For example, the company must make technical decisions regarding a product's compliance before it can negotiate pricing and terms and conditions. Similarly, a vendor's high price may cause the technical team to choose a less expensive but still compliant product. A problem in one area could cause the team to miss the proposal due date, which could render all the team's hard work worthless, because the government cannot accept late proposal submissions. Therefore, the people selected for a proposal effort must be able to work well under pressure and understand the interdependent nature of their work.

People Branch Out Beyond Their Area of Expertise on a Proposal Effort

People are selected to work on a proposal effort because they bring a certain expertise to the team. However, although someone may be initially selected for his or her talent to develop the technical solution, that person will also be required to provide assistance in resolving cost, contractual, and management issues. This broadening of skill sets may seem somewhat intimidating at first, but proposals are, for most people, one of the few working opportunities in which people feel pushed to their limit.

Customer Requirements Evolve

Finally, while all these challenges are going on internally, chances are that the customer is further refining its requirements. The customer can submit changes to the requirements any time during the procurement process. Customer changes require the team to re-group and re-position itself to meet the emerging requirements.

Tight deadlines, people who haven't worked together before doing things that they may not feel totally comfortable with, and evolving customer requirements all make for a dynamic, challenging environment within which to create a proposal. The following section discusses how a proposal is developed.

Proposal Process

The proposal process is complex and highly integrated. It contains many steps that the proposal team must conduct to turn in a responsive, compliant proposal to the customer. The steps are as follows:

- Revisit the bid decision
- Conduct high-level solution development
- Validate make or buy decision
- Select internal team
- Establish external team
- Develop proposal outline
- Assign a person to each outline section
- Prepare customer questions
- Develop and document the technical and management solutions

- Develop and document any other proposal sections
- Develop oral proposal
- Develop price proposal
- Develop the contracts volume
- Review proposal
- Produce and deliver the proposal to customer

Revisit Bid Decision

The previous chapter discussed reviewing the draft statement of work. As an initial step in preparing a proposal, the team must conduct a careful analysis of the final statement of work. Because the customer can change as little or as much of the proposal as it wants between the draft and final stages, often companies will conduct another bid decision to ensure that they still wish to pursue the program. If the team's analysis results in continuing the bid decision, the team will continue its proposal development work. If the analysis directs the team to end the bid, all team members are notified and work on the effort ceases.

As the team reviews the draft RFP, it begins designing the solution and lining up potential subcontractors. When the final RFP is released, the team must determine if the changes in the customer's final RFP represent a significant enough change in requirements that the company is unwilling or unable to put together a responsive proposal in the time allotted.

Conduct High-Level Solution Development

The most time-consuming part of proposal development is developing a solution. This is because any RFP requirement may have multiple solutions available. Deciding on the best solution for the customer is a matter of insight and interpretation of the customer's needs. Which solutions the company chooses determines whether it wins or loses the contract. Therefore, the company usually goes through several iterations of the solution before it makes a final solution.

The key to solution development is that the solution be developed, reviewed, and approved *before* the proposal writing begins. However, the proposal team cannot sacrifice missing the proposal deadline as it searches for the perfect solution. The team must strike a balance between design iterations and choosing a solution so that it can begin writing the proposal and start production.

The term *solution* in this book has several distinct aspects:

- The *technical solution* is developed in response to the customer's technical requirements and is documented in the proposal's technical volume.
- The *management solution* describes how a company will manage and operate the contract after award. It is documented in the management volume of the proposal.
- The *business solution* is the way in which a company prices each solution component. It is documented in the price volume of the proposal.
- The *contractual solution* describes a company's and its subcontractors' willingness to comply with a customer's terms and conditions. It is documented in the contracts volume of the proposal.

Each of these solutions is highly interrelated to the others. For example, the technical solution describes the products and services necessary to meet the technical requirements. The management solution describes how that technical solution will be delivered. The price volume provides prices for the technical and management solution components, and the contracts volume describes the terms and conditions under which the solution is offered.

Select the Internal Team

Selecting the appropriate people to handle the functions required in a proposal effort is imperative to proposal success. The abilities of the proposal team members can either make or break a procurement effort. When considering candidates for proposal positions, the company should remember the characteristics inherent in any proposal effort. The following section discusses the optimal size for a proposal team.

Size of a Proposal Team

The size of the proposal team varies based on the company's size, the size of the deal, how important the deal is to corporate objectives, and the role the company plays (e.g., subcontractor, prime contractor, or teaming partner). A company working as a subcontractor may dedicate only one or two people to a proposal effort to assist the prime contractor. A prime contractor working on a large, strategic deal, however, may involve up to 100 employees to complete the proposal. Most proposal efforts have between five to 30 members.

The proposal team does not require all of its team members for the duration of the proposal effort. Typically, a few people are involved in the beginning during the marketing and draft RFP analysis phase. After the customer releases the RFP, the bulk of the team members are added to develop the solution and to write the proposal. As the review process begins, team members are dismissed until only a few critical members remain. These members will remain with the proposal effort throughout the customer-questions process. The team is cut again so that only the members directly related to the best and final offer (BAFO) development (if a BAFO is required) remain. If the company wins the award, the team then quickly grows to begin work.

Key Positions on a Proposal Team

Although companies vary in how they organize their proposal efforts, there are some standard functions that must be completed on every proposal effort. On smaller proposal efforts, one person may perform several or all of these tasks. On larger programs, some of these tasks may require multiple people to work on a single task. The company should keep in mind that this is how a *prime contract proposal team* functions. The prime contractor may ask subcontractors for help to fill some of the roles. Having the subcontractor involved in the process early on helps improve commitment to the program and allows the subcontractor to understand how the prime contractor will operate after receipt of the award. Similarly, the subcontractor may have a similar smaller organization set up within its own company to complete the tasks required by the prime contractor.

The Appendix provides a detailed description of the functions that must be performed on most proposal efforts and the title most companies give to each person performing a function. Figure 1 presents a sample organizational chart depicting the functions needed on a proposal effort.

Work Delegation between the Prime Contractor and Subcontractor

Figure 2 summarizes the functions that are typically performed by the prime contractor and subcontractor teams. Keep in mind that the roles and responsibilities are defined between the two parties; for example, the subcontractor could be responsible for proposal production in which case the production team would reside in the subcontractor organization.

Figure 1. Sample Large Proposal Organization

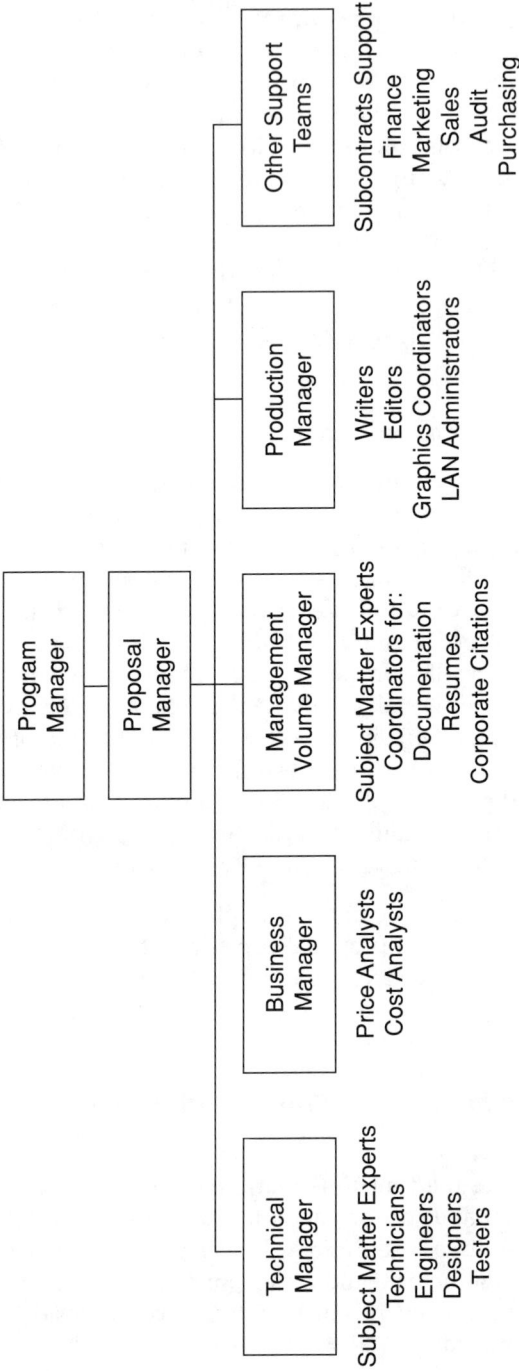

Figure 2. Work Functions for Prime Contractor and Subcontractor

Function	Prime Contractor Team	Subcontractor Team
Program manager	X	X
Technical manager	X	
Technical team members	X	X
Management volume manager	X	
Management volume team members	X	X
Business manager	X	
Business team members	X	X
Contracts volume manager	X	
Contracts team members	X	X
Purchasing representative	X	
Government compliance	X	
Sales team members	X	X
Demonstration team members	X	X
Production team members	X	

Establish the External Team

Early in the procurement process, the company determines how much of the solution it can provide and how much of the solution must be contracted out. Often, the company decides that it is more cost effective to contract out certain components rather than produce them or develop the capability to produce them in-house.

After the company decides to bid on a program, its next task is to determine how much of the program requirements can be done using internal resources and how much of the program must be accomplished using external resources. Internal resources must be budgeted, allocated, and scheduled and will be reviewed in the next section. As we discussed in Chapter 1, external resources are used in various levels of relationships: one time purchases, purchase orders, suppliers, teaming partners, and strategic alliances. Because of the complexity of these topics, they will be discussed in the chapter titled "Subcontract Development." For purposes of this chapter, which describes the overall proposal process, understand that the prime contractor would go through many of the steps outlined in "Subcontract Development" at this point in the proposal process.

Develop a Proposal Outline

Early on in the process, the proposal management team must finalize the proposal outline. In government RFPs, the outline is defined in Section L and the company should follow the outline prescribed. In commercial RFPs, the outline may or may not be defined. If it is, the proposal team should follow the customer's outline precisely because this is how the customer expects to see the information requested. If the contractor presents the information in a different manner, the customer may not be able to locate the data and the contractor's evaluation will suffer as a result. In the cases where the outline is not defined, the company must develop its own outline. This usually is a time consuming exercise because every team member will have a different idea about how the requirements should be addressed. A basic rule of thumb is to present the proposal in the order of the statement of work. At least this way the customer can look back at its own document to determine approximately where in the company's proposal the information can be found.

Determine Person Responsible for Each Outline Section

Once the outline is established, the proposal management team decides on who has the expertise to complete each section. This person will typically analyze the requirements, research solutions, select the best solution given the requirements, test the solution (if possible), write about the solution, and prepare to modify or defend the solution if needed. The people responsible for the outline can either be the company's team members or potential subcontractors. (**Note:** The term *potential subcontractors* is used because until a subcontract is actually signed, they are not technically subcontractors. Signing of the subcontract occurs much later in the process.)

Prepare Customer Questions

The company and potential subcontractors work together throughout the proposal process to develop questions for the customer. Typically, the customer will allow a certain period during which it will entertain questions from potential contractors. It is important that the company team ask questions as soon as it has them during the procurement cycle so that it get a better understanding of the customer requirements. Questions can cover technical, management, contractual, or business considerations. The customer then decides how it wishes to handle the answers. It can either provide its answer to just the company requesting the information or the customer can provide the answer to all the soliciting companies. The customer can choose any of the following options:

Discussion   The customer can elect to have a discussion with either the company submitting the question or with all the soliciting companies to answer the question. The discussion may be held at the customer's location or through a videoconference or teleconference.

Bidders conference   Sometimes the customer decides to conduct a bidders conference at which it answers all the questions submitted to date. The customer usually does not attribute the questions to the originators in hopes to preserve any competitive advantage a company may be trying to assert.

Formally documented   Some governmental customers and commercial companies answer all questions and provide the answers in a written document to every company. The customers can either send out their answers manually by giving a hard copy of the answers to each interested company or it can posted the answers on its Web page so that anyone interested can access the information.

Develop and Document Technical Solutions and Management Solutions

When a company selects a subcontractor for its team, the subcontractor works directly with the company to develop the proposal. The tasks outlined in the following chart are shared by the company and the subcontractor, and each party is responsible for its particular piece of the solution. The subcontractor may have representatives on both the technical and management teams.

Task Summary Chart for Technical and Management Proposal Sections

Although the process for developing a proposal is discussed in general terms in this chapter, Figure 3 presents the specific steps that the technical and management team members must complete to develop the solution for a particular component. The figure provides a summary of the tasks that need to be completed and who on the technical or management team completes them.

Technical and Management Solution Process

After carefully analyzing the customer's RFP, draft RFP, or design requirements and understanding how the customer will use the

Figure 3. Tasks to Complete the Technical and Management Proposal Sections

Task	Technical Solution Responsible Party	Management Solution Responsible Party
Finalize Solution Components	Technical team manager	Management team manager
Assign Each Component	Technical team manager	Management team manager
Gather Information	Technical team member	Management team member
Conduct Make or Buy Analysis	Technical team	Management team
Attend Bidders Conference	Technical team manager	Management team manager
Submit Questions to Customer	Technical team	Management team
Ensure Proposal Team Understands Solution	Technical team	Management team
Assess Effect of Teaming Partner	Technical team	Management team
Evaluate Vendor Proposals	Technical team	Management team
Test the Solution	Technical team member	Management team member
Finalize the Solution	Technical team	Management team
Document the Solution	Technical team member	Management team member
Develop Processes		Management team member
Develop Resumes		Management team member
Complete Past Performance Citations		Management team member
Review the Solution	Technical team manager	Management team manager
Incorporate Solution Changes	Technical team member	Management team member
Track Solution Changes	Technical team member	Management team member
Conduct a Compliance Review	Technical team	Management team
Turn Over Proposal Section to Production Team	Technical team member	Management team member

particular product or service, the team can design the technical and management solutions. All members of the solution design team must understand the customer's requirements and the overall solution design. As each component becomes workable, the team should continually validate it against the requirements and the rest of the solution to ensure a compliant end result. Solution development is evolutionary—the major components are determined, and the solution at the highest level is determined to be viable. Then, as each of the subcomponents is determined, each is validated against the evolving components from the other areas.

The subcontractor is key to the technical and management solution development process because it understands its product or service and how it can be used in the customer environment. The subcontractor also knows the competition for its solution component and can address the features of its solution that differentiate its product from the competitors' products and how the customer can benefit from those features.

The steps necessary to complete a solution are as follows:

Finalize solution components.   A top-down approach to solution development works best if the team analyzes the business problem that the program is designed to solve. By breaking down the total solution into its components, a subject expert can develop a solution for his or her functional area and then ensure that his or her solution is integrated with the total solution. Finalizing solution components is easier if the customer released a draft RFP or RFI documents.

The subcontractor is helpful in this process because it knows its product line, the capabilities of each product, and which product would be best suited to meet the customer's overall objectives. Multiple subcontractors often may work with a prime contractor to figure out the best mix of products and services to offer the customer.

Validate make or buy analysis.   The next step for solution development is to validate the make or buy analysis for each solution, as discussed in Chapter 3, to determine if the company wishes to produce the product or provide the service using internal or external sources. Once the RFP is actually released, the company may realize that it cannot meet the customer's requirements and decide to work with a subcontractor. Or, the company may not be able to locate a subcontractor that it can work with so it may decide to do the work internally.

Assess what each teaming partner will bring to the solution.   If the company will have a teaming partner for the program, the company should determine early on what parts of the solution the partner will provide. This decision occurs before the solicitation process begins so that the team sends solicitations only for those goods and services the team requires.

Assign each component. The technical or management team manager assigns each component to a subject matter expert to develop the solution. The subcontractor may be responsible for the sections of the proposal pertaining to its solution components.

Gather information to develop a solution. Many types of information are necessary to develop a solution, such as information about the customer, technology, competition, and past contract experiences.

Ensure all team members understand the customer's requirements and overall solution design. All members of the design team must have an overall understanding of the customer's requirements and how all the components fit together in the solution design. By understanding the big picture of the solution design, team members can develop individual solution components that are more closely integrated.

Conduct the solicitation process. The teams must evaluate vendor proposals for compliance as part of the solicitation process. The solicitation process helps determine which vendors will provide the necessary products for the solution. This process is described in Chapter 9.

Test the solution. Ideally, the team should test the solution before it submits the proposal. Although it is feasible for some components to be tested, time and resource levels do not usually permit the testing of every aspect of most solutions. However, the proposal team should feel confident that the solution will work as stated.

Finalize the solution. The team must finalize the technical solution. Once this is done, the writers can begin writing the proposal. If the solution is not finalized, writers will have to continually rewrite to accommodate product changes. If the solution continues to change up until the time of submission, the chance for submitting an inconsistent proposal becomes greater.

Manage change to the solution. Although a company strives to finalize the technical solution, outside influences will require changes to the technical solution. Any of these events could require changing the technical solution:

- Customer amendments that either add or change requirements
- Vendors' products that cannot meet the government requirements
- Vendors that are apparent winners as a result of the solicitation process but that are unable to reach a working agreement with the company

The team should monitor these areas and any others that may create change so it can prepare for any changes instead of being surprised by them.

Conduct initial reviews. The review process helps develop a better technical solution. The team should conduct multiple reviews as it develops the technical solution: one to ensure the solution will work; one to review themes and discriminators; and one toward the end of the proposal process to ensure each requirement has been addressed. Reviews are described in detail later in this chapter.

Write Proposal Sections

Once the solutions are defined, the team is prepared to begin writing the proposal sections. Outlined below are the steps to this process.

1. **Provide writing assignments to the proposal writer.** The writer could either be the technical team expert assigned to develop a solution component or a technical writer who is brought in to write a section and who has no involvement with developing a solution. The writer can begin preliminary data gathering and developing an outline, but he or she cannot complete the proposal until the solution is final.

2. **Provide information packet to writer.** The proposal manager needs to give the writer an information packet that includes the following items:

   - *Proposal outline*—The proposal outline illustrates how each section fits in the proposal.
   - *Approximate page length for the section*—Page limits may be determined by the customer in the RFP or by the proposal manager. The proposal manager may determine how long a section should be based on the degree of importance it receives in the customer's evaluation criteria.
   - *Proposal writing conventions and standards*—Give the writer a style guide that contains proposal writing conventions and

standards. The style guide should dictate the names the company intends to use throughout the proposal, such as the team name, product names, or version numbers. Providing a style guide will help ensure consistency throughout the sections of the proposal. A consistent proposal will help the evaluator understand what the company is proposing and limit the number of questions the contractor receives based on ambiguous data.

- *Format considerations*—The customer may dictate the format for the proposal in the RFP or the proposal manager may need to determine format standards, such as type font, margin width, headers, or footers.

- *Graphics guidelines*—The customer may dictate the format for the proposal in the or the proposal manager may need to determine graphics guidelines, such as graphics size, shape, or font size.

3. **Gather additional information.** Besides the information the proposal manager provides, the writer needs general proposal information to write his or her section. This information includes:

- *Customer information*—Information about the customer's environment and requirements is necessary for the proposal writer to develop a compliant, responsive proposal.

- *Solution information*—Information about the solution components is necessary to highlight the solution features that are particularly relevant to the customer's environment.

- *Competitive information*—Information about the competitors is necessary to develop win themes and discriminators for the proposal.

- *RFP citations*—The writer must know which RFP sections contain requirements that must be addressed in a particular section of the RFP.

4. **Develop a section strategy and outline.** A strategy and outline help the writer define the key components that should be discussed and make writing the proposal easier. The strategy and outline also assist in the review process to ensure consistent information is being provided across proposal sections to help sell the team's solution. Sometimes companies will develop proposal themes or win themes and emphasize them in their proposals. These themes are developed throughout the pro-

posal so that a consistent message is portrayed. Each proposal section is used to develop or validate that theme. The writer develops a strategy and outline for the section that includes:

- An understanding of the customer's requirements.
- A detailed description of the technical solution proposed.
- Customer issues and the specific features, benefits, and discriminators of the team's solution that address those issues.
- Specific demonstrations of the proposal's strategies and themes (e.g., if commitment to quality is a proposal theme, the team needs specific measurements provided in this section to substantiate the proposal theme). Other approaches that may substantiate themes include:
  — Past contract successes
  — Results of product studies
  — Reasons why alternative approaches will not work
  — Description of the solution features and the benefits the customer receives from them
  — Description of the items that discriminate or differentiate the team's product from its competitors' products
  — Description of the proof for the section or how it can convince the customer to buy the solution (e.g., photographs, graphics, statistics, comparison charts, and trend data)

A *customer issue* is any underlying want, desire, or need that drives the RFP requirements. For example, the previous contractor's shoddy workmanship might be a customer issue. This issue may drive the customer's requirement that a contractor "Shall maintain a defect rate of 5 percent or less throughout the contract." The team's response could be to outline how quality measures will be implemented and to illustrate the features of its solution. Next, the team could provide a commitment to zero-defect manufacturing, which may be a key discriminator of the company's solution that distinguishes it from its competitors. Finally, the team may provide a description of how its quality measures decrease the defect rate and how having a zero-defect contractor will be beneficial to the customer.

5. **Review strategies and outlines.** The proposal outlines are reviewed by the management team to determine whether the

order, content, logic, and strategy emphasis are appropriate. The team reviews the outline because it is easier to review than the detailed writing.

6. **Complete writing the proposal.** After the outlines are developed, reviewed, and approved by the appropriate team, the writer can finish writing the proposal.

7. **Conduct a requirement compliance check.** Before the proposal is produced in its final form, the team should review each requirement and response to ensure that the document is compliant. For example, if the proposal has gone through multiple reviews and rewrites, it is possible that responses to requirements were omitted. The team should review the document to ensure that all requirements are addressed and that they are addressed in the order suggested by the customer.

8. **Turn section over to the production team.** Once the proposal is finished, the production team reviews the proposal for final edit, graphics, and production.

Develop Unique Components of the Management Solution

This chapter has thus far discussed the items most typically required in proposals. However, customers may have unique requirements that the company will have to include in the proposal. Additional tasks that the customer may ask the management team to accomplish include the following:

Select Appropriate Past Contract Experience

Sometimes customers will want proof that the company has done work that is similar in size and scope to the work the customer is requesting. In such cases, the company can use contract performance citations to highlight the specific details of work it successfully performed for another customer. Some companies keep their contract citations in databases so they can quickly and easily access the information for prospective customers. The degree of detail a customer will want to see in a contract citation varies; typically, governmental customers require more detail than most commercial customers. The proposal team will want to highlight its subcontractor's past contract experience as well to validate that it is capable of providing the products and services required.

Types of information that can be included in the contract citation include:

- Project name
- Contract term
- Contract value
- Customer name
- Contact information
- Summary of work performed
- Customer benefits
- Technology used

Additional Information Typically Required on Contract Citations for Government Contracts

Because of the government's increased emphasis on past performance, the proposal team needs to gather a lot of data from previous contracts to meet proposal submission requirements. Data that the governmental contractors frequently request from companies include:

- Number of contract modifications issued
- Net fiscal result of the modifications, both positive and negative
- Effect of each contract modification on schedule or performance
- Number and type of engineering change proposals submitted
- Number of waivers and deviations requested
- Length of contract
- Number of late deliveries

Select Appropriate Resumes

Another task that the management team may need to complete is providing resumes of the people assigned to work on the contract if it is awarded to the company. If the company will need to submit resumes, the team will need to select people with the skills that match the customer's or program's personnel requirements. The resumes will need to be formatted according to the customer's specifications. Each customer has its own format for how the resumes must be submitted. The company should develop a template based on the customer's requirements and ask each selected person to revise his or her resume based on that format. The customer may request resumes from the subcontractors working on the contract as well.

If the RFP states a requirement for resumes, the company must first determine what type of resumes the customer is requesting. Sometimes the customer only wants to evaluate sample resumes, or examples of the types of skills possessed by the people in the labor category that the company is bidding on. When the company provides sample resumes, the company does not need to guarantee to the customer that those specific people will be available to work the program. More frequently, however, the customer may require the resumes of some or all of the key people who will be working on the contract. The customer may request that each person sign his or her resume. By signing, the person agrees to work on the particular contract for the period of time stipulated, barring unforeseen circumstances.

The government, in particular, tends to be very specific about its required qualifications, as such, the team must be equally specific in providing people with the required skill sets or education levels. If the management team does not meet the government's requirements, the government may issue deficiency reports or deem the company's offer as insufficient because the people the customer is proposing do not have the necessary skill sets or education levels.

Develop Detailed Plans, Processes, and Procedures

By providing details on how the team intends to manage every major component of work required under the contract, the company shows the customer that the company can perform the work if it is awarded the contract. Subcontractors and teaming partners may help in determining plans, processes, and procedures because they may have some techniques that are particularly useful.

The types of processes that the company may include in the management volume are training, documentation, project reporting, subcontractor management, delivery order processing, deliverable development and production, task order development, maintenance, manufacturing, management reporting, and customer assistance.

Sample Training Approach

- Introduce the training approach
- Provide success stories of previous training efforts, including customer, training objectives, results, and numbers of students
- Describe training issues important to the customer

- Describe how the company develops training courses
- Describe the media used to deliver the courses
- Provide resumes of key course developers and instructors
- Describe each course in the suggested curriculum
- Present course development and review cycle
- Explain quality assurance measures taken to ensure course effectiveness
- Present student feedback mechanisms employed
- Explain methods to keep the course current
- Describe the training materials available for the course
- Present sample materials
- Describe corporate training facilities

Develop Work Breakdown Structure (WBS)

The management team should begin working on a WBS if the customer requires one, or if the company determines that a WBS is an appropriate method for capturing costs. A *WBS* hierarchically characterizes all the work that must be done on a program as well as the resources, schedules, and costs associated with completing the tasks.

The first step in developing a WBS is to identify the major functional areas of the program. Then, within each functional area, the management team identifies the tasks that make up that function. Each subtask required to complete that task is then defined. The company can decide how many times tasks should be broken down and subtasks defined. The contract's complexity and the level at which the company chooses to manage costs drive the amount of detail in a WBS. One benefit of a WBS is it captures costs at the lowest level and can be used to estimate the next level of costs. Task details, including assigning resources, establishing dependencies between functions, and developing a schedule are tracked in a project management system. This level of detail allows a manager to budget costs across the contract in the proposal development phase and then ascertain at any time whether a function is being performed at, below, or above its designated costs.

A WBS also provides valuable input to the customer. The customer can determine the actual costs to perform a function and can easily decide whether it should continue to allow the contractor to perform the work or pursue other alternatives.

Develop the Contract Functional Organizational Chart and Staffing Levels

Most RFPs require companies to depict how they will set up the contract organization and explain where each function will reside in their organizations. Once the company has done this, the management team works with the other proposal team members to determine the resources required to run the contract after award. The management team also determines whether these resources will come from internal or external sources.

Gather Corporate Statistics

The customer may require information about the company's financial and personnel status. This information may include total revenue over the last defined period of years, percent of total revenue that is government business, annual turnover rate, lines of business currently being pursued, and other financial indicators to show corporate stability. The customer will want this information from the prime contractor as well as the subcontractor.

Plan for Contract Deliverables

Contract deliverables are required throughout the life of the contract. Many deliverables are cyclical; for example, monthly status reports or quarterly reviews. Other deliverables are one-time only, such as system test plans. Still others are driven by specific contract events. For example, an engineering change proposal may be necessary whenever a new product is considered for the contract. The customer may require deliverables as separate contract line items that have prices assigned to them, or the customer may require deliverable development as part of the program-management costs associated with running the contract.

Not all customers require deliverables. If the customer does require deliverables, the company should determine the level of effort required to complete the deliverables. This level of effort, in terms of people and resources, gets translated into costs, which must be shown in the price proposal. In addition, if the company uses subcontractors to help complete the deliverables, their involvement must be stated in the statement of work in the subcontract. The company can estimate the level of resources required for completing a deliverable by doing the following:

- Reviewing other corporate contracts that have deliverables to understand the estimating techniques employed

- Requesting subcontractor input

- Analyzing the deliverable requirements and comparing the activity required to other similar corporate tasks to help determine an appropriate amount of time and resources (For example, if the deliverable is for preparing and delivering meeting notes, the company can just determine how long it typically takes to develop and disseminate meeting notes for internal corporate meetings.)

In some government RFPs, deliverables are referred to as contract data requirements lists (CDRLs). The company must review two documents for each CDRL required: the standard CDRL form and the Data Item Description (DID) form. The standard CDRL form requires the following information: the CDRL name, delivery dates, recipients, and the corresponding DID number. The DID form details the specific data elements included in each CDRL delivery. Both of these documents must be reviewed to determine correct staffing levels for completing the CDRL. Copies of the deliverable and DID information are in the RFP or can be obtained through the Government Printing Office (GPO).

Establish Subcontracting Plan

Government RFPs will typically require two types of subcontract plans. One is contained in the contracts volume and for it the company must delineate specifically how much revenue is intended for each subcontractor, whether the subcontractor is a small business or a small and disadvantaged business, and what percentage of the deal each company receives. The other subcontracting plan may be required if the management volume addresses how subcontractors were selected to be on the team, what work they will perform on the contract, and how their performance will be measured. The company can get the information for this section by reviewing the justifications written up in the solicitation stage of the procurement and speaking with the subcontractors.

Develop Oral Proposal

To expedite the proposal process, the customer may require the contractors to provide oral proposals in place of some or all of the written proposal. In an oral proposal, the customer issues a RFP as it normally would, but it allows the offerors to submit either part of or all of its proposal orally to the evaluation team. The customer records the oral presentation using either videotape or audiotape so that it can preserve each company's performance to help to resolve any disputes that occur during the evaluation and selection process.

The Federal Acquisition Streamlining Act (FASA) gave government evaluation teams the ability to conduct oral proposals. As more and more procurement officials get used to the new format and see the benefits of using the approach, more and more procurements will be conducted using this format.

Why Should Customers Use Oral Proposals?

Oral proposals minimize the amount of paperwork that is generated when producing a proposal and evaluating its contents. Written proposals can be a few pages long to thousands of pages long depending on the size and type of procurement. Once the customer receives a company's proposal, the customer must evaluate the RFP and source selection plan (SSP) requirements against each contractor's proposal to determine if the proposed response is compliant. If the company neglects to provide certain information or if its response is ambiguous, the evaluator issues questions to the company to give it an opportunity to rectify the problem. If the company fails to answer the questions completely or further convolutes the issue, the customer may issue another round of questions or it may lower the proposal evaluation score because of the incomplete response. All of this exchange of paper takes time and effort away from designing a better solution and determining the best price for the solution.

In traditional government procurements the problem is heightened because the contractors may not speak with the evaluation team during the selection process so as to not violate the Procurement Integrity Act provisions. The Act prohibits (1) contractors from obtaining and government officials from providing source selection information; (2) contractors from offering or government officials from accepting bribes; and (3) contractors from offering or government officials from accepting job offers. Because conversations between the government evaluation team and offerors are non-existent in traditional procurements, some of these issues can also serve as protest fodder after award if the issues are not handled appropriately.

Oral proposals minimize all of the paperwork, time, resources, and confusion by putting the evaluation team in the same room with the people who will run the program after contract award. It gives the customer an opportunity to see the people who will actually work on the contract, test their knowledge of the program and technology requirements, and have the contractor answer its questions immediately.

Overall Process

Define the solution.   The company goes through many of same the steps listed earlier when it develops the solution for an oral proposal. Except that once the company develops a solution for an oral proposal, the company must determine how to best present the solution so that it meets the customer's requirements and illustrates the depth and breadth of the technical team's talents.

Understand the customer's requirements for oral proposals. Because of the varying requirements and enthusiasm for oral proposals among customers, the company must carefully evaluate the customer's RFP requirements to determine how much of the proposal must be submitted orally. Some customers are testing the oral-proposal format by requiring a written proposal to restate everything that was covered in the oral presentation. Other customers require certain parts to be presented orally and the remaining parts be provided in a written format. Some customers do not accept oral proposals. In a government RFP, Section L of the RFP will state specifically what the government expects to see and how it expects to see it.

Select the presenters.   The company must determine who the customer expects the company's presenters to be. Some customers will allow companies to use whoever they want to present the technical solution. However, more customers are requiring that companies use the people who will actually be working on the contract after award to present the oral proposal. This is important information because the company must not only decide who has the technical knowledge and management expertise to run the contract after award, the company must also make sure these people possess good communication and presentation skills. If all of these talents do not exist in one person, the company must work with the person with solid technical knowledge and management expertise to help him or her refine and hone his or her communication and presentation skills. A company may choose to use some of its subcontractors because they have expertise in a particular area.

Determine the presentation medium.   Because of technological advances, the company has many different options for the oral presentation medium. However, before selecting a medium, the company should determine the customer's requirements. The customer may state that the oral presentation must be done in person at its location. If this is the case, the company can decide whether it wishes to present using overhead slides or a multimedia computerized presentation. When the customer does not dictate how the oral proposal must be conducted, the company can select other options, such as interactive teleconference, real-time Internet-based chat rooms, or video technology.

Define standard presentation formats.   Unless formats are strictly defined by the customer, the company should define standard formats that each of its presenters must follow in making their presentations. The presentation formats should follow the customer's proposal instructions and evaluation criteria and consider the presentation medium. In addition, the customer may place time limits on the company's oral presentation.

Develop draft presentation and script.   As soon as possible in the proposal process, the proposal team should develop a draft presentation and script. A draft presentation and script help to fine tune the solution and give presenters documents that they can begin reviewing and rehearsing.

A draft presentation and script provide the following benefits:

- They help solidify the solution.
- They help illuminate holes in the solution.
- They provide the review team with a preliminary presentation and allow the team to identify technical problems, presentation issues, and marketing opportunities.
- They give the presenter a head start in working on his or her script by capturing the issues stated by the team during the preliminary presentation.
- They help to develop timing and topic transition issues.
- They help meet a customer deliverable if the customer requires copies of the presentation slides before the oral proposal presentation.

Review, rehearse, review, rehearse.   The company has a lot at risk when it sends people in to make an oral proposal. The company basically gets one shot at getting it right. Evaluators try to ask questions that will expose problem areas and risk mitigation strategies.

The evaluators have the benefit of surprise when evaluating the company's proposed solution because the presenter has no idea what the evaluator will ask, and the presenter may say something inadvertently to discredit his or her team. This is a great deal of pressure to put on a few people, especially if their previous positions may not have provided them the training to do well in high-pressure situations.

There is hope, however. The proposal team must review the materials and help the presenters rehearse their presentation. These reviews must focus on technical, business, contractual, management, and marketing issues. The rehearsals help the presenters in two ways: it lets them fine tune their presentation and provides them with opportunity to answer ad hoc questions from the review team to prepare them for the actual government evaluation panel. Some companies use videotapes or outside presentation consultants to help identify presentation weaknesses.

Develop a backup plan. Even though the company may prepare its first-string presenters well, the company may lose its competitive position if the presenters cannot attend the oral presentation. For this reason, the company should have the presenters' scripts carefully detailed and develop a strategy for backup presenters.

Prepare any handouts and additional material. The company can prepare information to distribute at the oral proposal presentation. Product drawings, industry reports, trend analyses, and sample reports are all items that may be useful to the evaluators during the oral proposal. The company should limit the information to only those things that help the customer evaluate the company's performance on the particular program requirement. Additionally, the customer may require the company to provide copies of the presentation slides before the oral proposal presentation.

Coordinate logistics. Once the customer informs the company that it has been invited to participate in an oral presentation of its proposal, the company needs to coordinate the logistics associated with the presentation. To do this, the company should finalize its list of attendees (which may be limited by the customer), transportation, equipment, and lodging.

Conduct oral presentation of the proposal. The next step is for the company's presenters to conduct the oral presentation at the location that the customer deems appropriate. The presenters must limit themselves to the time designated by the customer. Government evaluators usually are adamant about time limits because they do not want to give one company an unfair advantage over another company.

Complete any follow-up required by the customer.   After the oral presentation, the customer may require the company to submit information related to its oral proposal. The customer may even issue questions that must be completed (either in writing or orally) by the company before the customer's evaluation. Additionally, the company may have to submit parts of the proposal (such as the price proposal or contracts volume) before or after the oral proposal presentation.

Information needed for an oral proposal presentation:

- Complete technical solution and management solution
- Any key personnel requirements from the RFP
- Any oral proposal presentation requirements from the RFP
- Presentation techniques
- List of the features and benefits of the proposed solutions
- Answers to questions likely to be asked by the evaluation team
- A solid understanding of the proposed solution so that presenters can answer ad hoc questions from the evaluators

Develop the Price Proposal

Contractual Implications of the Price Proposal

The customer evaluates the companies' proposals to determine which company provides the products and services that represent the best overall value for the customer. To accomplish this task, the customer evaluates each company's solution in relation to its price. The technical proposal and management proposal contain the company's technical and management solutions, which are needed to develop the price proposal. In a product procurement, the price proposal must provide a price by year for each product or service that the company offers during the contract. In a labor procurement, the price proposal must include an hourly rate for each labor category the company proposes for each year of the contract.

The price proposal has the following contractual implications:

Assumptions made in the price proposal will drive decisions made on the account.   The decisions the company makes for developing the price proposal will establish the operating guidelines under which the contract will operate. For example, if the company estimates that two people will be needed for the program and the contract requires three people to actually perform the contract work, the third person's salary will come directly from the company's profit.

Solution and associated prices become the ordering menu for the contract.   The prices the company bids for the products and services are the prices that the company is committed to for the duration of the contract. Although the contract modification process exists on contracts, the customer ultimately decides whether contract modifications will be accepted. Therefore, a company that offers steep discounts on product prices in its price proposals in order to win the procurement will be obligated to provide the products at those prices for the duration of the contract, or until a contract modification is made.

Accuracy of the costs will drive whether the account will become profitable.   The more accurate the company's costs are in the price proposal, the better the chance that the account will operate profitably after contract award. This is why it is so critical that the company capture the price of all solution components described in the technical and management proposals in the price volume. Any solution component that is not priced must still be provided to the customer on a firm fixed contract, but the customer will assume that the offeror is providing the component at no charge. This means that the cost for that item comes out of the company's profit.

Costs and Prices

There are two terms that are used throughout this chapter that require definition: *cost* and *price*. *Cost*, from the perspective of a company acting as the prime contractor, represents the dollars that the company must actually spend to provide the goods and services required. These costs can include subcontractors, products, raw materials, internal support group labor, and other direct charges. To determine *price*, the company first adds these costs to its general and administrative (G&A) and overhead costs. Then the company adds its profit to these costs to determine the price for the goods or services it will provide to the customer. From the perspective of a company acting as the subcontractor, *cost* represents the dollars that the company spends to purchase the raw materials to make its products or the salaries it must pay people bid on the program.

Again, to determine price, the company acting as prime contractor first adds to these costs its G&A and overhead costs. Then it adds its profit to determine the price for goods or services it and the subcontractor will provide to the customer.

Additional requirements for a federal government contractor:

- Provide a proposal that is reasonable, accurate, and competitive.
- Price the company's solution in a manner that is compliant with the RFP.
- Price the company's solution in a manner that is attractive to the government.
- Provide an audit trail of each price given to the government.
- Provide cost and pricing data if requested by the government.
- Ensure that the solutions defined in the technical and management proposals match the cost elements defined in the price proposal.

Initial Offering Could Be the Only Offering

Many times the customer will decide that the original prices obtained through the initial proposal submission are too high or need modification. In these situations, the customer will ask the contractors that are still within the competitive range to submit a best and final offer (BAFO). The company should realize that both the commercial customer, through its desire to conduct an expeditious procurement, and the government, through its procurement reform and acquisition streamlining efforts, are moving toward a first and final offer (FAFO). In such cases, a contractor will have only one chance at giving the customer its best price. The company should keep this in mind when preparing its first price proposal submission, because the company may not get a chance to modify its proposal for a second chance at the program. For details on how to lower the initial proposal price, review the strategies outlined later in this chapter.

Overall Process

The overall process for developing the price proposal includes the following steps:

1. **Understand what and how the customer is buying.** Team members must understand the technology and services that the customer is buying and the contract type the customer is using

to procure the goods and services it needs. Pricing research and developing programs is significantly different from pricing products. Similarly, pricing a firm-fixed-price contract is different from pricing a cost-plus contract.

2. **Complete a competitive analysis.** Before the company spends much time and effort on bidding the program, it must realistically assess how well it will do in the procurement. To do this the company must determine how much its competitors are likely to bid versus how much its own prices are likely to be. The company must keep in mind that its own bid price must be high enough in order to manage the program after award yet low enough to win the procurement. If it looks as though the company cannot offer a competitive solution, it should not bid on the program.

3. **Develop a plan for how to pursue this piece of business.** As the company prepares to make its bid decision, it must plan how to win the procurement. The plan may include special marketing arrangements or strategic alliances with companies to allow the company to be more competitive. It is important that the business team members understand such relationships and the effect they have on the program pricing. A teaming partner or subcontractor can play a critical role if it can provide competitive prices, because with its help the overall team has a better chance at winning the procurement. However, each teaming partner or subcontractor must decide for itself how much it can lower its prices to remain competitive while still retaining a high enough price to cover its costs and a profit.

4. **Determine components of the solution and the person responsible for each**. The technical and management teams identify subject matter experts for each solution component. The business team needs to understand who is responsible for each component so the cost analyst responsible for a solution component knows who to go to for technical clarifications.

5. **Provide cost data for the bid decision.** The management team needs financial information to make its bid decision. Often, the business team supplies B&P budgets, potential contract revenue estimates, and financial assessments of the risk required to win the contract as input to the bid-decision process. The team is basically trying to answer the question, "Knowing what our costs will be and our assumptions about what our competitors will bid, do we have a good chance at winning the pro-

gram?" If the answer is no, then the company should not bid on the program.

6. **Gather information to cost the solution.** The business team must have the complete and current technical and management solutions for the price proposal and must work with the technical and management teams to understand the cost information that needs to be collected. The business team needs the following information: vendor name, product name, product version, product features, and unit prices by year for each solution component. Any extra services, such as training, maintenance, and documentation, are usually priced separately. Some companies keep this information in a database so that all proposal team members can have access to it. This becomes particularly critical if the solution changes frequently. On labor contracts, the company should provide hourly rates for each job category for each contract year.

Subcontractor Data

Once the business team has the correct solutions from the technical and management team, it needs to ensure that the appropriate cost data is available from the vendors. A subcontractor will provide data about its products and services to help the company acting as prime contractor determine if it can conduct the program at a price that can win. Product literature helps the business team determine which features the subcontractor bundles in the product price. A governmental customer may also require commercial and GSA price lists from the proposal team. These price lists are used by the government to determine if the price is reasonable. If the government requires these lists, the business team works with vendors to obtain the necessary information. In addition, the subcontractor will know how the competitors in its particular field might bid a product, which will help the prime contractor determine its overall price strategy.

Market Studies, Industry Research, and Trend Analyses

The business team uses market studies, industry research, and trend analyses to determine pricing strategies. These analyses help the business team identify risks associated with pricing strategies as well as methods to mitigate those risks. Strategies used on previous programs also provide a valuable resource for determining pricing strategies.

Develop Estimates

Estimates are used by the business team to project the costs over the life of the contract. Products or services obtained from subcontractors will normally be guaranteed through life-cycle contract pricing in the negotiated subcontracts. In such cases, the team uses the subcontracted prices as estimates for the contract. However, the business team must estimate other proposed items that are not covered in subcontracts, such as those provided by the prime contractor or products that will not be purchased in significant enough quantities to merit a subcontract relationship. Some of the items that the business team should consider when establishing estimates include the following:

- Everyone responsible for making estimates must use the same bases for estimates. For example, total number of labor hours in a year must be consistent throughout all estimates.
- Estimates must be time phased over the life of the contract to support contractual requirements.
- The business team must document its estimating methodology, rationale, and assumptions for audit purposes.
- Categories for cost estimating, which include:
  - Labor (e.g., hours, skill level required, labor rates, and task to be performed)
  - Other direct charges to the contract (e.g., computer usage and packaging materials)
  - Travel (e.g., air fare, per diem, car rental, number of days, number of people, location, and purpose of trip)
  - Subcontracted labor (e.g., hours, skill level required, labor rates, and task to be performed)
  - Product-related cost (e.g., research and development, cost of materials, cost of production, and specifications)

Develop Cost Model or Understand How the Customer's Model Works

The *cost model* is the tool that drives the development of the price proposal. The cost model may either be developed internally for a specific program, provided by the customer, or developed internally to handle all contracted programs. If the cost model needs to be developed, the business team should make sure it has the following four areas:

- The model must be able to report the information in the format described in the RFP requirements because that is how the customer expects to see the price proposal.
- The model must be able to capture the data items required to adequately represent costs. For example, if the customer wants the contractor to offer quantity discounts, the cost model must show how the company acquired the discounts.
- The model must have the flexibility to run what-if scenarios. This feature becomes particularly useful when the company defines best and final offer targets for vendors.
- Ideally, the model should interface with other corporate systems, such as the budgeting system, so that the costs to manage the program can be translated into the operating budget for the account after contract award. Also, if the customer requires the contractor to use a work breakdown structure for defining the work, the cost model should be able to feed cost type information into that system so that the costs for each component of the work can be determined.

Not only is it important for the business team to review these main areas to identify all the requirements for the cost model, it is imperative that the team understand the relationship between each of the data elements. Completing a data flow diagram that outlines what data are needed for each calculation will not only help define the system, it will also help troubleshoot problems down the road. Additionally, should the customer require changes to the price exhibits (which it frequently does), it will be easy for the team to add new modules to meet the new required functionality if the system is documented from the start.

The task of developing a cost model lessens significantly if the customer issues an electronic model that generates cost exhibits automatically. The business team must still validate the customer's model before keying in cost data to ensure that the model performs as expected. Everyone is capable of making a mistake, and evaluators are often required to quickly complete a system, so they may not have had test it thoroughly. The team should share any problems it identifies with the customer so that the problems can quickly be resolved.

In addition, if the company already developed a cost model for another program, the model may already have some of the capabilities built in. In this case, the business team may only need to add to the model the capability to report information the way the new customer expects to see it on the program.

Communicate to Subcontractor How Cost Data Should Be Provided

If the company will be working with a subcontractor, the company must inform the subcontractor on the customer's costing requirements so the subcontractor provides pricing that is consistent with the customer's costing requirements, otherwise the company's proposal will be evaluated as non-compliant. This is particularly important for a government program if the subcontractor submits its final price only to the company and its price build up directly to the government. The company needs to work with each subcontractor to ensure that the company obtains the proper cost data so that the business team can prepare an acceptable price proposal. As the procurement continues, the business team will need to know what specific details are required from each vendor so the company can price its portion of the solution. The customer, for example, may require such unique terms and conditions that the subcontractor's commercial price for the product is no longer applicable. In this situation, the subcontractor would need to develop a price for its product on this program alone, although, through FARA, the government is trying to mirror commercial terms and conditions to the greatest extent possible so it may not ask for unique conditions as much as it used to.

Participate in Solicitation Process by Evaluating Vendors' Cost Proposals

The company acting as a prime contractor uses the solicitation process to ensure that the goods and services offered to the customer represent the best overall value. The business team evaluates the cost proposals submitted by the vendors to help determine cost competitiveness. For government programs, in order to comply with CPSR requirements, the business team must document why one vendor was selected over another vendor based on financial merits. Cost analyses, prices analyses, and price negotiation memorandum are all examples of the documentation that the team can use to substantiate its decision. The solicitation process is described in Chapter 9.

Conduct Risk Assessment

Most customer programs have an element of risk for the contractor team. Adequate return on investment, parts availability, and poor performing subcontractors are just some of the risks that a company acting as prime contractor must deal with to bid a program; however, the company can mitigate some of the risks. One way of doing this is by establishing a mitigation plan. The company does this by having the business team determine the dollar value associated with each. To do this, the team gathers information, identifies what the risk components are, and determines methods to mitigate the risks so that the company can remain profitable. The inputs to this assessment include:

- Size and complexity of work
- Type of contract
- Effect of contract clauses, such as acceptance, liquidated damages, warranty, invoicing, payment, and insurance requirements
- Cost/risk area analysis, such as initial capital expenditures, minimum quantities, and avenues for future opportunities

The company can also mitigate risks by using carefully worded subcontracts. A subcontractor that provides products or services is in the best position to ensure that those products and services meet the customer's requirements. If they do not, the subcontractor should be responsible for fixing the problem and suffering any financial loss associated. To ensure that happens, the company should add a clause in the subcontractor's contract stating its work responsibilities and the financial repercussions of not meeting its responsibilities. Such a clause will not obsolve the company, however, and it must accept the responsibility for fixing the problems that fall within its area of expertise, such as systems integration or program management.

Capture All Costs in the Cost Model

Although the business team conducts a competitive analysis early in the bidding process, the analysis is constantly reevaluated throughout the proposal process. As costs are accumulated, the business team captures them in the cost model. By having costs readily available in the cost model, the business team can quickly determine how close it is to the competitive range. Based on this information, the management team may need to reevaluate how it intends to deliver the solution required.

Develop All Parts of the Price Proposal Submission

To complete the price proposal, the business team must collect data about the direct costs incurred on a contract, such as:

- Direct labor
- Fee/Profit
- Other direct costs (ODCs), such as:
  — Subcontracted items
  — Standard commercial items, such as hardware, software, and maintenance
  — Other costs, such as special tooling, travel, computer, or consultant services; packaging; and royalties

In addition, for government programs, the company must obtain components of the price proposal from the disclosure statement the company submits to DCAA for approval. These standard rates include:

- G&A costs
- Overhead
- Facilities capital cost of money

Begin Developing Pricing Strategies

Pricing strategies help the business team meet the competitive range target. Strategies may be based on technology trends, assumptions, market studies, or customer information. These strategies may be applied across the entire solution or applied to selected components.

Assist in Modeling Competitors' Solutions

Sometimes, the proposal team will want to try to determine what the competitors will offer in their solutions. After the technical team determines the components of the competitors' solutions, the business team may be asked to model the competitors' solutions to help the proposal team know what price target needs to be beat.

As the business team gains more information about the company's competitors and the customer, the competitive range becomes a price target that the company strives to meet to have a good chance at winning the procurement. The business team establishes a price target by analyzing the components of the solution and then making some assumptions as to what products the competitors will bid to meet the requirements. After the products are defined, the team makes additional assumptions about the strategies competitors will use to price their product offerings. GSA schedules, Freedom of Information Act (FOIA) requests, and other pricing data are all useful tools in defining the prices the competitors will use. The business team adds these solution component prices to obtain the overall price target. Once the overall target for the program is established, each component of the solution must be assessed as to whether it can be provided for the cost allotted to it. The team reviews this process at the component level and at the whole program level to determine if and where the company wants to take risks to win the procurement.

The company should keep in mind that as it prepares a competitive analysis to determine a price target to beat, its competition is doing the same thing. As more data becomes available about the company and its teaming partners, the company's competitors are changing their targets to reflect the new information. Companies use as much information as they can get to help them price a procurement to win.

Find Out If the Team Made the Competitive Range

The process of gathering and validating cost information occurs continuously throughout the procurement process. The objective of collecting this information is to determine whether or not the company's team can provide the requested goods and services at a price that is within the competitive range for the procurement. A customer determines the competitive range for a procurement based on the following sources:

- The results of the should-cost analysis it conducts before it releases the RFP
- Contractor proposal prices
- The amount that the customer is authorized to spend on the procurement
- Results of the initial review of each contractor's technical and management solutions
- Results of industry analysis, government price schedules, commercial prices lists, etc.

The FARA's efficient competition clause has given the government the right to limit the number of contractors' proposals it should consider for award. The government can even limit the number of companies that actually receive the RFP if it suspects a high volume of proposal responses.

It is difficult for the company to ascertain exactly what the competitive range will be on a procurement; however, based on its own industry analysis, the company can reasonably determine whether its price will be within the competitive range.

Manage Change to the Cost Model

As changes are made to the technical and management solutions, the business team will need to update the costs in the cost model to reflect the current solution. If a new vendor is added, the team will need to request a price proposal from the new vendor and to analyze it.

Conduct Reviews of the Cost Model Data

The business team needs to constantly review the cost model data to ensure that the appropriate components from vendors' proposals are costed in the solution. If the company is working on a large deal with hundreds of products, it is easy for the company or the team to overlook a feature that is required for the solution to work.

Finalize the Application of All Pricing Strategies

Before the business team submits the price proposal, the team needs to review with upper management how the team will apply the pricing strategies to ensure support for the post-award pricing. The prices the team submits will be the prices that will exist on the contract. It is important that the team price the contract appropriately and that everyone understands the potential risks to which the company is committing.

Review technical and management proposals to ensure all costs have been captured.

The business team should check one final time and make sure there is a corresponding price in the price proposal for every component listed in the technical and management volumes.

Begin Production

Once the review process is completed, the business team can print and verify the cost model reports. The price proposal is then turned over to the production team.

Information needed to develop the price proposal:

- Current technical and management solutions
- All parts of a price proposal submission
- Product literature and cost data from vendors
- Market studies, industry research, and trend analyses

- Estimates
- Cost model
- Risk assessment
- Competitive range determination
- Cost or pricing data

Develop the Contracts Proposal

Customers require a company to submit a contracts proposal, which outlines the contractual obligations under which the company will provide the products or services. The customer wants the contracts proposal because the RFP, including the amendments and modifications made during the discussions phase, plus the company's proposal, including proposal updates and responses to questions, will eventually become the contract. *Therefore, the customer uses the contracts proposal to ensure that the contractor understands that it is accepting the requirements of the RFP for the life of the contract.* Sometimes, the customer will include a draft contract to the company to mark up and sign as part of its original proposal submission. This is because sometimes the customer may issue an RFP, receive a vendor proposal, and immediately co-sign the contract and a contractual relationship would exist between the customer and the company. More typically, the customer will enter into question, discussion, and negotiation phases, but it is not obligated to do so.

Overall Process

The overall process for writing the contracts proposal is as follows.

1. **Determine type of contract.** The contracts team determines the type of contract the customer used to understand which clauses the company will need to comply with and to determine which clauses the company will need to pass down to the subcontractor. The contracts team also ensures that the subcontractors submit pricing based on the contract type. For example, pricing a firm-fixed-price-commercial-items contract is different from pricing a cost-plus development effort.

2. **Analyze effect of FAR requirements.** On government programs, the contracts team must review the FAR requirements and explain the implications to the rest of the proposal team. FAR requirements have significant implications to the success of the contract.

3. **Work with proposal team to identify a potential subcontractor and write statements of work.** The contracts team works with the proposal team to identify a potential subcontractor. An important step to this process is to document the statement of work for the subcontractor. This will become the basis for the subcontract. The contracts team must then finalize which contract terms and conditions should be flowed down to a subcontractor. The clauses that should be flowed down are those that the prime contractor cannot observe without subcontractor support. All terms and conditions relevant to a subcontractor's product should be flowed down in the subcontract. Once the team has developed a specific subcontract, the team is ready to negotiate with vendors. The contracts team may ask other proposal team members to review the subcontract to ensure that it represents the understanding between the two parties. Oral agreements must be documented in the subcontract if they are to be contractually compliant. Additionally, the contracts team must relay information about the clauses that the subcontractor will not uphold so that the proposal team can estimate the risk associated with such exceptions.

4. **Communicate issues to the customer and work to resolve them.** The contracts representative is usually the single point of contact between the customer and the company. In that capacity, the representative communicates any issues the company has to the customer. The contracts representative often works with the customer to resolve open issues by gathering information on any outstanding issues from precedent set on previous contracts.

5. **Write contracts volume.** A commercial customer typically wants to see any exceptions and possibly a draft contract as part of its contracts-proposal requirement. The government tends to ask for more information, which a commercial customer could also request.

   The contracts team compiles all the data and completes the contracts proposal by:

   • Determining any exceptions to the customer's terms and conditions

   • Collecting representations and certifications from vendors if required by the customer

   • Making representations and certifications on behalf of the prime contractor

- Completing a SB/SDB plan with actual business base percentages for government contracts
- Completing the responsibility statement
- Completing the draft contract, if required

Exceptions *The customer also requires the company to state in its contracts proposal if it intends to take exception to any term or condition listed in the RFP.* The customer evaluates any exceptions the company takes to the RFP requirements and determines the dollar effect of those exceptions. This dollar figure typically gets added to the company's bid price. The customer then carefully evaluates all exceptions taken by all offerors to determine which company, in light of all factors considered, represents the best overall value to the customer. The company should be wary of taking exceptions because by doing so, it may be eliminated from the competition. Also, the company must fulfill any exceptions taken by the subcontractor in its proposal.

Representations and certifications As part of contract performance, the government will expect that the prime contractor and its subcontractor abide by the representations and certifications they made during the proposal process. In addition, if the customer requires certification to ensure products provided on the contract meet evolving government or industry standards, the contractor is expected to keep its product current so as to remain compliant.

Degree of compliance with SB/SDB plan The government has small business and small and disadvantaged business goals that it must meet. It usually passes down those requirements to federal contractors. As part of the proposal evaluation process, the government reviews how close the company comes to meeting the goals set forth in the solicitation and to what lengths the company went to find qualified SB/SDBs. Ways that companies can find SB/SDBs to work with include:

- Reviewing databases of small companies
- Working with the Small Business Administration
- Determining what companies are currently subcontracted to the agency
- Reviewing previous SB/SDB relationships
- Evaluating capabilities listed on homepages on the Internet

Responsibility statement The government reviews the responsibility statement provided by the company to determine the company's ability to perform the work. Later in the evaluation process, the government conducts a site visit to review the company's facilities, processes, organization, subcontract agreements, and so on.

Performance risk As part of the government's increased emphasis on a company's past performance record, the government has begun two initiatives to validate the company's competence in performing the required work. See section above outlining the types of information required on government past performance citations to discover what is part of a performance risk assessment.

Draft contract The government will review the company's proposed contract to determine if the company has changed any language in the contract or added any new language to the contract. This evaluation will help the government to determine the similarities and differences between bids so that a fair comparison can be made between two similarly scored proposals.

6. **Prepare transmittal letter and turn over contracts proposal to the production team**. The contracts team completes a transmittal letter that will be used as a cover letter to the customer. The letter includes the following information:

- Name of company submitting the proposal
- Volumes of the proposal provided at this time (in the event that there are different delivery dates for each volume of the proposal)
- Any exceptions taken
- Any other issue that the RFP says to address in the transmittal letter

The transmittal letter is usually accompanied by a separate document stating the date and time that the proposal was delivered to the customer. This document acts as a receipt in the event that the proposal was hand-delivered to the customer site. By requesting a signature, date, and time stamp from the person receiving the proposal, the company has proof of the date and time that the proposal was delivered.

Review Proposal

The company must ensure that it provided a solution for each requirement in the RFP. In order to accomplish that task, the company typically conducts a variety of reviews to ensure:

- Each requirement is addressed.
- The solution provided for each requirement will work.
- Information is presented in the format outlined in the RFP.
- Information is presented in a clear, understandable manner to help facilitate easy evaluation.

Overall Process

The company should conduct the first set of reviews already described—individual, marketing, technical, management, oral proposal, and pricing—as the proposal is being written and costs are being collected so that changes can be suggested and incorporated. The final reviews—internal proposal team and the total proposal—should be done after the proposal is complete so that the proposal team can verify that all requirements have been addressed.

These reviews do not have to occur as separate activities. Sometimes companies will merge marketing, technical, management, oral proposal, and pricing reviews and invite subject matter experts from each discipline to participate. On the flip side, a particularly difficult proposal may require multiple reviews before it can be considered compliant and responsive by the evaluation team.

At the conclusion of each of these reviews, the reviewer should meet with the proposal team representatives to discuss specific recommendations for a specific section of the proposal or for the entire proposal. The team should document the recommendations and list specific steps required to make the document more appealing. The team representatives should then determine which of the recommendations should be acted on based on the time remaining on the proposal effort and the amount of unfinished work at that point.

Conduct Individual Reviews of Each Section

The purpose of the individual reviews of each section is to prepare for the more formal reviews, which are discussed later. Throughout the proposal process, writers conduct individual reviews of their sections before the formal review to ensure their sections meet the customer's requirements and the team's objectives. Writers may also review the sections with their manager before the review.

Conduct Marketing Review

The purpose of the marketing review is to determine if the proposal accurately covers the concerns that are most important to the customer. By ensuring the customer's needs, wants, and desires are addressed, the proposal has a better chance at being deemed compliant and responsive during the evaluation.

Even though the proposal can become a contractually binding document, it is still a sales document. As such, the company wants to present its goods and services in the best, possible manner. Conducting a marketing review allows external proposal team members the opportunity to see the claims being made and to assess how the customer will receive them.

The typical participants in a marketing review include:

- Program manager
- Marketing manager
- Technical and management team writers
- Experts who understand the customer environment

The process for a marketing review includes:

1. Agreeing in advance on what the marketing themes should be for a particular proposal effort
2. Communicating those themes to the section writers so that they may apply them in their sections
3. Reviewing outlines or storyboards to see how the writers applied the themes
4. Working with writers to make the themes stronger by providing statistics or other factual statements that lend credibility to the claims being made

Conduct Technical or Management Proposal Review

The purpose of a technical or management review is to solicit input from outside sources to review the validity, accuracy, and feasibility of the solution being designed. The goal is to ascertain whether the solution will work as intended for the customer's requirements. Typically, an internal review made up of proposal team members is conducted before an external review, which includes people who are not on the proposal team.

The participants for the internal review include the:

- Program manager
- Proposal manager
- Technical manager
- Subject matter experts/technical writers

The participants for the external version include:

- All participants from the internal review
- Representatives from the teaming partner and subcontractor organizations
- Experts representing each area required in the RFP

The process for a technical or management proposal review includes:

1. Providing a program overview (if the review includes external people)
2 Reviewing the customer's requirements for the volume
3. Providing flow charts of each major process or functional area on the contract
4. Providing descriptions of the overall solution
5. Discussing each requirement and stating how the solution meets the requirements
6. Reviewing the strategies and win themes that will be used throughout the proposal that provide the rationale for why the customer should pick the company
7. Identifying open issues so that any of the experts may suggest alternative solutions
8. Allowing the writer to work with the experts to get hands-on help with the open issues
9. Conducting a reviewer assessment during which the reviewers provide their overall comments and suggestions to the proposal management team for improving those areas that may cut across multiple functional areas

Conduct Price Proposal Review

The purpose of the price proposal review is to:

- Ensure that the vendor quotes collected represent the products and services used in the solution.

- Validate that the minimum vendor offering available to meet the requirement is used.
- Ensure that the labor required to complete all services required on the contract is estimated.
- Ensure the cost model works as intended with the appropriate loads applied.
- Ensure the cost model provides the data required to meet the customer's submission requirements.
- Assess if and how the company can make money on the contract after award.

The typical participants include the:

- Business team
- Business manager
- Technical team
- Technical manager
- Management team
- Management volume manager

The process for a price proposal review includes:

1. Providing each technical and management writer with the costs that have been captured for their solution component.
2. Allowing the technical and management writers to validate these costs by reviewing the vendor quotes, estimate sheets, and assumptions.
3. Reviewing any discrepancy with the management team for resolution.
4. Requesting the business team provide any additional quotes from the vendors.
5. Incorporating changes into the technical, management, and price volumes as deemed appropriate.

Conduct Oral Presentation Review

The purpose of the oral presentation review is to ensure that the team selected to conduct the presentation can accurately describe the solution, answer evaluations questions, and represent the company in the best possible light. Reviewers who meet the following qualifications should be selected:

- Know the solution and know if it is being presented accurately
- Do not know the solution so they can determine if it is being presented well
- Know what type of questions the evaluators may ask and can answer them well; also good at answering questions on-the-spot
- Have good overall mannerisms, word choice, knowledge, and presentation skills and can project the marketing messages strongly

Conduct Internal Proposal Team Reviews

The purpose of internal proposal team reviews is to:

- Correct any inconsistencies between sections and volumes. This effort alone will reduce the number of questions the customer issues to the team.
- Ensure that all managers understand how the program will run after contract award so that staffing and resource estimates are assigned appropriately.
- Ensure that what is described in the management and technical volumes is costed in the price proposal; otherwise, the company could lose money and never recoup its costs.
- Ensure that no required function to run the account is overlooked. Sometimes major topics can get overlooked because a writer thought that another writer was handling the topic in another section. The more experts the company has review the proposal document, the better chance it has of providing a thorough document.

The participants in an internal review include:

- Managers representing each functional area
- Writers who are writing large portions of the proposal

The typical process for the internal proposal team review includes:

- Providing copies of the entire proposal document to internal review team members
- Setting aside a day to complete the review so that interruptions are minimized

- Allowing reviewers to keep an action-item task list that needs to be accomplished to make the document complete

- Reviewing the action item lists with the appropriate writers at the conclusion of the review

- Ensuring changes are made to the proposal document before submission

Conduct Total Proposal Review

The purpose of the total proposal review is to concentrate on how the evaluation team will perceive the proposal. At this point in the process, design issues are all resolved and the document is in near final form. The review should primarily focus on how each of the functional areas is represented and if all the customer's requirements are addressed. The total proposal review should be held while there is still time to make minor modifications to the proposal and should include many of the same individuals from the previous reviews. This continuity between review team members allows for an efficient review focused on the task at hand rather than getting people up to speed on the approach.

The participants for the total proposal review include:

- All proposal team writers

- All proposal team management

- A subset of all review team members, particularly those who provided useful feedback

Produce and Deliver Proposal to Customer

The production team ensures that the documents written by the technical and management teams get incorporated into the final proposal that will be submitted to the government. The production team begins its work early on in the proposal process by establishing standards and formats for the writers. At this point in the process, the production team conducts the following tasks:

- *Make decisions about artwork to be used in the proposal.* The production team must decide if:

  —Proposal and corporate logos will be used throughout the document

  —Color or black and white artwork will be used

  —Proposal covers and spines will contain artwork

Once these decisions are made, the team must orchestrate how the artwork will be completed.

- *Receive documents from the team members.* The production team receives electronic copies of the documents from each team member and formats the material as required by the RFP.

- *Produce graphics.* Any graphics required are submitted to the graphics department or to an outside company for development.

- *Send documents to editors.* Editors ensure that the document is grammatically correct and that formats are consistently applied to text and graphics.

- *Send edited copy back to writers for review.* Typically, the editors will have queries that need to be answered by the writers. In addition, writers must review edits that have been made to ensure the content has not been altered.

- *Merge text and graphics.* Once the text is finalized, graphics are incorporated into the document at the appropriate locations.

- *Send merged copy back to writers for review.* The writers should review the copy one last time to ensure that the graphics have been incorporated into the appropriate sections.

- *Order and receive all necessary supplies.* The supplies necessary for producing a proposal include paper, binders, tabs, packing boxes, tape, labels, and acetate sheets.

- *Prepare document for duplication.* Add a table of contents and list of exhibits to the camera-ready copy of the proposal. Ensure headers, footers, and page numbers are correct on all pages. After reviewing the proposal for accuracy, duplicate and bind the document.

- *Conduct a quality review check of the entire proposal.* Once the proposal has been assembled, each copy should be quality checked to ensure all pages are adequately duplicated and in the right order.

- *Assemble all documentation.* If the RFP requires various volumes of documentation, the production team must determine a method to label and catalogue these documents to make it easy for the evaluation team to refer to them.

- *Box and label all copies of the proposal and supporting documentation.* Each box should contain a list of the contents within the box and should be appropriately labeled.

- *Deliver or ship the proposal.* Proposals may either be hand-delivered or shipped via a commercial carrier.

- *Maintain an electronic copy and hard copy of the proposal in a secure location.* It is important that the proposal team keep a copy of the proposal exactly as it was submitted to the government. This allows the proposal team to answer any questions posed by the government during the post-submission period.

The production team needs the following information:

- All technical volume sections
- All management volume sections
- All contracts volume sections
- All price volume sections
- Any other sections required by the RFP
- Any documentation required by the RFP
- Proposal preparation instructions

Prime Contractor Considerations

Determine Amount of Subcontractor Involvement

The company acting as prime contractor has overall responsibility for all the steps in the review process. But like an orchestra conductor, the company must direct a team of internal and external sources to produce a solution that is harmonious with the customer's environment. To do that, the company must decide how to achieve that delicate balance between prime contractor and subcontractor that leads to a winning performance or in this case, a contract. The balance is delicate because there is always more at stake than just winning the contract.

Subcontractor Prices

The company must determine how much of the business it wishes to keep for itself and how much it wishes to subcontract to another company. Part of this decision is made using a make or buy analysis: if the company does not have the internal capability to provide the product or service, it must, by necessity, subcontract the work to another company. However, the company must realize that the price it can offer the customer for a subcontracted product or service may be higher than that proposed by a company that provides the product or service internally. The higher price results from the fact that the subcontractor adds a profit to the price it submits to the company and then the company also adds a profit to the price it submits to the customer. This double profit margin could make the company's prices too high to be competitive.

Revenue Sharing

A second issue arising for the company is whether or not there is enough work that can be done internally to motivate the company to prime the deal. Marketing and proposal development can be expensive propositions. If the company must subcontract out a large portion of the contract, then the company must also give away part of its profit from the contract There is a certain point at which the company would decide that the investment to prime the deal is not worth the contract risk or minimal revenue after award.

Company Value

The company has to be very clear about the value that it brings to the customer through the contract. A prime contractor that subcontracts out all of the work and just tacks on an exorbitant program-management fee just to run the contract will probably have to answer some customer questions about what the customer is getting for paying the program-management fee. Just as a prime contractor looks for the value a subcontractor brings to the team, the customer is looking for the value the prime contractor brings to the team. A company acting as prime contractor must clearly articulate the products or the meaningful services it will provide on the contract. Otherwise, the customer may decide to contract directly with the subcontractor and write out the prime contractor all together.

Other Deals in the Pipeline

The company is not making a decision to bid on a particular program in a vacuum. A company typically reviews tens to hundreds of deals at any point in time. However, this does not mean that the company will always have many great contracts to bid on. The company may experience lean years in which it bids on contracts that it would never had considered during more prosperous times. Either way, the company must cultivate relationships with potential subcontractors early in the process in case the company decides to bid; however, do do not string along the subcontractor if the company decides not to bid on a program.

Subcontractor Involvement

The company must decide how much it wants a subcontractor to be involved in the marketing and proposal development process. Sometimes a subcontractor brings fresh ideas, innovative approaches, and genuinely better ways to do things. Other times, a subcontractor does not have the expertise that the company is looking for. Also, each subcontractor that the company uses will not typically have the same level of input on the prime contractor team. The company will determine each subcontractor's level of involvement based on each subcontractor's level of expertise.

Following are some tasks that could be shared with subcontractors:

- Writing proposal sections
- Developing strategies
- Reviewing the proposal
- Sharing customer information
- Sharing competitor information
- Developing products
- Integration
- Technical or management services
- Advertising
- Marketing
- Producing the proposal
- Research and development
- Independent test and validation
- Involvement in other programs
- Demonstrating the product
- Oral proposals
- Pricing strategy

Partners Today; Competitors Tomorrow

The reason a prime contractor has such a challenge in determining how much involvement it should allow the subcontractor to have is because a subcontractor could be working with you on a program today and competing against you tomorrow on another program. Some of the tasks that could be shared with the subcontractor could expose a great deal of information about the company's business, which would be extremely useful to a competitor. The more areas that the subcontractor is involved in, the more of a chance it has to garner the company's secrets, which it may (but shouldn't because of the non-disclosure agreement) use in its own repertoire of competitive tools.

Partners Today; Competitors Today

Another problem that complicates the prime contractor-subcontractor relationship is that the subcontractor can be supplier selling to the company and its competitors on the same deal. Although every prime contractor wants an exclusive subcontractor relationship to help its competitive position, sometimes a subcontractor work with multiple prime-contractor teams pursuing the same deal to improve its chances at winning. If a subcontractor is working with multiple prime contractors, the company acting as prime contractor must decide how involved it wants subcontractor to be in the proposal process. As a competitor, the needs to protect its own competitive position, so it may not be able to let the subcontractor get too involved in the program for fear that its strategy may be leaked to the competitor.

Breakout Work between Subcontractors

Another key issue for the company is to decide how work will be divided among subcontractors, particularly if two or more subcontractors can provide the same type of product or service. This decision can be difficult because each subcontractor is trying to get as much of the program as it can so it can grow its own business base. The best approach is for the company to define the roles and responsibilities early on in the relationships so that each party knows what they are responsible for providing. It also helps if the company does not make promises it cannot keep. For example, on an indefinite delivery/indefinite quantity contract, a prime contractor should not promise 60 percent of the training work to one company and 40 percent to another when the customer has total flexibility with regard to when it wants classes scheduled. In such cases, the prime contractor wants to make sure its subcontractors are each prepared to provide training as soon as possible, that way if one cannot provide the training, the other subcontractor will. It does not make sense to promise one subcontractor 60 percent of the training if it cannot provide the training at a particular time and the other company can. In addition, if the subcontractor that was promised 60 percent of the training repeatedly cannot deliver the training at designated customer times, it could potentially harm the relationship that the prime contractor has with the customer.

Unfortunately, subcontractors push to get percentages from prime contractors as part of their contract to improve their internal business case. If the company's subcontractor requires percentages, the company should mitigate its risks by putting in language that suggests alternative courses of action in the event that the subcontractor cannot meet the customer's requirements.

Effect of Strategic Alliances

In today's marketplace, companies frequently form strategic alliances for just about anything: product development, services, research, distribution, and marketing, to name just a few. These alliances are usually developed because they benefit both companies. However, sometimes strategic alliances force the company to do things "in the interest of good will in the alliance" instead of acting on what is best for the program that the company is working on. Strategic alliances tend to be rather all-encompassing, and the proposal team may be forced to work with the strategically aligned company even if its not in the team's best interest to do so.

Interrelationship of Programs

Another area that a prime contractor must consider when working with a subcontractor is the relationship that the subcontractor has with the company on other programs. In order to help secure a solid competitive position, the prime contractor may merge the requirements from multiple programs and work with only one subcontractor for all the programs. In return for this larger business potential, the subcontractor should provide greater discounted prices or more advantageous terms and conditions. So the prime contractor may consider sacrificing some contracts in order to work on a larger set of lucrative contracts.

Working with Subcontractors

A prime contractor also needs to keep in mind how much time it takes to work with subcontractors. There is a great deal of time involved in the marketing, discussion, negotiation, instruction, follow-up and buy-in that the prime contractor must commit to each subcontractor.

If a subcontractor is new to business, the contractor will need to provide even more detailed instructions. Too often, a prime contractor assumes that a subcontractor does business in a similar fashion only to find out later that there are major discrepancies. The value of clear communication cannot be overstated. The contractor needs to communicate clear instructions to the subcontractor on how the customer or the company wants something done. If the subcontractor delivers an end that does not satisfy the customer's or company's request, the company should consider the following explanations:

- The instructions were not clear.

- The instructions were given to someone who was not doing the work and that person did not clearly communicate the instructions.

- The subcontractor does things a certain way regardless of how others want things done.

- People doing the work are not familiar with the program requirements.

- The subcontractor had other priorities so it could only meet the minimum requirement.

- Multiple people on the proposal team are providing direction to multiple people on the subcontractor's team.

- The subcontractor made a strategic decision to support the program at a minimum level, believing the company gave it too much work to do on the program.

- The usual problems occurred: human error, technology glitches, and personality conflicts.

Subcontractor Considerations

Subcontracting is a wonderful option for companies interested in getting into a business area without all the risk associated with being a prime contractor. However, subcontracting is not without its own set of challenges that must be carefully evaluated before a company decides to subcontract. Some of those considerations include the following:

Decide How Much the Business Is Worth

As discussed earlier, the prime contractor must decide how much involvement it wishes to have from the subcontractor. Likewise, the subcontractor needs to decide if it is willing to provide the level of support requested from the prime contractor. For example, a subcontractor may be working with a prime contractor that just wants generic product descriptions and prices or the contractor may wants the subcontractor to be intimately involved every step of the way. In the first case, the cost of sale is minimal; in the second case, the cost of sale is much greater. To determine if the cost of sale is too great to even be considered, a company should conduct a return on investment and an opportunity cost analysis (described in the following paragraphs). After these analyses are performed, the company can decide if this is the best opportunity for it to participate at that particular time.

Return on Investment Analysis

A return on investment analysis consists of reviewing how much money the company will have to spend to get the business versus how much money the company can realistically expect to earn if the company and the prime contractor win the contract. When deciding how much money will be needed to win the program, the company should analyze its involvement in each stage of the process and look at how many people will be needed to do the work plus their salaries for that period of time. People that the company may need to consider include representatives from technical, management, business, legal, and other support organizations. Expenses for any travel, proposal duplication, producing the product, providing technical support, and other costs associated with turning in a proposal to the prime contractor and conducting the after proposal submission activities (described in the next chapter) must be included in the analysis. The company then needs to compare these expenses to how much it can reasonably hope to make on the program. The company does this by analyzing the revenue, expenses, profit, contract type, prime contractor's business case, and subcontract terms and conditions. It then factors that number by a win factor. A *win factor* is the percentage the company assigns to the win probability. For example, if the prime contractor is the incumbent, has a great relationship with the customer because of stellar contract performance, and is typically the low cost provider, the company might assign a win probability factor of 90 percent (i.e., the company is 90 percent sure that it will win the contract). However, if the prime contractor is trying to get its first contract with the customer and entered the marketplace within the last few years, the company would set its win probability at a much lower percentage. After the company figures out how much it will cost to bid the program and how much it can reasonably expect to make, the company needs to assess other factors than financial ones. For example:

- How will the deal help the company's overall marketplace growth?
- How will this subcontract relationship affect the other subcontract relationships the company has with the prime contractor?
- Are the company's employees currently fully utilized? If they are not and the company is paying them anyway, the company should take advantage of the opportunity to work on the program.
- How does the program help the company meet its other goals and objectives?

Opportunity Cost Assessment

Another part of the equation is the opportunity cost assessment. An *opportunity cost* is basically an analysis that answers the question "If I wasn't pursing this opportunity what opportunity would I be pursuing and which opportunity has the greatest benefit to me." To answer this question the company compares the return on investment analyses for multiple deals to determine which deal has the greatest payoff in terms of financial and strategic benefits.

Another factor that should be considered in the opportunity cost assessment is how much training the company needs in the marketplace. When a subcontractor is heavily involved in helping a prime contractor with a program, the subcontractor learns a great deal:

- Makes customer contacts
- Makes prime contractor contacts, from which it learns processes and procedures and technical strategies
- Meets other subcontractors working, which provide it with more program contacts and the company learns processes and procedures and technical strategies at the subcontractor level
- Acquires a detailed understanding of how the program will run after contract award
- Learns competitor information

The company can use the information it learns to pursue future business opportunities. In addition, a proposal effort can help get the company's team members up to speed quickly on contracting and the marketplace in a potentially inexpensive manner. Finally, if the company demonstrates strong abilities through its greater program involvement, it can gain other business opportunities. The key is to decide if the benefits outweigh the risks.

Working on Multiple Prime Contractor Teams

Another issue that a company needs to address is when a subcontractor is involved in multiple prime contractor teams pursuing the same customer opportunity. These relationships can get tricky if they are not managed well. One method of managing the relationship is to ask the subcontractor to sign a non-disclosure agreement, which prohibits the subcontractor from sharing information from one prime contractor with another prime contractor. A subcontractor that has or is perceived to have shared inappropriate information with a competitor will probably be kicked off the team or, at a minimum, not be asked back to pursue other business opportunities with the offended prime contractor. To help segregate efforts on a prospective proposal, a subcontractor may have different people working on each team the subcontractor works with so that there is no perceived or real conflict of interest. Or the subcontractor may elect to offer the same products, terms, conditions, and prices to each prime contractor team to simplify the relationships. However, this approach does not bode well for the prime contractors that are trying to differentiate themselves from their competitors.

Doing Things the Way the Prime Contractor Wants Them Done

A subcontractor is often used by the prime contractor to garner some of the skills the prime contractor is deficient in. The opposite situation can exist as well: the subcontractor could have a great deal more experience in developing business opportunities or proposals, so the prime contractor stands to gain the most from the subcontract relationship. The bottom line, however, remains the same: the subcontractor must abide by the way the prime contractor wants to run the program. Some prime contractors need a lot of help and they willing accept their subcontractor's help; some prime contractors don't need or want any help from their subcontractors. This can present a frustrating experience for the subcontractor, particularly if the subcontractor has more experience than the prime contractor.

What the Subcontractor Will Need to Provide to the Prime Contractor

The types of services and support that the subcontractor may provide to the prime contractor have already been discussed. Now we need to discuss the specific deliverables that the subcontractor must provide to the prime contractor in order for the prime contractor to submit a proposal to the customer. From this list of deliverables, the only item that is typically solely required on federal government contracts is the representations and certifications that a subcontractor makes to the prime contractor.

Technical Solution Write Up

The subcontractor must provide the prime contractor with information about the technical solution that the subcontractor is proposing. This information can be submitted as a formal proposal or in a less formal manner. The prime contractor needs the technical solution to develop its proposal to the customer. The prime contractor will normally want something in writing, as opposed to a verbal submission, in case there is an issue after contract award about the subcontractor's performance.

For a government contract, the prime contractor will typically require a formal response. The subcontractor needs to submit a formal response because the government will review how well the prime contractor follows the government's purchasing guidelines using a Contractor Purchasing System Review. See Chapter 9 for more information.

Technical Literature

The subcontractor also provides technical literature to the prime contractor to use for its own reference and to give to the customer for clarification. Technical literature consists of brochures, product specifications, product data sheets, user manuals, and installation manuals.

Prices

The subcontractor must provide its price for providing its services or providing the product. These prices may be based on commercial list prices or GSA schedule prices, or may be developed solely on the terms and conditions of the program. Prices typically are given for the life of the contract unless other provisions have been made.

Prices are given per product or service or labor hour for each year of the contract and include any necessary escalations or discounts granted. For commercial contracts, the final price is all that is required. For government contracts, price buildup (e.g., cost, G&A, overhead, profit, and fee) and supporting documentation may be required.

Integration Support

If the contract requires products to work together, the subcontractor must be willing to assist in developing a solution with the prime contractor. The subcontractor must do this because it best understands how the product works and how the service is supposed to be provided. Solution-development support could take the form of remote or local access to systems or technical expertise. The subcontractor may need to provide demo products or gratis licenses to products to ensure that all of the subcontractor's products work together as intended.

Draft Subcontract Revisions

As discussed in Chapter 9, a subcontract is not typically signed until after the prime contract has been negotiated. However, during the early stages of the process when the prime contractor submits a proposal to the customer, the prime contractor still needs a commitment from the subcontractor that it will provide the products and/or services as required. The subcontractor must demonstrate its willingness to accept the customer's requirements and a draft subcontract is one way to do this. A draft subcontract outlines all the terms, conditions, and requirements that the prime contractor wants the subcontractor to accept during contract performance. The subcontractor reviews the draft and indicates any revisions by marking up the document. The subcontractor submits its prices about this time. Once this is done, the two can begin negotiations and either reach fruition in a subcontract that is ready to be signed or reach an impasse and have a list of open, non-agreed upon issues. If they are not significant, these issues will be resolved after contract award. If they are significant, either one or both of the parties may decide to back out of the relationship.

Representations and Certifications

Representations and certifications are used by the customer to require the prime contractor to claim as true certain facts about itself.

The prime contractor cannot make many of these representations and certifications unless it imposes the same requirements on its subcontractor. Representations are most predominantly used in government contracts and seldom used in commercial contracts.

Following are some typical representations and certifications that the prime contractor and the subcontractor may need to make:

- Has a drug-free workplace
- Is an equal opportunity employer
- Has procurement integrity
- Has small business certification
- Has 8(a) or small and disadvantaged business certification
- Abides by Buy America Act provisions
- Adheres to industry standards (e.g., ISO 9000 or SEI CMM level)

Resumes

The subcontractor may be required to submit resumes of key individuals who will work on the program after award. Also, if the prime contractor flows down a key personnel clause to the subcontractor that requires that the customer approve a resume before the individual begins work, the subcontractor needs to comply. If the clause also requires the key individuals to work on the contract for some period of time (e.g., 90 to 180 days), the subcontractor and the prime contractor are bound to this requirement.

Past Performance Citations

Customers that request past performance contract citations typically want them from the subcontractors as well. If the subcontractor has performed well on past contracts, this will not be a problem. However, if the subcontractor has not performed well, there is a great possibility that the subcontractor could lose the program for the prime contractor. To make sure that the subcontractor does not cause problems on a proposal, it should always provide excellent service on existing contracts. Consistent good work will also ensure the subcontractor future contracts, and that message applies to prime contractors as much as it does to subcontractors.

Willingness to Answer Any of the Customer's Questions

As discussions between the prime contract and the customer begin, there may be issues about the subcontractor's portion of the work.

The prime contractor is in no position to make commitments on behalf of the subcontractor unless it is authorized by the subcontractor to do so. Therefore, the subcontractor must be willing to assist the prime contractor in answering any of the customer's questions about its offering and to help in any way it can to win the procurement.

Government Considerations

The proposal development phase for a government customer has the following unique considerations:

Quantitative Evaluation Criteria

The Government Performance Results Act (GPRA) requires each governmental agency to develop metrics and objectives for each aspect of business and to report on how well it is doing in meeting each objective. GPRA is tied to an agency's strategic planning, return on investment (ROI) analysis, and capital budgeting initiative. GPRA requirements are starting to flow down to contractors, and they are being asked to describe how their proposals will meet the GPRA requirements and to determine metrics that should be used to quantify the value the contractors will add to the governmental agency either through a positive ROI or improved cost management through performance-based contracting.

As a result of these quantitative evaluation criteria, a prime contractor may ask a subcontractor to help develop, abide by, and work to improve metrics in areas for which they are responsible. Some governmental agencies and commercial companies (and state agencies) are even taking these quantitative evaluation criteria one step further and are requiring contractors to get paid out of the savings that they generate on their programs. This means that if a contractor's solution doesn't work as intended, then the contractor doesn't get paid. One good side effect is that because a contractor is taking on more of the risk, the government is allowing higher profit margins.

Provide Exactly What Is Requested or Make an Exception

This concept was discussed in Chapter 1. The government applies the doctrine of strict conformance to its contracts (i.e., the contractor must deliver exactly what is called for in the contract). This requirement is passed on to subcontractors as well. A subcontractor cannot assume that it can swap out an older generation product for a newer generation product. Nor can it assume that if it stops manufacturing a product, that it is no longer obligated to provide that same product to its prime contractor to provide it to the government customer. The subcontractor may help the prime contractor develop a proposal to replace products on the contract, however, the government has the final decision as to whether the modified contract is acceptable.

Deliver Proposals on Time

Although commercial customers may be sticklers for deadlines also, the government requires that all proposals be delivered on time. A proposal that is even minutes late will not be considered for award. Some prime contractors pass this requirement down to the subcontractors as well and require the subcontractors to submit their proposals by a certain date and time in order to be considered for award.

May Need to Submit Prices Directly to the Customer

As discussed earlier, the government customer may require more financial data and supporting documentation for a contractor's prices than a commercial customer. Some subcontractors do not feel comfortable (and with good reason) submitting costs, G&A, profit, overhead, and FCCOM rates to the prime contractor to use in its proposal to the government. Because the data is required, some subcontractors opt to provide the prime contractor with final prices and to provide the rest of the confidential data to the government directly under separate cover. *Separate cover* just means that the subcontractors' prices will be submitted separately to the government and will not arrive with the prime contractor's proposal.

Two Types of Specifications

The government issues RFPs with two different types of requirements or specifications: performance-based or design-based. The distinction between each of these is critical when resolving any potential disputes during contract performance.

Performance-Based

Performance-based specifications leave the details of performance up to a contractor's discretion so the contractor assumes responsibility for achieving stated performance requirements. The government states the standards or performance requirements a contractor must meet and then leaves all the details of solution up to the contractor. The contractor must then deliver a solution that meets the stated performance requirements or face contractual remedies. An example of a performance-based specification is when the government requires that a system provide 10-second response time to its users. The requirement does not state what the system components should be, it just states its requirement in terms of end-user functionality.

Design-Based

In *design-based specifications,* the government details the manner or the method of the contractor's performance so the government is responsible for any omissions or errors in the specifications. In these specifications, the government conducts all of the system design activities and it determines the specific components needed to address its requirements. For example, the government needs Pentium II processors with 6GB of storage, 350 MHz processing speed, and 64MB memory. A contractor then puts together a solution based solely on the government's design and as long as the contractor delivers exactly the products stated in the proposal it cannot be held liable for the solution not working as intended.

DCAA Approval

The G&A and overhead rates are developed before pursuing government business. The FAR section on Cost Accounting Standards delineates the expenses that a company can charge back to the government in the form of overhead and G&A rates. The company sets up its accounting system to capture costs in a manner appropriate for government business. The company then submits a disclosure statement to the Defense Contract Audit Agency (DCAA) outlining which expenses are included in its G&A rate and which are included in its overhead rate. Once the DCAA has reviewed and accepted the rates, the company then uses these established rates to bid government programs. The company may periodically review the actual expenses that make up these rates to ensure that the rates are still appropriate. If the rates are not appropriate, the company can submit new rates to the DCAA for approval. Once the DCAA reviews and approves the revised rates, the rates are considered provisional and are used for bidding purposes. After the company incurs the costs that make up the G&A and overhead rates, it can recompute the rates to become final rates. The company then charges the government these final rates and the company must either credit the government's account if the rates are lower than expected or charge the government more if the rates are higher than expected.

5 AFTER PROPOSAL SUBMISSION

Chapter 4 discussed how a proposal is developed and delivered to the customer. Sometimes that is all that needs to be done: A customer receives and evaluates the proposal, it awards the contract, and the contractor begins work. A more likely scenario, however, is that the customer has some questions about the proposal or would like to alter the solution. Sometimes the customer wants to see the solution demonstrated or wants to negotiate certain portions of the contract. Other times the customer believes the proposal prices are too high and want the companies to submit best and final offers (BAFOs). For these and other reasons, a company will have to handle some after proposal submission tasks, which are discussed in this chapter. Chapter 5 discusses the following:

- How to respond to customer questions
- How to respond to customer amendments
- How to prepare for and conduct a live test demonstration
- How to finalize a competitive target
- How to prepare for and conduct discussions with government customers or negotiations with commercial customers
- How to prepare and submit a BAFO
- How to conduct tasks associated with an award

A company and its subcontractor need to work together during the after-proposal-submission process because the decisions made during this time will become part of the final contract negotiated between the customer and the company. The company will want to ensure it has its subcontractor's buy-in and approval before making commitments at this stage of the process because the company could be left particularly vulnerable during contract performance if it made unsupported decisions about the subcontractor's performance.

Answering Customer Questions and Responding to Proposal Amendments

Questions, Clarification Reports, and Deficiency Reports

After the customer receives the company's proposal, it begins the evaluation process. The first step of this process is to compare the proposal to the RFP requirements and the source selection plan to determine if the solution proposed by the contractor is compliant. If the customer's evaluator decides, based on his initial reading, that the solution is compliant, then he assigns a score to that section and the evaluation process is finished. If the evaluator cannot decide whether or not the customer's solution is compliant, further action is usually taken. In such instances, the first step is for the customer's evaluator to issue a question to the company. Government customers refer to this process as the clarification report (CR) and deficiency report (DR) process. The government uses a CR when the solution requires clarification; It uses a DR when it deems the proposed solution to be non-compliant. When a company receives a CR or a DR, it goes through a formal response process, including solution review and perhaps alteration, writing the response, updating the proposal, and reviewing the responses before it submits them to the government customer in writing. In some instances, the government will allow a company to provide oral responses to the government's questions, but more typically responses are requested to be in a written format so they can become part of the contract file.

Commercial customers typically adopt a less formal approach to questions because they do not have to deal with any potential protests as government contractors do. Because a commercial customer can basically make an award to anyone it wishes, it can conduct the question phase orally or ask for a written response and at any time it deems appropriate.

Another method of responding to a proposal is to issue an amendment. A commercial customer or a government customer can issue an amendment when it wants to change part or all of the RFP. The customer may have reason to modify, remove, or add requirements to the solicitation document or RFP, such as technology advances, vendor questions, new regulations, changes in the cost model, or the inability of all offerors to meet a certain requirement. The customer communicates these changes only to offerors that are within the competitive range.

Overall Process

The company responds to questions and amendments in basically the same way: acknowledging receipt of the document, assessing its effect on the solution, restating or redefining parts of the solution, documenting those changes in the proposal, and submitting the changes to the customer. The following process for responding to customer questions would accommodate government customer and commercial customer proposal responses that must be submitted in a written format. If a company will not need to submit a written response, it will still need to complete the thought process and solution work.

Receive Questions or Amendments from Customer

The customer issues questions to evaluate each contractor's response to the requirements. The customer may issue questions at any time after the proposals have been submitted. As discussed in the following sections, the customer may issue RFP amendments during the procurement process after it has released the RFP. In this case, the customer may issue an amendment because it has questions about the contractor's understanding of the amendment. The customer may issue questions many times throughout the procurement cycle and they usually are specifically developed for and issued to the company that the customer received an inadequate proposal from. Therefore, not every company will receive questions.

Similarly, the customer may issue an amendment at any point in the procurement process to inform contractors of a change in RFP requirements. Commercial customers may choose to issue the amendment either verbally or in a written format; government customers typically release all amendment information in the form of a written document that is either sent to the companies that are within competitive range or posted on the agency's Web page.

Acknowledge Receipt

For government programs, the company must inform the program's contracting officer (CO) that it received the documents using the procedures prescribed by the RFP. The typical method of acknowledging receipt of questions is a phone call or fax to the CO stating that the company received the documents. To acknowledge receipt of amendments, the company must send back a signed Standard Form 33 to the CO before, at, or after proposal submission.

Review the Question, the RFP Requirement, and the Proposal to Determine the Issue, or Review the Amendment to Determine Effect

The customer issues questions to a company in one of three ways:

1. Paper format

2. Electronic format using a diskette, which contains all the questions for a particular company

3. Electronically, via electronic commerce (EC), electronic data interchange (EDI), or the Internet

Some customers will inform a contractor orally of a problem in its proposal and require the company to respond to the question in a proposal update.

The customer's question report should contain the following information:

- Contractor's name or identifier
- CR/DR tracking number
- RFP section number that corresponds to the requirement of the response in question
- Contractor's proposal section number that corresponds to the response in question
- Description of the specific issue with the response
- Description of what the contractor needs to do to fix the problem area

Questions may be issued on any section of the proposal or procurement activity, including the technical, management, contracts, or price volumes; the live test demonstration; the site visits; or as a result of the performance risk assessment group evaluation. When a company's proposal team receives questions, the team must review the relevant RFP requirement, proposal section, and issue being raised to determine if it affects the solution as proposed. In some cases, the issue may be resolved with a brief explanation; for example, the customer may have become confused because the company used two different names for the same product throughout the proposal. The customer's response would be to explain the inconsistency in a memorandum. Other times, the company must change its solution to accommodate the customer's issue.

When the customer issues an amendment to a company within the competitive range, it does so in one of three ways:

- Electronically, via the agency's Web page from which the company may download the changes
- Paper format, with only the changed pages provided to the company
- Electronic copy, via diskette containing the entire revised RFP

A customer attaches a Standard Form 33, which serves as a transmittal cover sheet, to an amendment and includes RFP update pages that have sidebars to denote any changes. A company must incorporate the updated pages into the original RFP and determine the effect of the changes to its proposed solution. In some cases, the company's response is not required, such as when the new requirement is already met by the company's existing solution and the company's proposal already states that the requirement can be met. If the proposal does not already state that the requirement can be met, or if new products must be offered to meet the additional requirements, the company must issue a proposal update.

Notify Subcontractors of Issues within Their Areas

The proposal team must review any CR, DR, or amendment that affects a solution provided by a subcontractor with that subcontractor to ensure that the solution proposed is compliant. In the case of a customer question, the subcontractor should write the first draft of the response because it is familiar with the solution and have the proposal team review it. In the case of an amendment, the subcontractor should assist the proposal team in updating the proposal to reflect accurate information. If a CR, DR, or amendment renders the subcontractor's solution noncompliant, the proposal team must find a new subcontractor with a product that meets the requirements.

Determine If Additional Items Are Required

Sometimes additional products are required to address the issue stated in the question or to meet the modified requirements of an amendment. If this is the case, the company must find another product on the market that can meet the customer's requirements and that complies with the rest of the solution. Once the company has identified this product, the proposal team must gather all the necessary data about the product to update the proposal and assess the cost effect of the new product. Some of the proposal sections that the team may need to update for a new product include technical data, pricing information, representations and certifications, management information, and documentation.

Assess Cost Effect

The proposal team must assess the cost of the new product in terms of its overall contribution to the bottom-line price. It does not make sense, for example, to add a superior technical feature if the associated cost takes the team out of the competitive range. However, if the new product is expensive and necessary, the team should cut costs in other areas to remain competitive.

Understand How the Customer Wants to See Changes

The RFP Proposal Instructions section may explain how the customer expects to see changes made. Sometimes the customer provides additional submission information in the cover letter with its questions or amendment. For CRs and DRs, the governmental agency usually expects a written response to the issue raised and proposal update pages. For amendments, the customer usually expects proposal update pages or a certification stating that no changes are required. The proposal team must provide the revision number, revision date, and highlighted revisions on each proposal page that is updated. The customer may want each revision on a different color of paper. Sometimes the customer wants the company to mark which revision was generated by each question. The customer may limit the number of pages used for proposal revisions. The customer does this so that companies do not submit a lot of pages after the customer has already conducted most of the proposal evaluations. If the customer limits page counts, the total number of pages that each volume may contain will be outlined in the RFP. The customer may also stipulate that only changes driven by a question or an amendment will be accepted and evaluated. This is to prevent companies from proposing a brand new solution.

Write Response

Once the proposal team reviews all the relevant documents and decides which solution changes are required, the team can formulate a response. When responding to customer questions, the company is usually required to provide a written response to each question. If the company does not understand the issue being raised in the question, it should seek clarification from the customer either verbally or in writing.

Determine Effect of Changes and Update the Proposal

Changes made to one section of the proposal typically affect the entire proposal. For example, when adding a new product to the solution, the following sections may require changes:

- *Technical volume*—All charts, text, and graphics that contain a description of the revised product

- *Management volume*—All charts, text, and graphics that contain a description of the support being provided for the revised product
- *Contracts volume*—Percentage of business for the company providing the revised product and small business status
- *Live test demonstration volume*—All test plans for the revised product, if required
- *Price volume*—All exhibits that provide unit and life-cycle pricing for the revised product
- *Documentation*—All user and system documentation, if required for submission
- *Executive summary*—The description of all solution components

Any of these changes typically mean that the company must gain additional information from its subcontractors to be eligible for award. A subcontract relationship could fall apart at this stage because more negotiations and reassurances will be needed, and the subcontractor may not be able to provide them. For example, if the customer believes that part of the solution provided by the subcontractor will not work, the company must either gain assurance from the subcontractor that the product will be modified to meet the customer's solution or the company will have to replace the subcontractor's product with another product.

Review Changes

Once all of the proposal team has answered all the questions and made the proposal updates, the team conducts a review of all the revisions to ensure:

- No contradictions exist between sections
- Changes have been made in all the appropriate proposal sections
- Changes made as a result of the questions do not contradict previously written sections
- All team members are aware of each revision and its effect
- All references to the old information have been removed

This review is critical because if changes are not made properly, more questions from the customer can result.

Produce Proposal Changes

Once the proposal team responds to all of the questions and updates the proposal, it can begin the production process. The production process entails editing the changes, making the changes to the proposal, formatting the proposal changes according to the customer proposal instructions, producing the requisite number of copies, and conducting a quality check of the final document. The customer typically wants each question, response, and corresponding page packaged together so the evaluators may review the effect of a change on the entire proposal. The company usually has to provide the same number of proposal updates as it did original proposals.

Submit Revised Proposal and Question Responses

The company must submit the revised proposal and responses to the customer by the designated date and time. The customer evaluators will review the changes and, if necessary, issue additional questions, which starts the process all over again.

Preparing the Demonstration

The customer may require the company to present a demonstration as part of the evaluation process. Demonstrations give the customer an opportunity to verify and validate the company's solution against the RFP requirements and to ensure that the company's solution will work as proposed. In addition, demonstrations give the customer the opportunity to ascertain the level of risk associated with the proposed solution. The company is expected to design and produce a technical demonstration that complies with the customer's demonstration requirements and present the proposal team in the best manner possible.

Demonstrations provide an excellent opportunity for company and subcontractor to work together and share solution information. The company may need to obtain product, technical support, marketing brochures, demonstrators, presenters, and subject matter experts from the subcontractor organization in order to make the demonstration a success.

Overall Process

Determine the Requirements for the Demonstration

Demonstrations vary in type, duration, and format depending on the customer and the solicitation requirements. Demonstrations can also vary as to when they occur; either before contract award, which will be the focus of this chapter, or after contract award. After contract award demonstrations are used when the program is large and has many components that require frequent updating. In such cases, the customer may require the company to present a demonstration each time the company adds a new component to make sure it works.

All of the subcontractor's products may not be needed for a demonstration. The company must decide, based on the customer's requirements, which, if any, of the subcontractor's product line is necessary for the demonstration.

Demonstration Types

The types of pre-award demonstrations include the following:

Unwitnessed demonstration   During an unwitnessed demonstration, the customer provides the test data to the company. The company conducts the benchmark without customer evaluators present and submits the results to the customer as part of the proposal submission. In such situations, the customer protects itself by inserting a clause in the contract that states that the product or system delivered under contract performance must achieve the same test scores as the unwitnessed test yielded. The customer may also require a witnessed demonstration after contract award.

Operational capability test   In an operational capability test demonstration, the customer gives each company a list of tests to perform either before the demonstration or at the demonstration. All contractors receive the same set of tests to perform, and the customer assigns scores for how well each contractor performed against a preestablished set of criteria. The customer's evaluator reviews the scores as part of the proposal evaluation process.

Contractor-driven demonstration   In a contractor-driven demonstration, each company is allowed to select what solution components it wishes to demonstrate. This type of demonstration is designed to give the customer an overall impression of the solution, but it does not provide the quantitative scoring opportunities that the operational capability tests provide. This is because a company can demonstrate the solution components that represent its offering in the best possible light and neglect to demonstrate those solution components that are not as advantageous.

In any of these demonstration options, the company may request help from the subcontractor. In the case of the unwitnessed demonstration, the company may flow down some customer requirements to the subcontract so that if the subcontractor's products do not work as intended, the subcontractor will suffer the ramifications.

Demonstration Length

Demonstrations vary in length from several hours to a month or more for large programs. The length of a demonstration can provide a significant competitive advantage for some companies. For example, a customer uses a lottery to determine the order in which companies will demonstrate. The demonstration is expected to last a couple of weeks and many companies are involved. Because of the duration of the demonstrations, some companies may have extra weeks or even months to prepare for their demonstrations. Such instances can provide a significant competitive advantage to companies; particularly when procurement events, such as proposal submission, question response, and demonstrations are occurring concurrently.

Review RFP Requirements for Demonstration

When the customer requires a demonstration, the customer usually provides demonstration requirements in the original RFP or through an amendment to all offerors. The customer may require each company to submit a demonstration plan as part of its proposal submission depicting what the team plans to demonstrate (if the customer allows the company to decide) or how the team intends to comply with the customer's demonstration requirements.

Develop a Plan for How to Conduct the Demonstration

Regardless of whether or not the customer requires a demonstration plan, the company's proposal team should develop a plan for managing the demonstration to ensure that the demonstration occurs flawlessly. The team has much riding on a successful demonstration, and the customer does not allow for makeup demonstrations in the event that the team's first attempt fails. The demonstration plan should contain the steps listed in this section with specific dates established for each step.

Determine Solution Components to Be Demonstrated

A major part of the demonstration plan is determining what components to demonstrate. The proposal team will want to highlight its company's strengths and demonstrate those capabilities that are superior to that of the competition, but what is actually shown will be driven by the customer's demonstration requirements. If the customer conducts operational capability tests, the team must demonstrate the solution components that correspond to the components required by the tests. If the customer allows for a contractor-driven demonstration, the team has much more flexibility in choosing what to demonstrate.

Assign Responsibility for Each Component of the Solution

The team should assign one person to each component of the solution to ensure that the component is ready on the day of demonstration. A knowledgeable person from either the company or subcontractor may be selected for a solution component. Some companies prefer to have each component covered by two people: one to handle the presentation (talks during the test describing all activities and answering evaluator questions) and one to handle the demonstration (shows how the product is intended to work). These two people must work closely to present a well-orchestrated demonstration.

Determine Degree of Readiness of Each Component

Determining the degree to which each component is ready for demonstration will require input from both the company and its subcontractors. To determine readiness, the demonstration team should develop test plans for each functionality that will be demonstrated and establish criteria to determine how capable the product is of meeting each requirement. If actual tests are required by the customer, the team can:

- Define all requirements related to a specific test.
- Develop a standard format for test plans.
- Develop test plans for testing how a particular product meets each requirement.
- Conduct a management team review of the test plans to ensure adequacy.

If actual tests are *not* defined by the customer, the team can:

- Develop a plan for how to demonstrate as many requirements of the RFP as possible given the time constraints.
- Select the solution components that will show the team in the best possible manner and develop a demonstration plan for them.
- Complete and review test plans as stated earlier.

The company's solution will always have areas that are not as strong as others. The best way for the demonstration team to handle this problem it to carefully analyze its solution's strengths and weaknesses, as well as those of the competition. This analysis will allow the demonstration team to emphasize the competitor's weaknesses and downplay its own. The team can also try to fix as many of the weaknesses as possible to lessen the effect of the problems on the solution. For this approach, the proposal team will need assistance from its engineering department for products developed internally and from teaming partners and subcontractors for products developed externally.

Submit Any Demonstration-Related Questions to the Customer

During demonstration preparation, the company should call the customer if it has questions. It is much better to get any open issues resolved before the demonstration than to present the demonstration in a manner that the customer did not anticipate. Typically, a governmental CO will require the company to submit the question in writing. The CO then answers the question in a formal amendment that it sends to all offerors.

Determine the Role of Subcontractors in the Demonstration

If products or services are provided by subcontractors, the demonstration team should consider asking representatives from those companies to participate in the demonstration. The roles of the representatives can vary depending on the demonstration requirements. For example, members from the teaming partner or subcontractor company could be identified as the responsible person for a solution component because they know the product best. Other roles representatives can fulfill include demonstration support, presentation support, integration support, background documentation support, helpline support, emergency support, and facilities and equipment support.

Locate Demonstration Space

The customer has the option of requiring that the demonstration occur at a customer or company facility. If the demonstration is to occur at the company's facility, the proposal team must locate enough space to handle the demonstration requirements. Typically, a minimum of three rooms is needed for the demonstration: one in which to conduct the demonstration, another for the support personnel required to conduct the demonstration, and the third for the customer evaluation team to conduct sidebars. The demonstration room must be large enough to handle the customer evaluation team, contractor support personnel, demonstrators, presenters, and necessary equipment. The customer often limits the number of company personnel allowed in the demonstration room at any one time. Support personnel, therefore, need an area in which to wait before conducting its piece of the demonstration or in the event of an emergency. The customer evaluation team usually requests a private area in which it can retreat each day before, during, and after the demonstration to compile notes, compare evaluation scores, and assign risk assessments. Also, if the customer requires or if the company chooses to demonstrate manufacturing facilities, then the demonstration team may need to organize a tour of the facilities.

Provide Amenities

Besides demonstration space, the proposal team will need to provide other amenities for the customer during the visit. Furniture, projection systems, maps of the area, telephones, secretarial support, PCs, and food may all help the demonstration run smoothly.

Develop Demonstration Documentation and Presentations

To present a polished demonstration, the team should develop a carefully defined agenda and use standard presentation and documentation formats. The agenda should follow the demonstration requirements listed in the RFP or, if the company can develop the agenda, it should match the evaluation criteria established in the RFP. An agenda will help the proposal team stay focused on what the customer wants to see, rather than on what the company wants to demonstrate, which may be of little interest to the evaluators and, therefore, doesn't keep the evaluators' interest. Following is a sample demonstration agenda that a company could use:

- Welcome and introductions
- Keynote address
- Technology presentations
- Solution overview
- Individual tests, presentations, or demonstrations
- Manufacturing facilities tour
- Scheduled breaks/meals

- Status at the end of each day
- Schedule for the next day's events

The agenda should also include time for the company to answer any customer questions either at specified points throughout the day or during a presentation. Sometimes the RFP states that the company has the opportunity to retest if the team fails a test the first time. If the customer allows retesting, it is usually permitted under strict conditions. For example, the customer may stipulate that testing will occur for eight hours each day. If the company completes all the tests scheduled for the day under the eight-hour requirement, the customer may allow retesting for any failed test during the remaining time, but the retesting may not exceed the eight-hour time schedule. The proposal team should also highlight any concerns the customer expressed during the demonstration. If the customer expressed any major concerns, the company may wish to present its position as an agenda item.

Once the team has prepared the agenda, it can establish standard formats for its presentations and documentation. Presentations include all formal addresses given to the evaluation team throughout the demonstration. Documentation includes any handouts, samples, and test reports that are provided to the evaluators as part of the evaluation process or as background information. The team should develop standard formats early on and provide them to the presenters and demonstrators. Standard formats minimize the amount of rework associated with taking existing presentation and documentation and reformatting it into the new standard demonstration format.

Once the formats have been established, the team and/or presenters can prepare scripts for each test or presentation. The degree of script writing depends on the presenters and demonstrators used. If the presenters and demonstrators have been working on the proposal and are familiar with the RFP requirements, little, if any, script writing may be necessary. If the team uses professional demonstration personnel, however, it may be prudent to write a script that tailors what is said about the product to target the specific customer evaluators.

Determine Contingency Plans

If the company fails the demonstration, the company's chances of winning the procurement are minimal. Therefore, the company should have contingency plans in place in case a component fails before or during the demonstration. The contingency plans can be having backup components available on site, having the technical experts at the demonstration in case there is a problem, or assigning backup personnel to conduct the presentation. All of these contingencies need to be worked out with the subcontractor early on in the process.

Determine Accommodations for the Customer

Usually, the customer will request a list of hotels in the immediate area of the company facility if the demonstration is scheduled over multiple days. Some companies put together visitor's guides outlining the restaurants and amenities in the area.

Ensure Demonstration Personnel Are Prepared

Demonstration personnel need to be prepared for the pressured environment of a demonstration. Written scripts, rehearsals (including videotaping, if necessary), and external reviews are all approaches to help demonstration personnel prepare for the actual demonstration. It is also important that all demonstrators and presenters understand the evaluation criteria so that they may emphasize those characteristics of the solution that illustrate the team's ability to meet the evaluation criteria.

Test the Solution and Finalize Demonstration

The proposal team will need to continually test the solution to ensure that it works as intended. Sometimes the team finds that changes are needed to make the solution functional. Any changes to the solution must be carefully documented in proposal updates. As discussed previously, the team must decide when to stop making changes and begin working on finalizing the solution for presentation. Once the team has finalized the solution, it will want to conduct a requirement compliance check to ensure all RFP requirements have been addressed.

Complete Production of Demonstration Materials

The last step is to produce the final version of all demonstration materials.

Conduct Demonstration

The team is now ready to conduct the demonstration. Any tests that the team fails should be retested, if the customer allows. The customer and company must agree on what tests were completed. The customer may share with the company which tests it passed and which it failed.

Answer Demonstration-Related Questions and Update the Proposal

The company will need to update the proposal if any of the following situations occur:

- Solution changes were made in preparing for, or as a result of, the demonstration
- The customer issues questions based on it the demonstration
- The customer asks questions at the demonstration, which the company wishes to clarify in the proposal

Answering demonstration-related questions ensures that the solution the company demonstrated is the exact solution that it proposed.

Finalize Competitive Target

Because of the highly competitive nature of customer procurements, many companies develop competitive targets. A *competitive target* is the price a company believes that its competitors will bid to win the procurement. Armed with a competitive target, a company then tries to get its own price below what it believes the competitors will bid to win the procurement. Developing a competitive target is both an objective and a subjective activity. It is based on actual numbers (where they exist) and on assumptions (when real data is unknown).

Selecting People to Work on the Competitive Target

The right people must work on the competitive target. Ideally, a company should select individuals who understand the technical solution being proposed and who have a broad understanding of the competitor's product offerings to work on the target. In addition, it is helpful if the people selected can conduct thorough research, because the competitive target team will need to uncover what companies the competitors are likely to team with, what their strategies for winning will be, and what price they are likely to bid. Although the technical team members probably possess these characteristics, it is best *not* to have them identify the competitive target. This is because the more the technical team discovers about the competitor's solutions, the more likely it might be not to develop a different solution for its own company's offering. Once the competitive target team has uncovered the competitors' solutions, the team might want to review its discoveries with the technical team. In this way, the technical team might be able to apply strategies that the competitive target team identified as part of its research.

Sometimes it is easier for a company to hire an outside market research company to conduct the research and provide a competitive target for a particular program. A market research company can provide good data, if the proposal team selects a market research firm that specializes in the solution germane to the program. If the firm selected has a database full of information it has gleaned over the last several years in an industry, then it makes sense for the proposal team to tap into these resources to develop its competitive target. Of course, the team should decide which alternative, developing the target internally or externally, will yield the best information at the most reasonable cost.

Subcontractors are a tremendous source of information for developing the competitive target. They can assist the company acting as prime contractor in identifying realistic estimates for what the competitors may bid for individual components on the program. The company can take the information gleaned about the individual components and estimate what the other companies will bid.

Steps to Develop a Competitive Target

Identify Major Solution Components

The company conducts several steps to develop a competitive target. First, it identifies the major solution components required to meet the requirements of the RFP. The company already did this when it developed its own solution, so that information can be provided by the technical team. For example, if the procurement was for information technology, the team might identify printers, workstations, and modems as the hardware components of the solution.

Select Competitors to Use for the Competitive Analysis

Next, the competitive target team reaches consensus on the one or two teams on which it would like to develop competitive targets. The company cannot conduct targets for all the competitors because it probably does not have the time or resources to develop a target for each program competitor. Therefore, the company should select the competitors that are strong contenders for winning the procurement. Once it has selected one or two companies, it develops models on the selected competitors.

Determine How the Competition Will Bid

The competitive target team needs to determine which pieces of the solution the competitor company will provide itself and which components it will likely contract out. In order to do this, the company needs to understand the competitor's product lines and how the products are configured. Next, the team determines which companies the competitor will work with for the solution components that will likely be contracted out. Understanding the competitor's strategic alliances, the companies it has teamed with in the past, and the companies it is conducting marketing activities with are all ways to determine this information.

Estimate Prices for Each Component

Finally, the team attempts to ascertain the pricing that the competitor will use for each component. Commercial price lists, GSA schedules, and data obtained through the Freedom of Information Act (FOIA) process are all ways to gather this data. The pricing information is the hardest to obtain. Oftentimes, the team will have to make some assumptions about what the competition will bid. Ideally, after the team conducts several competitive target analyses, it has data that it can use to pursue future programs.

Finally, the competitive target team estimates the loads that the competitor will use on the products and services it offers. *Loads* are percentage rates that include general and administrative (G&A) costs, overhead costs, and a fee. Once all the component prices and rates have been established or estimated, the team adds them together to equal the competitive target for the program.

Validate the Competitive-Analysis Target

Developing a competitive target is an evolutionary process. Once the team has captured all the initial data, it reviews the data with internal and external people to try to validate as much of it as possible. As more information becomes available about the competitor's solutions, the team adds that information to the competitor model to develop the competitive target.

By now, the company's technical and business teams have developed and priced the solution offering. The competitive target team then shares the information it obtained with the technical and business teams. If the competitor is using strategies that would prove useful to the proposal team, the proposal team may implement them. In addition, the technical and business teams review each solution component to determine if the current product offering is cost competitive.

At this point, an education process occurs. The technical team may try to convince the competitive target team that the price it has established is unreasonably low. The technical team will cite solution components that could not be offered for the price that the competitive target team established. The competitive target team also tries to justify why the numbers it has developed are the price to beat. There is typically give and take on both sides and then the information is presented to upper management.

Upper management uses the information provided by the competitive target team and the business and technical teams to determine the price the company should offer for its products and services. The company wants to offer its solution at a price that covers its costs and makes a profit. The strategy and gaming occurs because the company wants to come in at a low enough price to win the award but high enough so as to secure as much profit as possible.

Conduct Follow-Up Activities After Contract Award

The company should review the competitive target after contract award to determine the lessons learned from the analysis. At this point in the process, the winning competitor's unit prices may be available through the FOIA process or through catalogues distributed to the customer. The company should use this data to update its competitive target files for future procurements. If the company is the winner, it should still analyze the losing company's total price with the competitive target established. Though detailed product pricing will not be available on the losing company's solutions, analyzing the competitors' total price with the competitive target will indicate how proficient the company is at establishing competitive targets.

Conduct Negotiations

Discussions and negotiations are designed to clear up any misunderstandings between the customer and the company before contract award. The customer expects the company to strive to resolve any open issues during the discussions phase. To do this, the company must solve open issues and develop alternatives for solution components, if necessary.

There are several points requiring emphasis in our review of the procurement's negotiations phase. First, governmental customers typically refer to the negotiations between the government and potential prime contractor as *discussions.* Discussions basically begin during the questions stage and can last up until BAFO. The commercial customer typically refers to a set period of time when the customer and potential prime contractor negotiate the contract. Secondly, the governmental customer may choose not to conduct discussions. If this is the case, the company should ensure the customer is aware of any open issues that the company believes need resolution at the time of proposal submission. The next round of discussions and negotiations usually occur before BAFO, so that the company can make any necessary proposal updates before the customer makes a contract award. However, some customers have, on occasion, conducted discussions after BAFOs were submitted with the apparent winners. In this latter scenario, the contractors are usually required to update their proposals to reflect the final negotiated contract between the customers as a result of the discussions.

The last point to understand about the customer's requirements for discussions is that the customer is not obliged to conduct discussions with every company. Typically, the customer will conduct discussions only with companies still within the competitive range, either in the interest of time for a commercial customer or to avoid potential protests after contract award for government customers. However, a customer may choose to not to have discussions with all parties, for example, when the customer conducts discussions with only the apparent winner.

Overall Process

The overall process for preparing for discussions includes the following steps:

Receive a Call to Discussions

If the customer wishes the company to participate in discussions, the customer will send a letter, or call the company, and provide the date, time, and location for the discussions. In addition, the customer will send a copy of the discussion agenda items to the company to assist it in its preparations.

Prepare Any Company Issues for Discussion

Once the company knows it is invited to discussions, it must prepare its items for discussion. Throughout the procurement process, the company should identify any issues that require discussion with the customer. Items for discussion could stem from confusion about a particular requirement or the company's desire to have certain requirements relaxed. For example, the proposal has a clause that requires the company to assume a great deal of risk. Because of it, the company must inflate its price to mitigate its exposure. The customer likes the company's solution, but cannot work with the company because its price is too high. In this case, the customer and company may be able to develop a mutually beneficial solution to the problem, perhaps by developing a risk-sharing scheme. The company may bring up issues during initial RFP evaluation, proposal development, demonstration, questions, marketing efforts, BAFO preparations, or during any conversations with the customer personnel.

Review and Prepare Responses to Any Items for Negotiation (IFNs)

Sometimes a customer will issue one more round of questions to a company to resolve any remaining outstanding items. This last round of questions may be called *items for negotiation*. IFNs are handled in the same way that questions are handled (i.e., the company reviews the issue raised by the customer, assesses its effect, develops a solution, and documents that solution in a response to the customer and in a proposal update).

Prepare Negotiation Strategy

Now the company is ready to compile all the information it developed for its negotiation strategy. The management team reviews its list of items previously developed, and decides which issues to discuss. The team then conducts research to determine the position the company wishes to take on a particular issue. These findings will then be presented to the customer. The company hopes to convince customer personnel to proceed as the company wishes. For key issues, the company may want to prepare several different solution scenarios in case the customer does not approve of the first option. Most importantly, the company should identify those issues that are most important so that it can discuss them first. The company should do this in case the customer sets a time restriction. It is also important to include subcontractors in the negotiation strategy preparation, particularly if they have issues that need to be addressed as part of the discussions.

Determine the Members of the Negotiation Team

Next, the company decides who should participate in the discussions. Typically, a company will select its contract representative as the spokesperson for the team. Other people the company may select to be on the negotiation team include the program manager, salesperson, and any other person who is an expert in the areas being discussed. The customer may restrict the number of people the company may have at the discussions. If this is the case, the company may bring as many people as necessary to the discussions and swap people in and out of the meeting as various topics are presented. The company may ask the subcontractor to participate in the negotiations or just exclude it.

Participate in Discussions

The discussions are held at the designated date, place, and time. The customer typically discusses its open items first. For commercial negotiations, the customer may choose to have any number of people present. For government negotiations, the contracting officer (CO) will conduct the discussions for the government and technical personnel are in the room only for the time during which technical discussions are held. When the business or contractual issues are raised, the customer has its technical evaluation team leave the room. This is because the customer wants its technical evaluators to select the best solution based on technical merit without regard to price or contractual issues. The contractor is not obligated to follow suit.

Discussions will continue until they are complete or until the customer states that time is up. Government customer personnel stay as neutral as possible during the discussions so as to not give one company a real or perceived advantage over another. The customer may not answer all questions raised during the discussions but will provide answers to the company's questions after the discussions are concluded. The customer may choose to continue discussions when the answers are obtained. These techniques are used to maintain the integrity of the procurement by keeping all companies on equal footing.

Work with the Customer to Develop a Negotiation Summary

At the conclusion of discussions with the government, either the customer or the company will develop a negotiation summary. If the company develops the summary, then the customer has the opportunity to review it before it is finalized. If the customer develops the summary, then the company reviews the summary before it is finalized.

Information about the discussions is disseminated in two ways. First, the information about relevant sections discussed may be provided to the teaming partners for their review. Second, the information from discussions is disseminated through a negotiation summary. The purpose of a negotiation summary is to provide an audit trail of the discussions in case any issue arises in the future. The summary contains the following information:

- Author
- Date
- Subject, including contract number
- Discussion's begin and end date
- List of personnel from both sides

Also included is a list of issues categorized in the following manner: contractual, cost related, technical, or miscellaneous. Each of the issues contains the related clause, brief description of the issue, highlights of the discussion, and a summary of the final text or how the contract will be modified.

Information helpful for discussions and negotiations include:

- Items raised by the proposal team throughout the procurement cycle
- Issues the customer has raised
- Data obtained during the CR/DR process
- Discussion agenda items issued by the customer
- Demonstration comments made by the customer
- Information on why the customer has concerns about an issue
- Data on alternative solutions to the issues
- Data to justify why the task must be completed in the manner proposed if the company does not wish to change its solution
- Information to rate alternatives; for example, what is the best, worst, and most-likely resolution to the open issue
- Information that helps the company understand bottom-line effect of an issue
- Information to prioritize the issues

Prepare Best and Final Offer

A best and final offer (BAFO) is typically the last formal information exchange before contract award. The customer asks for BAFOs only from those companies that are still within the competitive range. Bear in mind that the customer could have made a second competitive range determination after the discussions phase to further limit the competition. The reason the customer conducts a BAFO is to secure the best value. Most times, this means that the customer expects the company to lower its prices for the goods and services it is offering.

The customer is under no obligation to conduct a BAFO. Sometimes it awards a contract based on a first and final offer (FAFO). For governmental contracts, the current FAR states that if the customer puts a clause in the RFP stating that the contract may be awarded without a BAFO, the customer may, but it is under no obligation to, conduct a BAFO. (Commercial companies do not have any such regulations to which to adhere.) If the customer does not include this clause, the customer must conduct a BAFO. Likewise, the customer may conduct more than one BAFO if it deems this necessary. If multiple BAFOs are required, all offerors within the competitive range may submit a revised BAFO submission.

The customer expects the company to update the proposal, if applicable, to provide best value pricing and to resubmit the cost proposal. When a company receives a call for BAFO, the customer typically gives the company a very short period of time to prepare its response. For this reason, most companies prepare their BAFOs long before the actual call to BAFO is received in order to have enough time to complete the response. Likewise, many companies will prepare BAFO plans in order to anticipate all the steps required to complete a timely, compliant response.

Overall Process

The overall process for BAFO preparation begins before the company receives a letter requesting its BAFO. For a large program, the proposal team may begin its preparations one to two months before it believes the BAFO is due. These preparations will occur as the team prepares for discussions and completing the CR/DR phase.

Prime Contractor Develops a BAFO Plan

Once again, a plan is used to develop a strategy for accomplishing a procurement task. The customer typically gives a company a very short period of time, usually several days to two weeks, to submit its BAFO. Because of this tight time frame and all the tasks that the company must complete before its submission, the proposal team typically develops a BAFO plan. The plan details the specific strategies, methods, and approaches that the proposal team will use on outside vendors to lower their prices. In addition, the team looks internally at ways it can reduce its operating costs once the contract is awarded. Part of this BAFO plan includes determining the risks that the company is exposing itself to and the techniques that it will use to mitigate those risks during contract performance. Many of the following steps listed are milestones for the BAFO plan.

Prepare Subcontractors

In order for the prime contractor to submit a lower, responsive BAFO submission, it must secure lower prices and, perhaps, better terms and conditions from its subcontractors. Obtaining approval a subcontractor's approval on innovative pricing approaches takes time to secure. Ideally, the company acting as prime contractor wants to give the subcontractor as much time as possible to secure the lowest prices it can.

If the company gets the subcontractor involved too late in the process, the subcontractor may not be willing or able to work on lowering its prices. The company can use the prices already the subcontractor already quoted and assume it can negotiate lower prices after award, but this strategy tends to leave the company out of the customer's competitive range because the prices are too high. Similarly, the company could assume it can get lower prices after award and discount the prices to the customer based on that assumption, but this approach is risky because the contractor has no guarantee that the subcontractor will lower its price.

Complete Validation of Competition Analysis Target

During this preparation phase, the team continues to validate the competition analysis target. As more information becomes available, the price the company believes it needs to beat may become more realistic. The company will not know the actual price until the contract is announced. The company's estimate serves to drive additional cost-cutting strategies for the BAFO team.

Validate Technical, Management, and Business Solutions

Before the proposal team begins extensive work on the BAFO, the team should ensure that it has the current technical, management, and business solutions. This step, coupled with reviewing labor estimates and validating subcontractor's proposals, is part of an iterative process. As requirements are further refined, labor estimates and product mix may vary and subcontractor's proposals may need to be updated.

Review Labor Estimates

Labor is typically one of the most expensive items on a contract. Even having just one extra person on the contract for the life of the contract can add hundreds of thousands of dollars to the proposal. Likewise, if the proposal team underestimates the labor requirements, the company could end up losing money during contract performance because additional personnel resources are required. Therefore, the proposal team needs to understand the exact number of personnel needed to run the contract and ensure that the appropriate labor costs are included in the price proposal.

Validate Subcontractors' Proposals

Another step in the BAFO preparation process is to validate the subcontractor's proposal. This is important because the subcontractor may have proposed more than what is required to meet a particular technical requirement. In addition, the technical team needs to ensure that the products offered will actually meet all the customer's requirements. The team needs to conduct several reviews:

1. Review the subcontractor's technical proposals against the team's cost proposal to ensure that what is proposed has an associated price.
2. Review the subcontractor's list of products against the actual RFP requirements to ensure that all requirements have been addressed.
3. Ensure that the accurate subcontractor costs have been used to develop the prime subcontractor's price proposal.
4. Determine ways that the subcontractor might be able to reduce its prices.

Negotiate with the Subcontractor

Once the team understands the subcontractor's proposal, the next step is to negotiate any outstanding issues between the company and the subcontractor. The company wants to help the subcontractor develop pricing strategies that can allow the company to be more competitive.

Request BAFO Pricing from Vendors

At the conclusion of discussions, the company typically asks for the subcontractor's BAFO submission. The BAFO submission reflects the products and prices that are incorporated into the subcontract between the company and the subcontractor. The team inserts the subcontractor's prices into the cost model and uses them as the basis for its price proposal to the customer.

Develop and Document Pricing Strategies

Ideally, once all the suppliers' prices are put into the cost model, the company will have a proposal that comes in under its competitive target. Seldom, however, is this ever the case. Usually, the company has to take some additional risk in order for the overall deal to come in under the competitive target. Management must understand and be willing to commit the resources necessary to manage the contract given the risks that have been taken to win the contract. Management must understand this as it conducts a management review of the pricing strategies and final BAFO price.

Price Reduction Strategies

Brian T. Fisher, in his article titled "Winning on FAFOs: A Proposal Manager's Tailoring Techniques" (*Contract Management*, May 1997), suggests two different types of price-reduction strategies: cost based and process based. For cost-based strategies, he suggests that the company:

- Reevaluate the direct labor structure
- Propose a low or negative rate escalation
- Reclassify indirect laborers into the direct cost pool
- Use a value-added general and administrative rate
- Reduce the proposed fee or profit

For process-based strategies, he suggests the company:

- Create a new business unit
- Base the proposal on aggressive performance data
- Use review teams

- Reduce indirect rates
- Outsource
- Replace existing employees with job shoppers
- Eliminate midlevel supervisors or managers

Components required to document pricing strategies:

- Statement of the area to which the pricing strategy is being applied (e.g., hardware)
- Actual strategy being applied (e.g., reducing product prices in the out years)
- Anticipated costs saved (e.g., $20 reduction per item in years two and three of a three-year contract multiplied by 100 items per year yields a $6,000 contract savings)
- Rationale for taking the risk (e.g., the price of hardware typically declines over time as newer technology is introduced into the marketplace)
- Risk mitigation strategy or how the company intends to make up the money it could potentially lose (e.g., if the contract contains a technology refreshment clause, the company may decide it will offer a new product in its place in the out years)

Receive Notification from the Customer If It Makes a Competitive Range Determination

As discussed earlier, the customer may make a competitive range determination at any point in the procurement cycle. If after discussions the customer does not believe that a company can possibly change its proposal enough to warrant award, the customer may make its first or second competitive range determination and eliminate non-responsive contractors from the competition.

Complete a Profile for How the Contract Will Do Over Its Life and a Business Case

A company typically develops a contract profile to determine when and how profitable a contract will be during performance. This information is used to ensure the company will not lose money on the proposal submitted. During contract performance, the company uses the profile for budgeting purposes and to establish how well an account is managing its costs.

In order to establish the contract profile, the team must determine a likely business case for the program. A *business case* is the team's best estimate at how many products and services will be purchased during the life of the contract. A team makes these assumptions based on actual RFP language, customer meetings, customer buying patterns, assessment of customer's need, and potential budget available. Subcontractors will request this information from the company so that the subcontractor can use the data internally to obtain the necessary approval for quantity discounts and better terms and conditions.

Receive a Call for BAFO from the Customer

Once the customer requests BAFOs from contractors still within the competitive range, it may allow a few days or a few weeks for BAFO submission. The customer may also include any final instructions to the offerors in preparing their proposals. (Notice how much work should be completed *before* receiving the BAFO call.)

Prepare BAFOs

The company makes several final checks to validate its readiness for BAFO submission. First, it ensures the cost model is in the proper format to meet BAFO requirements. Frequently, the customer will ask for additional data to be provided at BAFO, such as GSA price lists or commercial price lists. The company may then be asked to give a discount percentage off those price lists in the price proposal. The company will want to quality check its costs. To do this, the company reviews what products have been proposed in the technical volume against the price quote submitted by the subcontractor and ensures that it is the same cost listed in the cost model. The company also validates its overhead, G&A, FCCOM, and profit rates and ensures they are applied appropriately.

Produce and Deliver the BAFO

Once the team has prepared its BAFO, the team prints it, reproduces it, packs it, and ships it to the customer by the due date. On government contracts, from this point until contract award, the company should not contact the customer. Any conversations between the company and the customer during this period may be questioned and become grounds for protest if a competitor should learn of them. Because protests are not an option for companies bidding on commercial contracts, contact with the customer after BAFO submission is not a problem on commercial contracts.

Prepare Audit Package

As the team finalizes its BAFO for a government program, the team should focus its attention on finalizing its files for the CPSR. Any contract purchase made during the audit period is subject to review. The team must ensure that the company's files are current as soon as the contract is announced.

Information needed for BAFO:

- The final solution so that the BAFO team prices the correct components.

- An idea of the acceptable price to the customer so that the team does not bid a price that is too high for the customer's budget.

- Information on the competition to determine what price the team should bid in order to price the program as competitively as possible.

- Trend analysis data gives the team an idea of the trends within a particular industry. The team can then decide the amount of risk it wants to take to win the program. It can do this by analyzing some widely accepted beliefs about what the future will hold so that it can price its products accordingly.

- Current rates disclosed to DCAA for overhead, G&A, and FCCOM are necessary to bid the program properly so that the company can later pass an audit for government contracts.

- Quotes from vendors that include the final discounts offered by the vendors for their BAFO submission so the company can develop its BAFO submission to the customer.

- Strategies on more efficient ways to conduct business that can help drive down the contract price (e.g., merging several program requirements to obtain discounts through economies of scale).

Conducting Tasks for the Award

Conduct Contract Start-Up Planning

The customer typically does not require a company to conduct account start-up planning. A contractor conducts account start-up planning because it is crucial to the success of the contract. Oftentimes, the customer requires the company to start work immediately after contract award. A contractor, more often than not, claims in its proposal that it has established processes and procedures to manage the program. The customer, therefore, expects the contractor to be able to immediately begin providing the necessary contract deliverables and to begin performing the work as stated in the proposal.

For the contractor to be able to begin working on the contract immediately, up-front planning is critical. This planning must take place before the contract is awarded so that the company can begin work immediately after award notification. The contractor must meet its requirements from the start to establish a solid relationship with the customer. If it does not plan for the contract, chances for initial customer satisfaction success is limited.

Start Up Planning: Main Objectives

The main objectives for the contract start-up planning process include:

- Preparing for deliverables
- Identifying personnel
- Establishing processes
- Understanding data requirements
- Establishing subcontractor relationships
- Establishing marketing channels

Prepare for Deliverables

In the RFP the customer states the deliverables it expects to see during contract performance. There are usually two types of deliverables: written reports and products. Written reports may be required one time only, periodically, or on some predefined schedule. The customer could require a few deliverables or hundreds. When the proposal team developed its management plan, the team considered what data was required for each deliverable, how often that deliverable needed to be produced, how many people were required to produce the deliverable, and how many people it would take to produce and review the final report.

Now the proposal team must determine precisely how these deliverables will be produced. It will need to answer questions such as the following: Will it need to develop a database to store all the data? Who will populate the database? Who has ultimate responsibility for each deliverable? What software package will be used to develop the deliverables? (The customer may require an electronic copy of the document, so it may tell the team which software package to use.) How will the quality control and management review processes work? How will the proposal team orchestrate delivery to the government? Will a draft be produced for the customer to review before it receives the final document? (Again, sometimes the RFP stipulates that this will occur.)

The other type of deliverable on a contract is the product that must be provided. A customer requires product deliveries to be made within 30 days after the contractor receives a delivery order. If, at contract award, the customer hands the contractor several delivery orders, the contractor is obligated to provide the ordered goods and services within 30 days of contract award. In order for the contractor to make these deliveries, the contractor must review delivery orders, create purchase orders for suppliers, manufacture and ship products, and pay invoices. The contractor must establish vendor contact points, ordering procedures, subcontracts, delivery terms, and shipping procedures so that orders can be processed in a timely fashion. In addition, if the products must be manufactured or assembled at the prime contractor's site, extra time must be built into the schedule for these tasks. To maintain control of all these processes, the contractor will have to track the data pertaining to each order. If the contractor fails to meet the customer's required delivery schedule, it could be terminated for contract default.

Identify Personnel

Finding well-trained, efficient personnel presents a major challenge to the new program team. Contract success depends on each person doing his or her job effectively and efficiently. Top-notch people may be scarce in a company, and even if they are accessible, they are typically so good that they cannot be extracted from the project on which they are currently working. However, it would not be prudent to have all the company's stellar performers work on one contract to the detriment of all the others. The program team must prepare alternatives for when it cannot get all the best people to work on the contract. For example, it could look for less-experienced people within the organization or try to hire people from outside the company.

Coordinating with subcontractors to get the specific expertise from its organization when and where the program team needs it is also a challenge the team will need to address. The subcontract should have clearly defined roles and responsibilities so that the subcontractor is prepared to meet the customer's objectives.

Establish Processes

The team needs to develop processes so the team performs tasks consistently in order to obtain consistent results. Processes are also important to reduce the training time needed for people new to the contract. The proposal team developed high-level processes when it developed its management proposal. Now the program team must decide the details of how each process on the contract will work.

The individual processes needed for a contract are numerous and are geared specifically to the requirements. The types of processes needed on most contracts are as follows:

- Contract and program training
- System training
- Product development
- Purchasing
- Invoicing
- Office administration
- Financial reporting
- Management reporting
- Customer reporting
- Vendor correspondence
- Customer correspondence
- Prime-contract administration
- Subcontract administration
- Customer delivery order
- Career development
- Employee appraisals
- Employee-salary administration
- Quality assurance
- Proposal development
- Contract modifications
- Time cards
- Travel-expense tracking
- Written-deliverable production

The company may have already developed some processes so the program team will just need to implement them on the contract. Not all of the processes will apply to a specific contract; for example, a labor-type contract would not require any of the processes for design and engineering.

The contractor or the proposal team should document processes so that they are not perpetually recreated. Processes will get refined over time as people get more sophisticated about the job requirements. As these processes are refined, the contractor may be able to save itself and the customer money through greater efficiency.

Understand Data Requirements

Once the team understands the deliverables it needs to turn into the customer and the processes required to manage those deliverables, it can then assess what data elements are required to support those activities. The program team should breakdown each deliverable into its data elements. Then the team should analyze each data element in terms of how it should be obtained. By starting off with the customer deliverables, the contractor can maintain focus on what the contract actually requires. The team may expand the data requirements after the process-definition phase if the team realizes that additional data is required to manage all the components of the contract.

Associated with the data required are the tools necessary to capture the data. Whether the team uses an internally developed database, spreadsheet, program management tool, or a combination of all three, data must be managed on the contract. Data must be accurate, easily accessible, and as integrated as possible. For example, if the database tracks all the steps in filling a customer order, ideally, the team would like the database to track all the contract financials as well. That way customer order data from the database does not have to be re-keyed into the financial spreadsheets before it can be used to develop a management report.

The team should store as much contract data as possible in one central repository that has the ability to generate programmed and ad hoc requests. This approach minimizes report generation because all reports are generated from the same data, it minimizes user training because users need to be trained on only one system, and it minimizes data correction because data only needs to be corrected in one system.

Establish Subcontractor Relationships

The team must accomplish two different tasks to establish subcontractor relationships: develop subcontracts and determine who in each subcontractor organization is responsible for helping the contractor meet the program objectives.

Throughout the proposal process, the subcontractor has worked on the team based on the contents of a nondisclosure agreement and a team agreement (which will be described in Chapter 9). By the end of the BAFO stage, the prime contractor and subcontractor companies should have reached agreement on price and any of the price-affecting terms and conditions. During this phase, the prime contractor and subcontractor negotiate all the rest of the terms and conditions for the subcontract.

Additionally, the prime contractor must understand how to accomplish program objectives through the subcontractor organization. Ideally, the prime contractor should know who in the subcontractor organization is responsible for:

- Subcontract issues

- Business issues

- Technical issues

- Marketing issues

- Purchasing and delivery issues

Overall Program Direction

By establishing these points of contact for each subcontractor, program team members can go to the right person within each of the organizations to get the program objectives completed.

Establish Marketing Channels

With the government's emphasis on indefinite delivery and indefinite quantity-type contracts, all the contractor actually wins when it is awarded the procurement is the right to sell its products and services. It is up to the program team to market its wares to the customer community if it expects the contract to be profitable. Marketing the contractor's products can be simple—rely primarily on word-of-mouth marketing—or complex—offer incentives to salespeople from subcontractor companies to push the products. Either way, the team's marketing efforts must be evaluated by comparing the money it costs to implement them versus the potential revenue streams they may generate.

Marketing efforts the team can use include:

- Trade show booths
- Trade magazine advertising
- Providing guest speakers at conferences
- Catalogues
- Brochures
- Internet advertising
- Product demonstrations
- Customer visits
- User meetings

Overall Process

To conduct contract start-up planning, the company and the program team conducts the following process:

1. **Ensure corporate support for the planning effort.** Planning efforts take time and money and are not typically reimbursable by the customer. Therefore, the company must decide if the plan is worth doing and the number of resources it is willing to devote to its development. Once the team has secured a corporate commitment to spend the funds necessary to develop the plan, the team is ready to select its planning team members.

2. **Select planning team members.** The program team members for a start-up plan should consist of individuals who will be responsible for bringing the plan to its fruition. Ideally, the team would have a representative from each functional area; however, that approach may be too costly for the company to implement. A more cost-effective approach would be to have three to five individuals who are responsible for key functional areas and who understand the contract as a whole so that they can develop a plan that is workable and makes good business sense. The individuals selected should have the ability to envision all aspects of the contract and should be able to logically think through the processes required to run a government contract.

3. **Develop the components of the plan.** The company can use whatever planning approach it deems necessary to develop a

workable, usable plan. Refer to Chapter 2 for a description of a generic planning methodology that can be adopted to contract start-up planning.

4. **Communicate the plan.** Once the plan is developed, the company must communicate it to the team that will implement it. The contract start-up plan may be shared with internal team members, management, and outside vendors. It may even be shared with the customer after the company is awarded the contract. As new team members are brought on board, the plan serves as a useful overview of the tasks that need to be accomplished for contract start-up success.

5. **Implement the plan.** The people assigned to implement the plan work on the projects defined and stay within the stated budget. If the customer delays the award, the company can work on refining the start-up plan or actually begin the start-up plan. Usually, the planning steps take longer to implement than anticipated. This is a natural outcome, particularly if the people who are working on the plan have never estimated resources or started up a contract. The team cannot predict how smoothly its plan will run. However, planning improves over time, and soon the team will reap the rewards of its labor.

6. **Develop and use feedback mechanisms to update the plan.** Periodically, the team should review the status of the plan. The team does this by developing feedback mechanisms and by assessing its performance against the mechanisms. In the case of assessing a start-up plan, the team can check if objectives are being met, if projects are being completed on time, if the stated number of resources are actually required for the project, and if the project is staying within budget. If the team answers any of these questions negatively, the team needs to reassess that particular area to determine what is causing the problem. Possible reasons include lack of knowledge by the planning team of the true resources required, members who are less-experienced than anticipated, or nonresponsive vendors. Feedback mechanisms allow the planning team to make changes in the plan so that the team can accomplish its intended purpose.

Receive Notice of Contract Award

When the customer makes an award to the procurement winner, the customer usually notifies the winner by calling the contract administrator of the winning company. The customer informs losing companies by phone calls or by sending letters. In rare instances, the customer does not notify the losers individually, and in the case of federal programs, the customer publishes the award in one of the procurement periodicals, such as *Government Computer News, Federal Computer Week,* or *The Washington Post.* A commercial company may just stop all communication with a company and its not until the company calls the customer does it find out that the customer made an award.

The customer may award the contract to multiple offerors. Some customers are using the multiple award contract vehicle much more frequently in its procurements. In fact, in government contracts, FASA legislation has mandated that all advisory and assistance procurements over $10 million dollars be awarded to multiple contractors. In these procurements, the customer stipulates in the original RFP that the award may be made to multiple contractors. In addition, the FAR encourages the customer to use multiple awards or indefinite-quantity contracts. Once the awards are made under these indefinite delivery/indefinite quantity (ID/IQ) task order procurements, each of the winning contractors must compete for work to be done under the contract.

Overall Process

The overall process that the company follows for notification of contract award is as follows:

Wait. Waiting for the contract award is one of the toughest tasks about the procurement. People will ask the team members daily, "Have we heard yet?" or "Do you think we won it?" If a company is not doing well financially, upper management may put increasing pressure on the team by stating how this procurement is a "must win." Rumors among contractors spread quickly, and the team may spend a lot of anxious moments second-guessing itself as to whether the strategy it used was the best one. If the customer runs into problems with the award, the announcement may even get delayed, so the company continues to wonder if it won. The only advice for this situation is for the team members to do whatever they can to keep their own spirits up until the award is announced.

Learn of contract award. The company will eventually learn when the customer makes the contract award. Typically, the customer publishes a schedule detailing when the award will be made. If the company has not been notified of an award by that scheduled date, the company may call the CO to determine when the award decision will be announced. The company will usually receive a letter or a phone call from the CO stating whether or not the contract has been awarded.

Determine if the company has won or lost the contract. The next steps in the process depend on whether the company won or lost the procurement. We will discuss the steps for the winning company first.

Winning Company

Execute Prime Contract between the Customer and the Contractor

The first step for the winning contractor is to execute the prime contract with the customer. Execution occurs after contract discussions have been completed. Discussions may have commenced before BAFO, in which case all that is left to do is for both parties to sign the contract. Discussions may also have been conducted after BAFO submission and after an apparent winner was selected. Again, the only task left to do in this situation is for both the customer and the winning contractor to sign the prime contract. However, the customer may wait to conduct discussions until after announcing the winner. If this is the case, the customer and the contractor complete their discussions, and pending satisfactory resolution of all outstanding issues, sign the contract.

Notify Relevant Parties of the Award

The most fun the contractor may have on a proposal effort is when it announces to the world that the team has won the procurement. The company should notify the following groups, at a minimum: upper management, proposal team members, teaming partners, subcontractors, newspapers, internal publication channels, and internal support groups. The purpose of this notification is to provide as much preparation time as possible to the groups that will support the contract. Each of these teams will need to begin preparations for providing resources to meet the first contract deliverable.

Implement Account Start-Up Plan

Once the award has been announced, the winning contractor team begins implementing the account start-up plan. Each of the steps discussed in the account start-up planning section discussed earlier must be completed in order to meet the initial contractual requirements.

Execute Subcontracts

Companies take different positions as to when to negotiate subcontracts. Most prime companies prefer the subcontract negotiations to occur before they submit BAFO pricing, so they have firm subcontractor pricing and understand the degree of risk to which their companies are being exposed. Subcontractors, on the other hand, prefer to wait until after contract award to negotiate the subcontracts with the prime contractors. Subcontractors believe they have more leverage after the contract has been made because the prime contractors has included the subcontractors' products and services in the proposals and, therefore, must provide the stated products and services. Subcontractors believe they can determine whatever price they want because the business is virtually guaranteed, at least for contract start-up.

Plan Win Party

At last it is time to celebrate. A win party is a way to publicly recognize the people responsible for the contract win. It allows team members to pat themselves on the back and reminisce about the long hours, the challenges, the heroes, and the seeming impossibilities that were overcome. It is a good closure for people. Although a party would make for a good proposal to contract transition, the proposal team members never work together again. Individuals go off to other efforts, and new people are brought in to work on the contract. The win party gives the recipients the feeling that the company really appreciates the effort that goes into winning new business. This appreciation is what builds employee loyalty to the company and gives them a reason to work on the next proposal effort when asked.

Win parties can be either a small affair with just the team members attending a luncheon or a dinner, or it can be a gala event with a theme, entertainment, and door prizes. Inviting spouses or significant others is a way of thanking them for the time that the proposal team members spent away from home. It also helps the spouses or significant others understand what their partners do at work. The size of the win party should be commensurate with the significance of the deal to the company, the amount of time the members worked, and the size of the deal. Dollars spent on the win party should be evaluated against the potential revenue that the contract will afford the company.

Public recognition of the team effort should be the order of the day. Public recognition of individual members is good provided that no one is left out. Gratitude speeches by top corporate people also emphasize what the team has accomplished.

In addition, there should be special, private recognition of outstanding contributors in the form of a special gift or bonus. Additional vacation days can be awarded to make up for all the additional work time required during the proposal effort.

Arrange Kickoff Meeting with Customer

Soon after contract award, the customer will usually schedule a kickoff meeting with the winning contractor. If the customer does not do so, the contractor should take the lead in getting this meeting established. Both parties need to understand how the contract will operate on a day-to-day basis.

The discussion items for the kickoff meeting include:

- Introduce management team members from both parties
- Determine appropriate ways to communicate with each other (e.g., phone, fax, or electronically)
- Review the organizational chart
- Discuss the first deliverables
- Conduct tour of contractor and customer facilities, if needed
- Instruct how to obtain badges for each site, if needed
- Discuss the specifics for how the contract will operate
- Obtain all customer furnished equipment
- Submit any contract deliverables that are due at contract award
- Review work breakdown structure, if required
- Determine access methods for systems that both parties need to use

On government contracts, the contractor may be required to provide a redacted copy of its proposal to the customer to use for FOIA purposes. FOIA allows any individual or business entity to request information from the customer, and for a modest fee, the customer will provide it. There are certain stipulations outlined in the FAR; for example, the information cannot be of a proprietary nature to give one company an unfair advantage over another. This is the reason that the customer allows the winning contractor to take a copy of its proposal and redact, or mark out, those items within the proposal that the contractor believes are of a proprietary nature. If the customer agrees, the redacted copy will used for any FOIA requests.

Ensure Procedures Are Established with All Subcontractors

As part of the contract start-up plan, the prime contractor discovered the points of contact within the subcontractor organization. Now it is time to work with those points of contact to determine how the purchasing and invoicing procedures will be implemented. For example:

- Will a forecasting process be used?
- Will a draft order process be used?
- Who should receive purchase orders?
- How will orders be received?
- Where will products be shipped?
- What is the method of shipment?
- When will products be accepted?
- When may invoicing occur?
- How will payment occur?

These discussions should occur initially with the subcontractor that is providing a large number of the products on the contract or that is providing products required for the first deliverable. Discussions can be held with the remaining subcontractors soon thereafter.

Transition All Proposal Files Over to the Account

After the award has been announced, all proposal files become the contract files. This includes all vendor correspondence, customer correspondence, final RFP, and final proposal. All data for the CPSR file, including solicitation; evaluation criteria; memorandum of negotiations; justification for why one vendor was selected over another, suspended, or debarred from listing; selection of a small or small and disadvantaged business; and price analysis must be retained by the team for the next review.

Losing Company

Notify the People Who Worked on the Program

The worst news that a proposal team can get is to find out that the program it worked so hard on for the last several months, or even years, was awarded to another company. It is a tough time—emotions run high, pride is crushed, and there are a lot of unanswered questions. Some commercial customers will explain why a company lost the program. The government customer gives formal debriefs to the losing contractor. It is important that the company take the information gained through this process and apply it to the lessons-learned exercise so that the company's next program can be a winner.

Schedule Debrief

In a government program, the company may request and be granted a debrief to more fully understand the source selection process. The information may assist the company in upcoming procurements.

Close Out Proposal Effort

As soon as the customer announces the award, the company should close out its proposal effort. Steps in that process include:

- Closing out cost centers
- Returning equipment to subcontractors
- Filing a copy of the proposal
- Finding other projects for the proposal team members
- Conducting a lessons-learned exercise
- Deciding what portions of the proposal might be re-used on other proposal efforts

Prime Contractor Considerations

Commitments about Subcontractors' Products or Services

There is a potential risk area for the prime contractor if it makes promises to the customer about the subcontractor's product without verifying the information with the subcontractor. On the surface, this prospect seems odd: Why would a prime contractor commit on behalf of its subcontractor? However, this often happens when the prime contractor prepares for BAFO or negotiations and tries to do everything in its power to secure the contract. Time frames are tight, contract details are complex, and the subcontractor isn't always available when the prime contractor needs it, so the prime contractor gets sloppy in good subcontract management techniques.

When this scenario occurs, the prime contractor risks performing the agreed upon task for the customer. This could be a dire situation if the contractor does not have the capability to perform the task. In such cases, it needs the subcontractor. The subcontractor may comply with the new requirements at no extra cost; it may comply with the new requirements but charge the prime contractor a higher price, or it may be unable to comply with the new requirements. If the subcontractor cannot comply, the prime contractor must either renegotiate with the customer (which is an unlikely scenario) or try to secure the compliant products or services from another subcontractor.

Level of Subcontractor Involvement

Once again the prime contractor needs to decide how involved it wants its subcontractor to be. The subcontractor knows its product or service best and, therefore, it can demonstrate, negotiate, or market it better than anyone. However, during proposal-submission activities the prime contractor and the subcontractor spend a great deal of time developing pricing strategies and negotiating, which involves revealing highly sensitive data. The prime contractor is in a vulnerable position because the subcontractor could be a competitor tomorrow, so the prime contractor may want to limit the subcontractor's involvement.

Short Time Frame for Negotiations

There is typically a brief period of time for negotiations, usually two weeks from the time a call to BAFO is made until BAFO is due. For a prime contractor that is working with many subcontractors, it must develop its strategies early and negotiate with each subcontractor quickly to ensure the BAFO is completed on time. A strategy that most companies use is to negotiate with the highest dollar value subcontractors first because price reductions here can greatly enhance the companies' competitive position. It is also a good idea for the prime contractor to use an effective cost reducing strategy as much as possible regardless of which subcontractor initiated it. For example, if a subcontractor offered documentation on CD/ROM to minimize documentation costs, the prime contractor might try to negotiate CD/ROM documentation with its other subcontractors.

Negotiation Timing

The best time to conduct negotiations differs for the prime contractor and the subcontractor. The best time for the prime contractor is before contract award so it knows its risk. When the prime contractor submits its BAFO, it may decide to trim its overall price to win the contract. In order to do this, the prime contractor must know exactly how much a subcontractor is willing to lower its prices so that the prime contractor knows exactly how low a price it can bid and how much support it will get from the subcontractor. On the other hand, the best time for a subcontractor to negotiate, particularly one that is working on multiple prime contractor teams, is after contract award so that it only has to negotiate with the winning contractor. In addition, the subcontractor is in a better position after the prime contractor submits the BAFO because the prime contractor is basically committed to using the subcontractor on the program. As such, the subcontractor's negotiation power is stronger after award.

The solution that most prime contractors and subcontractors reach is to negotiate prices and price affecting terms and conditions before BAFO submission and negotiate any other terms and conditions after award without changing prices.

BAFO Requirements

The prime contractor has to ensure that it complies with the customer's requirements in the BAFO. Some customers believe that the contractor basically has one shot at getting the solution right: at initial submission. When the customer asks for BAFOs, the customer may only allow a prime contractor to change prices and not any component of the technical or management solution. If the customer adopts this approach to the BAFOs, the prime contractor must inform its subcontractor that its initial submission cannot be changed, so the subcontractor should be prepared to work with its solution for the duration of the contract.

Prime Contractor: Single Point Contact

Before initial proposal submission, the company can initiate conversations with the customer. Once the initial proposal is submitted and during the after-submission activities, the prime contractor becomes the single point of contact with the customer for questions, live test demonstrations, discussions/ negotiations, pre-award visits, amendments, and BAFO call. The prime contractor decides how much information it should share with the subcontractor. Any questions that the subcontractor has must go through the prime contractor. Basically, the prime contractor is the conduit of information because it must funnel information from the government customer or commercial customer to the subcontractor and from the subcontractor back to the customer. If the communication process breaks down, the program is in jeopardy.

Prime Contractor: Single Point of Accountability

The prime contractor is responsible for doing whatever it takes to win the program. Its company and its subcontractor are depending on it to do so. As the single point of accountability, the prime contractor must ensure that the decisions that it makes are for the good of the whole team. Similarly, it frequently must choose between its corporate interests and the goals of the procurement team. It also must ensure that any changes made to the program are communicated among the team members. Typically, any change has a "domino effect" within a program: one change necessitates several other changes throughout the process. The prime contractor must understand the program enough to know who is affected by any changes and inform them so that they can take appropriate action.

Subcontractor Considerations

The following are some subcontractor considerations:

- Statement of work should clearly reflect the work of the subcontractor
- Ensure that all the products and services you are selling appear in the statement of work
- Determine if the prime contractor has negotiated items out of the subcontract to lower the contract price
- Determine if changes to contract necessitate that you end the contract
- Determine if you can negotiate for additional products and services after contract award (Make sure prime contractor is amenable to that approach.)
- Prices
- Prime contractor is under a lot of pressure to lower contract price; Subcontractor must decide how competitively it can price its product
- Future sales
- Future relationships
- Ability to perform at lower prices
- Do not assume prices can be modified after contract award

Government Considerations

Pre-Award Audits

On a government program, the government may conduct pre-award audits of the prime contractor and subcontractor. These audits can include the facilities, management structure, rate structure, and financial stability of the companies. If the government conducts a pre-award audit, it will notify the contractor that an audit will take place by calling the company or sending a letter. The government will tell the contractor what information is required before the audit. The contractor collects that information and submits it to the government auditor, who will review it and then inform the contractor of the date, time, and data required for the on-site audit. The contractor gathers this additional data and hosts the auditor. The auditor reviews and evaluates the data, prepares a preliminary report, and returns the data to the contractor. Several weeks later, the contractor will receive the audit report, highlighting any findings, suggested improvements, and course of action.

Types of information that may be required for an audit are as follows:

Company overview

- Company history
- Services or product lines
- Description of whether the company is a manufacturer or a regular dealer
- Description of whether the company is a proprietorship, partnership, or corporation
- Sales volume and government business percentage
- Organizational chart
- Description of the facilities

Scope of solicitation

- Product or service in solicitation
- Type of contract
- Value of contract
- Brief description of how solicitation will be executed

Technical

- Resumes of key personnel
- Number of personnel at the facility
- Employees listed by location and their skills and expertise
- Organizational chart

Facilities

- Equipment at location and equipment used for this solicitation
- Location dimensions
- Current equipment load capacity and projected load
- Condition and age of the equipment
- Capital equipment, facilities, special tooling, and test equipment required
- Plant and equipment layout
- General safety structure and control

Labor/Personnel

- Manpower on hand or required for this solicitation listed by occupation
- Data on any unions
- Production control
- Milestone chart and plan of how the contractor will control the program
- Past contract references

Purchasing and materials

- Purchasing system description
- Deliverables
- Long-lead items
- Materials processing description
- Dollar-level thresholds
- Vendor control

Subcontractors

- Bids, deliveries, and teaming agreements

- Subcontractor deliverables
- Subcontractor's function description

Performance record data

- Provide similar or same closed contract data
- Provide open contract data
- Provide pending proposal contract data
- Contract data

Wage Determinations

The government protects certain job classifications under the Service Contract Act and requires contractors to pay its employees the rates stated in the wage determinations. Wage determinations are established by industry and only certain labor categories are covered by the Act. Any contractor with employees performing work that has an established wage determination and is covered by the Service Contract Act must pay those employees the established wages. If the prime contractor must meet the wage-determination requirement, it will typically flow down the requirement to the subcontractor. If a contractor or subcontractor does not pay the employee the minimum rate established in the wage determination, the company faces significant penalties.

Subcontracting Plan

Because the SBA has requirements for each governmental agency on how much of its contracted business must go to small businesses (SBs) or small, disadvantaged businesses (SDBs), an agency will typically flow down these requirements to prime contractors competing for work with the agency. The prime contractor uses a subcontracting plan to inform the government agency how dollars available through the program will be disbursed to each of the participating subcontractors. This plan identifies which subcontractors are part of the prime contractor's solution; whether they are large, SBs or SDBs; and how much of the contract will be awarded to them. The governmental agency reviews the plan and the government either accepts it or rejects it. The agency also uses the subcontracting plan to monitor the prime contractor's promises of business to SBs and SDBs. The governmental agency could limit the award-fee portion of the contract if the prime contractor fails to meet the goals set forth in the subcontracting plan. If the prime contractor does not satisfy the government's RFP requirements for percentage of SBs or SDBs, the government will require documentation in the subcontracting plan of the methods employed by the prime contractor to secure SBs and SDBs for the program team.

Past Performance Review

Subcontractor's past performance is reviewed as part of the prime contractor's proposal. Therefore, it is important that both the prime contractor and the subcontractor realize that their performance on all current contracts affect their future business—both separately and jointly.

Government Evaluation Techniques

Conduct Best-Value Analysis and Assign Risk Dollars

In a best value procurement, the customer awards the contract to the company that submits the proposal that represents the best overall value to the customer in terms of technical, management, and price considerations. In addition, the customer evaluates any exceptions the company has taken to the contractual terms and conditions. This is significantly different from when the customer evaluates the proposals based on price only, in which case it ensures each company meets the minimum mandatory requirements and then makes the award to the lowest bidder. During a best-value procurement, the evaluation team reviews the technical, management, and contracts volumes of each company's proposal and identifies the strengths and weaknesses of each. Then the customer assigns risk dollars to each company's proposal to compensate itself for any inherent weaknesses in each proposal. For example, if offeror A has a 2,000-hour mean time between failure (MTBF) and offeror B has a 4,000-hour MTBF, the customer would have to replace offeror A's product two times as often as it would have to replace offeror B's product. Therefore, the customer would add the cost of these additional products into the price proposed by offeror A. After all these adjustments are made to each offeror's proposal, the customer awards the contract to the offeror with the lowest revised proposal price.

Prepare Backup for Award Decision and Receive Approval for Award Decision

The customer typically prepares all the documentation to support its award decision before announcing the procurement winner. This is done to prepare for the customer's upper-management's internal review of the final award decision to can ensure that the winner was selected without bias. In addition, the customer, under the FASA regulations, must conduct a debrief with any offeror that requests one. The backup materials are used during debriefs to lend credence to the customer's decision. The customer also uses backup material to defend its award decision should a losing company protest the award.

Because FASA states that an offeror must request a debrief within three days of the award and the customer should grant the debrief within five days of the request, the customer must prepare its debriefing materials before announcing the award. Items typically included in a debrief include:

- Description of the offeror's deficiencies
- Overall evaluated cost and technical ratings of all offerors
- Ranking of all offerors
- Answers to a company's questions
- Rationale for the award

Debriefs

Schedule a Debrief

The customer allows all losing companies to schedule a debrief. The company should request a debrief as soon as possible upon hearing of the contract award. According to FASA legislation, the company must request a debrief, in writing, within three days of the contract award. The customer must schedule the debrief within five days after receiving the request, if possible.

Determine Debrief Attendees

The company usually decides how many people it wishes to send to the debrief. The company may want to send only a few people to contain costs. Typically, a company will send the program manager, salesperson, technical manager, contracts person, and one other person. The company wants to send people who can listen to what the customer is saying with a genuine attitude of trying to understand the customer's basis for award. The information gained will be used as the basis for whether or not the company will choose to lodge a protest. One or two members of the debrief team should have not been involved directly in the procurement so that they can listen to what is said as objectively as possible.

Determine Questions the Team Would Like Answered

If the company conducted an extensive competitive analysis before contract award, the team may have some specific questions about the winning team's solution. For example, the team may be aware that a component of the winner's solution does not meet the requirements. The team will want to raise such concerns during the debrief. The team should also question any inconsistencies during the debrief.

Attend Debrief

Debriefs are given so that the company can learn how its proposal compared against the customer's source selection plan. Typically, the customer will provide the company with its proposal's high-level scores and list its strengths and weaknesses. The customer will also provide the rationale for its award decision. Company representatives are free to ask questions, the answers to which the debrief team may or may not have at its disposal.

It is important to maintain a professional atmosphere during the debrief. Even though the company may be genuinely upset at the result of the procurement, the customer evaluators were just doing their job the best way they knew how. In today's procurement, protest-ridden environment, customer officials spend a lot of time checking and rechecking their work so as to avoid a protest. If there is a valid reason for protest; for example, if the customer evaluation criteria said that the most emphasis will be given to price and the company's proposal represented the lowest price, the company may have a valid reason for protesting. However, seldom are protest issues so obvious.

Another reason to keep the meeting professional is that these people are still your customers. They will send out other procurements, and the professional stance the company takes when it loses a procurement could set it in a better light for a future procurement.

Debrief Losing Contractors

The customer conducts debriefs with all losing offerors that request a debrief. There are several purposes to the debrief, such as that the customer needs to:

- Explain its award decision rationale to the company.

- Inform the company that its proposal was evaluated fairly and according to the source selection plan.
- Discuss the weaknesses of the company's proposal.
- Mitigate, as much as possible, the company's need to protest.

The FAR has been updated as a result of FASA and clearly details the information that the customer must provide to the company during a debrief.

Protests

Decide Whether or Not to Protest

Protests, unfortunately, are a reflexive response for some companies after they hear they lost a procurement. On the down side, a protest is an expensive proposition for a company, protests annoy the government agency, they can affect future procurements with the same agency, and they can take a lot of time to resolve. On the positive side, the company could get a decision in its favor and receive the benefits of a contract award.

The company can protest to the General Accounting Office (GAO) or other channels if it believes that it was treated unfairly by the procuring agency. The GAO tends to be the most popular option available for companies and will be discussed in this section. FASA has made some changes in the protest area. For example, if a company decides to protest, it must send a letter to the GAO within 14 calendar days from the date the company discovered or should have discovered the basis for protest.

Additionally, if the protester is seeking a stay on the work currently being done by the winning contractor, the company must submit a request to the GAO by the later of either ten calendar days after award or five calendar days after the debriefing date offered by the customer. A stay is useful for the protester because it encourages the customer to quickly assess the merits of the protest so that work can commence on the program. It also precludes the winning contractor from becoming so entrenched in the customer's environment that it no longer makes business sense for the GAO to even think about reissuing the award. The GAO grants an automatic stay upon request.

Another change is in the area of protester cost recovery. The customer used to pay the winning protester's actual and reasonable costs. These costs included attorney fees and consulting fees. The FASA now allows the customer to cap the dollar amount that a protester can charge the customer for attorney fees to $150/hour and for consulting fees at about the equivalent of "the highest rate of compensation for expert witnesses paid by the federal customer." (Sections 1403 and 1405) This regulation places more financial burden on the contractor for protesting because attorneys and consultants specializing in federal customer protests typically charge much more than these amounts. The limits on the attorney rate is relaxed for small businesses.

The company must have an attorney when filing a protest because of the protective order policy. In the normal course of conducting a solicitation, a company provides detailed proprietary information that the customer reviews when making its award determination. The protester must have this information to determine if it should lodge a protest, but releasing that information to a protester could be detrimental to the company whose information is being disclosed. The customer gets around this problem by issuing a protective order on proprietary information. A protective order gives attorneys (either working inside the company or outside the company) the right to view the material and report back to the protesting company whether they believe the protest has any merit. The attorneys are forbidden from discussing any of the specific data observed so as to not give the protesting company information that it could use on a future procurement. However, the protester can direct its attorneys to ask to see certain types of information during the discovery phase of the protest.

Although the GAO tends to be the most likely place for a company to begin the protest process, other protest vehicles are available at other points of the procurement cycle:

- The contracting officer and the agency are available for all protests
- U.S. district courts are available for post-award protests
- U.S. Court of Federal Claims is available for pre-award protests

The General Services Board of Contract Appeals (GSCBCA) used to hear protest claims; however, the FARA removed the GSBCA as a protest vehicle. Each of the options listed above differs in terms of when the company may lodge a protest, what evidence is available to the protester during the discovery phase, and the standard to which the protester must prove it has been wronged.

Depending on the basis of the protest, the number of firms protesting, and the customer's requirements, potential outcomes of protests include:

- The protest is dismissed and the award decision stands
- A settlement is made to the losing company
- A deal is struck between the winning contractor, the protesting contractor, and the customer for the work to be shared
- A requirement is set for all of the companies to redo the BAFO, and the customer awards the program to the company that gets the highest score based on the source selection plan
- The procurement is canceled
- The procurement is reissued with a new set of requirements, and all companies interested must resubmit new proposals

Stay Abreast of Potential Protests

Protests can occur at any time during the procurement process, but they typically occur within ten days after the customer awards the contract. This is because a protest may be lodged ten days after a company determines there has been some perceived wrongdoing. Typically, when a losing company hears of the award to another company, the losing company may feel that just because it didn't win, a wrongdoing must have occurred. For many losing companies, lodging a protest is a knee-jerk reaction.

The winning contractor should be concerned about protests. First, protests put the original award in jeopardy. Second, they divert customer resources away from the new program objectives and focus them on resolving the protest. Third, a stop work may be issued, which basically stops all contract work until resolution. This means that the winning contractor may not spend any additional resources on the customer contract because it will not be reimbursed for them. This puts the winning contractor in a precarious position: It would like to have the additional time to prepare its team for contract start-up, but none of the work done is reimbursable. Also, the winning contractor fears that the resources it has already procured to support the new program will be lost to other, more stable projects within the company.

Another item to note is that protests may be resolved quickly, particularly if they are deemed to have no merit, or if they may take a long time to resolve. Additional companies may join the protest effort if they feel it has merit.

The FASA legislation, by requiring the customer to provide debriefs to losing companies and by strengthening the penalties associated with erroneous protests, is attempting to lessen the number of protests lodged.

Customer Review and Evaluation

The customer's review and evaluation of the price proposal begins early in the procurement cycle and continues until an award decision is made. The steps of the customer's evaluation include:

Customer conducts market research.   As a result of FARA legislation, the customer is required to review products available in the commercial marketplace to determine whether or not they meet customer requirements. This is done to secure a competitive price on commercially available products rather than pay a price premium for products that meet stringent customer requirements.

Customer conducts should-cost analysis before receipt of proposals.   During the time of RFP development, the customer conducts a should-cost analysis to determine what the program should cost the customer to perform. This is done in conjunction with a company's make or buy analysis (i.e., when the company decides whether internal resources or external subcontracted resources should be used to complete the program). To conduct a should-cost analysis, the customer determines all the components of the solution and conducts phone solicitations and market research to determine a realistic cost estimate for each solution component.

Sample price exhibits may be requested.   To ensure that the company will provide the data required for the customer evaluation, the customer may require the company to submit sample price exhibits. In sample price exhibits, the company is expected to print out all pricing reports using actual product names, descriptions, features, and bogus prices. The customer uses these sample price exhibits for two purposes:

- To validate that the company correctly interpreted the price proposal instructions, and

- To provide the customer's internal technical evaluation team with a list of solution components that do not have prices attached to them. The customer does not want the technical team influenced by the companies' prices.

Customer conducts cost analysis/price analysis.   After the customer receives each company's price proposal, it conducts a cost and price analysis. For a cost analysis the customer analyzes component costs to determine reasonableness at the component level. For a price analysis, the customer reviews the total price for the company to determine reasonableness. The customer will discuss significant discrepancies between the cost and price analyses and the companies' price proposals with the company.

Customer may issue questions on price proposal.   Once the customer reviews a company's price proposal, the customer may issue clarification and deficiency reports to communicate any problem areas to the company.

Price may be the only item that can change at BAFO.   The company should be aware that the customer may stipulate that price may be the only item that can change at BAFO. This means that product changes, new approaches, or component upgrades may go unevaluated if they are submitted with the company's BAFO submission. If this clause does not exist in the RFP, the company may issue proposal updates to reflect new information during the solicitation process. The customer will evaluate the changes and adjust its evaluation score accordingly. If the clause exists, the customer will only evaluate changes and adjust evaluation scores up until it requests contractors to submit best and final offers.

Risk determination assessment and associated dollars.   As the customer evaluates the company's proposal, the customer will determine if any components of the offered solution represent a significant risk to the customer. In a best-value procurement, the customer is entitled to add dollars the final company's bid price to compensate itself for the risk it could assume by accepting the company's risky solution.

Justification.   The customer must be prepared to justify its award decision in the event of a losing company protests. In addition, FASA requires the customer to provide specific details about why a company did not win the procurement, which is used during the debrief process.

PART III

PERFORMING THE CONTRACT

6 Contract Award and Start-Up

Contract start-up includes pre-contract award activities and contract initiation. This phase lasts several months before contract award until several months after contract award. During contract start-up a company typically develops a start-up plan, which outlines the details of how the company will start the contract work. Frequently, a customer will require deliverables within the first 30 to 60 days after contract award. A company that prepares and establishes operating procedures with the contract core team, internal support team, and subcontractor teams will be well-prepared for contract start-up after contract award and will begin the customer-contractor partnership on a positive note.

Contract Start-Up Characteristics

Contract start-up is a fast-paced, rapidly evolving, and dynamic time. It requires a great deal of communication and teamwork. The team working on the contract start-up should consider the following:

- The prime contract is still being negotiated.
- If it is a government contract, a protest may need to be resolved.
- Plans have not been finalized so there are still plenty of unknowns.
- A customer relationship has not been established.
- Typically, knowledgeable personnel are not available to work on the contract. The team spends a great deal of time trying to locate people to work on the contract.
- Service level agreements have not been established with internal support teams.
- Subcontracts are still being negotiated.
- Subcontractors may not identified their personnel.
- Many people need training, yet the team must balance completing important work with taking time for training and the cost of training.
- Communication channels within the organization are not established so problems can take longer to resolve.

- There is a lack of adequate operations procedures.
- Financial controls are being established.
- Customer sales probably are not coming in as fast as the company would like.
- Marketing channels within the organization need to be established.
- Automated tools to easily capture the information are not established.
- A process for developing deliverables has not been established.
- There may be a lack of facilities, technology, and equipment.
- The team may need to prepare for audits if it is a government contract.
- There are minimal program and contract changes.
- It is typically a risky time on the contract, because if the team is not careful, it could overrun its budget or establish standards that are too high (expensive) for customer satisfaction.

Contract Start-Up Process

Implement the Start-Up Plan

Nothing impresses a customer more than a team that can start working on the contract soon after contract award. A team that can get delivery orders and quickly fill them establishes itself in a positive light right from the start. In order for a team to do that, however, it must have worked on a start-up plan before contract award and decided how the contract would operate. Although this planning effort is beneficial, it is conducted at the company's risk because it could lose the award and have wasted valuable time and money establishing a start-up plan; however, if the company wins the contract, the effort proves invaluable for establishing good customer rapport early on in the contract. This positive feeling that the customer acquires for the contractor usually translates into add-on business opportunities and new customers.

When the company learns that it won the award, it begins implementing the plan. Careful coordination between the prime contractor and its subcontractor must occur for a successful start-up.

Finalize Prime Contract

The *prime contract* is the contract that exists between the prime contractor and the customer. It is negotiated just before or after contract award. The prime contracts represents the understanding between the customer and the contractor of how the program will operate and the tasks that must be completed for the program's success.

Develop Prime Contract

In the negotiated procurement process, the awarded contract results from a multiple-step process and incorporates the following information:

RFP + Winning Contractor Proposal + Negotiation Results = Contract

The RFP includes the original RFP and all its amendments issued by the customer throughout the solicitation process. The company's proposal includes the original proposal plus all its updates. The contract includes all items negotiated between the parties before award.

The RFP issued contains the following:

- Lists the supplies or services the customer requires
- Describes the specific technical requirements the contractor's solution must meet
- States the packaging and marking requirements for product delivery
- Describes how and where the contractor's goods and services will be inspected and accepted
- Identifies how the contractor's deliveries and performance must be accomplished
- Provides data on how the contract will be administered
- Lists any applicable special contract provisions
- Lists the FAR and other applicable regulatory clauses (on a government contract)
- Provides attachments that are useful in bid preparation and contract administration (e.g., technical drawings, glossaries, and deliverable requirements)
- States the representations and certifications that the contractor must make

The parts of the contractor proposal that are often incorporated into the final contract, if they are required by the RFP, include the following:

- Description of how the contractor will meet the technical program objectives
- Description of how the contractor will manage the program
- The specific goods and services provided by the contractor and the price for each item
- Description of contract deliverables
- Description of any other section deemed appropriate by the customer

Items that are included in solicitation amendments and proposal updates include issues raised during:

- Contractor questions and customer responses
- Customer question phase
- Live test demonstration
- Discussions
- BAFO

In addition, the summary negotiation memorandum is included from the negotiation process. This document is prepared by either the customer's or the contractor's personnel involved in the negotiation discussions and its contents are mutually agreed upon.

Negotiate the Prime Contract with the Customer

The company's negotiations on the prime contract with the customer can occur just before contract award, at contract award, or even after contract award. It is best for both parties to complete negotiations as soon as possible and to ensure that all open issues get resolved before the contract is signed.

Prime contract negotiations may result in changes to the subcontracts. If so, the company must clear such changes with the subcontractors before the company can agree to them.

Provide Copies of the Contract to Relevant Parties

The prime contractor provides copies of the contract to the people on the team who must have them. For example, managers and internal support team members typically require copies. The contract is referred to throughout the life of the contract as a guidebook for how things are to be done on the contract. Any substantial deviations from the contract must be cleared with the contracting officer or customer before implementation. A prime contractor may share part or all of the prime contract with its subcontractor.

Capture the Contract Baseline in an Automated System

The company should capture the contract baseline, which are the products, services, prices, and quantities that it and its subcontractor offer, in an automated system. This will allow everyone on the contract to know what products and services were proposed and what the customer can order. The baseline may be modified throughout the life of the contract. (For more information on contract baselines, see Chapter 9.)

Establish Customer Relationship

There are several steps to building a good customer relationship during contract start-up.

Conduct a Contract Kickoff Meeting

After the contract is awarded, the customer and prime contractor conduct a contract kickoff meeting. A contract kickoff meeting is an opportunity for the key people from the customer's and the contractor's organizations to meet each other and discuss how the contract will operate on a day-to-day basis. The meeting may consist of site tours of both the customer's and the contractor's locations, a review of the initial deliverables, and a discussion about the time frames for performance. The meeting is usually held within the first few days of the contract. The prime contractor may decide to invite key subcontractors to participate in the contract kickoff meeting.

Establish Points of Contact within Both Organizations

One of the first tasks in establishing a good customer relationship is to establish relationships between people performing similar functions on the contract. For example, the customer's contracts person should work with the contractor's contracts person on most contractual issues. The customer's program manager should work with the company's program manager on most technical and service issues. A similar relationship should exist between the business and technical teams of both organizations. These relationships help to resolve issues in each of the functional areas by the people who are most qualified to solve the problem. Understanding who the proper decision maker is for any type of problem is key to establishing a good customer relationship. Keep in mind that on government contracts, if any of these discussions result in a change to the contract requirements, the contracting officer must approve the change because he or she is the only person who can commit the government.

Understand What the Customer Is Being Evaluated On and Help the Customer Succeed

A key component in the customer-contractor partnership is to make both teams successful. A contractor that does everything to make its customer look good cannot help but look good itself. A positive customer perception leads to add-on business and new customers, both of which help the contractor meet its goals for revenue and contract growth. The customer is evaluated on certain components of its job. It is useful for the contractor to understand what the components are, how success is obtained, and then work with their customer to attain those goals.

Select People to Work on Contract

The success of any contract depends on the quality of its people. If the people are committed to a successful contract, they will do everything in their power to make it a successful contract. Managers and team leaders need to select motivated employees with the talents and skills necessary for the contract. Then the team needs to motivate and challenge the people so that they will continue to stay that way.

The people who work on the contract can come from three different sources:

- Contract core team members who work full time for the prime contractor on this particular customer program
- Internal support team members who work part time for the prime contractor on this particular customer program
- Subcontractors who work for outside companies and who were brought on to support the prime contractor

Contract Clauses Affecting Personnel

Key Personnel Clause

The key personnel clause frequently appears in RFPs. The clause states that certain positions on the contract are to be designated as *key* and that designation requires the people in those positions to meet certain additional criteria. The clause is designed to give the customer some additional control over the people selected to work on the contract and to ensure the contractor provides the caliber of people on the contract that was stated in the proposal. When the clause exists, either the customer may designate which positions are key or it may let the contractor decide which positions are key. Typically, the positions that the customer wants to designate as key are management and specialized technical positions. The clause may have different components; for example, the customer may require that it be given resumes for key people so that the customer can review the resumes before the key people begin work on the contract. The key personnel clause may also require the contractor to keep key personnel on the contract for some period of time, for example, 180 days. This means that unless the person is seriously injured or leaves the company, the company must use the person on the contract in his or her key position. The customer may even request that the person sign a letter of intent as part of the original proposal.

The prime contractor must understand the implications of this clause when bidding on the initial proposal. The key personnel clause prevents a company from bidding the same stellar performers on several contracts containing the clause, because if the company wins more than one contract, those people could not meet the provisions of the clause. For example, the key personnel promised could not work on two contracts if there was any overlap in the 180-day window for performance (assuming they were bid on both contracts full time). If the company does not provide the people it promised, the company will lose the contract based on default.

Key positions are *contract-wide,* meaning that either prime contractor or subcontractor personnel may fill the positions. The prime contractor must ensure that all parties understand the implications of the key personnel clause when bidding on the contract so as to prevent any problems with contract performance. The prime contractor should flow down this clause to subcontractors if they are providing labor on the contract.

Resume Review Requirement Clause

Sometimes, even without a key personnel clause, the customer will require that it review the resume of any person the company wishes to have work on the contract. If the contract has a resume review requirement clause, the company must build in enough time in the delivery schedule so that it can select a person and provide his or her resume to the customer for review before performance begins. The company has to ensure that its subcontractor team members realize this necessity.

Locating and Selecting Appropriate Personnel

Identify Personnel

The first task in locating people to work on the contract is to determine what functions are required on the contract and for each one develop accurate job descriptions that reflect the experience, skill levels, education requirements, and abilities required of a person to be successful. Job descriptions should be written and/or reviewed by the manager of the functional area. If the customer has provided job descriptions as part of the contract, the company should use them to secure the necessary personnel. Otherwise, many companies have developed generic position descriptions that can be used as a basis for determining the types of skills that should be required.

Internal applicants   The ideal candidate for a position on a contract is one who is qualified to do the work, understands the customer issues, can get along well with the other team members, and is willing to put in the long hours necessary for a successful contract start-up. It is even better if the person will work on the contract in the same capacity that he or she did during the proposal-development phase. Unfortunately, people do not always come in ideal packages. Less-experienced people within the organization are easier to secure to work on the project because their talents are not yet in high demand. There is an additional benefit: These people are already prime contractor or subcontractor employees. They have an established network of contacts and resources that will help them on the new project. Junior employees will require initial training, just like anyone new to the procurement, on the program, customer, and solution. In addition, if they are at the apprentice level, the junior employees will need additional training on how to do their job.

The manager can use a variety of approaches for locating internal candidates. He or she can post the job descriptions on bulletin boards, rely on word of mouth, use an automated job posting system, or depend on the internal recruiting department to find appropriate applicants.

External applicants   Another option is to hire people from outside the prime contractor's or the subcontractor's organizations. This approach requires a much more detailed strategy. Conducting job fairs, reviewing the personnel department's resume file, placing advertisements in newspapers and industry journals, or relying on employee referrals are all approaches to locating qualified applicants. The team needs to advertise and interview early on so it can find a good match for the program. The team is not likely to hire anyone, however, until after contract award. The problem with this is that the person being considered may not want to wait until contract award for a job and may instead accept another company's offer or, at a minimum, the team will have to wait until the new employee gives notice to his or her employer.

Although the team may end up with a more qualified candidate when it recruits an external employee, this approach may leave the team without the critical resource that it needs during the first several weeks of the program. Because a team is typically more selective when hiring people from outside of the organization, the candidates selected probably won't need to be taught how to do their job, however, they will require initial training on the program, customer, solution, and the company. Another drawback to external employees is that they do not have the network of resources within the company to rely on as perhaps an internal person would.

Because they are less experienced than their colleagues or new to the organization, junior people or people from outside the organization may welcome the chance to shine on a brand new effort. Contract start-up is an exciting, dynamic type of project. The team basically creates something that was not there before. The company wants people on the team who are willing to seize the challenge and do everything possible to make it a success.

Task-Order Staffing

Some contracts, in whole or in part, have a task-order component. When the customer does not know all the projects that require contractor support at the time of RFP release, it will add a task-order component to the contract. Task orders allow the customer to decide during contract performance when and what the contractor needs to support the contract. Task-order contracts allow the customer to get the right resources when it needs them without the risk of having to pay for them as full-time employees.

In the RFP for a task-order contract, the customer will usually provide sample tasks of the type of work the contractor will need to provide. The RFP also stipulates the contractor's bid rates that are commensurate to the job descriptions listed in the RFP. In bidding on a task order during contract performance, the contractor reviews the task-order requirements and determines the types of people necessary to do the work. Then, using the preestablished bid rates from the original proposal, the contractor puts together a proposal including a schedule and the costs necessary to do the work.

Management Issues Surrounding Task-Order Contracts

Although task orders are an ideal way for the customer to get the exact contractor resources just in time for the work needing to be done, task-order contracts require adept management skills on the contractor side. Some of the management issues the contractor will have to handle are as follows: First, the contractor must find personnel resources with the right skills to work on the contract. Task orders can vary in length from several weeks to several years, are sometimes extended, and can require the support just about anywhere. As such, the contractor must also locate people who are willing to work in a temporary duty (TDY) status for an undetermined amount of time wherever the customer requires the work to be done. This lack of job security is not exactly what some people are looking for when they are in search of a job. Hopefully, the challenges of the job, the salary, and the opportunity to travel and work on other task orders will motivate some skilled people necessary for task-order business.

The second issue is what to do with people when the task order is complete. Ideally, the prime contractor would like to "borrow" the necessary people from other organizations to work on task orders because borrowed resources can return to their regular jobs after the task order is complete. However, although this approach is great for the task-order contract, the providing contract is down by those resources until the people return. This means that the contractor may not be able to meet its customer requirements and/or will experience a revenue shortfall because it cannot bill for those people while they are not on the contract. Borrowing employees may work if the providing contract is experiencing a slow period or if its people require certain hands-on skills that can be provided through the task-order experience.

Frequently, a contractor will subcontract out task-order work and retain the management and oversight function. This approach allows the contractor to pay for the personnel resources only when they are required and not to be burdened with the expense when the people are not needed. Another approach that contractors use is to develop a task-order personnel pool so that if one task-order contract is not using the resources, perhaps another contract can use the resources. This approach minimizes the amount of downtime for the people and shares the burden of expense across multiple contracts.

The bottom line is that task-order contracts must be carefully entered into and managed if they are to be successful. Prime contractors must know the level of support that can be provided by each subcontractor so that it can determine if it has the staff necessary to commit to a task-order contract.

Resume Database

When the customer issues a task order, the contractor has very little time, usually 30 days or less, to locate, interview, and provide the necessary people to perform the work. If the contractor is using subcontractors, the contractor must decide which subcontractor has the required expertise and then work with it to determine appropriate people and availability. For these reasons, many contractors have adopted the resume database approach as a tool to fill positions on task orders.

In a resume database approach, the contractor collects resumes of people who have skills that are appropriate for contract work. The resumes can come from internal resources or from subcontractor organizations. When the customer issues a task order, the prime contractor can quickly scan the database to determine who has the requisite skills to perform the job. Although this approach minimizes the time it takes to locate appropriate people to work on the task order, just like any automated system, its value lies in the quality of the data within the database. If people keep their resumes current and if the system has query capabilities that are easy to use to locate qualified people, the system is a good management tool.

Select Internal Support Team Members

Internal support team members are team members who work with the contract core team to support the customer contract. These people can come from any type of functional area (e.g., management, engineering, production, marketing, sales, task-order support, legal, contracts, executive leadership, financial management, or human resources). Internal support team members are used on an as-needed basis to provide expertise or personnel to the contract core team. The team will need more members at the beginning of the contract, fewer during contract performance, and the number of members will decrease again during contract shutdown.

Reasons to Use Internal Support Teams

Internal support teams are in place for several reasons:

- They have experts in particular functional areas that can be used on contracts.
- They have a corporate knowledge repository within that particular functional area that can be tapped when solving problems.
- They have standards, policies, and procedures in place to be able to quickly accomplish the task at hand.
- They minimize the need for the contractor to have each contract acquire its own expert to perform the specialized work.
- They can better leverage the people with the expertise across multiple contracts so that one contract does not have to absorb all the costs for the expertise, particularly during downtime.

The value of the internal support team members lies in the degree to which they are included in the daily activities of the contract core team. If a good communication channel exists between the contract core team and the support organizations, the support team members probably will be able to contribute their expertise without much lead time. If communication between the groups is lacking, the internal support team's value is diminished because of the time it will take to get the team up to speed before it can solve a problem. If this lead time takes too long, the contract core team may consider doing the work, albeit not as well, without the expertise provided by an internal support team.

The contract core team needs to keep the internal support teams informed of specific contractual requirements. The internal support team needs to understand the requirements and develop and maintain the expertise that the contract needs. This degree of integration requires the core team to work with the internal support teams before contract award, during the proposal phase, when duties and responsibilities are agreed on between the organizations. Once the contract has been awarded, the organizations should meet periodically to discuss upcoming requirements throughout the life of the contract.

Internal Support Issues

Up until this point we have assumed that internal support team members are from the prime contractor organization. However, subcontractors that have a great deal of involvement in a prime contractor's program may also set up core teams with additional help provided by internal support teams from their own organization.

The key issues surrounding the internal support team at contract start-up include service level agreements, single point of contact, scoping out the project, and hiring enough of the right people. The following sections review each of these topics in more detail.

Service Level Agreements

Service level agreements are contracts between the contract core team members and the internal support team members. Similar to a subcontract, a service level agreement basically states what each party will bring to the relationship and what each party is supposed to do to fulfill the relationship. Many companies do not engage in service level agreements because of the belief that a formal agreement is not needed between members of the same corporation. This belief can cause trouble for the contract core team throughout the contract's period of performance. If the internal support team should be downsized or become the victim of budget cuts, the contract core team will need some document by which to demand and receive service. Likewise, if there are personnel changes in either the internal support team or the contract core team, a service level agreement states the relationship between the two parties so that there can be no confusion between the parties as to what is expected.

The service level agreement should state, at a minimum, the period of performance, the place of performance, the work that will be done by the internal support team, the contract core team responsibilities, the fees that will be charged for the work performed, and any flow down clauses from the prime contract.

Assigning a Single Point of Contact to a Contract

The internal support team should assign a single point of contact to the contract so that all issues between the internal support team and the contract core team can be directed and resolved at one place in the organization. The single point of contact can then determine what the requirements are from the contract core team and then locate the necessary resources within the internal support team. By having a single point of contact, the person assigned to this role understands the issues facing the contract core team and can be proactive in anticipating and meeting the requirements. This person is typically invited to planning sessions and inventory or workload forecasting meetings to provide input.

Scoping Out the Level of Effort

The service level agreement is also useful for the internal support team to scope out the level of effort required on the contract. Usually, support teams are required to provide resources to multiple contracts within the company. The internal support team needs to do an accurate job of scoping out the level of effort for each contract and ensuring that the resources do not overlap between contracts. Although this task seems simple enough, it is one of the most difficult for the internal support team to accomplish.

Locating the Right People

Once the internal support team understands and reaches agreement with the contract core team about the level of effort required, the support team can begin looking for and hiring the right people for the organization. Ideally, the internal support team would like to understand the requirements of all the teams it supports so that it may find candidates that have the skills to support multiple contracts, if necessary. Staffing the support team is a double-edged sword: the team wants to have the people available as soon as possible after the contract is awarded, however, if it staffs too early and the contract is not won, it is left with a surplus of people in the organization. Usually, internal teams working with the company's human resources department will make contingent offers to a person based on whether the company wins the contract and hope that the person does not take another job in the interim.

Continue Work with Subcontractors

Negotiate Final Subcontracts

At this point in contract start-up, the prime contractor wants to ensure that all subcontracts have been negotiated and executed so that both sides are protected as work for the customer commences. The process for getting subcontracts signed is discussed in Chapter 9.

Working with Subcontractors

The key step to working with a subcontractor is to ensure that it is included in all relevant contract start-up activities. The subcontractor needs to know when delivery orders or task orders are obtained, contract training initiatives, review and approval cycles on deliverables, and any other contractual requirements surrounding its products and services. As the prime contractor prepares to manage the aspects of the new program, it must consider the subcontractor in each stage. For example:

- Will the subcontractor be located at the customer or contractor site? If so, they need to be included in facility, equipment, and support estimates.
- Will the subcontractor help market the contract? If so, it needs the contract literature and demonstration products to help its marketing.
- Will the subcontractor be responsible for providing input to deliverables? If so, it needs to understand the review cycle, format considerations, and customer requirements.
- Will the subcontractor help in user support functions? If so, it needs training on customer requirements, contract objectives, and product capabilities.
- Will the subcontractor be offering new products and services to the customer? If so, it needs to work with the prime contractor to get those new products and services on the contract through the proposal process.
- Will the subcontractor be trying to forecast revenue for its own company's financial forecasts? If so, it needs to have forecast and projection information from the prime contractor.

Conduct Start-Up Training Initiatives

Training is a complex, evolving, and far-reaching initiative. It occurs at many different levels, among various teams of people, and during multiple points in the contract. Training can have different focuses and can be accomplished using many methods to achieve its objectives.

Recipients of Training

Customers

Various people need to be trained during a contract. First, there is customer training. Training may be paid for by the customer if a contractual obligation exists to provide certain types of training.

Alternatively, or in addition, the contractor may offer customer training to ensure that the customer understands the contractor's product or to educate the customer on the benefits of the solution proposed. This type of training is usually provided by the contractor at its own expense or it may be recouped through a program-management charge.

Contract Core Team

Next, the contract core team receives and conducts training. It may receive training from the internal support teams on corporate policies and initiatives or from vendors on new technologies. Similarly, the contract core team could conduct training for the customer on product specific attributes or for the subcontractors on how the contract operates.

Internal Support Team

The internal support teams also receive and conduct training. They need to understand the customer's environment and they get that training from the contract core team. The teams may also educate the contract core team and the customer on techniques and procedures within their discipline.

Subcontractors

Finally, the subcontractors receive and give training. Again, the contract core team needs to educate them on contract basics and potential revenue opportunities, and the subcontractors may share information on new customers and new technology available through their companies.

Types of Training

Different types of training occur on a contract. This section discusses some of the major training initiatives that can occur on a contract.

Job-Specific Training

Job-specific training is the training that a person needs to know how to initially do his or her job. It also includes follow-on training, which helps the person do his or her job better as the contract progresses. The types of job-specific training required on a contract vary with the requirements of the contract.

Customer

Customer training consists of providing a description of how the customer is organized, what it is trying to accomplish with its program, how the team will meet its requirements, and how the customer relationship will be developed. It is intended for everyone on the program team so that each person gets a big picture of how to best do his or her job to meet the customers' goals and objectives.

Roles of Team Members and How the Contract Operates

Team members must be educated on the roles of each organization within the contract, such as customer, contract core team, internal support team, and subcontractors, as well as the specific roles that each person within those organizations perform. The training should be updated as roles, responsibilities, and procedures within the organizations change. Usually the following items are reviewed:

- How delivery orders will be reviewed and managed
- How products and services will be ordered from subcontractors or provided with internal resources
- How order, delivery, installation, acceptance, and invoicing will be tracked
- How new products and services will be added to the contract
- How customer deliverables will be prepared
- How the prime contractor will review deliverables before they are delivered to the customer
- How other day-to-day procedures will operate

Customer Operating Style and Requirements

Subcontractors, internal team members, and contract core members should all be educated on how the customer operates and what their requirements are as they evolve throughout the contract. Because the prime contractor is ultimately responsible for the customer relationship, the contractor should dictate how the contract will operate in light of the customer's operating style and requirements. This training may continue if the customer's environment is rapidly changing; for example, new reporting structures, new regulations, or new ways of doing business.

Methods

This section discusses the many methods that can be used to deliver the training.

On-the-Job or One-on-One Training

The most basic of all training is considered on-the-job training. On-the-job training usually consists of one or more experienced employee reviewing the procedures with a new employee for accomplishing a certain task. After this review, the person being trained gets several opportunities to complete the task himself or herself receives constructive criticism from his or her trainers. As the trainee gets more experience, he or she receives fewer critiques and reviews until the trainee obtains mastery.

Classroom

Classroom training implies the traditional instructor paired with a given number of students in a class. Lecture, hands-on experience, interactive question-and-answer periods, audiovisuals, workbooks, and assignments are all approaches used to impart knowledge in a classroom setting. Technology is extending the classroom boundaries. Teleconferencing, video, Internet, and satellite technologies allow students and teacher to be together in real or virtual time at the same location or not. Classroom training is particularly useful to help the prime contractor's or the subcontractor's team members learn about each other's product lines.

Computer-Based Training

In traditional computer-based training (CBT) a computer is used as the medium through which information is imparted. Carefully designed programs allow the student to review the course material, complete exercises, assess mastery, and complete remedial work, if needed. CBT used to be mainframe-based and required access through a terminal; today, a lot of training is available on floppy disk, on CD-ROM, or through the Internet and it can be downloaded to any computer.

Interactive Uses of the Internet

Technology has once again simplified training and ordering initiatives. Using Homepages and chat rooms, people can solve specific problems or even ask questions and receive answers in real time.

Additionally, customers can even place orders using the Internet. Some vendors provide this service free as a discriminator for their product.

User Meetings

Customer- or contractor-sponsored user meetings give both teams the opportunity to meet and exchange ideas about the products or services being offered on the contract. Because user meetings are typically used for information processing systems, system fixes, short cuts, future enhancements, and creative applications are all topics that are discussed at the meetings.

Procedure Manuals

Vendor-provided or user-created procedure manuals are valuable aids to the people working on the contract. In addition, the manual help new people on the contract by giving them a starting point to garner knowledge. Two important things to remember about procedure manuals: (1) they must be kept current because out-of-date procedure manuals are useless and (2) they can be maintained through various channels, such as hard copy (paper), electronic media (floppy disk or CD-ROM), or on-line (stand-alone information system or on the Internet). Everyone on a contract team can use procedure manuals. Sometimes it is useful for the teams to share the procedure manuals so that adequate information and controls can be established for each member to accomplish his or her task. For example, subcontractors should understand how the prime contractor places orders and makes payment so that the subcontractors can ensure timely action with order processing. Likewise, it is useful for the prime contractor to understand how a subcontractor calculates warranty and maintenance on its product so that the customer obtains adequate coverage at the least cost.

Contract Overviews

Contract overviews are typically developed by the prime contractor and are used to train the core team, internal support team, and subcontractors about how the contract operates. The contractor also develops a modified version, which contains all the products and services and how to order them, to be used primarily with the customers. Contract overviews are usually designed as flip-chart presentations. Some companies put their contract overviews on videotape so that film from actual customer locations or vendor manufacturing processes can be incorporated.

Catalogues

Catalogues are a particularly useful tool for educating the customer on what is available on the contract and is used primarily on indefinite delivery/indefinite quantity type of contracts. Catalogues can be either hard copy (paper), electronic media (floppy disk or CD-ROM), or on-line (stand-alone information system or on the Internet). Like procedure manuals, catalogues must be kept current otherwise customers will never know the new product offerings or current prices.

Technical Briefings and Position Papers

The contractor will probably schedule technical briefings and/or develop position papers throughout the life of the contract. These services are used to educate the customer on the latest technology available or on improved methods for accomplishing contract work. To complete one of these services, the contractor must stay abreast of changes in the industry and in technology. After careful review and analysis, the contractor determines how, or if, these changes affect contract work, or if the changes can be incorporated to improve contract performance. If the answer to either of these questions is yes, the contractor usually presents its preliminary findings to the customer at a program review or other meeting. If the customer concurs, the customer may request that the contractor spend the time and resources to prepare a technical briefing and/or a position paper to summarize its findings. As a result of technical briefings and position papers, the customer may alter the way things are accomplished on the contract, such as adding or deleting products and services from the contract because of improved methodologies or new products that are available.

Contract Start-Up Training Issues

There are several key training issues that must be managed during contract start-up: total number of people to be trained, developing training, and the costs of training. The next section discusses each of these in detail.

People in Need of Training

When a contract begins, the most people probably know is how to perform their specific functions. The contractor must train them on how the contract will operate, the customer's requirements, the role of each individual, and many other areas. Sometimes a contract team has a very inexperienced member on the team, and that person may have to be trained to do his or her job as well. Because of the quick nature of contract start-up, the person has to be trained in a relatively short period of time so that he or she can begin participating as a team member to get the contract goals and objectives accomplished.

Developing the Training

The next major obstacle to overcome is training development. Developing training is a costly initiative, albeit one that reaps great rewards, but one that needs an investment in both time and resources. During contract start-up, people do not have much time available. Usually, everyone is so focused on meeting the contract deliverables that no one wants to focus on training people. The problem is that a contract has so many people in need of training and no one available to develop or conduct the training. Any training efforts that are initiated during this period are typically those required to support the customer. As the contract work progresses, people start to have more free time, and the appropriate level of time and resources can be dedicated to developing the training. The training has to occur— the sooner, the better. The sooner people are trained, the sooner they can accomplish tasks as opposed to spending their time and energies focused on how to accomplish some task.

Costs Associated with Training

As discussed earlier, training is an expensive proposition, particularly if the courses need to be developed in-house. Fortunately, many vendor-specific classes exist that can teach people how to use the products provided on the contract. These classes allow contract personnel to get the training they need when they need it most. In these situations, the contract management team must balance work needing to be done with the time taken out for training and the cost of training.

Develop Communications Channels

Communication on a contract is integral to its success. A contract needs good communication among its members (customer, contract core, internal support, and subcontractor) and between the contract's team and outside groups (the customer's and contractor's executive management teams). To ensure that communication is effective on the contract, the contractor should ensure that the right type of information is communicated to the people who need it and that appropriate communication channels are established.

Types of Information That Need to Be Communicated

The types of information that need to be communicated will vary from contract to contract. The following lists of some of generic types of information that are communicated:

- How the contract operates
- How the customer operates
- Status of customer projects
- Changes in customer requirements
- New customer requirements
- New technology and how it can be implemented
- New products and their applicability
- Personnel changes
- Order dates
- Delivery dates
- Acceptance dates
- Information about other contracts
- Information about other customer projects
- Contract financial data
- Subcontractor information

Who Needs the Information

The people who need the information on a contract will vary as well. Typically, the following people need information about the contract:

- Customer
- Customer's executive management team
- Contract core team personnel
- Internal support team
- Prime contractor's executive management team
- Subcontractor
- Subcontractor's executive management team
- Field personnel

Methods of Communication

The methods of communication will also vary. A key to effective communication is selecting the communication channel that will be used by the intended audience. For example, it does not make any sense to transmit information in hardcopy format to an executive manager if she prefers to receive information electronically. The following are communication methods that the contractor can use:

- *Training*—As discussed earlier in this chapter, communicating with people through training programs is an effective way to give everyone a baseline level of knowledge. More detailed classes can be developed for people who need more detail on a subject.

- *Team meetings*—Used within each of the functional areas of a contract, team meetings allow information to be disseminated quickly to everyone. Any issues raised at a team meeting can be addressed immediately or followed up on in later meetings.

- *Status meetings*—A method to stay current on a particular contract project is the status meeting. Status meetings can be held on one or more projects. To make the meetings effective, all the people necessary to approve or implement decisions in the meeting should attend.

- *Managers' meeting*—Typically held once per week, managers' meetings are useful in communicating critical events occurring on the contract so that the managers can implement strategies to respond.

- *Program reviews*—Many customers like the idea of monthly or quarterly program reviews during which the contractor and customer discuss how projects are going and any future requirements.

- *Contract deliverables*—The contract may require, or the customer may prefer, contract deliverables, such as monthly status reports, to inform the various customer groups about the progress to date on the contract.

- *Local or wide area networks*—Technology allows people on the same team to exchange information electronically. Local or wide area networks help significantly with work-flow management because documents can be created, edited, and reviewed on-line without hardcopy print out.

- *Team newsletters*—A way to keep everyone informed about what is going on in the account from both a professional and personal perspective are team newsletters. Published monthly or quarterly, team newsletters highlight significant contract accomplishments, stellar performances by contract team members, and even birth or marriage announcements.

- *Electronic mail*—E-mail allows people to exchange information electronically. Mail messages or whole documents can be sent between team members or to people outside of the team. Electronic mail also allows for an audit trail between the customer and the contractor.

- *Customer homepage*—Internet homepages are used within customer organizations and contracting communities to provide program or product information. Oftentimes, contractors will install a homepage filled with information about its products and capabilities so its customers can expedite their training on a new system.

- *User groups*—Originally started in the information technology community, user groups are forums for similar types of people to exchange information and ideas. Typically, all the people using a similar database or spreadsheet package would get together on a quarterly basis with the original product developer to discuss technology enhancements, bug fixes, or creative uses for the software.

- *Internet*—The latest and fastest growing communication channel is the Internet. Not only can people use it to send e-mail messages or documents, the Internet (with its various search engines) can be used to access information stored in databases around the world. Subcontractors use homepages to provide an overview of their companies and product lines. Prime contractors use homepages to advertise and to take orders for contract products and services. Even agencies use homepages as a public relations forum to highlight their missions, purposes, and key people.

- *Voice mail*—Another fast-growing communication channel is voice mail. Voice mail can allow private messages between individuals or can broadcast messages to many users simultaneously.

- *Fax*—The fax machine was one of the original solutions for information on demand. Fax machines allow people to exchange information within minutes.

- *Automatic downloads*—Sometimes it is easier to develop programs that will download information from one system and
  upload it onto another. This minimizes the time it takes to
  rekey the data, minimizes errors in data entry, and allows
  people to focus more on what to do with the data.

Communication Lines

The contractor will need to decide on what type of communication
lines will work best on the contract. For example, a formal approach
like contractor program reviews with the government may be appropriate, or an informal approach like asking the subcontractor to tell
the prime contractor about new capabilities within the industry.
Some of the basic communication lines that occur on most contracts
include the following:

- The customer needs to communicate program changes to the
  prime contractor and the prime contractor needs to communicate the changes to the subcontractor.

- The subcontractor needs to communicate product changes and
  enhancements to the prime contractor and the prime contractor
  needs to communicate them to the customer.

- Personnel changes need to be communicated to all parties concerned.

- Funding changes need to be communicated to all parties concerned.

- The contract team needs to communicate financial information
  for all functions on the contract to executive management.

- Processes and procedures need to be communicated to all parties concerned.

- The customer needs to communicate order information to the
  prime contractor and from the prime contractor needs to communicate the information to the subcontractor.

- The subcontractor needs to communicate delivery information
  to the prime contractor and the prime contractor needs to be
  communicate the information to the customer.

Now that we have covered what communication needs to be
exchanged, which team members need to be involved, and how that
information gets communicated, we are ready to discuss some key
communication issues surrounding contract start-up.

Contract Start-Up Communications Issues

During contract start-up there are basically two key issues surrounding communication: determine the information requirements and establish the communication channels.

Determine the Information Requirements

A key to good communication during contract start-up and throughout the life of the contract is to determine to whom to communicate and what information to communicate. Not all customers need detailed contract data; similarly, prime contractors may need to ensure that they get a great deal of data from their subcontractors. The key here is to decide who needs information, what level of detail they need, and how often they need the information.

Establish the Communication Channels

Once the team understands who needs information and what information they need, the team can begin developing the most effective communication channels through which to relay the information. First, the team needs to look at the communication requirements across the entire contract to determine similarities in the information required. Then the team needs to determine an effective way to deliver that information (e.g., on-line systems, broadcast voice messages, or status reports). Once the team determines the most effective way to deliver the information, it must determine if the methods selected will work logistically in the organization. For example, does everyone have a compatible machine to get to data on on-line systems or does everyone have voice mail? These logistics may require that the team select a less effective communication channel in order to get the information out. Finally, the team must establish the communication channels. It must decide who is providing the information, verifying its accuracy, packaging it for dissemination, following up with the recipients to answer questions, and providing updates to the information. Establishing communication channels is the longest process to develop and should be done in conjunction with other information requirements needed on the contract, as discussed in a future chapter.

Benefits of Good Communications

Although establishing good communication may seem like a timely process during contract start-up, it has many benefits:

- People will have the information they need to run their portion of the business right from the start.

- Errors are more likely to be caught early in the process, when they can be corrected easily, because there are multiple people involved in the review process.

- People are more productive because they can focus on the information they are receiving and not on how to get the information.

Managing Information, Processes, and Deliverables

The *deliverable* is the document, product, or service that the contractor must provide to the customer as defined in the contract. If the contractor fails to accurately provide deliverables, on time and within budget, the contractor is in default of the contract and may be terminated. Due to their contractually binding nature, deliverables drive what information the contractor needs to collect and the procedures that the contractor must establish to collect that information.

Information is necessary to produce and manage deliverables. Information generally falls into three main categories:

1. Information that must be produced on the contract and provided to the customer in some form, either through oral, written, or electronic means

2. Information that is used internally to produce the information that is provided to the customer

3. Information that is used internally to manage the contract

Processes are the methods the contractor uses to collect the information necessary to produce and manage deliverables. Processes are descriptions of what needs to be accomplished and integrated across functional areas (e.g., the process for delivering orders, which requires involvement from the technical and business teams in order to be successful).

Contract Start-Up Issues

Establish Deliverable Schedule

Because each deliverable is on its own time schedule (i.e., weekly, monthly, as-needed), the program team needs to develop a master schedule that plots out all contract deliverables through some point in time (i.e., one year or end of contract). The master schedule needs to include all the interim milestones, such as production points.

Determine Deliverable Requirements

The contractor then must review each of the deliverables to determine the requirements contained in each. Either the customer or the contractor defines the elements of each deliverable. The contractor should review the deliverable requirements so that they can be included later when the data requirements are defined.

Determine Person Responsible for Each Deliverable

Equally as important to determining deliverable requirements is assigning one person to each deliverable. Deliverables that are to be completed by committees seldom get accomplished. Although one person has ultimate responsibility for the deliverable, many people on the contract will probably be required to support its development and completion.

Determine Review Process for Each Deliverable

The team must also determine the review process for each deliverable, both from an internal and an external perspective. Internally, the program manager, technical manager, and business manager, at a minimum, should review each deliverable before it goes to the customer. Externally, the customer may want to conduct a preliminary review of the deliverable before it receives it in final form. Other reviews include an editing review, a data accuracy review, and a production control review.

Determine Data Requirements

Once the schedule has been developed, the team should determine what data items are required for each deliverable. The data items should be compiled across the entire contract. They should include not only those needed for producing the deliverables but also any items needed to manage the deliverables. The data requirements should include who needs the data, where the data needs to come from, how often the data is needed, and what reports are necessary to relay the data.

Establish Methods to Collect, Retain, and Report the Data

After the data requirements are established, the team needs to determine methods to collect, retain, and report the data. Usually, a team will elect to use some sort of management database with query and reporting capabilities. These systems are costly to develop and sometimes an existing system can be modified to support another contract's requirements.

Determine Procedures

Once the deliverables, data items, and systems are in place, the team needs to develop procedures to ensure that data items are collected and deliverables are completed in a timely fashion. These procedures need to be communicated to all parties involved with producing deliverables and collecting data.

Establish Effective Financial Measures and Controls

In order to reach its goals of establishing customer partnerships, developing its employees, or maintaining shareholder trust, a company must make money and continue to make money in order to exist. A company uses financial data to indicate if:

- A project is over or under budget
- A contract or part of a contract is profitable
- The company can get the necessary capital to grow its business
- The company can use its existing cash flow to pay its expenses
- A contract's product line is cost competitive as compared to products on other contracts
- The return on investment is worth the cost of the investment
- The company can declare a dividend on its stock
- A contract can provide a product or service more cost effectively
- A contract's revenue is proportional to its expenses

Evolution of Financial Management on a Contract

The following sections discuss how financial management evolves on a contract.

Pre-RFP Analysis

First, the team analyzing the draft RFP made the first attempt at determining how much it would cost to bid on the contract to determine if it was worth the up-front investment. Then the team analyzed at a higher level what it would cost to run the program and what the potential revenue stream was for the contract. The team assessed how much of the business would be done internally and how much would have to be subcontracted. Also in that analysis, the team determined if any "deal killers" or clauses existed that would cause the company not to bid on the contract because they represented too much risk for the company. The team needs to spend quality time on the initial analysis because it determines, to a large extent, whether the contract becomes profitable later on. The last aspect that the team focused on is what the competitors were likely to bid. The team needed to determine if the competition would come in with a bottom-line dollar amount that the company can beat. Although the team does not have all of the contract details at its disposal, by conducting a careful analysis at this point the team can discover many of the issues that could cause contractual problems later on. Unfortunately, many companies skip this careful analysis, and focus only on the large dollar revenues that could be associated with the contract and overlook the risk that it must take to win the contract.

Bid Decision

The company will go through a formal bid decision process after the final RFP is released. The team's bid decision analyzes all the items listed earlier as well as a few other items, such as the strength of the team's product compared to that of its competitors. The team looks at how the company will mitigate any risks associated with winning the contract. It reviews whether the company has the skilled people to staff the proposal and the resulting contract. The team also looks at two questions regarding the financial revenue stream: When will the contract become profitable? What the is financial value associated with the risks taken? The answers to these questions will give the executive management team the rationale for bidding or declining to bid on the RFP.

Proposal Process

When a company decides to submit a proposal in response to a customer RFP, the company carefully analyzes the products and services necessary to meet the contract requirements. Once the team understands the requirements, it can determine its cost for providing those goods and services. To those costs, the company adds the rates for general and administrative (G&A) cost and overhead costs. On government contracts, these rates are pre-established with the government through its disclosure statement to the Defense Contract Audit Agency (DCAA). Finally, the company adds a certain percentage of profit to the contract costs. The product and service costs, G&A costs, overhead costs, and the fee equal the price the company offers on the contract. These prices are then multiplied by the total estimated quantities that the company believes it will sell under the contract. This document becomes the price proposal to the customer.

BAFO Submission

The company may have the opportunity to submit one revision to the price proposal if the customer requests a best and final offer (BAFO). This is the company's opportunity to lower its prices by determining more efficient ways to conduct business and by renegotiating lower prices with subcontractors. If the company can lower its prices, the company can offer a more attractive and competitive bid; However, the company must weigh the value of winning the contract against the risk of managing the contract with lower prices.

Outlook Process

While the company is conducting its BAFO submission, the company establishes the outlook. For the outlook, the company prepares a summary of the expenses and revenues that will become the operating budget for the contract. The outlook assumes when the contract will start, when expenses will be incurred, and when revenue will be received. At the time of contract award, the outlook becomes the operating budget for the contract.

During contract performance, actual expenses are compared to the budget. If expenses are higher, the contractor must cut costs elsewhere to maintain the same profit margins that were projected in the financial outlooks before contract award. The contractor must then modify the operating budget and explain deviations each month or quarter throughout the outlook process. The outlook process serves two purposes:

1. It allows the contract management team to modify the estimated data contained in the operating budget, which was developed before contract award, with actual data that is based on real contract sales for the current quarter and more realistic projections about the sales for the next quarter. The team will need to explain any deviations between the projected and ac-

tual amounts because the company relies on the financial information provided by the contract to make its financial decisions.

2. It allows the company's management team to determine how well it is doing financially across all contracts so that it can make appropriate decisions when it hires new personnel, builds a new facility, obtains financing, grows the business, or declares a stock dividend. Similarly, if the company, as determined by the outlook process, will not be profitable, the company can institute cost-cutting measures or new revenue generating schemes.

In conjunction with the outlook process, the company's management team may need additional financial indicators to determine where and how the company can improve profitability. These ad hoc requests can range anywhere from how many days it takes for a customer to pay an invoice to the amount of overall contribution a contract provides to the company's bottom line.

Financial Data Tracking

In order to continue profitably, to conduct a timely outlook process, and to prepare any ad hoc reports necessary for the management team, the contract team needs to track the following information:

- Customer delivery order quantity and prices to ensure that they match the prime contract
- Purchase orders to subcontractors to ensure that they match the quantities on the customer delivery order and the prices on the subcontract
- When delivery of the products and services is made and acceptance is obtained so that invoices can be generated
- When customer invoices are paid
- When subcontractors' invoices are paid
- The number of hours worked and invoiced on the contract
- The raises given to people on the contract
- Any expenses made on the contract

In addition, the contract may employ its own strategies for increasing profitability, such as:

- Decreasing expenses by downsizing personnel or lowering dollars spent to manage the contract

- Generating additional revenue by increased marketing efforts
- Improving productivity by completing and implementing the results of a work process analysis

Contract Start-up Financial Management Issues

Understand the Contract

The first task for the contract team is to understand how the contract operates; for example, when must products and services be delivered so that liquidated damages are not incurred? How soon after delivery will the customer accept products? How soon after the customer accepts the deliverables can the invoice be processed? When will the company get paid? What are the terms and conditions for each of the subcontractors? The answers to these questions will help the team more accurately assess its revenue and expenses.

Understand What Drives the Outlook Process

People working on the contract should understand the basics of the outlook process (e.g., when revenue and expenses are accrued, when labor hours are recorded in the system, and when invoices are processed) so that all team members can do their part to accurately capture the data necessary for the financial management process.

Understand the Company's Financial Indicators

Because each company measures success differently, the program team must understand which financial indicators are important to the company. The company's emphasis on these indicators may change over time; for example, a company interested in acquiring another company may be interested in cash flow, whereas a company interested in capital expansion may be more interested in contract backlog.

Set Up Data Systems on the Contract to Track Financial Data

Once the contract team understands the contract, the outlook process, and the company's financial indicators, the team can set up data systems to capture and report financial data. Equally important to setting up systems to capture and report financial data are controls to verify the accuracy of the data being reported. These controls can be both automatic (built into the system) and manual (requiring human intervention) to verify the data.

Set Up Procedures to Keep Track of All Financial Paperwork

Coupled with the automated system to capture and report financial data is the paper trail that the contract team must retain on the contract for audit purposes. This paperwork must be maintained throughout the life of the contract for two reasons: (1) If the company is working on a government contract and the contract is audited, the government auditor will need to review these files and (2) at contract closeout, the paperwork will help substantiate the contractor's claim for final payment.

Understand What Other Company Groups Are Involved in the Financial Process

Because each company is set up differently, there is no standard format for financial data management. Some companies have all financial control maintained with the contract team, other companies prefer to segregate responsibilities to ensure accountability through a series of checks and balances. When the contract team uses an internal support team to manage the financial data on the contract, the contract team must work with the other team to determine how the contract will work and to determine each team's responsibilities. The contract team needs to establish these processes right from the start so that critical financial management procedures are followed and so that data does not fall through the cracks.

Establish Marketing Methods

The discussion on marketing in Chapter 3 focused on the activities that occur before contract award. This discussion focuses on marketing activities that occur after contract award to grow the business.

Effect of Contract Type on Marketing Efforts

In a firm, fixed price contract, the company does not to conduct marketing, except to grow the business in new areas. With such contracts, the governmental customer provides a statement of work in the RFP, to which the company proposes a fixed price. The contract between the government and the company is to get the stated work done for the stated price. If the government has additional requirements, however, the company may find it prudent to market its capabilities to the government agency in an effort to grow its business.

In an indefinite delivery and indefinite quantity contract, or a cost-plus contract, all the company actually wins when it is awarded the procurement is the right to sell its products and services. In this case, the team must market its wares to the customer community if it expects the contract to be profitable. The company is interested in growing the contract because it represents additional revenue, increased business, and a justification for the bid and proposal dollars spent on winning the procurement. The government, too, may be interested in buying as much as possible off the contract because the contract allows it to procure the goods and services necessary to implement its program.

Methods to Grow the Business

The company can use two methods to grow the business through marketing efforts. The first is to grow the business that the company has with its existing customers. In this case, the company could rely on its superior quality and service from to market itself and sell additional product and service. Although the company may use some of the marketing channels listed in the following section to inform its customer of new product and service offerings, a company's reputation goes a long way in driving whether the new product and service sales come to fruition. The second method the company can use to grow the contract business is selling to new customers. This technique requires much more up-front effort than the first method and can employ any of the channels listed in the following sections.

Establish Marketing Channels

Marketing channels, or methods to sell products and services, can be simple or complex. For example, the company could rely primarily on word-of-mouth or it could offer incentives to salespeople from subcontractor companies to push the products. Either way, marketing channels must be evaluated by assessing the money it costs to implement them versus the potential revenue streams they may generate. Most companies adopt a mixture of different marketing channels to obtain maximum penetration of the market. Marketing channels during contract performance may include the following:

- Trade show booths
- Trade magazine advertising
- Providing a guest speaker at conferences
- Catalogues
- Brochures

- Internet advertising
- Product demonstrations
- Customer visits
- Technology papers
- Marketing calls
- Subcontractor marketing
- Identifying and responding to customer needs
- Customer endorsements
- Previous reputation
- User meetings

Who Conducts the Marketing Efforts?

The marketing efforts are conducted by several different groups. For example:

Contract or company marketing or sales team   Many companies refer to marketing and sales as two different initiatives within a procurement cycle. The term *marketing* is used to describe all the activities that occur to establish and build customer relationships. Once the relationship is established, the sales team comes in and presents the company's product and services and closes the deal. Some contracts have their own dedicated marketing and sales people; other companies have a centralized marketing and sales team that supports all contracts.

Executive management team   Sometimes the executive management team performs the marketing function by establishing high-level relationships with the customer's executive team. For example, the executive management team may accompany the sales team to a company-sponsored customer demonstration or the executive management team may call on senior customers to discuss product offerings across multiple contract vehicles.

Marketing or sales support   The support team does a lot of the background work for the marketing or sales team. Tasks such as developing brochures or advertising, coordinating trade shows, and creating homepages are all completed by the marketing or sales support team.

Contract core team members   The contract core team tries to grow the business through the service it provides on a daily basis. Besides conducting user meetings and responding to customer requirements, contract core team members may develop technology papers, conduct marketing calls, staff trade booth exhibits, or analyze customer needs to determine better or more efficient methods to meet them. It is through the efforts of the contract core team members that customer endorsements are obtained.

Subcontractors Subcontractors can provide a great deal of support in marketing the products and services on the contract. Many subcontractors have preestablished networks within the customer community that they can tap into to sell off the contract. The subcontractor is usually happy to provide this service because it yields increased revenue and profit if its marketing efforts are successful.

Key Issues

Consolidated Marketing Approach

A consolidated marketing approach is warranted given the number of professionals engaged in the marketing effort. It can really annoy a government customer, or any customer, when multiple representatives from the same company show up to sell their products; particularly, if it is evident that the company representatives don't realize that the other company representatives already paid a visit. This shows professional discourtesy. A much better approach is for the marketing team to develop a consolidated marketing approach among several contract vehicles so that a minimum number of people are visiting with the customer and a company-wide marketing strategy is being implemented, rather than one contract vehicle working at odds with another contract vehicle.

Decide How the Team Brings Value to the Customer

Another professional discourtesy that a company can commit is to show up at the customer's office with no clear idea of how the company or the contract vehicle brings value to the customer. Careful preparation, which includes understanding the customer's requirements, reviewing the company's product and service offerings, and determining how the company can add value through its products and services to meet and surpass the customer's requirements, is integral to establishing a solid customer-contractor partnership.

Ask What the Customer Needs

An often overlooked marketing strategy is to ask the customer what he or she needs and then listen to the answer. Too often, companies assume they know what is best for the customer, and sometimes they may. However, the customer probably knows how to solve its own problems better than a contractor ever will.

Make Frequent Contact

It is important that the marketing team maintain contact with the customer through periodic marketing visits, follow-up phone calls, and correspondence to stay involved in the customer's business. Such actions make the customer feel that the company cares about the customer's efforts and reminds it that the company is ready and willing to help out.

Get Involved at the Strategic Level

For a true customer and contractor partnership to exist, the contractor should try to get involved in strategy meetings, customer planning sessions, and other events that allow members to talk about what will happen in the future. The more the contractor knows about the customer's business base, both now and in the future, the more the contractor can assist the customer in meeting its goals and objectives.

Develop a Marketing Plan

Although the team has won the contract, the company should still make a concerted effort to market regularly to the customer. A marketing plan helps the team focus on which customers should be marketed, what is the best way to market to them, when is the appropriate time to market to them, why the company should market to them, what the strategic significance of marketing to those customers is, and where the company plans to target its marketing efforts.

Anticipate the Customer's Requirements

A contractor that simply responds to customer's requirements does not provide the same level of service as a contractor that anticipates the customer's requirements. Staying on top of the customer's environment and understanding the drivers and effects of change allow the contractor to be an effective partner.

Always Follow Up on Customer Requests

Although it may sound like a simple business principle, many individuals in companies do not realize the significance of following up on customer requests, responding to customer phone calls, and keeping the customer informed of project developments. This communication strengthens the bond between the customer and contractor and establishes the contractor as a cut above the rest. This is paramount to contractor success.

Contract Start-Up

Locate and Educate Field Personnel

It is important that the company be closely located to the customer or give the appearance that the company is always close by. This makes the customer feel that its problems can be resolved quickly. Sometimes, companies locate marketing personnel close to key customers. These marketing people may support multiple contract vehicles. If this is the case, the contract core team should educate the marketing people on the contract so that they can accurately represent the team's product and service offerings. By keeping the marketing team informed of changes in the customer's approach or political structure, the contract team can gain additional business opportunities. By educating the marketing people on the contract's success stories, they can look for work that is closely aligned with the strengths of the contract team.

Establish Marketing Strategy and Approach

Many different approaches to marketing are discussed in this chapter, but a key to marketing success is targeting specific strategies at specific opportunities. The individual marketing plans developed for each contract should support the company-wide marketing strategy. By leveraging the resources, relationships, and technologies across the contracts, the company gains much for a relatively minimal investment.

Determine How Subcontractor Marketing Will Occur

Part of the marketing strategy may include subcontractor marketing. A subcontractor usually has preestablished relationships, approaches, and success stories that the contractor can leverage to obtain new business for the contract. Although the prime contractor has ultimate responsibility for the customer relationship, the subcontractor can be used in either direct or indirect customer marketing opportunities. The contractor should work out the details of how subcontractor marketing will occur up front; for example, who will call on who and how contract solutions should be presented.

Establish Customer Relationships

A key to contract start-up marketing is to establish the customer relationships, particularly if the company has never worked with the customer before. The contractor should learn if the company or the subcontractor has an existing relationship with the customer and when the relationship can be leveraged. The company will need to understand the customer's organizational chart, program goals, and contract options. The company should learn where the customer is located and schedule trips out to the site to understand site-unique attributes. Taking the time up front to get to know the customer and what it is looking for will help the contractor target specific products and services to specific customer audiences.

Encourage Team to Be Successful

The contract team's daily work will influence future sales. If a customer is happy, it will tell others and perhaps they can then become future customers. The contract core, internal support, and subcontractor teams must understand how influential their daily work is to the future success of the contract. The contractor should establish quality control measures early on and stay committed to improving the service levels provided on the contract.

Understand the Contractor's Capabilities, Contract Vehicles, and Pricing Strategies

Finally, it is important during contract start-up for the contract team to understand all the company's capabilities, because the team can never be sure when a customer will want to expand the contract to include additional capabilities. Similarly, the team should stay informed about alternative contract vehicles and pricing strategies that could be applied in the event that the existing contract vehicle does not work (e.g., perhaps a customer project is outside of the scope of the contract).

Facilities, Technology, and Equipment

Several items must be in place as soon as possible after the company is awarded a contract and must be present throughout the life of the contract: facilities, technology, and equipment. Although the specific requirements will vary from contract to contract, this section discusses some of the special considerations that should be given to these topic areas.

The first step, determining the requirements for facilities, technology, and equipment, is accomplished while the contract start-up plan is being developed.

These requirements may be dictated by a number of items, such as:

- Prime contract requirements
- Solution requirements
- Customer preferences
- Teaming relationships
- Company standards

Determine Physical Location of Contractor Site

Depending on the nature of the program work and the number of customer sites involved in the contract, the customer may require the contractor's office location to be either on site, within close proximity to the customer's site, or wherever the contractor chooses to be located. Being located on site fosters a greater team relationship because both customer and contractor are working side-by-side to accomplish the work at hand. However, this approach is not always possible or desirable. For example, the customer's site may be too small to accommodate the contractor's employees, or the team members may need access to their own internal equipment or resources, which they cannot access at the customer site. The next best option is locating the contractor site within close proximity to the customer's site. This way, both customer personnel and contractor personnel can quickly meet to resolve problems or to drop in on each other to work on tasks. The hardest customer relationship to maintain is one in which the customer is located a great distance from the contractor and all face-to-face meetings end up being events that must be planned and orchestrated.

The customer may dictate where a contractor facility must be located in relation to its own facility (e.g., within a 30-minute drive). Similarly, the contractor may have a standard technology platform to which all contracts must adhere. Such requirements should all be included in the contract start-up plan.

Determine How to Secure Facilities, Technology, and Equipment

During contract start-up, the prime contractor must expeditiously locate facilities, technology, and other equipment in order to get the team functional as soon as possible. Some contractors have a temporary site where they keep their existing equipment that they use when a contract begins. They then move the team to a more suitable location several months after contract award. Although this is not an ideal situation, a temporary site prevents prime contractors from having to spend time and resources to secure facilities, technology, and equipment that they may not need if they do not win a contract.

A contractor may not have to procure the facility, technology, *and* equipment. The contractor could lease a facility if the contractor doesn't own one. Or, the customer or subcontractor may allow the prime contractor to share its facilities. Likewise, technology and equipment may be already owned or leased by the prime contractor. Similarly, the customer may provide government furnished property (GFP), or the subcontractor may provide demonstration models of equipment to the prime contractor at no charge.

The prime contractor must consider what the contract core team, internal support teams, subcontractors, and maybe even the customer needs when the contractor develops the facility, technology, and equipment requirements. The contractor should consider staffing projections and the number of pieces of technology or other equipment when determining the size of the facility. For example, if the customer wants a conference room in which to conduct meetings at the contractor location, the contractor will have to ensure that the facility it selects has one. Internal and external requirements must be included in the contract start-up plan.

If the prime contractor must procure the facilities, technology, and equipment, it should conduct a lease-versus-own analysis to determine the most cost-efficient manner in which to obtain the items. The contract team will usually need to work the finance department and senior management to make these decisions.

Secure Facilities, Technology, and Equipment

Once the prime contractor knows what facilities, technology, and equipment it needs and determines the most cost-effective manner in which to obtain them, it is ready to implement the procurement portion of the contract start-up plan. After obtaining financial backing from the company, the contract team procures the necessary items needed to work on the contract.

Understand the Government's Requirements for Government Furnished Property

If the contractor will have any GFP on the contract, it should take special precautions to understand how the government expects the equipment to be obtained, maintained, and returned. If the government's procedures are not adhered to, the government can charge the contractor to replace the item(s).

After Submission Proposals

Even after the team has put together a winning proposal that has resulted in a signed contract, there are still opportunities for the contract team to create proposals. New product additions, changes to the contract, and task-order requests all require the contract team to create proposals for the customer to evaluate. This section reviews how task-order and after-contract award proposals are developed and fulfilled.

Task Orders

Contracts may have a task-order component. Some contracts are dedicated only to task-order work. Task orders are used because the customer, at the time of RFP release, really did not know what specific tasks it needed the contractor to perform. Task orders are a way for the customer to decide "as it goes" what work needs to be done. They also allow the customer to negotiate the labor and resources necessary to perform the work with the contractor when the work is needed.

Task orders may be *firm, fixed price,* which means that the contractor is required to complete the stated amount of work for the price that was mutually agreed upon. Task orders may also be *cost-plus,* in which the contractor is guaranteed of getting its costs paid for, but its profit margin may decline if the work costs more than originally intended. Finally, level-of-effort task orders allow the customer to keep the contractor on retainer by ordering a given number of products for the year. As work is required, the customer asks the contractor. This last approach is similar to keeping the contractor on retainer.

Process for Developing Task Orders

The customer and the contractor typically establish a process similar to the one described in this section when there is a task-order component to the contract or if the entire contract is dedicated to task orders. On a task order-type contract, the labor categories and hourly rates are established during the proposal process and agreed to during contract negotiation. The customer tries to have several contract vehicles or multiple contractors on the same contract vehicle. That way it can run a competition to decide who can do the work in a manner that represents the best value to the customer and, thereby, wins the right to do the work on the task order.

Customer Determines the Need

The first step in the task-order process is for the customer to decide what it needs to have done. The customer submits a statement of work outlining its requirements to the contracting shop.

Customer Conducts a Solicitation

The contract shop then looks for contract vehicles that have task-order components capable of doing the work. The contracting officer (CO) may decide to run a competition among three different contract vehicles, or all the contractors on a multiple award task order contract, or among three different company's GSA schedules. The statement of work is sent to the three offerors, and contractors' task-order proposals are due back by a certain date and time. If the contractors have questions, the answers are provided.

Company Prepares Task-Order Proposal

The company receives the task-order request from the customer, determines the scope of the effort, and determines if subcontractor support is required. As part of its proposal, or a subsequent contract modification, the company negotiates labor rates with various subcontractors. Working with the selected subcontractors, if necessary, the company develops a task-order proposal. The task-order proposal contains the company's technical approach, estimated labor and resources, suggested milestones, terms and conditions, and price, besides any specific requirement the customer has for the proposal.

Customer Receives Task-Order Proposals

On the designated date, the customer receives the task-order proposals and begins its evaluation. The proposals are evaluated from a technical, price, contractual, and management perspective. The customer may decide to award the contract based on original proposals, or it may decide to hold negotiations and a best and final offer. In the end, the company submitting the proposal that represents the best overall value to the customer is awarded the task order. The winning contractor then receives a delivery or task order for the work. (Some customer use the term *delivery order* for all orders; other customers use the term *task order* for labor and *reserve delivery order* for products and services ordered off the contract.)

Company Develops a Plan for Completing the Task-Order Work

In preparing the proposal, and in anticipation of winning the work, the company develops a plan for completing the task order. In the plan, specific individuals are identified, subtasks are determined and assigned, project budgets are developed, outside resources are estimated, other direct charges are considered, and milestones are established. If an internal support team will assist in providing personnel for task orders, the company contacts the team, and the people are scheduled. The company may consult a skills database that has the resumes of all the people who could be potentially used on a task order to locate appropriate resources in the contract core, internal support, and subcontractor organizations.

Contractor Begins the Task-Order Work

The contractor can begin work once it has obtained the people and resources for the contract. Usually, the contractor establishes one or multiple cost centers so that the costs for each task order are segregated and easily managed. The contractor must track all labor and resources used on the task order. The customer usually requires notification when 75 percent of the labor hours have been exhausted on a task order. The contractor completes the task or provides the level of effort necessary for the task and usually submits DD250s (or some other form of acceptance document) on a monthly basis (or whatever time frame is agreed to with the government) to obtain acceptance so that it can invoice the customer and get paid.

Contractor Completes Task-Order Work

The contractor continues on with the task order, submitting DD250s for labor and other direct charges, generating invoices, and receiving payment until the task order is complete. The customer may require a final document, presentation, or other product at the end of the effort. Again, the contractor should obtain acceptance on this document or some form of recognition that the customer has approved the work done on the task order for final contract closeout efforts.

After-Award Proposal Efforts

Reasons for New Proposals

This section discusses some of the reasons why an after-award proposal is required.

Adding new products to the contract As discussed in the earlier chapters, the contractor must deliver the products and services that are stated in the contract baseline. If it delivers anything that is not on the contract baseline, the contractor is in default of the contract and may not be paid for the products delivered or the services rendered. The contract may require the contractor to add new products; for example, the governmental customer may have a technology refreshment clause that basically states that the government expects the contractor to update the technology on the contract when it makes good business sense to do so. Similarly, the contract may include a product substitution clause that gives the contractor the right to substitute products that are no longer manufactured with products that provide equal or greater functionality for the same price as was agreed to in the original contract. Finally, there may be an (value) engineering change clause that encourages the contractor to develop more efficient methods of conducting business; the customer may even share some of the cost savings incurred by using the new method with the contractor. If such clauses exist in the contract, the contractor has the right to submit a new proposal to add new products to the contract.

Contract change If the contractor wishes to make a formal request to change a part of the contract, it must submit a proposal. For example, if the manufacturer changed a model number, the contractor would have to submit a proposal stating that change, the reasons for the change, the benefits to the customer in making the change, and the costs associated with making the change.

Process for Developing a Proposal

The process for developing a proposal includes several steps that occur over a short time—from one to two weeks—or, depending on the proposal's complexity, may take several months to complete.

Establish the contract baseline The customer established the contract baseline by using the price and technical volumes of the customer's proposal. When negotiations were completed between the customer and the contractor, contract line item numbers (CLINs) were established to track each product or service offered on the contract. The contract baseline is usually kept in some automated system that tracks the CLIN, product or service description, quantities, and out year prices. In addition, supplier information, such as subcontractor name, subcontract number, model number, description, out year prices, special terms and conditions, mailing address, and point of contact, for that particular CLIN is maintained in the automated system for when the customer needs to develop purchase orders.

The contract baseline is important for several reasons:

- It represents what the contractor is contractually obligated to provide throughout the life of the contract.

- It represents what the customer may order (i.e., if an item is not in the contract baseline, the customer cannot order it).

- It represents what the contractor must provide in filling a delivery order from the customer. If the contractor cannot deliver the exact make and model number stated in the contract baseline, it must receive a waiver or deviation from the customer subject to the its approval. (Waivers and deviations are explained in Chapter 1.)

- It provides a central repository of ordering information for the contract by stating what the customer can buy and where the contractor intends to purchase the items necessary to fill the order. It usually includes not only how products were offered to the customer but also how subcontractors offered their products to the prime contractor. This information is vital in resolving contractual and subcontractual issues throughout the life of the contract.

- It can automate many of the routine purchasing functions.

Understand the contract baseline   Before the contractor embarks on proposing new products or services, it must understand what is in the contract baseline. The contractor must understand what the products and services are used for and how to customize a system for its customer's environment using the components from the contract. Only after a thorough understanding of what is available in the contract baseline can a contractor understand new requirements or useful additions to the baseline.

Needs assessment   Once the contractor understands the contract baseline, it can look for better and more efficient ways to meet existing or new requirements. The contractor can add new products or services to the contract baseline using the proposal process. The first step in developing a proposal is to determine the customer's need. This needs assessment can occur through a variety of channels: user meetings, problem calls to the help desk, training initiatives, one-on-one customer meetings, installations, program reviews, or ideas from subcontractors.

Conduct technical research   Once the contractor determines the need, it then conducts technical research about the requirement. How can that the requirement be addressed? Are additional products needed to meet the requirement? The contractor conducts some initial research by reviewing industry periodicals and talking to subcontractors and other subject matter experts about the problem and potential solutions.

Develop a white paper to determine customer interest   Usually at this point, a contractor has asked the customer whether it has an interest in the contractor pursuing this effort. If the customer is remotely interested in the topic at hand, it will typically ask the contractor to prepare a position paper outlining the problem and potential solutions. It may also ask the contractor to make a recommendation on the method to pursue. If the customer is not interested in the contractor developing a solution to a perceived problem area, the contractor ceases its efforts on the problem. If the customer is interested, the rest of the process commences. In such cases, the customer will probably direct the contractor as to the course it would like the contractor to take. For example, should the product be leased or purchased? Which vendors should be considered? What technical specifications should be used to evaluate the technical capabilities? What source selection information should be used to determine a winner? How should the solution be proposed? These are all questions that the contractor would like its government customer to answer.

Gather information   The contractor collects information a second time; this time to actually run a procurement. Additional vendor meetings are held, subject matter experts are consulted, alternative approaches are considered, and the customer's suggestions are reviewed. This data gathering is usually done before a proposal kickoff meeting so that there are facts to review at the meeting.

Conduct kickoff   The next pivotal step in the proposal process is to conduct a proposal kickoff meeting. Based on the data that has already been collected, the team determines if the source for the product or service is internal or external and establishes the schedule for the procurement.

If the product will be bid using internal resources, then no procurement needs to be conducted. Instead, the team needs to make internal assessments from the technical, engineering, manufacturing, business, management, and contractual perspectives before it can submit a proposal to the customer.

If the product will be bid using external sources, then the team must conduct a procurement. In order to conduct a procurement, the team must complete the following steps:

1. *Identify potential sources*—The first step that the team must complete is to identify potential sources for the product being procured. The company can find sources through many different channels: trade booth exhibits, purchasing files, industry magazines, sales contacts, subcontractor reference, etc. Once the companies that make the product are identified, the team should contact each to determine if it is interested in bidding on the new piece of business. The goal for the company is to find at least three companies willing to bid on the procurement so that the company can demonstrate that it held a competition.

2. *Develop RFP*—The next step is for the team to develop the RFP document. The RFP typically contains:
   - A cover letter explaining the procurement
   - Technical specifications
   - Pricing instructions
   - Proposal preparation instructions
   - Terms and conditions under which the product must be proposed
   - Representations and certifications
   - Evaluation criteria

3. *Develop source selection plan*—The contract team must then develop a source selection plan to use to determine the procurement winner. Based on the customer's requirements, the source selection plan assigns points for each facet of the solution based on the degree of importance to the customer. Typically, the plan has points assigned for the management, technical, contractual, and business solutions proposed.

4. *Conduct solicitation*—The team sends the RFPs to the companies interested in bidding on the procurement. The companies are notified of the date that questions must be submitted and the date that proposals are due. If any company asks a question, the contract team must develop the answer and send it out to all bidders. All proposals must be received by the date and time stated; otherwise, they are deemed noncompliant.

5. *Evaluate the proposals*—Next, the team evaluates the proposals received from the companies. The evaluations are based on the weight given to each evaluation criterion in the source selection plan. Representatives from the company from each of the key functional areas (e.g., technical, management, business, and contracts) evaluate the sections of proposals based on the source selection plan.

6. *Conduct strategy session*—The team then convenes a strategy session. Each evaluator reports his or her findings for each proposal. Points are tallied based on the scores given in the management, contractual, technical, and business assessments. At this meeting, the apparent winner is determined. The term *apparent* is used because, until a final agreement has been reached between the prime contractor and the potential subcontractor, the company cannot be deemed the winner. If there are problems during the negotiations, then that subcontractor could bow out and the number two or number three company could actually win the procurement.

   Also during this strategy session, the team determines how it intends to propose the new product or service to the customer. The team decides how it will be propose the new product to the customer, under what terms and conditions it will be proposed, what maintenance or support will be offered with the product, and how it will be priced.

7. *Negotiate with the supplier*—Before the team submits a proposal to the customer, it is best for the prime contractor to complete negotiations with the supplier and either develop a new subcontract or modify an existing subcontract with that supplier. This protects both the customer and the prime contractor by documenting the agreement that describes how the products are being offered and priced to the prime contractor.

8. *Develop the proposal to the customer*—The next step is for the team to develop a proposal to the customer outlining its offer. Typically, a proposal contains:

- A cover letter outlining the offer
- A proposal overview that contains a description of the existing customer situation, the product or service being offered, a description of how the new product or service will fit in the existing customer environment, and the features and benefits of the solution
- A technical description of the products or services
- Prices and quantities for the product through the end of the contract
- The terms and conditions under which the product or service is offered
- Any relevant contract modification data
- Any relevant technical literature
- The life cycle costs of the old versus the new solution

9. *Negotiate with the customer*—After the customer reviews the prime contractor's proposal, it will do one of three things: (1) Decide that it has the interest and funding to implement the solution and will enter into negotiations with the contractor, (2) decide that it does not have enough information to make a decision and go back to the contractor for additional detail, or (3) decide that it does not have the funding or interest in the solution change and will inform the contractor to cease all efforts.

   Keep in mind that the contract states whether after-award proposal efforts are paid for by the contractor or by the customer. It is in both parties' best interest to determine as early as possible in the process whether there is funding and interest in the project so that money spent on resources is not wasted on either side.

10. *Receive the contract modification from the customer*—After negotiations have been completed, the customer will send a draft contract modification to the contractor for review. The modification usually contains the CLINs, descriptions, quantities, and out-year prices on the prime contract that are deleted as a result of this modification. The modification also contains the CLINs, descriptions, quantities, and out-year prices for the new products added as a result of the modification. The technical proposal, terms and conditions, and other relevant parts of the contractor's proposal are incorporated as well. The contractor

will make any appropriate changes to the document and return it to the customer. If the customer agrees with the contractor's changes, it will sign the modification and reissue it to the contractor. Once the contractor signs the modification, it is formally part of the prime contract.

The contractor then inputs data from the contract modification into the system that tracks the contract baseline. Old CLINs are deleted and information about the new CLINs is added. Not only are the new CLINs, description, quantities, and out-year prices maintained in the system, but is should also keep track of supplier information for that particular CLIN, such as subcontractor name, subcontract number, model number, description, out-year prices, special terms and conditions, mailing address, point of contact, and other relevant information for when purchase orders need to be developed.

11. *Receive the delivery order for the new item from the customer*—The step that the contractor is waiting for is when it actually receives a delivery order from the customer for the new product or service. When the contractor receives the delivery order, it checks the contract baseline to review the delivery order for accuracy and to ensure the exact CLIN, description, and price are stated on the delivery order and that the quantity is still available on the contract. If the delivery order is for products previously added and there were no remaining quantities available for purchase on the contract, the contractor could decide whether it wants to sell additional quantities for the same price. If so, the contractor would have to submit a proposal to add additional quantities to the contract. Once the customer accepts the proposal and issues a modification, the contractor can sell the government the products requested. If the contractor decides that it can no longer offer the products for the stated price, it must conduct a solicitation to allow vendors to compete for the new quantities to be added to the contract. The prime contractor would then repeat the steps listed earlier for developing a solicitation and a proposal to the government.

12. *Generate purchase orders*—Once the contractor has a valid delivery order, it uses its automated system to generate purchase orders for the products listed on the delivery order to its subcontractors. The prime contractor must deliver products and services in accordance with the contract, for example, if the contract states that the contractor has 30 to 90 days from the date on the delivery order to deliver the products and services,

the contractor must abide by that time frame. If the contractor fails to deliver the goods and services within the designated period of time, the contractor usually must pay liquidated damages. *Liquidated damages* are designed to compensate the customer for the loss of productivity incurred when the contractor fails to complete a contract task. Because it is difficult to ascertain the exact amount of money the customer loses when a contractor fails to complete any given task, the customer and contractor agree during contract negotiations on a set amount (e.g., the contractor will pay the customer $500 per day when the contractor is late with a delivery or if its system fails to perform). What usually happens is that the contractor doesn't actually write the customer a check, but rather deducts the amount equal to any liquidated damage settlements from the total invoice for that period. Knowing this, the prime contractor negotiates a lesser period of time with the subcontractors for them to deliver products and services. This is because the prime contractor assumes it will take a few days on its part to log the delivery order, review it for accuracy, and generate the purchase order.

The purchase orders going to the vendors contain the following information: prime contractor name, address, point of contact, product model number, description, pre-negotiated price, quantity, customer name, address, special delivery instructions, subcontract number, special terms and conditions, required due date, and maintenance requirements. The system is typically set up so that a CLIN on a delivery order triggers purchase orders to be sent to all vendors supplying parts for the CLIN. The prime contractor negotiates with the subcontractors ahead of time if special packaging or shipment to a staging area is required.

13. *Subcontractor delivers product or services and receives payment*— The subcontractor delivers the products or services by the requested due date. Either the prime contractor accepts them at its facility or they are accepted as part of an overall shipment directly to the customer. Once acceptance is obtained on the products or services or whatever event has been agreed upon in the subcontract, the subcontractor may invoice the prime contractor for products delivered or services rendered. The prime contractor acknowledges the receipt of the goods and services within its own company's systems, approves the subcontractor's invoice for payment, and generates a check either manually or through electronic funds transfer to the subcontractor.

14. *Prime contractor tracks the revenue and expense*—The prime contractor then tracks the revenue and expense associated with the
delivery order in its financial records. This information feeds
into both the contract's and company's financial management
systems.

Contract Start-Up

Understand What Is on the Contract

As was discussed earlier, it is important that the program team
understand what is currently in the contract baseline. By understanding the baseline, the contractor can formulate solutions to
customer's problems with existing components.

Understand the Items on the Contract That the Contractor Would Like to Change

There is inevitably some items on the contract that the contractor
wishes to change because the company took a great deal of risk on
these items in the pricing strategy. Pricing items low to win the
business is a risky proposition because the customer has the final say
as to whether products or services can be changed after it awards the
contract. The contractor could be forced to live with the prices in the
proposal for the duration of the contract. The contractor's low prices
could cause the customer to use the contract to support all of its
requirements for that product, and the company could even be forced
out of business if its pricing is too aggressive. The contractor must
know which items on the contract represent that kind of risk. The
contractor should consider ways to propose new products with new
pricing to mitigate the risk. One way is finding a more efficient
alternative. Or, the contractor could scale down the marketing efforts
associated with the riskier products. Being aware of the problem
areas helps the contractor determine ways to mitigate the risk.

Learn About the Customers and Their Requirements

Contract start-up is the time to get to know the customers—the ones
that will be buying products and the ones that will be buying task-
order services. The contractor should make an effort immediately
after contract award to visit each of the customers, or at least the
main customers, to demonstrate the products and services available,
to suggest task-order projects, or to recommend new technologies for
the customer's environment. This exploration time will give the

contractor a good understanding of who the customers are and what their requirements are for now and for the future. This information helps the contractor with ideas of future proposal suggestions. It also allows the contractor team to know what skills will be in demand so that it can begin locating and training the required personnel.

Determine How Task-Order Work Will Be Divided among the Subcontractors

Another effort that the contractor should do before contract award or during contract start-up is to determine how task-order work will be divided among the subcontractors. Each subcontractor is typically brought on the team to handle some specialized work so that when the prime contractor receives a task order, the contractor immediately knows where to get the support needed. Selecting a subcontractor when multiple subcontractors have expertise in the area requested in the task order is a more difficult situation. The prime contractor needs to decide which subcontractor is selected to perform the work based on past experience, lowest price, availability, or some other criteria. The contractor should decide this before it receives a task order so that the subcontractors know when work will be awarded to them. The last thing a prime contractor needs is for subcontractors to lodge protests to the prime contractor or to the customer for work being accomplished under the contract.

Prime Contractor Considerations

Decide How Involved It Wants Its Subcontractors

At each stage of the procurement process, a prime contractor must determine how involved it wants its subcontractors to be with the program. The prime contractor-subcontractor relationship may vary depending on how well the two companies get along, the degree of trust that has developed between the two companies, and the degree of comfort that the customer has with the subcontractor.

Clearly Define Subcontractors' Relationships with the Customer

The prime contractor must decide how involved it wants its subcontractor to be with its customer. This decision has logistic, contractual and business implications. From a logistic point of view, the customer should have a single point of contact. That single point of contact should be one in the prime contractor's organization. When other people have real or perceived authority to obligate the prime contractor, problems occur. From a contractual point of view, there is privity of contract between the prime contractor and the customer not between the customer and the subcontractor. Therefore, it is important that the two parties involved in the contract (the prime contractor and the customer) work to resolve any issue between them. Finally, from a business perspective, a subcontractor could get so involved with the customer that the customer decides to stop working with the prime contractor and contract directly with the subcontractor. In this case, the prime contractor loses the business all together.

Educate Subcontractors on Expectations and Manage Subcontractor Performance

The prime contractor must educate subcontractors on how it should perform its work or deliver products on the contract. If the products or services provided by the subcontractor are not compliant, the prime contractor needs to inform the subcontractor. The subcontractor then needs to take the necessary steps to rectify the situation. Problems can occur when the prime contractor does not educate the subcontractor, or does not state its expectations, or fails to inform the subcontractor of substandard performance. Problems result because the subcontractor believes that everything is fine with its service performance or product delivery, and its substandard level of service becomes the norm. Meanwhile, the prime contractor, and possibly the customer, gets more and more annoyed at the level of service and may initiate contractual remedies to fix the problem. If the problem should escalate to the litigation phase, the subcontractor may fall back on precedence: it delivered the same product or service that it has always delivered and it was deemed acceptable and now it is not.

Beware of the Double-Edged Sword

As was mentioned earlier, the key to contract start-up is to quickly get the contract team functional so that it can meet the customer's requirements and establish a good relationship with the customer. However, the contractor has to know the contract requirements and understand when it is doing tasks that are above and beyond the contract. The contractor must provide only what is required on the contract, because in its zeal for doing an excellent job for its customer, the contractor may take on additional tasks that the contract does not require. This is not to say that the contractor shouldn't try to accommodate any government customer's onetime requests for additional support. Providing extra services could strengthen the customer-contractor relationship, however, if the customer expects the contractor to fulfill all of the customer's onetime requests, the contractor may take on too many extra tasks and find that it may need additional staff or resources to accommodate all the contract requirements and all of the extra tasks. Providing extra resources for the additional tasks causes the contractor to lose money and may require the contractor to ask the customer for additional funds. If the customer does not want to ask for additional funds, it could discuss with the customer scaling back the levels of support to only those outlined in the contract. Either of these situations could strain the customer-contractor partnership. So, although the contractor should do what is necessary to establish a good customer relationship, it should not take on additional tasks until after careful evaluation of existing contract resources.

Subcontract Changes Due to Prime Contract Negotiations

The prime contractor may need to make certain concessions during contract negotiations that will affect the subcontracts that it has already negotiated or is in the process of negotiating. The prime contractor must be careful about the contract concessions it accepts or makes because they could affect the prices it received from the subcontractors (and subsequently built its own prices upon). The best thing for a prime contractor to do is to verify how the concessions will affect the subcontracts and decide whether it or the subcontractors can cover the changes before the prime contractor commits to the changes with the customer.

Subcontractor Considerations

Decide How Much It Wants to Provide

During contract start-up, the subcontractor is busy trying to get a new contract established with a prime contractor. Before the subcontractor finalizes the subcontract, it must decide how much it wants to support the prime contractor in order to grow the contract versus how much that support will cost. For example, the prime contractor may need marketing support from the subcontractor. That support could take the form of:

- Providing product literature
- Providing product demonstrations
- Conducting program overviews at customer locations
- Marketing the contract as part of other sales calls
- Conducting specific marketing calls to support this contract
- Developing position papers on customer issues
- Providing CD-ROM catalogs
- Advertising
- Hosting joint trade booths at industry conferences

The term *marketing support* can mean a lot of things. Some of the items that are considered marketing support can be accomplished with minimal cost; others require a great deal of labor, time, and expense in order to accomplish. The subcontractor must decide what level of support it wishes to provide the prime contractor to make these types of things happen. That decision will be based on:

- Cost of the resources required to accomplish the task
- Current revenue stream of the contract
- Current revenue stream of other contracts
- Availability of resources
- Contractual obligations

Another key component is the profit margins on the subcontract. If the subcontractor is getting low margins on one subcontract and high margins on another subcontract, it would probably put its resources into marketing the other contract because the potential payoff is higher.

Second-Hand Information

An initial problem that occurs on many new subcontractor-prime contractor relationships is second hand information. The prime contractor is the conduit of information from the customer to the subcontractor. In that capacity, the prime contractor must ensure that it stays focused on satisfying the customer and provides the subcontractor with enough direction so that the subcontractor can help the prime contractor satisfy the customer. Unfortunately, communication is not typically as great as it needs to be, and the prime contractor tends to not want the subcontractor in on planning meetings with the customer because it wants to establish itself as the single point of contact. Consequently, some things do not get the care and attention that they need in the beginning so subcontractors may be asked to perform on tasks that were not clearly defined.

Government Considerations

Redacted Contract

The government may get a request through the Freedom of Information Act (FOIA) soon after it awards a contract for information pertaining to the award. Therefore, the government usually asks the contractor to submit a redacted contract, or a copy of the final contract that the contractor has gone through and marked out any proprietary information. By marking the contract, the contractor can protect data it believes is sensitive, and the government can promptly respond to any FOIA requests made. The prime contractor needs to discuss any proprietary subcontractor data with the subcontractor before releasing the subcontract to the government.

Additional Requirements

When working with a governmental customer, the prime contractor may have additional requirements imposed on it, which it may flow down to the subcontractor. For example, the government may conduct pre-award audits, site surveys, or inspections to ensure that the prime contractor and the subcontractor are performing according to contract. Because of the "long arm" of the government customer, it is allowed by regulation to impose additional contractual requirements on the companies that it does business with.

Interface Requirements

The government is moving toward a much more integrated contractor community because it believes that when contractors work with rather than against each other, the government stands to gain. As such, the government may direct the prime contractor to work with certain companies on projects or require subcontractors to share information with other companies that they normally wouldn't be inclined to do so. These interface requirements are all part of the government's efforts to streamline procurements and lower acquisition costs.

Audits

Government Authority

The government conducts audits because it must ensure the contractor complies with all federal regulations. Compliance is required before contract award, during contract performance, and after contract shutdown. The government authorizes regulatory agencies, such as the Defense Contract Audit Agency (DCAA), the Defense Plant Representative Office (DPRO), the Defense Contract Management Office (DCMO), the Inspector General (IG), and the Government Accounting Office (GAO), as well as the contracting officer (CO) or the CO's representative (COR), to conduct audits. The regulations that govern audits are found in the Federal Acquisition Regulation (FAR), the Defense Federal Acquisition Regulation (DFAR), and any other agency-specific regulation, particularly the sections dealing with cost accounting standards. In addition, the contract may stipulate other audits that can be conducted throughout the life of the contract.

Expected Contractor Response

The contractor is expected to understand what type of audit is being required, work with the government to determine the types of information necessary before the audit, host the government auditors when they come on site, provide all the requested information, and implement the recommendations made by the auditors during the audit. If the contractor fails to provide all requested information or alters the information, the act is considered lying to the federal government and calls for criminal prosecution.

Specifically, the contractor may be called upon to:

- Demonstrate an accurate audit trail detailing cost build up of the prices in the proposal.
- Provide documentation for each subcontractor price.
- Demonstrate that its employees are filling out time cards accurately.
- Prove that the expenses used to determine overhead and G&A rates are accurate.
- Demonstrate that the company has the financial, physical, and personnel resources to carry out the requirements of a contract.

- Demonstrate that the company either conducted or could prove exemption from competitive procurements in selecting sub-contractors.

- Demonstrate that the company followed its own purchasing procedures.

Types of Audits

There are several different types of audits that the government can conduct. The more frequently occurring audits are discussed in this chapter and include unallowable costs audits, contractor purchasing system reviews, time card audits, and final payment audits.

Unallowable Cost Audit

The government conducts an unallowable cost audit to ensure that the contractor is only charging the government for costs that are allowed under the contract and federal regulations. An *unallowable cost* is any cost which, under the provisions of any pertinent law, regulation, or contract, cannot be included in prices, cost reimbursements, or settlements under a government contract to which it is allocable (FAR 31.001). The government uses three different tests when it conducts an unallowable cost audit: whether the cost is allowable, reasonable, and allocable.

The term *allowable* means (1) a cost that is not specifically unallowable by regulation (e.g., bad debts, contributions, cost of alcohol, entertainment, fines, penalties, idle facilities, interest, lobbying costs, and losses on other contracts), (2) a cost that is not specifically unallowable by contract (e.g., on some contracts the cost of doing proposals for add-on business is allowed and on other contracts it is not), and (3) finally, a cost that has limited allowability (e.g., bid and proposal, independent research and development, travel, public relations, training, relocation, and precontract costs).

The government determines if a cost is reasonable if, in its nature or amount, it does not exceed that which a prudent person would incur in the conduct of competitive business.

A cost is *allocable* if it is chargeable to one or more cost objectives on the basis of relative benefits received. This means that if a company conducts commercial and government contracts, it must allocate the overhead costs associated with performing the work in equal proportion to the business base. So if the business base has 60 percent government business and 40 percent commercial business, the government would expect to be allocated 60 percent of the overhead costs in the rate structure.

Contractor Purchasing System Review (CPSR)

The purpose of a CPSR is to ensure that when the contractor purchases products and services on behalf of the government, that the contractor spends the government funds appropriately, adheres to government purchasing regulations, and follows corporate purchasing procedures. CPSRs are conducted at least every three years, and if the contractor passes, the contractor does not have to get administrative contracting officer (ACO) approval to purchase items on behalf of the government. All direct purchases made during an audit period are subject to review.

When the government auditor conducts a CPSR, he or she reviews the following information:

- Purchase request
- Solicitation
- Government supplier letter
- Representations and certifications
- Subcontracting plan
- Proposal
- Evaluation/source selection
- Nonselection of SB/SDB
- Cost or pricing data exemption
- Cost or pricing analysis
- EEO clearance for subcontractors
- Flow-down clauses
- Negotiation memorandum
- Other requirements

Time-Card Audits

The government is also concerned about how accurately people who work on government contracts fill out their time cards because labor is one of the largest expenses on a contract. Usually, contractors assign billable and nonbillable cost centers to the employees working on a government contract. Employees are then required to fill in their time cards with the appropriate number of hours and the appropriate cost center for the time they worked each day. When employees are working directly on the contract, they charge their time to a billable cost center; when they are completing professional development training or attending a company-sponsored event, they charge their time to a nonbillable cost center. In addition, companies develop detailed operating guides for directing employees on what cost center to use for each government contract and educating them on how to properly complete a time card.

The government is concerned about both unintentional errors, such as using the wrong pay codes on a time card, as well as intentional errors, such as recording direct labor to the wrong contract or to a nonbillable account. As such, many contractors will assign someone to conduct internal reviews of time-card procedures and the accuracy of employees' time cards to ensure that the company passes a government audit should one be conducted. The government can, for example, come to a contractor location to ensure employees are actually at work performing the assigned jobs and properly recording their time.

Labor Audits

The government also audits the contractor's labor, G&A, and overhead rates to ensure that cost build ups are accurate. These reviews are typically conducted by the DCAA when the contractor submits a disclosure statement. The government may also review the labor proposed on a contract to ensure that the people being bid have adequate skills to perform the work. The government is mainly interested in the contractor's internal control systems, management policies, accuracy and reasonableness of cost representations, adequacy and reliability of records, financial capability, compliance with cost accounting standards clause (FAR 52.230–1) for noncommercial items, and compliance with the defective pricing clause (FAR 52.215–22).

Final Payment Audit

The prime contractor may be entitled to a final payment for products delivered and services rendered. Because overhead and G&A rates that are used in any given year are *provisional*, meaning the contractor has to wait until the end of the year after all expenses have been calculated to determine what the true rates are for the year, the government reserves the right to audit all contract files and rate build ups up to seven years after the close of the contract before it makes final payment to the contractor. This audit requires that all subcontracts be closed to ensure that the subcontractors will not come back to the prime contractor for remuneration. It also requires that the prime contract be closed to ensure that the prime contractor will not come back to the government for remuneration.

Overall Process for Audit Preparation

The CO determines the need for an audit on a particular contractor or potential contractor. The CO requests the appropriate audit agency and informs it of the company and the reason for audit. The government audit agency or CO notifies the contractor that an audit needs to be conducted. A letter is sent stating the type of audit, the documentation required, the date of the audit, and any personnel who needs to be made available during the audit. The government may ask for documentation and summary information before the audit. Then the contractor collects all the necessary information and prepares it for the government audit. The key is to provide exactly what the government is asking for in an easy-to-use format. The contractor hosts the government auditor and reviews the information with the auditor. The auditor may ask additional questions or may take all the documents back to his or her office for a more in-depth review. If requested, the contractor provides any additional information the auditor needs to make an evaluation. At the conclusion of the audit, the auditor may choose to review preliminary results with company representatives. The government audit agency completes its audit and recommendation and informs the contracting officer of the results. The contracting officer shares this information with the contractor. If questions about the contractor's ability to perform the work arise, the government may ask for additional information as part of the audit.

Contractor Techniques for Audit Preparation

Audits can either be initiated for a single contract (e.g., a pre-award survey) or across multiple contracts (e.g., a CPSR). Although audit requirements vary, there are several techniques that can assist the contractor in preparing for a government audit.

Determine the Contract Type for Each Contract

The government has a shrinking auditing capability. The demand keeps rising because more and more contracts are being let, yet government dollars supporting audit agencies are declining. Therefore, the government must determine the areas that present the most risk and focus on correcting any problems in those areas. For example, fixed-priced contracts tend to be more risky for the contractor because the contractor will get the agreed-upon amount of money for the work done regardless of whether it costs more or less to actually complete the work. So, typically, minimal investment is made by the government in auditing downtime contracts. In a cost-plus contract, however, the government is at a greater risk because the contractor will always get its expenses paid. So the government will spend money auditing those types of contracts because the government is more vulnerable.

Understand Which FAR Clauses Are Applied to the Contract

In order to know what the government expects of the contractor, the contractor must pay particular attention to which FAR clauses are applied to its contract. The FAR clauses govern the contract. They are incorporated into the contract by title only; however, they are read in totality into the contract. The cost accounting standards are particularly useful in preparing for a government audit because the contractor must have a DCAA-approved cost accounting system to work on government business. The DCAA will work with new businesses to help them ensure that their cost accounting system is compliant.

Understand How Contracts Are Priced

The team must understand how the solution is priced, where risk was taken, what assumptions were made, and how estimates were developed. The company should be able to answer these questions for all the contracts it has been or may be awarded. The team must understand how the company is disclosed to the DCAA because sometimes companies have rates for multiple divisions disclosed to the DCAA. The team must use the correct overhead and labor rates.

Understand What the Auditor Wants to See When He or She Conducts an Audit

No matter what type of audit the government conducts, the contractor must understand up front what the government is coming in to audit. The contractor should also talk with the auditor before his or her arrival to understand exactly what pieces of information he or she is looking for. Some contractors will give the auditor the opportunity to "look at everything," and the auditor ends up finding problems in other areas that were not even intended in the original audit. Once the contractor knows the type of audit and what the auditor wants to see, it should make an effort to organize the data in a way that the auditor can quickly get through it. This will allow the auditor to do his or her job quickly and easily. Also, by organizing the information, the company can see what pieces of data it is missing before the auditor sees it, and the company can rectify the situation (if possible).

Ensure Team Understands the Solicitation Process for CPSR

To pass a CPSR audit, the team must know how to conduct solicitations in accordance with corporate purchasing guidelines. The team must document its procurement steps and analysis. It is best to document these procurement steps as they occur because if much time elapses, people forget why they selected one subcontractor over another. During proposal efforts and contract performance, technical, management, contracts, and business people all conduct solicitations. Because this is not their normal job (usually reserved for purchasing agents), team members need to understand how to structure, run, and evaluate procurements.

Because many competitions are run during the time of proposal preparation, the team should ensure that the files are in order as they are completed, or as soon as the contract is awarded. This is because the contractor does not know when the government is likely to show up to conduct a CPSR. As soon as purchases are made under the new contract, it is eligible to be part of the next CPSR. So a new contract with incomplete competition files could jeopardize the entire company by failing a CPSR. If the company fails its CPSR, every government contract could be required to obtain ACO approval before purchasing any products and supplies for a government customer.

Ensure Team Collects Proper Cost Documentation

Again, collecting cost documentation occurs primarily during proposal preparation and periodically throughout contract performance. Getting vendor quotes in writing and documenting basis of estimates, bills of material, the application of pricing strategies, assumptions, cost and price analyses, life cycle impact cost analyses (after contract award), and commercial, GSA, or other price comparison lists are all examples of cost documentation that the team needs to retain.

Prepare for the Pre-Award Survey

The team needs to collect all the data that the government requests in the pre-award survey letter. This audit is basically an information audit and the data necessary can quickly be pulled together. If everything is organized in an easy-to-understand format, the auditors oftentimes will just stop by to pick up the prepared information and take a quick site tour. Then they will evaluate the data back at their offices and call the contractor if there are any follow-up questions.

Contract Start-Up Audit Issues

Ensure audit information is collected from the beginning of a contract The information that is needed within the company to pass an audit includes:

- Copies of any RFPs on which the company is bidding
- Copies of any proposals the company has submitted
- Copies of any contracts the company has won
- Cost detail for any submitted proposal
- Cost estimating forms completed on any labor contracts or proposals
- Pricing strategies and justification used on any proposal
- Historical data maintained on any existing contract
- Vendor quotes for any proposal submitted either pre-award or post-award
- Contractor's financial history and other data required for a pre-award survey
- Contractor's cost accounting system to gain DCAA approval
- Corporate disclosure statement to the DCAA
- Corporate bid rates approved by the DCAA, which may change periodically so copies of all rates should be kept
- Basis of estimate for proposed labor rates, hours, subcontracts, and materials costs
- Corporate financial statements stating information about the contracts
- Contractor purchasing procedures and subcontractor selection information

Develop tools to support the auditing effort There are several tools that are useful for audit preparation, such as an established purchasing system that will pass CPSR and that includes standard forms and procedures to make vendor selection documentation easier and helps to streamline the purchasing effort. Financial systems that adequately capture, report, and allocate costs for government contracts are necessary both at a company level and for individual contract reporting. Likewise, a labor reporting system that can help track and manage labor hours used on contracts is important so that the correct cost centers are charged for hours worked on a contract.

Establish cost centers to track allowable and unallowable costs The team needs to establish a cost center structure, or a series of accounts to which time and costs can be charged. Cost centers can be specific to a project, team, individual, or functional area. If the team is using a work breakdown structure approach to contract management, it makes sense to tie the cost centers to the work breakdown structure. What drives the cost center structure is how closely the management team, contract, and customer require the expenses to be tracked. Ideally, the team wants these cost centers established right from the start so that everyone can use them when they work on the contract. Otherwise, there is a significant amount of effort to change any incorrect cost centers to the correct ones.

Ensure team members understand how to fill out time cards appropriately Tied closely to establishing cost centers is educating all the team members on how to fill out time cards correctly and what cost centers to use to charge their time and other expenses. People need to understand how to code regular work and sick, vacation, holiday, and administrative time. They need to understand that time cards need to be completed on a daily basis and that it is a criminal offense to lie on a time card. They need to understand how to receive and submit time cards so that someone can key the hours worked into the labor tracking system so that invoices can be generated to the government customer.

Audit Outcomes

There are four potential outcomes of an audit:

1. The contractor passes the audit and no further action is required. This means that the government allows the contractor to pursue other federal business and to receive payment for products delivered and services rendered.

2. The contractor could partially pass the audit and receive a provisional approval with the stipulation that certain recommendations must be implemented before a full approval can be given. In this situation, the government auditor may schedule

another interim audit to come in and review the progress that has been made toward implementing the recommendations.

3. The auditor may need additional information or a follow-up audit to determine whether the contractor passes or fails. If this happens, the contractor and the government auditor will need to repeat all the steps outlined above.

4. The contractor is deemed unacceptable and any of the following penalties can be imposed, depending upon the severity of the situation: negative media coverage, stop payment action, fines and interest, criminal prosecution, suspension from government business, debarment from government business, disapproval of purchasing system, notification of all present and prospective customers of unapproved rating, no further awards or follow-on business recommendations, or a requirement for administrative contracting officer approval before any purchases are made.

7 CONTRACT PERFORMANCE

Contract-Operations Plan

The duration for contract performance is several months after contract award through six months before contract shutdown. The basis for contract performance is the contract-operations plan. The team developing the contract-operations plan should outline how the contract will operate on a daily basis. The team should use the contract start-up plan as a starting point for creating the contract-operations plan. The start-up plan identifies the processes, procedures, and tasks that are required to establish the account. When the contract start-up plan was developed, there were still many unknowns about the optimum way for the contract to operate. The contract-operations plan, which is developed several months after the contract is initiated, allows the team members sufficient time to discover the best ways to accomplish the tasks required by the contract.

The generic planning approach described in Chapter 2 can be used to develop a contract-operations plan.

Contract Performance Characteristics

During contract performance there is usually a stable operating environment. Many of the problem areas have been worked out; now it is a matter of fine tuning each of the areas. In developing a contract-operations plan, the team should consider the following issues:

- The prime contract is established and modified any time changes are made to it.

- Contract operations, marketing, customer, and financial plans are periodically reviewed and updated; other plans, such as those for task orders or new product proposals, are conducted repeatedly throughout contract performance as new task orders or proposals are required.

- The contract-operations plan should delineate the functions the contract requires and include a description of who will provide support and how the support will be provided. Support can come from the contract core team, internal corporate support organizations, and subcontractors. Personnel descriptions should be consistent with individual development plans for contract team members, internal memorandums of understanding or service level agreements on relationships with internal support organizations, and teaming agreements and subcontracts.

- A good customer relationship can be established through quality contractor performance; if the contractor does not have a solid track record of success, then an environment of mistrust may permeate every business transaction.

- Core team members are efficient in their jobs and may make suggestions on how to streamline efforts. If the contract is long term, original team members may want to move into other positions, either on or off the contract. The team will then need to replace the team members and train new members on their positions on the contract.

- Internal support groups will also have personnel turnover, so the contractor should have service level agreements established so it can continue to get the level of support necessary to run the contract.

- Subcontracts are established and modified as changes are made to them. The prime contractor and subcontractor will want to stay on top of any outstanding business, technical, or contractual issues as they occur.

- Training for original team members is focused on refining skills, preparing the members for new levels of responsibility, and cross-training. Training is conducted by each part of the organization: customer, core team members, internal support members, and subcontractors.

- Formal communication channels are clearly established (e.g., the team knows how to disseminate information using team meetings, program reviews, or internal newsletters).

- Procedures are established, refined, and act as a guidebook for new people on the contract. The degree of diligence in adhering to procedures allows for a smoother contract closeout.

- Contract performance requires diligent tracking of costs so that problem areas are quickly discovered and resolved.

- Sales stem from past performance, established customer relationships, add-on work, branching out to new customers, and subcontractor sales.

- Data requirements are known and automated tools are established to easily capture the information. Usually, a data control person ensures that information is accurate and reliable. The contract-operations plan describes the types of data necessary for the execution and management of the contract.

- A process for developing deliverables is established and automated tools are used to obtain the information.

- There are probably adequate facilities, technology, and equipment.

- Audits on government contracts will occur periodically. If the team ensures contract work, time cards, and subcontract files are completed accurately and documented appropriately, the company will not need to be as concerned about audits.

- Program changes occur periodically—more frequently in some industries, such as information technology—so the contractor needs to coordinate between the program shop (with the funding) and the contract shop (with the authority) to make program changes.

- The contractor has to mitigate risks taken during proposal development; however, the company still expects a profit, the customer still expects satisfaction, and people may be required to do more with less.

Process

Manage the Prime Contract

Live by the Contract

The *prime contract* is the document that governs performance on the contract. The contractor needs to ensure that it provides products and services in accordance with the contract. If the contractor delivers non-compliant products or performs in a manner not stipulated in the prime contract, the customer can terminate the contractor for default.

Modify the Contract as Needed

The customer and contractor must be diligent about modifying the contract as necessary to reflect the current relationship. Modifications are driven by changes in prices, schedules, products, model numbers, and terms and conditions. Modifications made to the prime contract should be incorporated to any relevant subcontracts as well.

Modifications can either be minor (e.g., changing a model number without changing any features and functions of the product) or major (e.g., adding a new product to the contract). A discussion about changes and modifying the contract is found later in this chapter.

Resolve Issues as They Occur

The contractor and the customer should resolve any contractual issues as they occur on the contract. Usually, there is a dollar effect associated with contractual issues. The contractor and the customer should resolve any contractual problems as soon as they occur because the people who know the most about the issues are still working on the contract. If the contractor or the customer do not resolve the issue right away, the team members who know most about the issue may leave and other people who have no historical perspective of the problem will join the contract.

Maintain Customer Relationship

Success during contract performance is largely attributable to how successful contract start-up is. If things start off well, contract performance can be a great time for the contractor. If the contractor is still trying to validate its worth and is still considered with skepticism by the customer, the contractor will have a harder time developing a customer and contractor partnership. This is not to imply that the contractor should not do everything in its power to improve the customer relationship—many contracts have started off poorly but then turned into success stories. Most contracts can be successful; success is driven by how much each side wants to obtain it. A customer wants the contract to be successful; it is paying a lot of money to ensure project success. A contractor wants the contract to be successful; its future revenue, contract growth, and future business depend on it.

Turn Around an Unsuccessful Contract

If the contractor finds itself engaging in an uphill battle to win back its customer, it can take several avenues to turn the contract around. For example, the customer could identify the areas of the contract that are unsuccessful and do everything possible to fix those areas. If the customer is upset because deliveries take too long, the contractor could conduct a work-process analysis to determine the steps of the delivery process and how it can be improved. (Work-process analysis is described later in this chapter.) In some cases, the customer would just need to quickly validate delivery and purchase orders, work with the subcontractors to decrease lead time, and understand customer requirements before the delivery order is issued to speed up the delivery process and to turn around a potentially dangerous customer situation.

If the contractor made an error or if a delivery will be late, the contractor should inform the customer right away about the problem, the effects of the problem, and how the contractor intends to fix the problem. If the situation is severe, consider giving the customer some product or service for no cost as a goodwill measure to help improve customer relations.

Continually provide top notch quality service in all areas of the contract. Nothing speaks more highly of a solid customer relationship than when the customer feels the contractor has the customer's best interests at heart.

The contractor should schedule a meeting between its top executives and the customer to discuss the problem areas between the two teams in an effort to work out an amicable solution for both sides.

Ensure the Contract Accurately Reflects the Relationship

The contractor should keep the contract *clean,* which means make sure the contract remains a "living" document that accurately reflects the relationship between the contractor and the customer. For example, the contractor should ensure that delivery orders accurately reflect the products delivered, that new requirements are documented, and that products and services receive customer acceptance. Although these contract administration details may seem trivial, accurate contract data files assist in the daily management of the contract and are invaluable at the time of contract shutdown. Further, the files keep the history of what has occurred on the contract and provide a reference point for new decision makers to the contract. (Techniques for good subcontract management are discussed in Chapter 10.)

Establish a Regular Meeting Schedule

The contractor should ensure that it conducts regular meetings with the customer. Some customers refer to the meetings as program reviews or account meetings; It doesn't matter what they are called as long as they are conducted on a regular basis. The meetings are good because they provide a forum to solve any systemic operational problems and to conduct strategical analysis about how the contract can better meet the customer's requirements. The contractor should manage the meetings carefully to prevent them from being perceived as a waste of time. One way to do this is to include the decision makers from both organizations, ensure the appropriate personnel are invited to address the issues on the agenda, schedule other meetings to discuss any of the topics that do not involve many of the participants, and keep track of action items and their resolutions.

Continue to Add Value to the Customer

The contractor must continually evaluate what value its team brings to the customer. Should the contractor get lazy in fulfilling this responsibility, the customer will more than likely find another contract vehicle from which to procure the necessary goods and services. Contracts that run for a long period of time are particularly susceptible to getting in a rut and providing the same old thing to the customer. Contractors with long-term relationships must continually assess what value they can offer above and beyond the customer's expectations to obtain and retain customer satisfaction.

Provide Quality Service

In a similar vein, the contractor must continue to provide and improve quality products and services if it wants to retain customer loyalty. The situation is the same as in the added-value discussion: if the contractor gets lax in maintaining and improving its quality standards, the customer will find another contract vehicle to use. Alternatively, the contractor that understands the customer's commitment to quality and enforces that commitment will gain follow-on business and a good reputation within the marketplace, thereby influencing future customers.

Manage the Contract So the Customer Does Not Have To

The contractor should be intimately involved in every area of contract management and should keep accurate records so that the customer can trust the contractor to manage the details of the contract. If the customer trusts the contractor at the detailed level, the partnership between the customer and the contractor strengthens, and the customer is more apt to trust the contractor's opinion with the larger strategic-level issues.

Follow-Up With the Customer

The contractor must continue to work on the customer-contractor partnership throughout the life of the contract. This means continuing to visit or to call all the customer sites and to follow up after work has been done or products have been delivered to determine if the service meets the customer's satisfaction. Quick checks such as these allow the contractor to know early on if there is a problem with the service levels and to determine a course of action for improvement. Quick fixes tell the customer that the contractor cares enough about the customer's business to ensure that purchases made under the contract are adequate for meeting the requirements.

Keep Track of Success Stories

As projects are successfully completed, the contractor should document what was accomplished during the customer-contractor partnership. Success stories are necessary for the contractor because they are tangible occurrences of the strength of the partnership and how the contractor's products and services helped the customer accomplish its goals and objectives. The contractor can share success stories with current or future customers in an effort to assist in growing its business. Success stories also acknowledge the customer's work and efforts. This recognition is valuable because some customer personnel do not get the recognition they deserve. Success stories, particularly when presented to the immediate customer's management team, help the customer receive credit for the work they did on contract to meet its or another agency's mission.

Partnerships Evolve and Change Over Time

The customer-contractor partnership, just like any relationship, evolves and changes over time. A contractor is typically not immediately invited to learn of the customer's strategic plans for the contract; instead, the contractor must build up a level of trust with the customer before the customer feels comfortable sharing its business strategies. Likewise, if a contractor violates that trust by broadcasting problems within the customer organization, and the customer learns of the violation, the customer-contractor relationship may deteriorate into a relationship that does not enjoy the benefits of a collaborative problem-solving effort. Partnerships change over time because people don't tend to stay in their jobs for a long period of time. People working for the customer or the contractor may get promoted or leave their respective organization and the new team members must continue the relationship. This new relationship may experience many of the same peaks and valleys until both teams feel comfortable with each other. When new partnerships must be forged, every process or contract precedent that has been established may be subject to review and change.

Manage Team

Once the contract has been fully operational for about six months, many of the contract start-up issues should be resolved: team members have been identified, customer relationships have been established, and people understand how the contract operates on a daily basis. It is now time for the management team to focus on some of the internal core team issues surrounding contract performance.

Work-process analysis is a way to reevaluate the requirements of the team to determine if the right people are in the right jobs. Work-process analysis can be done at the prime contract level or at the subcontractor level.

Work-Process Analysis

Once the contract is operational for six months or more and the team has determined what has to be accomplished and how it should be accomplished, the contractor should determine if work is being done in the most efficient manner possible. In the haste of contract start-up, the contract team may have misplaced some functions within the organization or the team may have omitted them. Perhaps work is not evenly distributed among people performing the same task within the organization. Maybe some key people are overburdened and some of their tasks need to be reassigned. The contractor should concentrate on process improvement or analyze what needs to be done and determine how it needs to be done.

Work process improvement, or business process reengineering, is a top-down structured approach to analyzing an organization's inputs, outputs, and processes in an effort to optimize the resources it takes to run the organization. Work process improvement analysis can be conducted with an outside consultant or performed by the team responsible for the work.

Consultants

If the contractor decides to use a consultant, the consultant usually brings a repertoire of tools to expedite the process. Usually, a senior executive within the contractor's organization sponsors the consultant. Once the organization and the consultant negotiate a contract containing performance requirements, deliverables, and a payment schedule, the consultant begins work.

The consultant typically collects written information first to get a feel for how the organization operates; for example, the business plan, contract start-up plan, financial goals and objectives, files, and organization chart, are all data that the consultant reviews.

Next, the consultant conducts interviews with key people in the organization to understand how work is accomplished between and within functions of the organization. What are the current processes? What are the steps necessary to complete each of these processes? How are data created? What is done with the data? When are data reviewed? How accurate are the data? Why are the data produced? Does data flow through the organization in a timely manner? What would expedite the data flow within the organization? How well are people within teams working together? How well are people from each team working with the other teams? Do the people have the resources, facilities, and equipment to do their jobs? The consultant notes any problems. The consultant stores any solutions mentioned by the interviewees during interviews for future applicability. The consultant does not act on each suggestion because he or she wants to keep an open mind during this information gathering stage. He or she does not want to be prejudiced by what one person in the organization believes is the solution because it may be totally erroneous to the organization at large. Or, the interviewee may have the answer to key problem areas, but until the consultant gathers the necessary data, he or she will not know whether the answer provided is the best one for the organization.

As the consultant gathers all of this initial data, he or she depicts how the processes are currently working. These drawings help the consultant see problems either between or within the functional areas of the organization. Functional problems usually occur within four areas: data, processes, personnel, and resources. Problems with data could include lack of data necessary to complete a function, data redundancy, untimely or inefficient data gathering, someone causing a data choke point, or inaccurate data. Problems with processes could include lack of steps within the process to complete it accurately, too many steps within the process to complete it timely, duplicative processes within one or more functional areas, inexperienced people implementing the processes, or erroneous processes that only serve to frustrate people rather than contribute productively to the contract work. Problems with personnel include personality conflicts, inexperience in the task at hand, lack of training, lack of big picture knowledge, or lack of understanding of what the other functional areas do with the information produced. Problems with resources include lack of resources, inappropriate resources, antiquated equipment, or insufficient facilities.

Depending on the types of problems the consultant finds, he or she may verify the data that he or she has collected with the executive within the organization who sponsored the consultant. The consultant does this to ensure that he or she is not completely off track in some area or to determine if he or she needs access to additional people within the organization to get a true understanding of what is going on. It also gives the sponsoring executive an idea of the types of problems that are perceived to exist within the organization. Usually, the sponsoring executive is high enough in the organization that he or she will not try to thwart the consultant's efforts. Rather, it is in the sponsoring executive's best interest to work with the consultant to determine the accuracy of the perceptions. Armed with this information, the sponsoring executive can evaluate the consultant's recommendations with a deeper understanding of why they were made.

Finally, the consultant makes recommendations to the organization based on the data collected and on his or her expertise with optimized organizations. The consultant or the sponsor presents the recommendations to senior management, and the internal management team decides which recommendations will be implemented. The senior management team then establishes teams to implement the agreed-upon recommendations within the organization. The management team should evaluate the recommendations to determine if they are having the desired outcome within the organization.

The benefits of using an outside consultant to complete the work flow analysis include the following:

- Daily work is minimally interrupted because the consultant only requires a small amount of time from the team to conduct the interviews and to gather data.

- The consultant brings work flow expertise and tools to expedite the process and may come up with better solutions.

- Sometimes improvements are more widely accepted when they come from an outside, independent source rather than from an internal, and perhaps biased, source.

The drawbacks of using an outside consultant to complete the work flow analysis include the following:

- A consultant can be rather expensive.

- The consultant does not have a historical perspective or a great deal of time invested in the organization to understand the environment and may suggest improvements that are great in theory but will not work in the organization.

- An inferior consultant could just paraphrase suggestions made from the team without applying much of his or her own expertise and knowledge to the problem areas.

The following section discusses the option of using an internal team for conducting the work flow analysis.

Internal Team

When an internal team conducts a work flow analysis, it uses a slightly different approach. The team typically has some form of corporate sponsorship, either at the executive level or from its immediate manager. An executive or a manager may have even suggested a work flow analysis.

First, the team gathers information. This stage requires less time than when a consultant is used because the team members typically understand what is trying to be accomplished. This information-gathering stage usually centers around sending some background information to all team members, such as an organizational chart, mission statements, business plans, and work flow diagrams. This is done to give everyone an overall understanding of the contract.

At the first work flow analysis meeting, each member or functional area reviews how work is accomplished in a particular area. Using work flow diagrams, the speaker reviews what information is required by the particular area, how the member processes the data, and what outputs are created in the area. The member should also highlight what components of his or her functional area are working well and which ones need improvement.

After each member has a chance to review his or her functional area, the team looks for redundant or inefficient processes. It looks for redundant or aberrant data collection. It looks for the ways to solve the problems in each functional area. It looks for many of the same problem areas that the consultant looked for. The only difference is that the internal people tend to get through this process more quickly because they already have an understanding of the organization.

Next, the team brainstorms to come up with alternative approaches to accomplishing the work. All approaches are captured, and then each is reviewed by the team. Because all team members are present, they can quickly evaluate the approaches to determine if they will work in the organization.

Then the approaches are turned into recommendations, inefficient processes are streamlined or eliminated, redundant data are no longer collected at multiple points in the process, and reasons are uncovered for why data are incorrect. The team recommends solutions for the problems in each functional area. Finally, the team develops plans for implementing the recommendations once management concurs with its solutions.

The benefits of a team that is disciplined enough to conduct the analysis on its own is that the overall data collection process takes a lot less time because team members already have an understanding of what needs to be done. The cost is usually less prohibitive because team members can work on these improvements as part of their daily job. Full team participation improves the likelihood that team members will accept and implement the recommendations.

The drawbacks of this approach include occasional petty differences between people on the team, which do not make for a productive exchange of information nor do they foster consensus. Also, the process takes time away from the daily work that needs to be done. The results, however, can more than adequately make up for any loss in productivity. Finally, the team may not have access to tools that could expedite the process.

Personnel Tasks Related to Work Process Analysis

Several people-related tasks may occur as a result of the work process analysis.

Simplifying Complex Work

Sometimes the work process analysis reveals that a complex portion of the work is not being completed properly or accurately. This situation may require the complex work to be broken down into its most basic tasks. Then, the simplified tasks may be redistributed among the team members. The benefit of simplifying complex work is that better control can be retained over the events making up the task.

Further Refine Job Function Specific Skills

During the contract start-up phase, management determined the positions necessary to meet contractual obligations based on the proposal the company submitted. Management defined the position descriptions, job requirements, and the previous experience necessary to complete the tasks for the contract. Once the contract has been in operation for a while, management should determine if the position descriptions accurately reflect the job that must be done, if job requirements must be added or deleted, and if the previous experience section description would give the candidate the necessary background to perform the job.

Refining job functions is necessary for several reasons. First, it gives the manager and team member a document upon which to base career development. If the team member lacks some of the skills necessary to perform his or her function, the manager can get him or her the additional training needed. Next, the manager and team member can use the document to develop performance objectives. Performance objectives need to be based on the actual job requirements so when the manager appraises the team member, the manager has something to use when he or she evaluates the member's performance. Finally, refining the job function produces accurate position descriptions, job requirements, and previous experience requirements in the event that a new person has to be hired to perform the job. If the job description is current, the manager has a much easier time comparing the job candidates' skills with the actual skills required for the job.

Determine If People Are in the Right Jobs

In the haste of conducting contract start-up, the contractor may have placed one or two individuals in inappropriate positions. Perhaps the person was overqualified or perhaps he or she was underqualified for the task at. Perhaps they person determined that he or she was not a match for the job. If any of these situations exist, the manager working with the member must determine:

- If the person wants to succeed in the position.
- If the person lacks specific skills and if additional training is available to improve those areas.
- If there is another function on the contract that the person could perform that is not currently filled, or if the position can be enlarged to include the talents of the additional person.

- If work can be redistributed to make the situation work with the existing people.
- If work processes can be redefined to make the situation work with the existing people.

If the options listed do not produce an acceptable solution, the manager must replace the person. The manager must also help the employee find another job and locate another qualified candidate for the position.

Give People the Opportunity to Further Refine Their Skills

After the work flow analysis, the contractor or team manager should start developing the skills of the people who perform tasks on the contract. Additional classroom training, computer-based instruction, mentoring, and temporary duty assignments on other projects are all ways that people can refine their job specific skills. People can also broaden their perspectives by engaging in educational efforts that reach out beyond job specific skills; for example, working on a degree at a local university or taking company-sponsored courses on topics such as time management, change management, or cultural diversity.

Cross-Train Employees

Cross-training means that employees are learning the jobs of fellow employees. Cross-training benefits the individual team member and the team as a whole. For example, cross-training:

- Provides back up capabilities to the team when one team member is not available.
- Gives people the ability to take on new opportunities while still getting work accomplished.
- Allows people to diversify and broaden their skills.
- Prevents boredom on the job because employees have new challenges in each area to meet.
- Prepares people for their next positions.

Replacing People

Another key personnel issue raised during contract performance is replacing people on the contract. Replacing people takes time and effort to ensure that qualified people are brought in to complete the contract work with minimal degradation of service levels.

Reasons for replacing people   People can be replaced on a contract due to either planned or unplanned events. Some unplanned conditions that can cause the need to replace people, are as follows:

- The person performing a job on the contract assumes a position elsewhere.
- The work that the person did on the contract is no longer required.
- A person's rising salary is higher than the bid rate for that particular job and is causing the contract to lose money.
- The person is not able or willing to be successful in the position and a more qualified person must be brought on the contract to perform the work.

Replacements can also stem from the need to develop personnel to keep their jobs challenging. This people-development initiative could prepare a person to take a job with a greater degree of responsibility or another job in a different discipline on or off the contract.

Effect on Service Levels

Service levels can be affected in several ways. For example, the individual who is being replaced may be looking for another job and is not totally focused on the job he or she is supposed to be doing on the contract. The team's productivity can be affected if a disruptive, disgruntled employee is on the team, if the team must do extra work to cover for a poor performer, or if the team must complete the work that is not being done due to a job position vacancy. Another distraction would be if the manager's time is diverted away from contract work in order to make the time to locate, interview, and select a qualified candidate. Or, the manager may be helping the replaced employee find a new job. Finally, the team's productivity could be affected while a new person is adequately trained to perform the task at hand. When a person must be replaced, it is best to act quickly and try to minimize the effect on the team.

Although some events prohibit employee development planning, the contractor or the team manager should continually assess the people performing in each of the positions to ensure they have the skills and resources they need to be successful. By keeping employee development plans current, the manager can proactively solve development issues before they become problems. Also, replacements can be made in a more orderly fashion by timing and balancing customer requirements with employee development needs.

Contract Clauses Affecting Personnel Replacements

When the contractor has to replace people on the contract, the contractor must follow several contract requirements that govern when, how, and with which people the contractor may use to fill the vacant positions. The key personnel clause may prohibit a person from being replaced within the first 90 to 180 days of the contract. Other contractual clauses may state procedures for replacing the key person; for example, the customer could require that it review the resume of any new person before the person begins work. The contract may also require that the contractor adhere to position descriptions, which state specific skills and education levels a replacement person must have before he or she is considered for a position.

Manage Internal Support Team Members

The contract performance period provides some interesting challenges for the internal support team—keeping people current in the discipline, providing opportunities to keep people billed out most of the time, finding time and resources to train people, and focusing on what core competencies the team should provide.

Getting People the Appropriate Experience to Keep Them Current

Keeping team members current in the discipline is a difficult challenge for the internal support team. Ideally, the team would like to have its members on the cutting edge of knowledge in most functions related to the discipline. Unfortunately, projects are seldom scheduled to allow all team members to gain this degree of knowledge. What usually happens is that people are assigned to a project for a long period of time and they become experts in one to two niche functional areas. Then the internal support team wants to use them for every other piece of business employing those functional areas. The specialized team members get bored with doing the same work and usually want additional challenges. The internal support team then faces a dilemma: Allow the team members to branch off in new areas to improve their career and be unable to provide the expertise for some contracts until new people are brought up to speed; or continue to use the people in the same functions and hope that they do not get so frustrated that they leave the company. Careful personnel management, such as billable or non-billable training, can mitigate some of these risks.

Keeping People Billed Out a Significant Amount of the Time

The internal support management team has an obligation to the company to keep its personnel resources working on the contracts as much as possible. For every hour that a person is not working on a contract, or billed out, the company must pay for that individual through its profits; The more people in this situation, the bigger the drain on profit. Although some investment is necessary and inevitable, the company's management and marketing teams should find additional business for the support organizations to keep them billable. Because of the rise and fall of internal support work load over a contract life cycle, the contractor should add extra people only if absolutely necessary.

Finding the Time and Resources to Train People

The flip side of trying to keep people billed out is that work may be so abundant that the team manager or the contractor may not have time to train people in new skills. As discussed earlier, people doing the same work for a long period of time can get bored. Allowing people to obtain new skills is important not only for employee development, but it allows the company to have the internal skills required to pursue new opportunities. Training people while emphasizing that people keep working on contracts so as to not affect the bottom line is a difficult situation. Several companies have taken a threefold approach. First, they decide to make a corporate investment in a certain amount of training per year per person. This training is nonbillable and everyone knows it will affect the bottom line—in the short run. However, the companies consider the training to be insurance for future business. Second, each company's management team looks to lower its profit potential in some areas by using less experienced people to support the experienced people in accomplishing the work. In some contracts, the less experienced people may be billed to the customer using a lower priced job category; in other situations, the company may make the investment of allowing the inexperienced person to work on the contract to gain the experience without charging the customer for the person's time. Third, each company encourages a lessons-learned mentality across the team. In such situations, people share their experiences and teach each other about new technology or new functional areas. By providing this direct-experience approach to training, coupled with hands-on opportunities, each company can grow its internal expertise with minimal corporate investment.

Determining What Skills the Company Is Willing or Able to Provide

Finally, the hardest job for the internal support team is to decide what the group is willing or able to provide. Because the team is trying to affect the company's bottom line as little as possible, the team tries to be "all things to all people." Although a can-do attitude goes a long way in a company, this approach can quickly deteriorate if the company tries to gain expertise in a wide variety of functional areas without developing any depth of experience in any one area. A successful approach to this problem is to align the support team's capabilities with the new business opportunities being pursued. Although this approach does not mitigate the risk associated with the current contracts, it allows the internal support team to position itself more closely along business lines for the future.

Manage Subcontractors

Subcontract performance begins either before or after the subcontract is signed. The subcontractor is at greater risk if it is performing work without a signed subcontract in place because the prime contractor is only under a verbal obligation to pay for goods or services rendered. In this situation, the subcontractor can mitigate its risks by ensuring a signed subcontract is in place between the subcontractor and prime contractor before any work commences. Subcontract performance may go on until the specific task contracted for is complete, or the subcontract may remain open until the end of the prime contract.

Contract Performance Issues with Subcontractors

During contract performance the prime contractor must maintain a close relationship with the subcontractor to ensure successful contract performance. Some of the things that the prime contractor can do to work with the subcontractor are discussed in this section.

Provide Ongoing Contract Status

The prime contractor needs to keep the subcontractor informed about customer program developments so that the subcontractor can plan additional support if needed. The subcontractor also needs to keep its upper management team up to speed about the customer relationship. By maintaining ongoing contract status, the subcontractor can more effectively support the prime contractor in meeting customer objectives.

Keep Lines of Communication Open

The prime contractor should keep lines of communication open between itself and the subcontractor. This means that the prime contractor should inform the subcontractor if things are going well or if the subcontractor is not performing up to the prime contractor's or customer's expectations. Keeping lines of communication open also helps to further the trust level between the two companies, so that if other opportunities come up, the teams are comfortable working with each other. Additionally, the subcontractor can relay information that is useful to the prime contractor.

Implement Training Initiatives

The training issues that are prevalent during contract performance are preparing people for new levels of responsibility, cross-training, updating training, and bringing new people on board. Many of the issues that are discussed in this chapter pertain to the customer, the contract core team members, the internal support team members, and subcontractors.

Types of Training Useful During Contract Performance

Cross-Training on Different Aspects of the Contract

Sometimes the individual teams working on customer business will allow their members to cross-train to learn how another area within their functional discipline operates. For example, the person who reviews delivery orders may learn how to conduct the purchasing function and vice versa. Cross-training allows people to broaden their skill bases while allowing the team to develop internal backup capabilities within its organization.

Product Specifics

The contractor typically must teach the customer about, how to order, and how to work the products it is buying. The contractor should cover support services, such as warranty, installation, troubleshooting, and maintenance, in the training. In addition, the contractor must train its own people and, potentially, the subcontractor's people who will be supporting the customer, on the products being offered on the contract.

Contract Opportunities

In addition to learning about what is on the contract today, contractors also need to teach the customer what could be available on the contract in the future. New technologies, new approaches, and new vendors all present alternative methods for the customer that could result in cost savings. The subcontractor needs to keep the prime contractor aware of changes in its product lines, and the prime contractor needs to educate the customer to understand how the marketplace is evolving to determine if, or what, new products should be added to the contract.

Contract Performance Training Issues

Preparing People for New Levels of Responsibility

After the team members have been working on the contract for one or two years, the original team members may be yearning for new opportunities or new levels of responsibility. It is now up to the individual team members to work with his or her manager to develop a career plan that lays out what the member's next career objective is and what training is required for the member to reach that goal. Ideally, the member's career development plans should have been developed during the contract start-up phase, but there is seldom time to focus on employee development when a contract begins. Career development plans may point to some general training requirements that many people on the contract need; for example, leadership training or professional development. Or, the plans may contain specific classes targeted at individuals to improve their productivity. During contract performance, workloads can be redistributed for a short period of time to allow the people the flexibility they need to get the training required.

Updating Training

Another key to a successful training approach is to periodically update training once it becomes outdated. The contractor can use refresher mini-courses that highlight changes for the people who have been on the contract a long time and need to know what has changed since they took the course. The contractor should use updated new courses for any new team members added to the contract.

Training New Team Members

During contract performance, original team members will move up in the organization to positions of greater responsibility. Other original team members may move off the contract entirely. In either of these situations, a position will become available that may be filled with someone outside of the contract organization or maybe even outside the company. When the positions are filled with such people, the team manager needs to recall the types of training that were useful to them when it trained the team for the contract and use those classes or training techniques to quickly get the new people up to speed. Once again, training is focused on acquiring skills needed to perform the job as well as on customer and contract specific training. If the new people are from outside of the company, they will need new employee training as well. This type of training is also done by each part of the organization (e.g., customer team, internal core team, support teams, and subcontractor teams), however, experienced team members often help new team members even if they are from different organizations.

Further Refine Communication Channels

If contract start-up has gone according to plan, and all the communication channels have been established, then the contract team needs to maintain the communication channels during contract performance and assess which communication channels need improvement. If the communication channels have not been established, however, the team will spend much of its time trying to keep everyone informed about what they need to do their jobs.

Maintaining Communication Channels

Although most of the work in defining and establishing communication channels is complete, keeping people enthusiastic about maintaining the communication channels is sometimes difficult. Some people may feel a need to slack off, or provide incomplete information, or lose the drive to ensure the information is accurate. When these events occur, the contract team should signal the management team that changes need to occur because problems are right around the corner if these attitudes continue. No contract can be effectively managed with incomplete or inaccurate data. When people do not have actual data on which to base their decisions, they begin to fudge the data to support their beliefs. Although hunches are sometimes accurate, many teams have found themselves in a lot of trouble both from a financial and a contractual perspective when they stopped worrying about the quality of the data being presented. Conducting spot checks on the data and rewarding people for accurately doing their jobs are two ways to verify the accuracy of the data and to keep people motivated in doing a good job.

Assessing What Needs to Be Done Better

Either in support of maintaining communication channels or as a function of streamlining contract operations, the team should periodically assess the communication channels to see if they are on target and meeting the recipients' needs. The recipients' requirements may change—maybe they don't require the amount of information they originally thought they needed, maybe they need even more data. It is worth the effort to periodically ask these questions because some data requirements may be eliminated, thereby easing everyone's workload; other data requirements may be automated, which also tends to ease people's workload; or other data requirements may have yet to be defined. The team could discover a change in logistics: perhaps the information is needed more frequently or perhaps it needs to distributed to a wider audience. The only way to answer these questions is to get the team members to look objectively at their areas of responsibility to determine what they need to do their jobs better.

Manage Deliverables

Produce Deliverables and Obtain Acceptance

The contractor is responsible for producing the deliverable in a timely manner and for obtaining acceptance. *Acceptance* is the contractor's signal that the customer has received and approved the deliverable. Acceptance also indicates that the contractor can submit an invoice for the deliverable.

Produce Data

Once the contractor has the systems in place, the contractor must ensure that the data are entered in a timely and accurate fashion. This data production process is critical because the team relies so much on the accuracy of the data; if the information is incorrect, the team may make wrong decisions.

Follow Procedures

Lastly, the team must follow procedures during contract performance. As new people are brought on board, they must be trained in the procedures of the contract.

Determine Methods to Improve the Process

Because of the close relationship between improving the process through work process analysis and personnel, this topic is discussed in detail earlier in this chapter.

Manage Financial Data

Assess Risk Items on the Contract

During the BAFO stage, the company may have taken on some risks by underpricing some products or services in an effort to gain the competitive edge. This strategy may or may not be a successful one for the company. If the company can renegotiate those items after contract award because the product is no longer manufactured (and the contract has a product substitution clause), or if the product has been replaced by newer technology (and the contract has a technology refreshment clause), and if the customer is willing to change the products, the contractor may experience little financial risk. If the contractor cannot renegotiate, the contractor may be forced to provide the products throughout the life of the contract for the low proposed price.

Contract performance is a good time for the contractor to assess if any of its product or service offerings represent a great financial risk and to determine if any contractual remedies are available to mitigate the risk.

Determine Ways to Improve the Contract's Performance on the Financial Indicators

Coupled with the risk-mitigation strategies is the contract core team's responsibility to determine ways to improve performance on the financial indicators. Examples of ways to improve performance include streamlining operations, improving productivity, and growing the business through revenue generation. Additionally, the team could improve contract performance by minimizing the amount of time that invoices are outstanding, ensuring that acceptance and invoicing occur in a timely manner, and billing the customer as soon as possible for services rendered.

Continue the Outlook and Budgeting Process

The outlook and budgeting process continues throughout the life of the contract. Any deviations between projected and actual expenses usually require an explanation. The team should also project new revenue or unexpected expenses for the upcoming quarter.

Continue Marketing Efforts

During contract performance, the emphasis shifts from identifying customers, core competencies, and contract details to maximizing the return in each of these areas.

Sustain and Build on Existing Customer Relationships

It is much easier and less expensive to maintain an existing customer relationship than it is to develop a new one. During contract performance, the contractor must be attentive and proactive to the requests of the existing customer base. The contractor may lose the customer if the contractor stops paying attention to the details of a good customer relationship. Maintaining existing customers helps grow the contract backlog and can keep the contractor's staffing levels constant.

Build New Relationships

Building new customer relationships helps the contractor grow the contract by providing new sources for revenue. New customers represent new challenges and new opportunities for the contractor's personnel to broaden their skills and to excel.

Grow the Product Line to Grow the Business

The more products that a company has on a contract that are competitively priced, the more likely that the contractor may sell those products to generate revenue (and hopefully, make a profit). Therefore, it is in the contractor's best interest to get as many products as possible on the contract. However, putting new products on the contract represents a certain amount of work for the customer in terms of evaluating the pricing and terms and conditions and for the technical team in terms of evaluating the feasibility of the product.

Additionally, the contractor will incur expenses as it prepares proposals to add the products, and those costs may or may not be passed on to the customer. The key is for the contractor to target the specific products and services that the customer has a need for and to work to get those added to the contract. The contractor should plan demonstrations or technical briefings to teach the customer about the newest technologies available. This helps the customer get what it needs and the contractor broadens its business base.

Tracking Success Stories Helps to Grow Future Business

Another key area for the contractor to track is the contract team's success stories. When the contractor works with a customer using the products and services available on the contract and helps the customer meet its goals and objectives, the contractor's team should document the effort in a summary. The contractor can share this summary with future customers to illustrate the value that the contractor provides. Sharing success stories is particularly useful when the contractor's people provide a value-added contribution to the customer's project.

Keep Customers Happy—Do Whatever You Can to Rebuild Trust If in Doubt

The contractor will sometimes fail to meet the customer's expectations for a project. It could stem from a difference in opinion, unclear requirements, or just a misunderstanding. Should this occur, the contractor must do whatever it takes to rebuild that relationship. One dissatisfied customer can do a great deal of harm to the contractor's reputation, particularly if that customer is consulted by prospective customers about pending future awards. The contractor may be able to resolve the problem by conducting a simple meeting, apologizing, or developing some contractual consideration. The contractor should take the necessary steps to fix problems.

Always Conduct Government Business Affairs Above Reproach

The worst thing for a governmental agency is to be featured on the front page of the *Washington Post* for contractual problems. Unfortunately, when contractors commit wrongdoing, the agency employing the contractor tends to get dragged through the mud as well. The contractor should not do anything that could harm its company's reputation or that of its government customer. Bribes, illegal actions, payoffs, and other tactics seldom work in the long run. The company could be banned from doing any government business if it is caught. It is best for the contractor to always conduct government business with the thought in mind, "Is this business transaction something I would mind having published in the *Washington Post*?"

Understand Who the Competitors Are, What They Are Offering, and How Their Prices Compare to Yours

The competitive environment changes almost daily. New contracts are awarded, new teaming relationships are established, old contract pricing changes, and new technology is introduced fairly regularly in today's environment. Each event can threaten the company's contract business. The company cannot stop any of these events from occurring: The customer will continue to award new contracts, teaming relationships will always evolve, competitors will change prices on their contracts, and new technology enters the market faster now than ever before. However, the savvy contractor knows who the competitors are, what they are offering, and how their prices compare to their own. Armed with this information, the contractor can mitigate its risk by deciding on which products or services it wants to compete and walk away from other business because the competitive prices are already too risky. The contractor can also use this information to determine innovative ways to offer its products and services to separate itself from the crowd; for example, it could offer longer warranties and decreased delivery times, or use leases.

Be Willing to Cut Profit When Needed to Get the Business

On commercial contracts, a contractor tries to get as high a profit as it can and still win the business. However, in the government marketplace, profit margins, for the most part, are capped at 10 percent. Some contractors are taking 4 to 5 percent profit margins just to stay in the government marketplace. This highly competitive state does not allow much room for error. It requires contractors to cut their margins even more just to stay competitive.

Keeping Costs Low Often Ends Up Being a Cost Shoot-Out

Even with best-value procurements, the government still is sharply aware of the bottom-line price. Commercial companies are also looking for good deals. Government agencies and commercial companies can shop electronically on the Internet to compare prices to find the contract representing the best value for the cheapest price. Therefore, it is in the contractor's best interest to keep its overhead rates as low as possible, to run the contract with as few people as necessary (in firm, fixed priced contracts) or with a full staff (in cost-plus contracts), and to negotiate the best deals it can with subcontractors.

Maintain Facilities, Equipment, and Technology

Monitor Requirements and Secure or Dispose of Additional Items, If Necessary

During contract performance, the staff will increase and decrease, the requirements may change, the technology may become outdated, or a host of other events can occur that will require the contractor's team to review its facilities, technology, and equipment requirements. Each time a requirement changes, the contractor conducts a similar analysis to the one presented earlier to determine the most cost-effective manner in which to obtain the items.

Arrange for Maintenance and Updates

The team is responsible for routine maintenance to the facilities, technology, and equipment. The team must determine when items should be replaced and updated. Migrations to new or upgraded technology platforms must be done in an orderly fashion to ensure data integrity, minimal downtime, and little disruption to the employees.

Continue Task-Order Work

Track Evolving Requirements

The contractor needs to track evolving requirements for both new products and new ways of conducting business during contract performance. The contractor should suggest alternative products and services to the customer. The contractor needs to stay ahead of the customer and anticipate its needs and define solutions. The more responsive the contractor is, the better chance it has at selling products off the existing contract baseline and adding new products to the contract baseline.

Complete Proposal Process

The prime contractor needs to complete the proposal process every time new requirements are defined. Hopefully, over time the contractor will understand its customer enough to know which requirements may get funded and which requirements will never get funded.

Look for Task-Order Opportunities

The prime contractor and the subcontractor need to look for task-order opportunities. The contractor cannot issue task-order requests for proposals to all task-order contractors; however, the contractor that lets it be known that it is interested in the upcoming workload may have a better chance at being selected to provide a proposal.

Complete Task-Order Proposals

The prime contractor must submit complete and accurate proposals when it bids on task-order business. Understanding the customer's environment and its specific requirements helps the contractor submit a responsive proposal. The contractor must answer all questions on a task-order proposal and explain how it intends to complete each requirement in the statement of work. Remember, a contractor can be thrown out of the competition because it just stated that it would comply with the requirements without stating how it would accomplish the tasks. Task orders are evaluated just like original proposals: They are sales documents used to convince the customer that the contractor team is the most capable partner in accomplishing the task at hand. The contractor's confidence needs to come across in the proposal.

Stay Focused on High-Quality Product and Service Delivery

Nothing will speak louder in marketing new products and services than the contractor's past performance. People choose the people they can rely on. If the contractor has provided stellar performance on task-order work or on the current contract work, the customer is more apt to select it over the contractor that has had shoddy past performance.

Manage Changes to the Contract

Changes That Occur in Programs

Changes occur in programs, pre-award and post-award. Program changes drive contract changes and can either originate with the customer or with the contractor. Contractor-initiated change must be approved by the customer on commercial business and the contracting officer on government business because he or she is the only person vested with the authority to commit the government.

Customer-Initiated Changes

Program modifications occur when the customer changes, among other things, any of the following items:

- Schedule
- Funding
- Regulations
- Personnel
- Contractor involvement
- Requirements
- Technological advances
- The need to correct performance problems
- Problems with the contractor's performance
- Customer reorganizations

Contractor-Initiated Changes

The contractor may wish to modify the program by making changes to the following:

- Schedule
- Support services (based on decreases in customer funding)
- Personnel assignments
- Subcontractor involvement
- Subcontractor additions
- Newly proposed solutions (either due to advances in technology or the need to fix performance issues)

Methods for Discovering Changes

This section focuses on how a customer and a contractor's team discover that a change needs to occur. Changes may be identified through:

- Program reviews
- Technological advances
- Marketing efforts
- User requirements
- Ease of use analysis
- Help desk issues
- Solution design flaw

Seldom does a change stand alone. If a change is made to one place in a program (even under a different prime contractor's contract), it may affect other parts of the program. For this reason, the contractor and the customer must look at a change from both a content point of view to determine if the change is valid in and of itself and from a context point of view to determine how it will affect the rest of the program(s).

Differences between Commercial and Government Contract Changes

Any change in the program typically results in a contract change. There is an important difference between contracting with the federal government and contracting with a commercial company with regard to changes. In the government arena, when the government makes a change under the changes clause, the contractor must implement it. In the commercial environment, a contractor is not obligated to perform work that is not specifically stated in the contract. Any modifications to a commercial contract must be agreed to by both parties. In a federal contract, the government can issue a unilateral modification that changes the contract, and the contractor must perform according to the new contract.

The government does realize that with this privilege it must compensate the contractor for any additional expense incurred for making the change. The government's position on contract changes is that if it issues a change under the changes clause, and this causes an increase or decrease in the contractor's cost or schedule, the contracting officer will make an equitable adjustment. This means that the contractor is obligated to perform the changed work but that the government will compensate the contractor if the new work causes the contractor's costs to increase or if the contractor needs more time to complete the work. Similarly, if the change requires less cost or less time, the government expects to realize the actual savings.

Types of Changes

Definitized vs. Undefinitized Changes

There are several different ways to categorize changes. First, there are definitized and undefinitized changes. *Definitized changes* are documented in a contract before the work starts. The contract modification contains definite terms, conditions, statements of work, and price. Definitized changes possess the least amount of risk for the customer and the contractor because both parties are aware of the contractual implications of the change. Such changes are better for the subcontractor as well because there is a contractual document that states that the work should be done and will be paid for.

A riskier approach is a undefinitized change. In this situation, the contractor and customer do not agree on terms, conditions, statements of work, and price before the work starts. All undefinitized changes eventually become definitized changes. In an undefinitized change, the customer and the contractor verbally agree on a statement of work, but terms, conditions, and prices are not negotiated. This approach is risky for the customer, the contractor, and the subcontractor. The customer or the prime contractor can protect itself from extravagant price risk by stating a not to exceed (NTE) amount in a letter to the prime contractor or subcontractor. The contractor, however, loses all its negotiating power for a higher profit because the risk associated with contract performance is minimized as the work proceeds. For example, if the contractor requests an 8 percent fee on a definitized change, it is negotiated up front and the contractor is guaranteed whatever fee is negotiated. In an undefinitized change, the contractor would be hard pressed to justify (not to mention the difficulty the customer would have in agreeing to) an 8 percent fee after the work has been completed. At that point, there is no contractor risk so the government would have no reason to pay the large fee.

Authorized vs. Unauthorized Changes

The government also categorizes changes as to whether the change is authorized or unauthorized. An *authorized change* is issued by the contracting officer under the changes clause in the FAR. Authorized changes are less risky for the contractor and the government because both sides understand what change is being made and how it will affect the program. Problems occur when there is an unauthorized change.

The contracting officer is the only person who can commit the government. When someone in the government, other than the contracting officer, initiates a change and the contractor acts on it, there is a problem. For example, a program manager tells a contractor to change a knob on an instrument from the contract-required 2" in diameter to 3" in diameter. The contractor assumes that the program manager can commit the government (which is not true) or that the program manager discussed the change with the contracting officer (which may be a wrong assumption). When a contractor acts on changes from someone other than the contracting officer, the contractor is at risk for the cost of making the change. This means that the contractor must pay for any costs it incurs for making the change because the change was not issued by the contracting officer. In order for the contractor to be reimbursed for its expense, it must prove that a constructive change occurred. This requires that the contractor initiate a claim and then the government reviews it and decides if the claim has merit. Time, effort, and expense are incurred on both sides. For this reason, it is imperative that the contractor immediately notify the contracting officer if the contractor has been ordered to make a change or if it perceives that a change is on the horizon. By acting as a liaison between the program manager and the contracting officer, the contractor reduces its own risk and minimizes the likelihood that a claim will need to be filed. Once the contracting officer is aware of the situation, he or she can take the appropriate steps to either stop the change from occurring or help to secure the budget necessary to make the change. Additionally, the contracting officer will work with the contractor to document the change in a contract modification.

Although commercial contracts are not governed by the FAR, a contractor can run into an issue with authorized versus unauthorized changes in a commercial contract as well. If the prime contract states that all direction should be in writing or given by the contract's office and the prime contractor acts on the authority of a program manager, the prime contractor is still at risk for performing an authorized change. Once again, the contract is the governing document for how changes are to be properly implemented on the program.

Cardinal vs. In-Scope Changes

Another way that the government classifies changes is to determine whether the changes fall within the scope of the original contract. Changes within the scope of the contract are referred to as *in-scope changes*. In these changes, the original intent of the contract has not been altered and the dollar value of the change is in proportion to the original contract. For example, the government released an RFP to paint ten rooms and contractor A won the contract. If the government asked contractor A to paint an additional two rooms, this would be perceived as an in-scope change. Chances are that contractor A would have won the contract whether ten or 12 rooms were in the original solicitation.

Changes that are outside the scope of the contract are referred to as *cardinal changes*. Cardinal changes can be difficult for the contracting officer to justify because contractors that did not win the original procurement tend to protest such changes. Using the earlier example of a government RFP to paint ten rooms and contractor A winning the contract, assume that the government decides to change the contract after award and adds that the contractor must wallpaper 20 rooms. This change would be considered cardinal because 20 rooms is twice the amount of the original contract and the job requirements changed. If the original RFP had stated that wallpapering would be required, other companies specializing in wallpapering would have bid on the contract. Similarly, companies that did bid on the original procurement could protest and say that had they known that the contract would have included wallpapering, they could have offered a lower price for the entire project.

The reason that cardinal and in-scope changes are important in the governmental environment is because of the potential protests they may bring. Because commercial contracts cannot be protested, a commercial customer can expand the scope of a contract to include anything it wishes. A government customer doing the same thing would be accused of limiting competition because, as in the above example, it could have competed the entire requirement at the beginning and awarded the contract to a more cost-effective provider that could provide both painting and wallpapering services. Once the government realizes a new requirement, the government would be better off conducting a second solicitation for the new products or services. This would minimize the chances of protests.

How Changes to the Program and Contract Are Communicated between the Customer and the Contractor

The methods to communicate change between the customer and the contractor during contract performance are multiple and varied. For government contracts, the "Changes" section in the FAR governs how changes should be implemented (FAR 52.243-4). The method selected should be tailored to the type of change so that long-term contract management problems are avoided. For example, some changes, such as a change in personnel, might be handled orally between the two parties, unless the contract has a key personnel clause that requires a formal change process. Other changes, such as adding new products to the contract baseline, are best handled through a formal negotiated change.

Any change that alters performance, terms and conditions, or price must be effected via a written contract modification. In this way, both sides acknowledge the change, negotiate the terms of the change, and the modified contract becomes the new baseline. The following section discusses channels through which changes can be communicated.

Contract Modification

Issuing a contract modification is the most formal way to effect changes to the contract. Contract modifications are commonly used for changes in funding, adding new products to the contract, and providing new work tasks. For commercial contracts, contract modifications are bilateral, meaning that both parties must agree to the change before it is executed. For government contracts, contract modifications may be unilateral or bilateral depending on the terms of the contract. Under a *unilateral modification*, the government issues the modification and the contractor is obligated to perform in accordance with the modification. Terminations or work stoppages are handled by unilateral modification. In a *bilateral modification*, one party typically generates a draft modification for the other party to review. Once both parties agree on the terms of the modification, the final modification is negotiated and signed by both parties. Additional detail is provided in FAR Part 43, "Contract Modifications."

Written Direction

Written direction, such as faxes, electronic mail, and formal letters, are all excellent ways to keep each party informed of changes in the contract. Written direction is particularly important when the change involves how work should be accomplished. Electronic mail is a quick and easy way to communicate between the customer and contractor because correspondence tends to be less cumbersome. For example, questions can be asked and answered quickly without the formality of a letter from contract office to contract office and direction is still provided in writing.

Deviation

A request for deviation is used by a contractor in a government contract to request a limited change to the contract when a product or service must deviate slightly from the original requirement. For example, 10-foot cables are specified in the contract but, for a limited period of time due to a supply shortage, the contractor must supply 12-foot cables. The contractor would request a deviation because although 12-foot cables can normally meet the specifications required for 10-foot cables, 12-foot cables are not currently on the contract and, therefore, deviate from the contract (FAR 1.4, "Deviations"). Deviations on commercial contracts are typically handled with a phone call between the two parties.

Waiver

A request for waiver is used by the contractor to request a change to a government contract when a product or service provided is slightly different from the product or service on the contract. For example, a task-order contract requires the contractor to submit resumes of all personnel working on the contract. If one job description requires a person to have a bachelor's degree in engineering, but the contractor has an experienced person who does not have a bachelor's degree, the contractor may submit a waiver asking permission to ignore the bachelor's degree requirement. In the waiver the contractor would explain that the individual was equally capable of performing the effort. The government has the right to accept or reject the request for deviation or ask for consideration if the government believes it is appropriate. If a contractor supplies a product substitute without obtaining the government's consent, the contractor is deemed noncompliant and the government can utilize contractual remedies, such as nonpayment or termination. On a commercial contract, waivers are typically handled with a phone call between the two parties.

Status Meetings

Status meetings can occur weekly, bimonthly, or monthly between the customer and contractor to review current contract conditions, upcoming program events, and any areas for improvement. The meetings provide a forum to discuss upcoming program changes to give the other party a chance to assess the effect of the changes before the changes are actually implemented. Unless formal notes are taken at these meetings, which are later agreed upon by both parties and which become part of the record, it is always a good idea to ensure any substantive changes are followed up in writing and agreed to by both parties.

Letter Proposal

A contractor can submit a letter proposal to communicate a change that does not affect the price of the contract, if the contracting office agrees to allow letter proposals. Typically, letter proposals are one to two pages, outline the salient points of the change, and state that there is no change in price or in terms and conditions. Because letter proposals usually indicate small changes, the customer can review letter proposals quickly and modify the contract. An example of when a letter proposal would be appropriate is when the contractor changes the part number on a product, which does not affect the price. Commercial customers and prime contractors tend to use letter proposals frequently to communicate changes to each other.

Oral Direction

Oral direction can be risky unless it is followed up in writing and agreed to by both parties. Oral direction is approved for use by the government during times of national crisis or emergency when the government must quickly procure goods and services from the contractor. Oral direction is used more frequently in a commercial contract than in a government one.

Minor Modifications

The contractor can easily make a minor modification to a contract. Typically, the prime contractor will either orally or in writing tell the customer of a minor change that needs to be made. The customer or the prime contractor develops the contract modification by stating the following information:

- Contract number
- Contract name
- Names of the two parties
- Date of modification
- Effect on contract requirement
- Effect on cost (usually $0)
- Effect on schedule
- Old item/new item
- Reason for modification

Both parties sign the document and the modification is incorporated into the prime contract. A minor modification is made to a subcontract in much the same way. Minor modifications typically are carried out between two commercial companies (prime contractor and customer or prime contractor and subcontractor) and the process is conducted in the manner described above, or bilaterally, which means that both parties sign off on the modification. However, if the contractor is working the government or with a prime contractor who is working with the government, the government has the right to issue unilateral modifications. In a *unilateral modification,* the government just signs the modification and it is incorporated into the contract.

Formal Proposal

The contractor must use a formal proposal to communicate more substantive changes in the program. For example, the contractor wants to add new products to the contract that are considered within the scope of the contract. The contract is for information processing technology, and the customer wants to add a database product to the contract. The prime contractor may either provide its own database product or provide a database product from another company. Either way, the company must justify why the chosen database product represents the best overall value to the customer. To add a new product to the contract, the contractor goes through the process described in the following section.

Process for Adding New Products to the Contract

As discussed in the earlier chapters, the contractor must deliver the products and services that are stated in the contract baseline. If it delivers anything that is not on the contract baseline, the contractor is in default of the contract and may not be paid for the products delivered or the services rendered. The contract may require the contractor to add new products; for example, the contract may have a technology refreshment clause that states that the customer expects the contractor to update the technology on the contract when it makes good business sense to do so. Similarly, the contract may include a product substitution clause that gives the contractor the right to substitute products that are no longer manufactured with products that provide equal or greater functionality for the same price as was agreed to in the original contract. Finally, there may be an (value) engineering change clause that encourages contractors to develop more efficient methods of conducting business; the customer may even share some of the cost savings incurred through use of the new method with the contractor. If these clauses exist in the contract, the contractor has the right to put in a proposal to add new products to the contract.

The process for developing a proposal includes several steps that occur over a short time (from one to two weeks) or, depending on the proposal's complexity, may take several months to complete.

Establish the Contract Baseline

The contract baseline was established using the company's price and technical volumes from the proposal it submitted to the customer. When negotiations are completed, the contract baseline is usually transferred to some automated system that tracks the product or service description, quantities, and out-year prices. In addition, supplier information for each particular line item is maintained. The system also should have the subcontractor's name, subcontract number, model number, description, out-year prices, special terms and conditions, mailing address, point of contact, and other relevant information for when purchase orders need to be developed.

The contract baseline is important for several reasons:

- It represents what the contractor is contractually obligated to provide throughout the life of the contract.

- It represents what the customer may order (i.e., if an item is not in the contract baseline, the customer cannot order it).

- It represents what the contractor must provide in filling a delivery order from the customer. If the contractor cannot deliver the exact make and model number stated in the contract baseline, it must submit a waiver or deviation to the government and wait for the government's approval. Commercial customers may give a verbal approval of the change.

- It provides a central repository of ordering information for the contract by stating what the customer can buy and where the contractor intends to purchase the items necessary to fill the order. It usually includes how products were offered to the customer and how subcontractors offered their products to the prime contractor. This information is vital in resolving contractual and subcontractual issues throughout the life of the contract.

- It can automate many of the routine purchasing functions.

Understand the Contract Baseline

Before the contractor proposes new products or services, it must understand what is in the contract baseline. It must understand how the customer uses the products and services and how to customize a system for its customer's environment using the components from the contract. Only after the contractor thoroughly understands what is available in the contract baseline can it understand new requirements or useful additions to the baseline.

Conduct a Needs Assessment

Once the contractor understands the contract baseline, it can look for better and more efficient ways to meet existing or new requirements. The contractor adds new products or services to the contract baseline by conducting the proposal process. The first step in developing a proposal is to determine the customer's need. This needs assessment can be conducted in a variety of ways: user meetings, reviewing problem calls to the help desk, training initiatives, one-on-one customer meetings, installations, program reviews, or ideas from subcontractors.

Conduct Technical Research

Once the contractor determines the customer's need, the contractor then conducts technical research about the requirement. How can that the requirement be addressed? Are additional products needed to meet the requirement? The contractor conducts some initial research by reviewing industry periodicals and talking to subcontractors and other subject matter experts about the problem and potential solutions.

Develop a White Paper to Determine Customer Interest

Usually at this point, the contractor has asked the customer whether it has an interest in the contractor pursuing this effort. If the customer is remotely interested in the topic at hand, it will typically ask the contractor to prepare a position paper outlining the problem and potential solutions. It may also ask the contractor to make a recommendation on the method to pursue. If the customer is not interested in the contractor developing a solution to a perceived problem area, the contractor ceases its efforts on the problem. If the customer is interested, the rest of the process commences. In such cases, the customer will probably direct the contractor as to the course it would like the contractor to take. For example, should the product be leased or purchased? Which vendors should be considered? What technical specifications should be used to evaluate the technical capabilities? What source selection information should be used to determine a winner? How should the solution be proposed? These are all questions that the contractor would like its customer to answer.

Gather Information

The contractor collects information a second time—this time to actually run a procurement. The prime contractor must run a procurement for a government customer; it has the option to run a competition for a commercial customer. If a procurement is held, the customer must hold additional vendor meetings, consult subject matter experts, consider alternative approaches, and review the government's suggestions. The contractor gathers data before a proposal kickoff meeting so that there are facts to review at the meeting.

Conduct Kickoff Meeting

The next pivotal step in the proposal process is to conduct a proposal kickoff meeting. Based on the data that has already been collected, the team determines if the source for the product or service is internal or external and establishes the schedule for the procurement. If the product will be bid using internal resources, then a procurement does not have to be conducted. Instead, the team must make internal assessments from the technical, engineering, manufacturing, business, management, and contractual perspectives before the proposal is made to the government.

If the product will be bid using external sources, then the team may conduct a procurement. In order to conduct a procurement, the team must complete the following steps:

1. *Identify potential sources*—The first step that the team must complete is to identify potential sources for the product being procured. The company can find sources through many different channels: trade booth exhibits, purchasing files, industry magazines, sales contacts, or subcontractor reference. Once the company has identified manufacturers, the company should contact each manufacturer to determine if it is interested in

bidding on the new piece of business. The goal for the company is to find at least three manufacturing companies willing to bid on the procurement so that the company can demonstrate that it held a competition.

2. *Develop RFP*—The next step is for the team to develop the RFP. The RFP typically contains:

- A cover letter explaining the procurement
- Technical specifications
- Pricing instructions
- Proposal preparation instructions
- Terms and conditions under which the product must be proposed
- Representations and certifications
- Evaluation criteria

3. *Develop source selection plan*—The contract team must then develop a source selection plan that will be used to determine the procurement winner. Based on the customer's requirements, the source selection plan assigns points for each facet of the solution. Typically, the plan has points assigned for the management, technical, contractual, and business solutions proposed.

4. *Conduct solicitation*—The company then sends the RFPs to the manufacturing companies interested in bidding on the procurement. The companies are notified of the date that questions must be submitted and the date that proposals are due. If any manufacturer asks a question, the contract team must develop the answer and send it out to all bidders. The company must receive all proposals by the date and time stated; otherwise, they are deemed noncompliant.

5. *Evaluate the proposals*—The company's team evaluates the proposals received from the manufacturing companies. The evaluations are based on the weight given to each evaluation criteria in the source selection plan. The team's representatives from each of the key functional areas (e.g., technical, management, business, and contracts) evaluate the appropriate sections of the proposals using the source selection plan.

6. *Conduct strategy session*—The team then convenes a strategy session. Each evaluator reports his or her findings for each

proposal. The team tallies points based on the scores given in the management, contractual, technical, and business assessments. At this meeting, the apparent winner is determined. The term *apparent* is used because until a final agreement has been reached between the prime contractor and the potential subcontractor, the company cannot be deemed the winner. If there are problems during the negotiations, it is quite conceivable that the apparent winner could bow out and the number two or number three company could actually win the procurement.

Also during the strategy session, the team determines how it intends to propose the new product or service to the government. The team decides how the new product or service will be proposed to the government, under what terms and conditions it will be proposed, what maintenance or support will be offered with the product or service, and how it will be priced.

7. *Negotiate with the supplier*—Before the contractor submits a proposal to the customer, it is best for the contractor to complete negotiations with the supplier and either develop a new subcontract or modify an existing subcontract with that supplier. This protects both the customer and the prime contractor by documenting the agreement that describes how the products are being offered and priced to the prime contractor.

8. *Develop the proposal to the customer*—The next step is for the team to develop a proposal to the customer outlining its offer. Typically, a proposal contains:

- A cover letter outlining the offer
- A proposal overview that contains a description of the existing customer situation, the product or service being offered, a description of how the new product or service will fit in the existing customer environment, and the features and benefits of the solution
- A technical description of the products or services
- Prices and quantities for the product through the end of the contract
- The terms and conditions under which the product or service is offered
- Any relevant contract modification data
- Any relevant technical literature
- The life-cycle costs of the old solution compared to the new solution

9. *Negotiate with the customer*—After the customer has reviewed the prime contractor's proposal, it will do one of three things:

- Decide that it is interested in the product and has the funding to implement the solution and will enter into negotiations with the contractor.

- Decide that it does not have enough information to decide and go back to the contractor for additional details.

- Decide that it does not have the funding or interest in the solution change and will inform the contractor to cease all efforts.

   The current contract states whether after-award proposal efforts are paid for by the contractor or by the customer. It is in both parties' best interest to determine as early as possible in the process whether there is funding and interest in the project so that money spent on resources is not wasted.

10. *Receive the contract modification from the customer*—After negotiations have been completed, the customer will send a draft contract modification to the contractor for review. The modification usually contains the product or service descriptions, quantities, and out-year prices on the prime contract that are deleted as a result of the modification. The modification also contains the descriptions, quantities, and out-year prices for the new products added as a result of this modification. The technical proposal, terms and conditions, and other relevant parts of the contractor's proposal are incorporated as well. The contractor will make any appropriate changes to the document and return it to the customer. If the customer agrees with the contractor's changes, it will sign the modification and reissue it to the contractor. Once the contractor signs the modification, it is formally part of the prime contract.

   The contractor then inputs data from the contract modification into the system that tracks the contract baseline. The contractor deletes old product or service information and adds information about the new products or services. Not only does the system maintain the new description, quantities, and out-year prices, but the system should also keep track of supplier information for that particular product or service. For example, the subcontractor's name, the subcontract number, the model number, a description, out-year prices, special terms and conditions, the mailing address, the point of contact, and other relevant information should be kept in the system for when purchase orders need to be developed.

11. *Receive the delivery order for the new item from the customer*—The step that the contractor is waiting for is when it actually receives a delivery order from the customer for the new product or service. When the contractor receives the delivery order, it checks the contract baseline to review the delivery order for accuracy and to ensure that the product or service description and price is stated on the delivery order and that the quantity is still available on the contract. If the delivery order is for products previously added and no remaining quantities are available for purchase on the contract, the contractor must decide whether it wants to sell additional quantities for the same price. If it decides to do so, the contractor has to submit a proposal to add additional quantities to the contract. Once the customer accepts the proposal and issues a modification, the contractor can sell the customer the products requested. If the contractor decides that it can no longer offer the products for the stated price, it must conduct a solicitation to allow vendors to compete for the new quantities to be added to the contract. The prime contractor would then repeat the steps 1 to 10 for developing a solicitation and a proposal to the customer.

12. *Generate purchase orders*—Once the contractor has a valid delivery order, it uses its automated system to generate purchase orders for the products listed on the delivery order to its subcontractors. The prime contractor must deliver products and services in accordance with the contract. For example, a contract states that the contractor has 30 to 90 days from the date on the delivery order to deliver the products and services. If the contractor fails to deliver the goods and services within the designated period of time, the contractor usually must pay liquidated damages if they are stipulated in the contract. Liquidated damages are designed to compensate the customer for the loss of productivity incurred when the contractor fails to complete a contract task. It is difficult to ascertain the exact amount of money the customer loses when a contractor fails to complete any given task. Therefore, the customer and contractor agree during contract negotiations on a set amount; for example, the contractor will pay the customer $500 per day when the contractor is late with a delivery or if its system fails to perform. What usually happens is that the contractor doesn't

actually write the customer a check, instead the contractor deducts the amount equal to any liquidated damage settlements from the total invoice for that period. Knowing this, the prime contractor negotiates a lesser period of time with the subcontractors for them to deliver products and services. The prime contractor does this because it assumes it will take a few days on its part to log the delivery order, review it for accuracy, and generate the purchase order.

The purchase orders going to the vendors contain the following information:

- Prime contractor name, address, and point of contact
- Product model number, description, pre-negotiated unit price, quantity, and total price
- Customer name, address, and point of contact
- Special delivery instructions, subcontract number, special terms and conditions, required due date, and maintenance requirements.

The contractor typically sets up the system so that when a product or service shows up on a customer delivery order, the system triggers purchase orders to be sent to all vendors supplying parts for that product or service. The prime contractor negotiates with the subcontractors ahead of time if special packaging or shipment to a staging area is required.

13. *Subcontractor delivers product or services and receives payment*— The subcontractor delivers the products or services by the requested due date. Either the prime contractor accepts them at its facility or the customer accepts them. Once the products or services or whatever event has been agreed upon in the subcontract are accepted, the subcontractor may invoice for products delivered or services rendered. The prime contractor acknowledges the receipt of the goods and services within its own company's systems, approves the subcontractor's invoice for payment, and generates a check either manually or through electronic funds transfer to the subcontractor.

14. *Prime contractor tracks the revenue and expense*—The prime contractor then tracks the revenue and expense associated with the delivery order in its financial records. This information feeds into both the contract's and company's financial management systems.

Prime Contractor Considerations

Managing Change

This chapter reviewed the components of effecting change. The initial contract represents everything agreed to at contract award. The contract must be modified to reflect any changes that occur during the program's life cycle. Program changes affect the contract between the customer and the prime contractor, however, each change must be approved by the customer before it is reflected in the contract. The bottom line for both the customer's personnel involved in managing the prime contract and for the contractor's personnel involved in implementing the prime contract is to *know the contract*. The other key is to keep the contract document updated with program changes. By knowing precisely what is in the contract, and by living up to the terms and conditions contained within it, most contractual issues are easily resolved.

Additionally, the prime contractor must keep the contract baseline current. If the baseline is in an automated system, the contractor should update the baseline to reflect any products or services that were added or deleted. The baseline should also reflect any changes in suppliers, model numbers, prices, features, or other requirements.

Modifications to Prime Contract May Necessitate Modifications to Subcontracts

A related issue to managing change is the responsibility that the prime contractor has to update subcontracts based on changes made in the prime contract. (The process for implementing a change in a subcontract was described in Chapter 9.) The contractor must realize that modifications to subcontracts may result in a higher price. The prime contractor must decide if it wishes to take on the risk or try to recoup additional funds from its customer. This decision will depend on the nature of the change.

Cash Flow Issue

A key issue for prime contractors during contract performance is cash flow. The prime contractor has to understand the conditions under which it will get paid by the customer. The acceptance terms, payment terms, payment medium (check or electronic funds transfer), return policy, and damages all determine when the prime contractor will actually get paid for products delivered or services rendered. The prime contractor also must be aware of the payment terms it negotiated with each of its subcontractors. If the prime contractor does not carefully manage these two aspects of cash flow, it could easily find itself operating with a negative cash flow if it pays subcontractors before it has received payment from the customer.

Obligation to Fulfill Prime Contract Requirements

The prime contractor has the sole responsibility of meeting customer requirements. If a subcontractor delivers a non-compliant product or inadequate service, it not only jeopardizes the subcontract it has with the prime contractor but it also jeopardizes the contract between the prime contractor and the customer. The prime contractor is ultimately responsible for ensuring quality products and services to its customer, even if the subcontractor fails to do so. Therefore, the prime contractor's first course of action is to do whatever it can to remedy the situation with the customer so as to not lose the contract. Then the prime contractor can always go back and use the contractual remedies available in the subcontract to secure quality performance or receive damages.

Growing the Contract

A prime contractor, just like a subcontractor, is interested in growing its business when it is awarded a contract. Contract growth can result in more revenue, greater marketshare, higher profit margins, more employees working on the contract, or a greater reliance on the contractor by the customer. This contract growth can occur in four ways: new customers, new products or services, lower expenses, or using expertise from previous contracts.

New Customers

Growing the business by adding new customers is driven by how the customer is organized. If the customer is one entity and other entities exist within the customer organization that need the same products or services, the contractor may be able to grow the contract by marketing to those other entities. In government business, the contractor may work with other agencies to get their requirements placed under the existing contract vehicle.

New Products or Services

The prime contractor can also grow the contract by offering new products or services (either its own or from its subcontractors). This technique is driven by what the customer wants added to the contract and whether the prime contractor makes a strong enough business case for adding the products or services.

Lower Expenses

Particularly on a firm, fixed-price contract, the prime contractor can increase its revenue by lowering its contract expenses. Of course, if the contractor cuts too many corners, the customer may complain about the quality of the contractor's products or services. The contractor can maintain service levels and lower expenses by hiring lower-priced personnel, streamlining operations, implementing cost-cutting measures, getting greater discounts from subcontractors, or reducing personnel.

Using Lessons Learned on Other Contracts

A related way in which to grow the business is by taking the expertise gained on previous contracts and applying it the current contract or new business opportunities. For example:

- Success stories gained on a contract could be used in marketing the company to other customers

- Effective streamlining efforts learned on a contract can be used on other contracts

- Practical methods that may or may not have worked on a contract can be tailored for other business opportunities

- People who have learned talents on a contract can be transferred to other contracts to utilize their talents

Subcontractor Considerations

Obligation to Fulfill Subcontract Requirements

The subcontractor is obligated to fulfill its subcontract requirements, even if doing so means that the subcontractor must pay more than it had originally intended. This is why it is important for the subcontractor, during price and technical proposal development, to determine the products, services, prices, and terms and conditions it can live with throughout the life of the contract. Just as the prime contractor may not have a chance to renegotiate the contract, the subcontractor also may not have a chance to renegotiate. The subcontractor must be willing to provide the products and services at the prices it stated or suffer the consequences of subcontract termination or assessment of financial damages.

Keeping Prime Contractor Informed

As mentioned earlier, the prime contractor must keep the subcontractor informed of changes occurring in the prime contract. The subcontractor also is responsible for keeping the prime contractor informed of news it hears about the program. If the contract has clauses that allow products to be changed because a product was discontinued or because of technological advances, the subcontractor must tell the prime contractor about:

- Discontinued items
- Changes in model numbers
- Technological advances

In addition, if the subcontractor's prices are high and remain stagnant, thereby causing the prime contractor's prices to be high, the customer may choose to procure the subcontracted goods and services through alternative methods. If the customer uses alternative methods, both the prime contractor and the subcontractor lose out on business. As such, the prime contractor and the subcontractor must periodically review their prices to ensure that they are still competitive in the marketplace because the customer is probably reviewing the marketplace.

Keeping the Prime Contractor as the Customer

It is in the subcontractor's best interest to keep the prime contractor as a customer because the prime contractor relationship could lead to new business under the existing contract or future contracts. In order to retain the prime contractor as a customer, the subcontractor must do whatever it can to instill trust between the two companies. Some things that do *not* instill trust between the two companies include:

- Marketing product or service sales to the customer without using the prime contract
- Sharing competitive information about the prime contractor
- Exploiting the prime contractor through price gauging or other improper business practices
- Forming strategic alliances with the prime contractor's competitors without giving the prime contractor advance notice

- Failing to perform subcontract obligations
- Allowing unqualified people to support the prime contractor
- Not keeping its commitments or meeting requirements

Successful Performance May Lead to New Opportunities

On a positive note, successful subcontract performance with a prime contractor could lead to new business opportunities, such as:

- Additional business under the current contract
- Future business relationships on other contracts
- Future strategic alliances between the two companies
- Subcontracting opportunities within the prime contract organization
- Information about business opportunities that the subcontractor can pursue through networking

In addition to the advantages that the subcontractor company enjoys from having a trusting relationship with the prime contractor, there are also individual gains to be had by building a trusting relationship with individuals from the prime-contractor organization. For example:

- Mentoring opportunities between the two companies in which each company can help teach the employees of the other company
- Career opportunities within the other organization
- Networking contacts so that the people within the other organization can be successful by having doors open to them that previously were not
- Marketing information about the competition or other customers
- Advance warning about product announcements or reorganizations that may help the individual gain a reputation for being "someone in the know"

Government Considerations

Termination for Convenience

Unlike a commercial contract, the government reserves the right to terminate a contract for the government's own convenience. This means that the contractor, through no fault of its own, is no longer required to work on the contract. The government may choose to terminate for convenience for a number of reasons, including:

- Change in priorities
- Change in program requirements
- Change in regulation
- Change in available funding
- National emergency

The government is usually willing to pay a contractor claim for an equitable adjustment surrounding the government's decision to terminate the contract for convenience. (See the following section on equitable adjustments.)

Must Have Funds to Authorize Performance

A government contracting officer must have funds available and appropriated before he or she can authorize a contractor to perform work. If a contracting officer or other government person authorizes work to be performed without available and appropriated funds, the person runs the risk of losing his or her job and criminal prosecution. This approach is different from the one in the commercial marketplace where an authorized person can give the contractor contingent approval because the project will probably be approved.

The government contracting officer's approval is solely based on the government's requirements. Sometimes, sales people, in an effort to meet "this quarter's quotas" for their own organizations, try to pressure the government to give the go ahead on a purchase order or task order. The government cannot do that. The only deadlines that the government is interested in are program delivery dates or end of government fiscal year dates.

Program Delivery Dates

The program manager decides when products and services are needed from the contractor. When a program manager decides products or services are needed, he or she will work with the contracting officer who will prepare the task-order request for proposal or the delivery order for products. The contractor will then have the ability to either bid on the work or provide the products and services. If a contractor wishes to make a sale, it must work with the program manager to make the sale occur.

End of Government Fiscal Year

The end of the government's fiscal year is September 30. When the government awards a contract, it requires the contractor to provide prices by government fiscal year. The contractor must provide a price for each product or service by fiscal year. The government does this for a very specific reason: its funding is appropriated by its fiscal year. A lot of contractor sales occur during the last week of September because the government is trying to spend the money that it was allocated by the end of the government's fiscal year. If an agency does not spend the money it was allotted, it will lose the money.

In addition, the government is trying to buy products and services at the lower prices that it may obtain by either buying the products in the former or latter fiscal year before the contractor increases its prices or before contractor discounts are no longer available.

Appropriations

The government also has one other issue it must contend with as it contracts: appropriations. In Department of Defense contracts, the government stipulates how money will be appropriated. For example, the contract may designate money to be available for only research and development, or to purchase items, or to operate and maintain the items. Appropriations limit the government customer from spending money erroneously, for example, items can only be purchased using purchase money.

Prime Contractor Has an Obligation to Meet Its Small Business and Small, Disadvantaged Business Goals

The prime contractor set forth in its proposal a plan to help the government meet its small business and small, disadvantaged business (SB/SDB) goals. During contract performance, the prime contractor must live up to the goals that it set forth in the proposal. This requirement may guide which subcontractor the prime contractor gives business to under the prime contract. If the prime contractor fails to meet its SB/SDB goals, the government could terminate the contractor for default (not likely) or it can limit the amount of profit and business the prime contractor gets under the contract.

Managing Change on Complex Programs

Additional caveats to changes in government programs that the contractor needs to address are discussed in this section.

Variances

The first thing the government does to manage change on complex programs is to determine how the proposed change will affect the cost and the schedule. The government uses variance analysis to ascertain whether a change has a positive or negative consequence on the cost and schedule of the program. A *positive cost variance* occurs when the actual cost for the work performed is less than budgeted. A *negative cost variance* occurs when the actual cost for the work performed is more than budgeted. A *positive schedule variance* occurs when the actual time to perform the work is less than budgeted. A *negative schedule variance* occurs when the actual time to perform the work is more than budgeted.

In order to determine the variance, the government must compare current conditions against how things are going to be as a result of the change. The government uses program phases and configuration management to help isolate and evaluate the proposed change.

Government Program Phases

As mentioned earlier, sometimes a change in one program affects other programs. In complex programs, the government typically thinks of a program going through four phases:

- Phase 0: Concept exploration and definition
- Phase 1: Demonstration and validation
- Phase 2: Engineering, manufacturing, and development
- Phase 3: Production and deployment/operations and support

The government works with the contractor during each of these phases to develop configuration baselines for three out of the four baselines. The Phase 0 baseline is known as the *functional baseline*, the Phase 1 baseline is the *allocated baseline*, Phase 2 does not have a baseline, and Phase 3 is known as the *product baseline*.

Configuration baselines are made up of configuration items. These items are units of work that satisfy some component of the work breakdown structure and are tied to a specific user requirement. When the government or contractor wants to make a change to a complex program, it must first evaluate how the baseline will be changed as a result of the proposed change.

Not All Changes Are Created Equal

The magnitude of the change can vary from having little affect to a profound affect on a program. The government classifies changes into two categories based on the effect to the program:

- Class 1 changes alter the form, fit, or function of a program component. For example, if the weight of a missile on a bomber program increases, this change could affect the aircraft, aerodynamics, and physical layout of the missile bay. Because of the far-reaching implications of Class 1 changes, the government typically requires that the change be processed through an engineering change process, which is discussed later.

- Class 2 changes are administrative changes that have relatively little affect on the other program requirements. For example, if the manufacturer of the knobs required in the cockpit goes out of business and the prime contractor secures another knob manufacturer whose knobs meet the same specifications as the previous manufacturer, then it is a Class 2 change.

Engineering Change Process

When the contractor is involved in a Class 1 change, it must present the engineering change to the Configuration Control Board (CCB). The CCB reviews the change and its implications on the program. Then it recommends to the government's program manager that the engineering change be accepted or rejected. The program manager either accepts or rejects the engineering change. If the manager rejects the change, the contractor ceases all work on the change. If the manager accepts the change, the contractor completes the engineering change proposal. The engineering change proposal is negotiated between the government and the prime contractor. The contractor is responsible for documenting any changes to the configuration baseline and work breakdown structures. As the change is being implemented, the government validates the contractor's change process to ensure accuracy. Once the change is implemented, the government evaluates the contractor's performance against the new baseline.

Equitable Adjustment

The government understands that it must somehow compensate the contractor for changes that the government mandates in a federal contract. Equitable adjustments are described in the Changes clause (FAR 52.243-1). An *equitable adjustment* is an amount equal to the difference between what a reasonable person believes is the amount it should have cost the contractor to perform the work before and after the change was made. The government allows a contractor to submit a claim in which it delineates the total amount it should have cost to perform the work and how much it will now cost because of the change. The government limits its liability by requiring the contractor to justify the costs as those that result only from the change and not those that are due to the contractor's failure to accurately predict its performance costs.

The prime contractor can also include any claims made by its subcontractor in the contractor's claim to the government under the changes or termination for convenience clauses.

Maintain Audit-Readiness

Most Audits Occur During Contract Performance

Most audits will occur during the contract performance stage of the contract because this is when most contract work is completed and auditable actions are likely to occur. The government may choose to come in for any of the audits already discussed in an earlier chapter, or the government may require an audit that does not fit neatly into any of the categories previously discussed. If the government suspects any contractor or government wrongdoing, it can call for an audit. Sometimes the Government Accounting Office or Inspector General may conduct an agency-wide audit that reviews all the contracts with that agency.

Conduct Quality Checks on Audit Information

The key to passing audits is to stay diligent on keeping the information current throughout contract start-up, performance, and shutdown and not waiting until the government schedules an audit before getting prepared. The contract team should conduct spot checks of CPSR, time cards, and proposal efforts to ensure compliance.

Prepare for the CPSR, Time Card, Labor, or Ad Hoc Audit

The contractor must understand exactly what the auditor is coming in to review so that it can supply useful information to the auditor. Typically, the contractor has to prepare its files by either tabbing or pulling out relevant sections for the auditor. The contractor may have to locate the files if they are spread out within the organization (i.e., some are retained by the internal support teams and some are retained by the contract core team). The contractor also wants to know what information the auditor will want to see so that it does not give too much information. Providing too much information is not wise because the auditor could review the information and find problems he or she was not even looking for.

Complete After-Audit Tasks

After the audit, the contractor needs to understand what the government's concerns are and determine how to fix the problem areas. Oftentimes, the auditor will say which specific parts of the process need to be rectified. Perhaps the process itself does not need to be fixed but its enforcement needs to be improved. After the contractor understands the concerns, it needs to develop strategies to mitigate those concerns and identify operating recommendations for correcting problem areas. Developing the strategies and identifying the operating recommendations is the easy part. The challenge comes in communicating, teaching, and implementing the changes across organizations. The time frame to implement these changes is usually pretty quick because the government auditor will be back to check on the progress of the implementation of the recommendations.

8   CONTRACT CLOSE OUT

The contract shutdown period is a time of tying up loose ends. Contract shutdown occurs once a contract term is over, after contract work is complete, when a contract option is not exercised, or a contractor is terminated for default. In a government contract, contract shutdown can also occur because the agency exercised a termination for convenience clause. The contractor is obligated to perform all contractual duties until the last day of the contract. On a government contract, the prime contractor must close out the prime contract with the government. In order to do so, the prime contractor must close out all the subcontracts with the subcontractors. The contractor must resolve issues so that the government can conduct its final audit so that the contractor can receive its final payment within seven years after the contract closes. On a commercial contract, the prime contractor typically chooses to work with the customer to close out the prime contract and the associated subcontracts to minimize the risk and exposure for all companies involved.

The duration of the contract shutdown varies depending on how long the contract has run; how many people are involved in the shutdown process; the specific contractual, company, and customer requirements; and how many open issues need to be resolved. Usually, a contractor can complete contract shutdown in 6 to 12 months, and the government has up to seven years after contract close out to complete its audit and final payment.

The prime contractor needs to work with the customer to establish a closedown plan that encompasses all the functional areas addressed in this book. The plan should include a schedule that states the customer's milestones for work completion, subcontractor release, and contractor transition to another contractor, if required. The customer has different options as to how it wants to end a prime contract. For example, the customer may release a follow-on contract, or the work may be completed and the customer no longer needs the contractor's services, or the contract may be extended for a short period of time until alternative methods for accomplishing the work are established. The customer must review all of these options with the prime contractor so that the contractor does not do anything that would impede the customer's actions. For example, if the customer wants to extend the prime contract for a short period of time, the customer should notify the prime contractor so it doesn't begin closing out subcontracts, because if the subcontracts had to be re-opened, the subcontractors may try to raise their prices. The customer and the contractor must maintain a close coordination during close out. One way to do this is to create a contract close out plan.

Characteristics

The characteristics of contract shutdown may include a decreasing workload and low employee morale because the contract is ending and anticipation over new career opportunities, however, the contractor is obligated by contract to maintain customer satisfaction. In order to maintain quality work during this possibly difficult time, the contract team should develop a shutdown plan. The team developing the contract shutdown plan should consider the following:

- The customer and prime contractor must close out the prime contract and all outstanding issues should be resolved. Closing out the prime contract typically requires that the prime contractor close out all subcontracts and that it resolve all outstanding issues with the subcontractors.

- A contract closedown plan is helpful to ensure that all customer and corporate objectives are met and to plan for a transition delay, if necessary.

- All contract work must continue while the team is downsized and as people pursue new opportunities.

- If the contractor has established a good customer relationship, then close out activities remain a team effort with both sides helping the other to get documents to complete their files. If a bad customer relationship exists, contract close out can be difficult as each side drags up old issues that need to be closed.

- The contractor must continue to meet contract requirements until the contract ends, because not only is it good business to do so, but also because terminations for default can still occur.

- Customer satisfaction is paramount. Sloppy work toward the end of the contract leaves a lasting impressions that the customer will remember when the contractor asks for recommendations on future procurements.

- The contractor may experience a surplus or a shortage of personnel at the end of the contract. The team must determine who is critical to the contract and provide incentives to those people so that they stay until the contract ends. Additionally, the team needs to help find new jobs for people.

- The contract must have internal support until the contract ends but then terminate the service level agreements so that it does not accrue additional, nonbillable charges.

- The contractor must close out subcontracts before closing out the prime contract and the contractor must resolve all outstanding issues. The customer may need to extend the subcontracts if the customer extends the prime contract.

- The contractor may need to provide training on resume writing and interviewing for employees looking for new jobs.

- Good communication needs to continue throughout contract closedown because people get more anxious when their future is uncertain.

- How well the team followed procedures while they worked on the contract will drive how successful close out will be (i.e., if the contract team consistently kept copies of all documents and filed them in a given order, all contract documentation should be easily retrievable for close out).

- Closing out issues typically have a dollar effect so the team must create a cost-efficient plan.

- The company's upper management is not as interested in the contract; everyone seems to be losing interest and is moving on to new deals.

- The customer's marketing efforts are now focused on trying to get products and services that were provided under the contract moved to another contract from which the contractor will be able to provide similar work.

- Automated tools, if used to capture information consistently and accurately, help tremendously in collecting the data necessary to closedown the contract.

- The contractor may need to provide deliverables up to the last day of contract performance. The contractor must continue to provide them even though the staff is shrinking.

- All facilities, technology, equipment, and any government furnished property must be transferred, returned, disposed, excessed, or given to charity.

- The contractor must retain an audit trail complete enough to merit final payment.

Though no one likes close out, the company can lose a great deal of money if the process is not managed successfully.

Process

Begin Shutting Down the Prime Contract

Understand Why the Contract Is Being Closed

Contracts close for a number of reasons: the work is complete, the customer decides not to renew an option year, or the contractor is terminated because it was in default of the contract. Each of these reasons for close out carries with it its own set of requirements for what tasks must be included in the shutdown. Many of the requirements are the same; for example, system access must be terminated and customer-furnished property must be returned. The company should find out what actions are required for contract shutdown based on the specific contract.

Determine Goals of the Shutdown

Once the contractor understands why the contract is being closed, it can then begin to determine the goals of the shutdown. Goals should be reviewed in terms of three perspectives: the customer, the prime contractor, and the subcontractor. For example, if the customer is pleased with the contractor's team's work, the contractor could make one of its goal be to have the team work on other pieces of business for the customer. If the contract work is not complete and the contract is about to expire, it may be in all parties' best interests to extend the contract. If a contract gets extended, the prime contractor will need to determine which subcontracts it needs to extend to support that effort.

Ideally, the contractor and its subcontractors would like to be able to keep as much of the contract work as possible after the contract closes. This is not always possible in the government marketplace because the government conducts a solicitation for a follow-on contract. However, there are instances when the contractor works with the customer to move portions of the work to another contract that the contractor has, or the contractor offers to move under a contract vehicle with another prime contractor just to be able to keep the work. The customer and the contractor must discuss special relationships and reach an agreement before the close of the contract.

Identify Information Requirements for Close Out

The customer and the contractor should work together to determine what information each side needs to complete its own internal close out procedures. By determining the requirements up front, both sides may be able to assist the other with any missing documentation and can complete an orderly transition. The types of data required for close out include:

- Contracts
- Subcontracts
- Agreements
- Modifications
- Task orders
- Delivery orders
- Purchase orders
- Correspondence
- Accounts payable records and backup data
- Accounts receivable records and backup data
- Audit reports
- Data on any claims by or against the company
- Copyright or patent data
- Contract performance data
- Insurance policies
- Inventory records
- Internal billing and back up
- Lease, maintenance, or service agreements

Continue Customer Relationship

The customer-contractor partnership may take several different turns at contract shutdown:

- It could disintegrate because the work is complete and there is no reason for the relationship to exist.
- It could carry on in a different contract vehicle.
- It could be suspended as the people involved in the relationship go on to other positions. The relationship could then get

reestablished between the same or different people who are now in different capacities within their organizations.

Whether the relationship continues depends on a number of factors, such as the stability of the customer-contractor partnership, the value the customer places on that partnership, if work needs to be done, and if the individuals are still working in a similar area.

Reasons for Maintaining Good Customer Relationships at Contract Shutdown

Good customer relationships take a long time to build; the customer should be careful to not damage its relationship with the customer at the end of the contract. The contractor must stay focused on maintaining a good customer relationship, at least until the end of the contract, for several reasons:

- It is the right thing to do.
- The customer can initiate termination proceedings if the contractor fails to perform.
- The customer can influence the contractor's future business opportunities.
- Close out efforts require the talents of both the customer and the contractor.
- Work may be able to be kept by the contractor using a different contract.

The following section reviews each of these reasons.

The Right Thing to Do

Maintaining a good customer relationship should always be paramount in the contractor's mind. Relationships are based on individuals trusting each other to do the right thing. Contract shutdown may represent a difficult time for the people working on the contract: they may be looking for other jobs, they may be tasked to work on other projects because their current project is ending, they may have anxiety about leaving their current job, or they may be so enthusiastic about the future that they don't want to look back at what has to be done to close their current contract. Regardless of the uncomfortable feelings some may be experiencing, the contractor and the customer should be committed to the relationship and preserve it.

Termination for Default

The contractor must meet contract requirements until the last day of the contract. If the contractor fails to deliver the goods and services up until the last day, the customer could terminate the contractor for default. Even if the customer does not resort to default proceedings, it is not in the contractor's best interest to have a stellar performance record throughout contract performance ruined in the last days, weeks, or months of the contract.

Contracting Officer Influence

On government contracts, the contracting officer can influence the contractor's ability to win future procurements by using the contractor evaluation sheets. The government customer fills out these sheets on a government contractor. Source selection authorities and procuring contract officers (PCOs) use the evaluations to validate the contractor's ability to perform on previous government contracts. If the contractor fails to meet contract requirements, the contracting officer could emphasize the poor contractor performance at the end of the contract and give the contractor low scores for delivery and performance. These low scores could cause the contractor to lose future procurements.

Close Out Is a Team Effort

It is in both the customer's and contractor's best interest to conduct a smooth close out. The customer has to ensure that the contractor will not come back to the customer with unresolved contractual issues several years after the contract has closed. The contractor also does not want to have any contractual issues remaining, nor does it want any of its subcontractors to come back with any outstanding contractual issues. To meet both teams' objectives, a cooperative effort needs to occur. If the contract lasted a long time, both parties will probably find gaps in their data files: the contractor may have information that the customer needs to closedown the contract, and the customer may have information that the contractor needs to closedown the contract. Events that occurred and need explanation during the close out process may not have been documented in the contract files. Both teams probably have pertinent contract, so both teams need to work together to ensure that both sides have the adequate documentation necessary for a smooth close out.

Moving Existing Work to Other Contract Vehicles

Because of the government's ability and current emphasis to maximize the use of contract vehicles to obtain the best value for the government, contractors have developed multiple channels or contract vehicles through which to procure goods and services. This is an opportunity for a contractor because when one contract ends, the products or services for that contract may be purchased through another contract vehicle. However, this process is not automatic. Because of the government's regulations, work may have to be recompeted among new and existing contractors. Whether the work can be done through another existing contract or if it must be won back through a recompetition, the contractor should begin developing its strategy for retaining the work early on before the contract close out actually occurs.

Manage Contract Core Team Personnel

During contract shutdown, the contractor must balance the work that must be done with the orderly downsizing of the staff. Although the task seems simple enough, conditions during contract shutdown make the period difficult for many people. However, the contractor must remember that contractual ramifications can occur if all contract work is not performed.

Contract Environment

Contract shutdown tends to be bittersweet. Bitter because team members are leaving a comfort zone that has been established on the contract. People, work, relationships, and customers are all established and familiar and the team members know how to effectively get their jobs done. Some fear the unknown regarding their next job. Then as the people on the contract begin to leave to pursue new opportunities, remaining team members may experience a sense of loss and the realization of the finality of the contract.

Contract shutdown is sweet because the team can take pride in a job well done. The contract has given individuals the skills they need to be marketable on their next career endeavor. New beginnings, new opportunities, and new challenges await the team members.

Contract Ramifications

In spite of the emotionally charged environment in which people are working, contract work still must be accomplished during shutdown. The team must complete daily contract work, provide deliverables, and attend customer meetings to meet the contract requirements. If this work is not accomplished, there are severe ramifications for the contractor; for example:

- The contractor could be terminated for default.
- The contractor could lose its good reputation that it has taken the entire contract to develop.
- The contractor could receive bad scores on contractor performance evaluations that will affect its ability to win future customer contracts.

Suggested Solutions

This section covers some key approaches to working with people during contract closedown to meet the contractor's need of maintaining good customer relationships and the team members' need of finding new job opportunities.

Agree on the Final End Date with the Customer

Contract shutdown could be driven by when the contract work is completed, termination, or the customer's decision not to renew an option year on the contract. Even if a contract is scheduled to be shut down, the customer may extend the contract because it has not established a follow-on contract or existing work is not complete. The actual end date of the contract may be somewhat flexible. As soon as reasonably possible, the contractor and the customer should agree on the actual end date of the contract. This will ensure that the contractor has adequate staff to work on the contract through shutdown.

Decide Which Functions Are Required Up to the End of the Contract

The contractor's management team should decide if all functions are necessary throughout contract shutdown. If the last deliverable is due 30 days before the end of the contract, the production team will still be needed before contract shutdown. Certain key people have to be available until the contract is shut down. The contractor's management team will have to devise an incentive program to encourage these people to stay on the contract until their talents are no longer needed. To solidify this decision, the team should create a list of all the people on the contract and the dates after which they are eligible for release from the contract.

Keep People Informed

Once the management team establishes the release date, it should inform the team members. This will give the members the maximum amount of time to prepare for their next career opportunity. Although the management team would like people to stay on the contract until their release date, employees will be looking out for their own best interests. If an employee finds a permanent position, he or she will more than likely take it regardless of his or her actual release date. This is understandable: Take a guaranteed position now rather than hope for a position to be available later. One way keep some of the employees is to ask them to plan their new job start dates to coincide with the dates that they are no longer needed on the contract. In this situation, everyone wins: Team members get new opportunities, and the management team has the resources it needs to complete the contract.

Decide Which People and Skills the Company Wishes to Retain

Ideally, the contractor would like to be in a position in which everyone on a closing contract is migrated over to another contract or support organization within the contractor's company. Depending on the size of the company, the number of existing contracts, and the number of people needing to be placed, this option may not be feasible. If the contractor cannot retain all of its contract people, it should decide which people or skills it should try to retain. Key managers, talented individual performers, or people with hard-to-find skills are usually the types of people the contractor wants to keep.

Inform Internal Teams that People Are Available

Once the contractor decides who should be retained, the next step is for it to try to find career opportunities for those people within the company. Recruiting efforts, internal job fairs, resume databases, and word-of-mouth are all techniques used to get people placed in new positions within the company.

Decide Which Benefits Are Available for People

If contract shutdown means that some people will lose their jobs within the company altogether, the management team must decide what benefits will be offered to those people leaving the company. Management should clearly communicate the benefits to the appropriate employees. Possible benefits include the following:

- Resume writing assistance, which could include a resume writing class or access to company resources to develop resumes
- Job placement assistance, which could include company-sponsored job fairs or time off for interviewing
- Severance package, which usually includes a certain amount of money for every year the person was employed with the company
- Early retirement options, which may grant employees bonus years to be added to their age and number of years of service with the company

If the total number of people being laid off at a particular contractor location is 75 or greater and the contractor is working on a government contract, the federal government has regulations about procedures that the contractor must follow. These regulations include notifying local social service agencies and publicizing the downsize.

Conduct a Closing Event

A completed contract represents a great deal of hard work by many people. In closing a contract, it is a good idea to have a celebration for those people who made the contract a success. The event allows people to bring closure to this part of their career and gives the management team the opportunity to give a well-deserved thank you for the efforts expended.

Close Out Internal Support Team Efforts

If the internal support team is carefully managed, contract shutdown should be an easy event. Part of carefully managing the internal support team is having the management team move people on and off the contract as necessitated by the work load. The management team is also continually looking for new business opportunities for the team to pursue. Careful management signals that contract shutdown is just another transition period for the people working on the contract as they move to other opportunities within the internal support team or other contracts.

Close Out Subcontracts

The last phase of the subcontract relationship is subcontractor close out. Part of terminating the prime contract is terminating all subcontracts. Termination of the subcontract can occur under normal circumstances—the contract is completed or the customer chose not to exercise an option. Likewise, the subcontract may be terminated due to the default of the prime contractor or for the convenience of the government. In any of these instances, termination proceedings begin.

Subcontractor's Role

A subcontractor's role during subcontract close out is as follows:

- Provide any outstanding deliverables
- Complete any outstanding contract work
- Return any customer-furnished equipment or information
- Return any prime-contractor furnished equipment or information
- Resolve any open issues between the subcontractor and the prime contractor
- Submit a final invoice for service rendered
- Submit any claims for equitable adjustment if the situation merits such requests

Resolving Subcontract Issues

Subcontract issues typically have a dollar effect. If the contract team was good about resolving financial issues all along, there will probably be no surprises at the end of the contract. Otherwise, money that is owed to the subcontractor will need to come out of the current budget even though the problem may have occurred years ago. Similarly, if the subcontractor owes the prime contractor money, the subcontractor will have to pay the contractor from the current budget. Though this may present a potential windfall at the end if either party is owed money, it is not a good idea to delay resolving financial issues. Delays could be caused by personnel changes; The new people are not familiar with the history of the issue and do not have any of the backup documentation for the claim. Another reason is that the subcontractor may have been merged, acquired, or gone out of business by the time of contract close out, thereby making resolution of issues even more complicated. For these reasons, it is best to resolve subcontractual issues as they occur and not wait until the end of the contract.

Complete Training Initiatives

As the contract is closing, the contractor's emphasis switches from learning about the current customer and contract requirements to future customers and contract requirements. If the contract work can be migrated to a different contract, then the contract team only needs to be trained on the new contract. If the contract work cannot be migrated to a new contract, then the team must be trained for new challenges and opportunities. There are two different emphases on training people during contract shutdown: training for new areas of responsibility and training on business skills.

Training for New Areas of Responsibility

As the contract is winding down, a careful assessment of each person's career development plan and resume should be done by both the individual and his or her manager. In this review, they should determine a career objective and what position could help the person meet the career objective. They should also review the person's experience to see what additional skills are required for the career objective. For example, an employee has been a technical person for the last five years and she wants to become a technical manager. If she has no managerial experience, she may need managerial training to become a technical manager candidate. If she needs a lot of additional training, she may need to take on another position before reaching her career objective. Once the manager and individual determine a career goal and the training needed, they can look for that type of position within the company.

If the manager and the individual find that only a small amount of training is required, they may determine methods through the current contract to get the person the experience she needs to apply for a technical manager position. For example, if she needs experience in conducting employee evaluations or in preparing budgets, the current contract may offer those training opportunities.

Training on Business Skills

The other type of employee development that occurs during contract shutdown training is business skill education. This training is focused on giving people the skills they need to look for another job, to write a clear resume, and to successfully complete an interview. These are skills that employees had at one time in their repertoire, but over time, and particularly if the contract has gone on for a long time, locating another job, writing a resume, and interviewing are all skills that many employees believe they need to update and practice. By allowing the human resource department or an outside organization to conduct training classes, the employees on a closing contract get the skills they need.

Manage Communications Efforts

Communication is key during the contract shutdown phase. To ensure that the contract shutdown occurs in an orderly fashion while maintaining the service levels required by the contact, there must be a close coordination between the customer and the prime contractor and the prime contractor and its subcontractor.

New Communication Link

The government's terminating contracting officer (TCO) and the prime contractor's point of contact during shutdown must forge a new communication link. These two people will need to pull the resources of both their teams to ensure all the requirements of shutdown are met and final payment can be obtained.

Shutting Down Communication Links

At the end of the contract, the customer and the prime contractor must close out many of the links that existed to support communication during the contract. For example, access to systems must be terminated on both the contractor and the customer side. In place of these communication links, the customer must determine alternative methods, such as using the contract, to secure the information that it needs on a daily basis.

Reestablish Communication Links among New Players

Another alternative to shutting down the communication links is to reestablish the links among new players from the prime contractor, the customer, and the subcontractor organizations. Perhaps portions of the contract work can be moved to another contract. In this instance, the communication links would need to be reestablished among the new team members.

Develop a Deliverable Audit Trail

Ensure Files Have a Complete Set of Deliverables

The contractor needs to provide a complete set of deliverables and acceptance documents as part of contract close out. The degree of difficulty with contract shutdown is directly related to the degree of adherence to the procedures established during contract start-up. If people follow the procedures, collect the data, and turn in acceptable deliverables, shutting down the contract is a quick and easy exercise. In this case, it would consist of archiving the documents and deliverables. If people don't follow procedures, or the collected data is inaccurate, or the customer does not accept the deliverables, then the contract team must go back and locate all the missing data elements before it can obtain final payment. This is particularly difficult to do when the contract has gone on for a long period of time and its original members are working on other projects.

Determine Which Data Need to Be Kept as Part of the Contract Files

Not all data maintained on the contract need to be kept as part of the contract files. Usually, the customer's terminating representative or the terminating contracting officer (TCO) in a government contract and the contractor's point of contact for shutdown meet to decide the list of items that are needed to meet both the customer's and the contractor's requirements for contract shutdown. This meeting should occur early in the close out process so that information needs are defined before people from either organization start leaving. When people leave, vital contract files potentially may be taken with them.

Prepare Files for Shutdown

The government, as well as individual companies, usually has specific requirements for file retention and archival during contract shutdown. These requirements will dictate where the files should be stored, how accessible the files should be, and who will be responsible for answering any customer questions during the allotted seven years the government requires for shutdown.

Shutdown Systems

The last step in contract close out is to shut down the systems that have been used to retain contract data. Both the customer and the contractor may have data systems at their locations. If the systems support multiple contracts, then the parties will only have to terminate the access of the employees working on the contract.

Finalize Financials

The customer and the prime contractor conduct contract close out for several reasons:

- The contract work has terminated and issues must be resolved.

- The customer wants to ensure that the prime contractor will not come back several years after contract award with issues to which it expects financial resolution. If the contractor did, the customer would be forced to pay damages out of its then-current-year budgets, which would lower the dollar amount it had for meeting that current year's objectives.

- The prime contractor wants to ensure that the subcontractor will not come back several years after contract award with issues to which it expects financial resolution. If a subcontractor did, the prime contractor would be forced to pay damages out of its then-current-year budgets, which would lower the dollar amount it had for meeting that current year's objectives.

- On government contracts, the prime contractor may be entitled to a final payment for products delivered and services rendered. Because overhead and G&A rates used in any given year are provisional (i.e., the contractor has to wait until the end of the year after all expenses have been calculated to determine what the true rates are for the year), the customer reserves the right to audit all contract files and rate buildups up to seven years after the close of the contract before it makes final payment to the contractor.

Determine What Financial Data Must Be Kept

In order to meet the financial objectives of contract close out, the contract team must understand what financial data must be kept in the archives as per the company and the contract. If the contract team has followed the procedures and if it checked the data for accuracy throughout the life of the contract, these tasks become rather simple for the team to accomplish. Similarly, if it kept the contract current and delivery orders were modified when they needed to be, the team probably will not experience many open issues that need resolution before contract close.

Ensure Cost Centers Are Closed

The contractor also needs to ensure that cost centers, which were set up to support product and service delivery and task-order completion, are closed. This is because any charge to the cost centers will continue to hit on the financial records of the closing contract. Expenses will continue to incur with no corresponding revenue, making the profit margins deteriorate. Additionally, there is a bigger issue in that when the contract is closed, there should be few, if any, charges made to the cost centers because the work is complete. Charging to these cost centers usually causes inaccurate invoices to be sent to the customer. The only way to fix the problem is to correct all expenses that hit the cost centers erroneously, which requires significant effort from the team to determine which expenses are erroneous and to which cost centers it should move the expenses.

The contract team should notify internal support groups that support product or service delivery that the contract is closing and that all work in support of the contract should stop. For example, if the contractor has an internal support team that buys spare parts to provide maintenance to the customer on the contract, the contract core team should work with the team to forecast what the exact requirements should be throughout the close of the contract. This effort will prevent the company from spending money on parts or updating training materials that will never be used.

Complete Marketing Efforts

Ensure Work Ends by Contract End Date or Can Be Moved Under a Different Contract Vehicle

Contract shutdown offers new challenges for marketing initiatives. The contractor could lose all the work it has because the contract has expired, or the contractor can look for other contract vehicles under which to complete the work. If the contractor cannot move its work to another contract, then the contractor must ensure all the work is complete by the contract end date or determine a way for work to continue after contract close out (with the contracting officer's approval). Not all work can continue after the close of a contract, but sometimes warranties, maintenance, or task-order work may extend past the contract end date. The contractor must discuss any of these options with the contracting officer before contract close out so that there is no interruption of service for the customer (or revenue for the contractor).

Figure Out What Can Be Sold Until the End of the Contract

Because all contracts are different, the contractor needs to determine if any components of the contract will extend to the end of the contract. For example, sometimes products and services are available for purchase through the end of the year before the end of the contract, and maintenance is available all the way until the end date of the contract. The contractor must know what can be sold through the life of the contract so that it can sell the maximum possible.

Market Services to Incoming Contractor

If the customer awards a follow-on contract, the contractor may wish to market its services to the incoming contractor. This approach benefits the existing contractor because it allows for follow-on work and it benefits the incoming contractor because it acquires people with current expertise in the customer's environment. The existing contractor may be able to solve service problems that the incoming contractor is unaware of.

Keep Track of Where the Customer Goes

If the contract ends, the contractor, at a minimum, should keep track of what is going on in the customer's environment or where the customer is reassigned. Previous customers can help with future business opportunities, particularly if the contractor performed well for the customer.

Close Down Facilities and Get Rid of Equipment

Determine a Schedule for When Items Are No Longer Needed

As discussed earlier, the customer may extend a contract or the work may be moved under another contract. The contractor should determine a schedule for when its items are no longer needed by the contract. Leased items should be returned to minimize any additional expense.

Dispose of Facilities, Technology, and Equipment

The contract team will need to dispose of facilities, technology, and equipment that was necessary to support the contract. Options for disposing of items include transferring to existing contracts, returning (if rented or borrowed) to original source, moving them with the people going to new opportunities within the company, saving them for new contracts, excessing them, giving them to a charity, or throwing them out.

Close Out Proposals and Task Orders

Ensure Acceptance Documents Were Obtained for Products or Services Delivered

The contractor needs to have documentation during contract close out verifying that the products and services delivered under the contract were the products and services that the customer ordered, that they were on the contract baseline at the time of order, and that the customer actually received and accepted them. The acceptance documents are the customer's way of informing the contractor that the products were approved and that it is acceptable for the contractor to invoice and receive payment. If waivers or deviations were used at any point of the contract, the contractor should include them in the contract files to demonstrate that the customer did make exceptions on a limited number of events. Additionally, the contract files should contain anything that the contractor gave in consideration for the right to substitute products or services that were not on the contract at the time the order was placed. For example, if the contractor offered an early delivery, an expedited performance schedule, or a delivery order discount on the non-compliant products, then this information should be in the contract files. (The government is not at liberty to grant waivers and deviations without receiving something in return from the contractor.)

Ensure All Task-Order Work Was Completed

The contractor must have documentation in its files that supports the fact that all task-order work was completed. The contractor should keep signed acceptance documents, copies of all deliverables made under a task order, and time cards and expense reports to substantiate who worked on the task order, when the work was done, how many hours were worked, what the expenses were, and what deliverables were provided.

Ensure Any Open Issue Has Been Resolved

The contractor should understand that an open issue occurs any time complete and accurate information is not available to support that products and services were delivered, or that task order work was completed. Sometimes the customer or the subcontractor will have copies of pertinent information that the contractor can get for its files. Sometimes the documents do not exist because acceptance was never obtained. The contractor needs to resolve or write off open issues at the time of contract close out.

Prime Contractor Considerations

The Contract Must Go On

The key thing for the prime contractor to focus on is that the contractual obligations must be carried out until the last day of performance. This means that even in the face of unenthusiastic employees looking for their next opportunity, a disinterested upper management team, and subcontractors that are focused on getting their next business opportunity, the prime contractor must focus on and meet the contractual obligations until the contract is officially over. If the prime contractor does not, it risks being terminated for default and receiving poor contract evaluations that can affect future business.

Other Opportunities?

The prime contractor with the support of the subcontractors need to evaluate with the customer whether or not the contract work is completed, and if it is not completed, they need to determine if the work can be moved to another contract vehicle. The customer has the ultimate decision to make based on:

- The prime contractor's and the subcontractors' performance during the life of the contract
- Program requirements
- Pending legislation (if the customer is a government agency)
- Internal direction (if the customer is a commercial company)
- Other contract vehicle requirements

If the work is completed, the customer may still choose to continue work with the prime contractor and its subcontractors by defining other requirements that the team can work on. A governmental customer has more restrictions imposed on it than a commercial customer would to do this kind of thing.

If the customer decides to continue working with the contractor team, it can simply cease operating under the existing contract on the contract end date and just begin issuing task orders or delivery orders under the new contract vehicle after the customer negotiates a new prime contract.

Ideally, the contractor team should strive for an ongoing customer relationship throughout the life of the contract. This is because it is much more cost effective to continue to gain business from a satisfied current customer than it is to secure new business from a customer with whom the team has never worked.

Close Out Timing

The prime contractor has to ensure that it stays in synch with the customer to establish mutually agreeable milestones for contract close out. The contractor needs to be particularly concerned with this issue, not only to maintain customer satisfaction, but to ensure that it does not incur any additional subcontractor expenses. For example, if the prime contractor closes out all of the subcontracts but the customer decides to do some extra contract work requiring one of the subcontractors, the prime contractor will have to renegotiate with the subcontractor. Those renegotiations will almost inevitably lead to a higher subcontractor price, yet the prime contractor will still be required to provide the product or service at the same prime contract price to the customer.

Subcontractor Considerations

No Other Chance at Recouping Payments

The prime contractor will probably require the subcontractor to sign a statement stating that no further payment is due under the terms and conditions of the subcontract before the subcontract is closed out. The prime contractor does this to protect itself from a subcontractor claim lodged months or even years after the subcontract has been closed. Even if the claim is legitimate, the prime contractor will probably not have any recourse to receive payment from the customer because the customer probably had the prime contractor sign a similar statement. (For government contracts, see the discussion below on the "M" accounts.)

Other Opportunities with Prime Contractor

The subcontractor wants to do everything it can to continue to satisfy the prime contractor even during contract close out. For all the same reasons that the prime contractor tries to maintain customer satisfaction, the subcontractor wants to do whatever it can to maintain the trust built up between the two companies during contract performance. This trust could result in new business opportunities that are mutually beneficial to both the prime contractor and the subcontractor.

Other Opportunities with Successor Contractors

When a prime contract ends, it would be nice if the contract work could continue with the same prime contractor under a different contract. Sometimes this is not in the best interest of the customer or the subcontractor. The subcontractor may learn that the prime contractor is not going after the re-compete business (for whatever reason) or that the customer is not likely to select the incumbent prime contractor even if it did decide to pursue the business. In these situations, the subcontractor should work with another contractor that is going after the follow-on business. The subcontractor has a strategic advantage because it has done the work and may provide a competitive advantage to the new contractor team.

Breaking Out

Another alternative for the subcontractor is to pursue the re-compete business as a prime contractor either working alone or subcontracting a portion of the work to another company. While the subcontractor worked on the contract, it got insider's experience on how the customer operates, strategies that work, and political issues that may affect the contract's success. Armed with this information, the subcontractor becomes a viable candidate to win the follow-on contract.

Government Considerations

Government Must Go through the Close Out Process

Although a commercial customer may choose whether to go through a formal contract close out, the government must go through contract close out. The reasons why the government must go through close out are as follows:

- Required by regulation
- To ensure that the prime contractor or its subcontractors do not lodge any future claims
- To ensure a clean contract file with all outstanding issues resolved
- To protect its future budgets (See the discussions below on final payment and "M" accounts.)
- Must complete close out procedures before the contract can go through a final audit, which is necessary in order for the prime contractor to receive final payment

Prepare for Audits

Conduct an Orderly Contract Close Out

The key to mitigating future contractual or subcontract issues is to conduct an orderly contract close out. This means resolving any outstanding issues. Contract issues could stem from a discrepancy in the contract or subcontract, a delivery issue, a performance problem, or incomplete contract files. The people who are working on the contract at the time of the issue are in the best position to make a business decision about how the issue should be resolved. The ideal situation is to resolve issues as they occur and not wait until contract close. If the contractor waits, the people involved at the time the issue was created will probably no longer be available. The existing contract people from the prime contractor, customer, and subcontractor organizations probably may not have all the facts to make a decision and may have to research for missing pieces of information. In this case, issue resolution ends up taking a lot more time and may not even be worth the effort. When many issues are still unresolved at contract close out, oftentimes, the damaged party just writes off the loss because the effort to recoup the owed moneys is negligible compared to resources required to resolve the issue.

Prepare for the Final Payment Audit

The final payment audit is usually coordinated with the company's financial group because it has most of the data on how records were kept, such as DD250s, invoices, and payments. The rest of the teams need to support the financial group by resolving issues, closing out subcontracts, and closing out the prime contract. In addition, they need to provide any information the financial group needs from their own files.

The contractor should provide a list of data that is necessary for shutdown to all employees working on the contract so that files are not accidentally thrown out when people leave the contract. Any documentation pertaining to how outstanding issues were resolved should be maintained, as should any documentation required by the company, the customer, or the contract. Customer-furnished equipment, information, and property should be returned or disposed of as per the customer's instruction.

Understand the Company's File Retention System

Once the contractor understands what the company's, the contract's, and the customer's requirements are for contract close out, the contractor needs to understand how its own company retains files. These files will need to be accessed periodically to answer any customer questions up to seven years before final payment is received. Many companies use off-site storage capabilities or company-owned, remote-site locations for storing data. The ease with which data can be located over the next several years depends on how well the contract team organized the information and how well it organized the storage facility.

Successful Shut Down Influences Future Contract Award Decisions

Another reason that the government wants to go through a formal contract close out procedures is to verify its opinion as to whether the contractor has performed all the contractual requirements of the contract. As part of the close out procedure, the government will evaluate the contractor on how well it met the program objectives and contractual obligations. The government will use the evaluation to determine whether the prime contractor will receive future government contracts. By going through the close out process, the government raises issues that help determine how to score the contractor on its evaluation.

Close Out Payment

The prime contractor must ensure that it has received a notice from its subcontractor that it does not require any further payments from the prime contract under their subcontract. The government will in turn require the prime contractor to sign a similar statement that the prime contractor will not try to recoup any additional payment under the prime contract. The statements are signed because M accounts were dissolved. M accounts were used by the government to pay for products provided or services delivered under a contract that had been completed. The government, upon receiving a contractor claim or invoice for payment, would secure the funds from the M account to pay the contractor. The government dissolved that aspect of the M accounts because it found that improper budgeting techniques were being used and the M account became basically a slush fund.

Today, if a contractor makes a claim on a former contract, the government must pay the contractor using current-year funds. This means that the projects the government had budgeted for the current year will be delayed because the money is being diverted to pay contractors for products delivered and services rendered on a closed contract. The government does not like this solution so it requires the contractor to certify that it has billed and received payment for all accepted products and services as part of the contract close out procedures.

PART IV

DEVELOPING AND ADMINISTERING THE SUBCONTRACT

9 SUBCONTRACT DEVELOPMENT

Selecting External Resources

A company acting as prime contractor has basically three methods to secure external resources: informal quotes, formal solicitations, and strategic selection. Though any of the methods can be used for each level of relationship (e.g., a one-time purchase or a strategic alliance), typically, the higher the level of relationship, the more likely that the company will use formal solicitation or strategic selection to secure external resources. Another basis for deciding which method should be used is whether the company's customer is a commercial enterprise or a governmental enterprise. Government customers tend to require prime contractors to conduct at least formal solicitations for products and services provided under the contract. Options available for solicitation methods are outlined in Table 1. Note that the shaded areas represent those relationships that typically become subcontracts.

Informal Quotes

The informal quote method is the easiest method to implement, however, the results may be somewhat inaccurate. A company obtains informal quotes by telephoning, e-mailing, or faxing the requirements to a supplier. Little dialogue occurs between the purchaser and supplier and, consequently, there is often a discrepancy between what is required and what is priced. If the customer is the federal government, informal quotes are often *not* used because they do not yield the substantive documentation required for a contractor purchasing system review (CPSR) audit.

Process

The steps in an informal quote process include:

1. The buyer develops a requirements document.

2. The buyer randomly selects 3 to 5 vendors for soliciting bids.

3. The buyer relays its requirements by faxing, e-mailing, or calling the vendors.

Table 1. Selection Methods for Each Relationship Level by Customer*

Customer/ Relationship	Informal Quote	Formal Solicitation	Strategic Selection
Government/ One-time purchase	X	X	
Commercial/ One-time purchase	X		
Government/ Purchase order		X	
Commercial/ Purchase order	X		
Government/Supplier		X	X
Commercial/Supplier		X	X
Government/ Teaming partner		X	X
Commercial/ Teaming partner		X	X
Government/ Strategic alliance			X
Commercial/ Strategic alliance			X

*Highlighted areas represent those relationships that are eventually documented in a subcontract.

4. The sellers either fax, e-mail, or call the buyer with their prices.

5. The buyer awards the contract to the seller with the lowest price.

Formal Solicitations

Once the company has identified the high-level solution components, the company conducts solicitations to determine the providers
of the goods and services required for the solution. Commercial
companies may either conduct a formal solicitation, such as the one
described below, or conduct a modified formal solicitation, selecting
components of this approach. A commercial customer cannot man-
date that a prime contractor use this approach, however, a prime
contractor often chooses to conduct a solicitation to obtain the best
overall price and value for its customer. Government customers
require that contractors spend government money (taxpayers' money)
prudently. As such, the government requires that large companies
solicit offers from providers of each product or service and determine which vendor offers the best value for the government. The
government does not require small businesses or small, disadvantaged businesses to conduct competitions, though they may be required to prove cost reasonableness. This solicitation process is outlined below.

Process

Determine Multiple Sources for Each Item

Once the company has identified the major components of the solution, the technical team develops a list of companies that could
provide each particular good or service. Typically, a company sends
out a different solicitation for each product or service it intends to
procure to support the customer's requirements. Sometimes, the
company will group related products and services into one solicitation to cut down on the amount of evaluation and management
needed for many different subcontractors' products.

A proposal team member can determine which companies offer a
particular good or service by reviewing the following:

- Past experience with a provider
- Corporate purchasing files
- Industry trade journals
- Customer preference

- Corporate teaming agreements
- Industry trade show exhibits

Develop Evaluation Criteria and Scoring Methodology (Source Selection Plan)

The company must decide how it will evaluate the proposals to select the winner. The evaluation criteria it develops should outline the solution features considered important based on the customer's request for proposal (RFP). In developing the scoring methodology, the proposal team assigns relative weighting factors to each component listed in the company's evaluation criteria. The evaluation criteria and scoring methodology make up the source selection plan. The *source selection plan* documents the standards that evaluators use to evaluate all proposals in a consistent fashion.

Examples of evaluation criteria that the company can use are as follows:

- Technical fit
- Technical quality
- Cost/Price considerations
- Degree to which a company steps up to the imposed terms and conditions
- Degree of risk associated with the solution
- Ability to meet the performance criteria
- Ability to meet the delivery schedule

Source selection plan components The components of the source selection plan include the following:

Source Selection Plan Overview

- Solicitation title
- Background—Provides the history of the procurement and how it ties to the prime contract
- Amendments—States if any amendments were made to the solicitation and why they were made
- Evaluation criteria—Provides a high-level overview of how the subcontractors' proposals will be evaluated
- Evaluation team members—Lists the people involved in the source selection and their area of expertise

- Procurement schedule—Lists any significant milestones in the procurement
- Award—Provides a brief description of how the award will be made

Source Selection Plan

- Objective—Describes what the procurement is designed to accomplish
- Type of procurement—Describes how the procurement will be operated and the items included in the solicitation package
- Description of the requirement—Describes the technical and management requirements
- Specification or product description—Describes the minimal acceptable technical standard that a subcontractor's product must meet in order to be deemed compliant
- Selection constraints—Describes the minimal acceptable management standards and contractual terms and conditions that a subcontractor must meet in order to be deemed compliant
- Product/Service schedule—Describes when the product or services are needed
- Evaluation criteria—Details how the subcontractors' proposals will be evaluated

Develop Solicitation Packages

Solicitation packages are the contractor equivalent to customer RFPs and are sent to vendors that the company identified as being able to provide a given product or service. Each vendor must decide whether or not to submit a proposal for consideration. There are several key components of solicitation packages, such as:

Cover letter   The cover letter provides information about the government program and solicitation requirements, such as:

- Project name
- Solicitation number
- Type of solicitation (e.g., firm fixed price, cost plus, or ID/IQ)
- Subcontractor proposal due date, time, and location
- Required format for submission

- Company's point of contact for any potential offeror questions
- Description of the parts of the solicitation package

Specifications The specifications are the technical requirements that come from the customer RFP that pertain to the good or service being procured. Depending on the nature of the solution, a company may need to add additional requirements to ensure the component works with other solution components.

Appropriate contract clauses for the subcontract Any contract clause from the customer RFP that the customer cannot perform on its own can be flowed down to the vendor providing the good or service to which that contract clause applies. For example, if the company must accept a contract clause that says, "All components of the solution must be fully operational 99 percent of the time or the contractor will be charged with damages," the company would want to flow down that clause to the vendors providing components on the contract. Unless the vendors make the same commitment, the company could potentially lose money. Additional flow down clauses include delivery requirements, acceptance criteria, and payment terms.

Scoring methodology The company should provide the potential bidders with information on how it will evaluate the goods and services. The company often will provide a synopsis of its source selection plan to potential offerors. By knowing up front the criteria by which a product will be judged, a potential offeror can determine if its offering has a chance of becoming part of the company's offering. If the vendor determines its product is not suitable, the vendor may decline to bid, thereby saving the vendor and the company time and money.

Representations/Certifications The government typically requires that the company make certain representations and certifications on behalf of the team and solution being proposed. In order to legally accomplish this requirement, the company must have the proposed subcontractor make the same representations and certifications to the company. A commercial customer may or may not require representations and certifications from the company.

Proposal instructions The format in which the company would like to receive each vendor's response is provided in the proposal instructions. Guidelines for the technical response, contract administration data, and cost proposal submission are described in the proposal instructions.

Send Out Packages

The company sends solicitation packages to the vendors it identified. Each vendor that receives a package decides whether or not to bid on the solicitation. If the vendor chooses to do so, it will prepare a proposal.

Answer Offeror Questions/Send Amendments, If Necessary

The potential subcontractor should have the opportunity to ask the company questions about the solicitation package. Clearing up any ambiguities between the company and the subcontractor is important for several reasons. First, once the company accepts a potential subcontractor's proposal and negotiates a subcontract, both parties are required to live up to the terms and conditions stated. Therefore, both parties should have a common understanding to minimize discrepancies. Second, allowing potential subcontractors to ask questions helps ensure that losing companies' protests are minimized because issues are identified and resolved early on in the process.

A company will answer most of the questions raised, but the potential subcontractor occasionally may raise issues that the company will need to address with the customer to obtain clarification. In addition, while the subcontractor is developing its proposal, and throughout the life of the procurement, the customer may issue amendments to the original RFP document. The company must review these amendments and send revised requirements to the potential subcontractor performing the contract work. Oftentimes, a subcontractor's product may be fully compliant with the original requirement, but the product becomes non-compliant due to an amendment to that requirement. The company wants to know as soon as possible if this is the case, because the prime contractor will need to find another subcontractor's product to meet the RFP specifications.

Receive Potential Subcontractors' Proposals

All offerors' proposals should arrive at the designated date, place, and time. The company may wish to time and date stamp proposals to avoid protests later from unsuccessful bidders that claim that the winning bid was untimely.

Evaluate Proposals

The company's proposal team evaluates the proposals from the offerors using the source selection plan. The proposals are evaluated from technical, management, business, and contractual perspectives.

Select Apparent Winners

The proposal team selects vendors and associated products and services based on the scores the vendors achieved in the evaluation process. The vendors selected are considered the apparent winners. The proposal team negotiates subcontract terms and conditions with the apparent winners. The team also should continue good communication with the vendors that were not selected in case the proposal requirements change or the company and the potential subcontractor cannot reach a common understanding during the negotiation process. In either of these cases, the second- or third-ranked vendor may become the apparent winner.

Ensure Documentation Is Completed for CPSR

For a solicitation run to support a government customer, the team must complete the CPSR documentation. The company must document the solicitation, evaluation, and selection of a subcontractor for CPSR. The CPSR is a way for the government to ensure taxpayers' money is spent prudently. The government sends a reviewer to a contractor's site to determine if the contractor's employees are following the steps in the pre-approved purchasing system process. The solicitation process is part of that review.

Note: The solicitation and selection process is used for most of the goods and services required on a contract. The company completes the process for each component while the company develops the prime proposal to the government. This makes for tight time frames in developing the solution.

Strategic Selection

Strategic selection is used most often when a company is interested in establishing a teaming partnership or a strategic alliance with another company. The FAR, Section 9.601, states that a "Contractor team agreement means an arrangement in which (1) two or more companies form a partnership or joint venture to act as a potential prime contractor, or (2) a potential prime contractor agrees with one or more other companies to have them act as its subcontractor under a specified government contract or acquisition program."

Both commercial and government customers, in addition to contractors, may find teaming agreements and strategic alliances advantageous for the following reasons:

- *Economic sense*—If the cost of responding to a solicitation and performing a contract is unduly restrictive, it may make economic sense for several companies to become teaming partners and share the burden.
- *Sharing technology*—The technologies required to perform the contract may not exist in one company.
- *Risk sharing*—Teaming allows companies to share the liability and the investment required to prepare a proposal and perform the contract.
- *Economies of scale*—If a company uses the same subcontractor on multiple deals, the subcontractor may give the company quantity discounts, thus, lowering the customer's cost.
- *Stronger overall offerings*—The combined team is greater than the sum of its component corporate parts.

Stages of a Teaming Partner/Subcontractor Relationship

The stages for building a teaming partner or subcontractor relationship include the following:

- Finding a company with which to team
- Selecting a company with which to team
- Getting-to-know-the-company phase
- Jockeying-for-position phase
- Semi-consummation of the deal
- Negotiation and execution of the final subcontract

The next section discusses each of these stages.

Finding a Company with Which to Team

A company can use many different ways to find another company to complement its team's offering to the government. For example:

- Customer-sponsored bidders conferences allow companies to identify other companies that are interested in the same procurement and that may be suitable teaming partners or subcontractors.

- Trade shows give companies an opportunity to meet potential providers for goods and services.
- Successful incumbent contractors currently working on a program within the customer organization may provide a competitive advantage to their teaming partners.
- Former business partners provide the additional benefit of previously negotiated subcontracts.
- The Small Business Administration (SBA) provides lists of companies meeting certain standard industrial codes (SIC) or industry classifications.
- Corporate marketing and purchasing departments develop relationships with many companies as a matter of doing business.
- Industry trade journals and periodicals provide overviews of successful companies within various industries.
- Personal recommendations, phone books, and the Internet are other resources for finding teaming partners.

Subcontractor relationships evolve over time. A company may begin searching for a subcontractor as soon as it hears of a business opportunity. Or the company could routinely interview companies with compatible product lines to understand the current technology trends and to assess each company's capabilities before an actual RFP is released. Because the stages of a subcontract relationship take time to progress, getting the preliminaries out of the way early paves the way for a future business relationship.

Selecting a Company with Which to Team

Once a company has identified the companies that provide the good or service required, the next step is to select the company with which to team. In all but the most limited circumstances, the government requires the company acting as prime contractor to conduct a solicitation to select the subcontractor that represents the best overall value for the government. The government reviews the company's ability to conduct solicitations properly by conducting a CPSR. At least once every three years, the company must demonstrate that it followed its DCAA-approved corporate purchasing guidelines, treated all companies in an equitable manner, and selected a company based on pre-established criteria. A commercial company does not limit its prime contractor when it selects a subcontractor.

There are many criteria that a company can use when selecting a subcontractor:

- Degree to which the subcontractor's product fits the company's solution, because a product has to be compatible with any other subcontractors' products the company selects.
- Degree to which the subcontractor's product is commercially available.
- Size of the subcontractor's company, because a small or minority-owned business may make the offering more attractive to a government customer because the partnership allows the government to meet its socioeconomic objectives.
- Degree to which the subcontractor gives the proposal team a competitive advantage, because the subcontractor may have attributes that distinguish it from its competition and are desired by the customer, thus, giving the team a better chance of winning the procurement.
- Degree to which a mutually agreeable deal can be struck between the subcontractor and the company, because if a deal cannot be struck, there is no sense pursuing the relationship.
- Price for goods and services offered, because many programs are awarded based on lowest price and a company needs a subcontractor on its team that will help meet this objective.
- A product or service that is technically superior to give the proposal team a competitive advantage.
- Willingness of the subcontractor to be on the company's team, because the relationship must be mutual for it to succeed.
- Ability to leverage existing corporate agreements between the subcontractor and the company, because, it is often easier to add business under an existing subcontract than to negotiate a new subcontract.

Getting-to-Know-the-Company Phase

After the company selects a teaming partner, the two companies must get to know one another. Although there is much public information available on most companies and their product lines, a true relationship between the companies cannot begin until they begin talking with one another. The purpose of these discussions is to determine if a mutually satisfying relationship can exist between the subcontractor and the company.

Nondisclosure Agreement

The first step in the getting-to-know-the-company phase is the non-disclosure agreement. Both companies sign nondisclosure agreements to keep the information discussed relating to the program confidential. Nondisclosure agreements exist because a company wants to keep its competitive position private but it needs to share certain information with the potential subcontractor in order to make a good business decision. Likewise, the subcontractor has certain information that it wishes to keep private but it needs to share with the prime contractor.

Share Information

The second step in the getting-to-know-the-company phase is to share information. In today's highly competitive marketplace, today's team partner could be tomorrow's competitor, so it behooves both parties to share the minimum amount of information to get the job done. The companies must decide how much information to share and when to share the information. Minimally, the company must share information that the subcontractor needs to make the program successful. The types of information that are exchanged during this period include product or service capabilities and discriminators, customer references, and the names and titles of key decision makers for both companies. As time goes on, information is shared on future product strategies, strategic marketing agreements, competitive information, and pricing data. Depending on the relationship level, the subcontractor may participate in the proposal-development process.

Jockeying-for-Position Phase

The jockeying-for-position phase follows the getting-to-know-the-company phase and seems to happen in every prime contractor-subcontractor relationship. Seldom is the arrangement perfect for both parties right from the start. Frequently, the company just wants parts from the subcontractor so that the company can keep the bulk of the revenue. The subcontractor, in an attempt to grow its business, wants more of its product line on the contract. This give-and-take goes on until the final subcontract is signed.

During this phase, each side tries to ascertain the other company's level of commitment to the deal. Each company wants the assurance that the other company will do whatever it takes to win the deal. Unfortunately, making this level of commitment to every deal a company pursues is a costly endeavor. Therefore, a company must decide which deals it pursues with this degree of veracity.

Semi-Consummation of the Deal

After jockeying for position, the parties reach the semi-consummation-of-the-deal phase. At this point, both parties believe that they can strike a mutually agreeable deal. Documenting the relationship now is useful because it allows each party to go back to its respective company with an agreement in hand to begin building internal support for the relationship. The semi-consummation of the deal usually occurs right before the release of an RFP, or shortly thereafter.

The document created during this phase may be called a number of things; Executive letter of agreement (ELOA), memorandum of understanding, teaming agreement, and draft subcontract are all terms used to characterize this document. The document basically states the following:

- Purpose of the relationship
- Title of the program being pursued
- High-level description of what the subcontractor will provide on the program, including technology exchange, proposal support, demonstration support, and post-proposal support
- Commitment that unless the actual RFP drastically differs from the draft RFP, the parties will pursue this program jointly
- Acknowledgment that if a company backs out of this agreement, it is not allowed to team on this same program with another competitor
- Effect of failure to agree on scope of work after RFP release
- Signatures of key personnel in both companies
- Best estimate of percentage of work for each partner
- Antitrust concerns

Negotiate a Subcontract

After a company has selected a subcontractor either through informal bids, formal solicitations, or strategic selection and the company determines that a subcontract is warranted (based on the criteria established in Chapter 1), the company and the subcontractor are ready to enter into a subcontract.

Develop Draft Subcontract

The draft subcontract is developed by the company acting as prime contractor and is based on the draft prime contract. The subcontractor has already seen parts of the subcontract: Requirements were part of the informal bid, or formal solicitation, or discussed as part of the strategic selection process. Terms and conditions were included in the solicitation document or the executive letter of agreement between the two parties. Prices were established as part of the proposal response from the subcontractor to the company. Now all this information needs to be pulled together into the actual subcontract that will exist between the company and the subcontractor.

Subcontract Components

The components of a subcontract will vary depending on the type so products and service being contracted. Some of the more common subcontract components are:

- Names of the two parties that are entering into the subcontract
- Definitions of key terms
- Scope of the agreement
- Term of the contract
- Purchase order issuance
- Purchase order acceptance
- Purchase order evaluation
- Purchase order cancellation
- Product transportation
- Product title
- Product risk of loss
- Right to cancel for delays
- Delivery lead time
- Inventory adjustment
- Discontinued products
- Time of performance
- Product requirements
- Product acceptance
- Product return
- Product documentation
- Documentation duplication
- Product-testing support
- Product training
- Proprietary markings
- Support services
- Technical information
- Engineering changes
- Defective product components
- Product incompatibility due to engineering change
- Prices
- Payments
- Invoices
- Taxes
- Changes to products

- Product upgrades
- Right to substitutes
- Warranty
- Proprietary rights indemnification
- Price guarantee
- Limitation of liability
- Termination of prime contract
- Termination for cause
- Initial dispute resolution by parties
- Prime-contract disputes
- Agreement disputes
- Continued disputes
- Miscellaneous

Component Responsibility

Both parties develop the subcontract in accordance with the prime contract. The company acting as prime contractor has a good idea as to what will be in the prime contract because of the customer's RFP document, which typically delineates all of the contract terms and conditions. To develop the subcontract, the technical team member puts together the statement of work or modifies the statement of work that was part of the informal bid, formal solicitation, or executive letter of agreement. Then the contract administrator adds the terms and conditions from the prime contract that the company must flow down to the subcontractor in order to reduce its risk. In addition, it will add any terms and conditions that are required by its own company when working with a subcontractor. The business team then adds the prices that have been submitted by the subcontractor through the informal bid, formal solicitation, or executive letter of agreement. Finally, the management team reviews the subcontract to determine any additional technical, management, business, or contractual requirements that should added to the subcontract.

Submit the Draft Subcontract to the Subcontractor

Once the company develops the draft subcontract that outlines the roles and responsibilities of each party, it submits it to the subcontractor. The subcontractor typically does one of two things:

1. It reviews the subcontract document, makes any changes it believes are appropriate, and forwards it back to the prime contractor, or

2. It ignores the subcontract document and sends back its own subcontract or master agreement that it expects the prime contractor to sign.

If the subcontractor responds in the manner outlined in the first option, the two companies have a much easier time negotiating because they are both starting from the same contractual document. If the subcontractor submits its own, new contract, the two will have a harder time finding the terms and conditions that they can both agree on because the parties are working with a new contract.

Develop a List of Issues

The company may give the draft subcontract to the subcontractor at any point in the procurement process after the company has selected an apparent winner or a teaming partner. Both parties then review the draft subcontract to determine if there are issues or discrepancies that are not currently resolved. Issues with the subcontract can exist in the following areas:

- Technical statement of work
- Terms and conditions
- List of products covered by the subcontract
- Prices
- Schedule
- Delivery location
- Payment terms
- Shipping responsibility

Negotiate

Because the draft subcontract lists the baseline of contracted products and services and the prices for each year of the subcontract, it is important that both sides work to obtain the best mutually satisfying relationship. To do this the parties should negotiate to find solutions that work for both parties. Negotiations are a highly creative process; but they are tampered with approval chains, personalities, corporate egos, and, typically, quick deadlines. In addition, the company is usually dealing with changes being made to the prime contract. Negotiations can serve to either excite or frustrate the contract administrators responsible for getting a signed subcontract.

Timing of Negotiations

Negotiations can begin at whatever point in the procurement process as long as both sides are willing to begin. Typically, it is not realistic to expect negotiations to be completed before the company submits the initial proposal to the customer. The company is usually too busy ensuring that the proposal is made on time and without mistakes to the customer. The company accepts a certain amount of risk with this approach because although it may have some price agreements with the subcontractor, typically, the parties have not discussed the terms and conditions at great lengths. If the terms and conditions do not affect the subcontractor's prices, the company is not assuming a great deal of risk. However, the company will experience problems if the subcontractor tries to raise its prices because it believes that the terms and conditions being imposed are too unique or contrary to its commercial practices. Increased prices may cause the company to either cut into its own profit margins or offer the subcontractor's products and services on the contract at a loss.

The subcontractor, of course, realizes the leverage it has if it delays the negotiation process until after either initial proposal or BAFO submission. The company has already committed to using the subcontractor's products and services to the customer, so the company will more than likely work to keep the subcontractor in the deal.

Why Problems Occur in Negotiations

Following are some fundamental reasons why negotiations can serve to frustrate the contract administrator or, even worse, why negotiations cannot be brought to a signed subcontract.

Win-lose mentality   Some people enter into negotiations with the view that if "I win, you automatically lose." This "me versus you" plays at our warrior instincts and we want to do everything we can to defeat our opponent. Successful negotiators realize that a win-win mentality by both parties serves to develop a stronger, mutually satisfying contractual relationship between the two parties.

Tactics   Hundreds of books have been written on negotiation tactics. Some of the popular tactics include:

- *Good copy/bad cop*—Two people from the same company assume the roles of the good cop and the bad copy and play the other party off each other. For example, "I'd be happy to do that but my technical director would never let me get away with that."
- *Contrived logistics*—One of the parties puts the opponent in the worse possible chair, facing into the sun, right before lunch-

time, and has the meeting take place in the controlling party's office. The controlling party hopes that the opponent will be so physically uncomfortable that he or she will give into anything just to get the ordeal over with.

- *Not presenting all the facts at once*—In this scenario, the controlling party asks for some minor concession, and another, and another, and another without presenting the big picture of what it is trying to get.

- *Car salesman technique*—One party keeps going back to some "higher authority" to get approval for what the opponent is asking for, which makes the opponent wonder why it is even dealing with the "lower authority."

- *Dramatic* —The party does things not because they will help move the negotiations in a positive direction, but rather for the effect of the action; For example, walking out of a negotiation or pounding a fist on the table.

The problem with tactics is that some negotiators spend so much time posturing and gaming the situation that they fail to work at the main issue at hand: negotiating a subcontract. In addition, many seasoned negotiators have either used these tactics before or are trained to not fall victim to them. As a result, when these tactics are used, they are rebuffed.

Successful negotiators treat each other honestly and with respect, even though they may not agree with the opposing party's position. They also try to do things that will help the build trust between the two parties and will overlook minor discrepancies for the good of the overall agreement.

Other company members making commitments Good contract administrators know that negotiations are a process that plays out until both sides believe that they have gotten a good deal for their company. People who don't negotiate on a daily basis believe that they must agree or disagree (in isolation) to the terms requested from the other party. For example, a technical manager working with a technical team member notices that the product doesn't perform one of the requirements and the manager agrees to accept the product anyway. Or, a program manager who makes commitments about how much of a deal a subcontractor will get without running the numbers or determining if he or she can realistically promise that business to the subcontractor. When such decisions, although they may sometimes be the right ones, are made without a negotiating team or a pre-established list of negotiation objectives, they tend to result in a subcontract that does not reflect the best interests of the company.

A good contract negotiator realizes that the deal must be evaluated in its entirety. Parts of a company's negotiation power are withered away by decisions made in isolation from the whole deal. When this happens, the company's starting position is not somewhere in the middle, but it is skewed to the team that gave away nothing before they came to the negotiation table.

Contract administrator gets involved in the program too late A contract administrator should be involved in a program from its inception. In that manner, the administrator can ensure that she captures the terms, conditions, and requirements that will protect the company. Too often, however, the contract administrator is brought in at the last minute to put a subcontract together even though she hasn't been privy to any of the prior discussions or decisions. What is even worse is when the subcontract is signed without a contract administrator and a problem develops that needs resolution. The contract administrator must then try to solve a problem that she did not develop and without an understanding of why terms, conditions, and requirements were written as they were.

Scope of authority of contract administrator Another issue that can hinder negotiations is the contract administrator's scope of authority. If a contract administrator is given little authority to agree to any changes to the subcontract, the whole process gets bogged down. A good contract administrator will sit down with the proposal team before negotiations and determine exactly what the team hopes to get out of the subcontract and will then obtain authorization to make those goals realities. Once this authority is given, the contract administrator will only need to obtain additional approval or authorization on contract terms, conditions, and requirements that are drastic exceptions. The contract administrator should be able to make small decisions during negotiations with the subcontractor.

Unrealistic expectations Another problem with negotiations is when companies enter them with unrealistic expectations. A company cannot assume another company will agree to things that do not make good business sense. A negotiation that becomes too one sided and results in a deal that is too good to be true probably is. The company that got the short end of the stick will probably try to get the contract modified to a more equitable position; and failing to do that, will resort to non-performance, which will lead to contract default. The company that got the better deal under the subcontract will then have to decide whether it wants to litigate, a process that tends to be more costly than the money owed under the contract. In this situation, nobody wins.

A good contract negotiator tries to ensure both sides get the bulk of what they want; compromises on the things that the parties cannot agree on; and sets the foundation for a strong, positive, trusting relationship between the two companies. To accomplish this, the contract administrator must work with the proposal team to manage expectations and set realistic negotiation goals.

Lack of objective measures or outside research Conducting outside research or determining how much similar items cost in the outside market is a useful exercise in establishing realistic negotiation targets. In addition, keeping in mind how unique the subcontract's terms and conditions are compared to those of comparable products will help the company determine how much profit it will require to accommodate the special terms and conditions.

No goals established In order to have a successful negotiation process, the company must have goals established. Unless the company team meets with the contract administrator and decides what it wants to get out of the negotiations, the administrator will have no way of determining whether or not the negotiations were successful. For example, if the administrator negotiates a 10 percent price reduction on a product, that may be either good or bad depending on how much the team actually needed a subcontractor's price to come in at based on the overall program costs. Had the administrator known the overall program costs, she may have found that 8 percent was all that was needed or that 15 percent is the only way the deal is going to be price competitive.

Another misconception that people have during negotiations is that price is the only thing negotiable. There are other components that drive the price that, if negotiated, would make the deal equally attractive. For example, if the subcontractor could bundle greater services or additional components with the product price, this could result in a better overall program price. Similarly, a subcontractor may be willing to give a lower price if other terms, for example, delivery were relaxed.

Sign Subcontract

A signed subcontract means that both parties have agreed to the terms, conditions, and requirements of the subcontract and are willing to commit to meeting them for the life of the subcontract. All negotiations have been completed and the approvals from each side's hierarchy have been sought and granted. Ideally, the subcontract should be in place by the time any orders are placed by the customer. This protects the company if the subcontractor fails to deliver the products or services as required and it protects the subcontractor if the company fails to pay for the products or services.

A signed subcontract represents a contract baseline that exists between the company and the subcontractor. A well-organized company has a signed prime contract that delineates the products and services that will be provided under the prime contract and prices for those items for the life of the contract. That prime contract baseline lists products and services that will be provided by the prime contract to the customer. The subcontract baseline consists of those products and services that will be provided to the company to support its customer for the duration of the contract. Ideally, every product or service provided to the customer and appearing on the prime contract baseline should either be provided by the company or provided by a subcontractor that is covered by a negotiated subcontract.

In a perfect commercial contract or, typically, in a government contract, the customer orders only items on the contract baseline and pays the price stated in the baseline. The customer does not order anything from the prime contractor that is not on the prime contract baseline. Similarly, the prime contractor takes the customer order for products and services on its prime contract baseline and either fills the order using its own products and services or places an order for the products and services with the subcontractor. The products and services ordered, of course, are on the subcontract baseline.

Subcontract Changes

The subcontract baseline can be changed through a formal contract modification process.

Items That Drive Change in Subcontracts

Because contract performance can begin before the subcontract is signed, changes can occur pre-award or post-award. Also, the parties may choose to sign the subcontract before the customer awards the prime contract. Items that drive change to subcontracts include the following changes:

- *Customer priorities*—If the customer's schedule changes, the prime contract will change, which will necessitate changes to the subcontract.

- *Subcontract requirements*—If the customer changes its requirements, it will either require additional products from the subcontractor (additional subcontractor business) or select features available from another subcontractor (deletes a portion of subcontractor business).

- *Prime contractor requirements*—If the prime contract requirements change to support alterations in the customer requirements, the subcontractor may lose or gain business.

- *Federal regulations*—Changes in federal procurement regulations can drive changes in subcontracts supporting government business.

- *New technology*—New technology can drive changes in a subcontract because the technology allows a subcontractor to add other products from its product lines to the contract.

- *Performance standards*—Performance standards drive subcontract changes because the subcontractor may be required to perform its work in a different manner to meet the performance standards.

- *BAFO strategies*—BAFO strategies may increase or decrease the scope of the subcontract to meet price targets.

- *Price competitiveness*—Price competitiveness drives changes to a subcontract because if a subcontractor cannot remain price competitive, the prime contractor may be forced to find a more cost-effective subcontractor.

Implementing Changes to Subcontracts

In the pre-contract award environment, the company communicates orally most minor changes that affect the proposal. This is not the best way to handle such changes; However, a lot of companies have difficulty formally documenting every change during the proposal-development process. The parties also realize that the final agreement that emerges will be documented in the negotiated subcontract between the company and its subcontractor.

The company should communicate major changes, particularly those issued by the customer, via formal notification. This is because the company needs to ensure that the subcontractor understands exactly what is expected of it so that the prices that the subcontractor submits reflect the true costs that the company will incur. This helps both the company and the subcontractor reduce operating risk.

In the post-contract-award environment, the subcontract normally has been signed. Any changes that occur to the subcontract after formal agreement are negotiated between the two parties and, if agreed upon, incorporated into the subcontract as a contract modification.

The process for implementing these formal changes is as follows:

1. Once a change is identified, the company reviews the customer's contract to determine which particular areas the change will affect.

2. If the change affects a subcontractor, the company's program manager or designated point of contact notifies the subcontractor's point of contact and describes the change and why it happened.

3. The subcontractor evaluates the effect of the change and determines if it can be implemented, as stated, or suggests an alternative.

4. The subcontractor submits its evaluation results to the company, and the company makes a decision from a technical and program management perspective.

5. The contract administrators from both companies are then asked to mutually determine the language to reflect the change.

6. The agreed-upon language is reviewed with both companies' program management teams to ensure it accurately reflects the change.

7. The new language is incorporated into the subcontract.

Some changes are far reaching and affect multiple subcontractors. In that case, the company needs to conduct the exercise with each subcontractor.

Problems That Can Occur in Subcontracts

Following are some problems that can occur in subcontracts.

Subcontractor or prime contractor does not meet the terms of the contract   If this is the case, then both sides must expend resources to document and resolve the issue. If the situation is severe, legal counsel may be required to help with arbitration or other dispute forums. This can significantly affect program success and the prime contractor's ability to meet customer requirements.

Privity issues The prime contract exists between the customer and the prime contractor. The subcontract exists between the prime contractor and the subcontractor. If the subcontractor interferes with the relationship between the customer and the prime contractor, problems can ensue because the subcontractor is violating privity of contract. This problem usually occurs when the subcontractor is located on the customer site. The customer may rely on the subcontractor's opinion rather than calling the prime contractor for its assessment. Similarly, a customer representative could instruct the subcontractor to perform a change in the contract that has not been authorized by the government's contracting officer for the commercial customer's contract office. Such situations cause problems for all parties, as the prime contractor is out of the information loop and cannot effectively manage the program. The prime contractor's risk results from its being under no obligation to provide whatever its subcontractor commits to the customer, yet the prime contractor is held responsible if the subcontractor acts in a manner inconsistent with the prime contract. The subcontractor assumes risk because it is making unauthorized commitments. The government risks program execution by not going through the proper channels to implement changes.

These problems can be avoided if the subcontractor makes a concerted effort to encourage the customer representatives to take any issues directly to the prime contractor. If this proves ineffective, the subcontractor should notify the prime contractor of ongoing issues that arise so that the prime contractor may take appropriate action with the customer. In this manner, the prime contractor stays in control, and all parties mitigate their risk.

Poorly drafted subcontracts Any subcontract that contains ambiguous language is bound to cause problems during program execution. Both parties must put in the time and effort to ensure the contract accurately reflects their working relationship. The subcontractor and the prime contractor should also assess areas on which the subcontract is silent. Although subcontract negotiations can be tedious at times, a well-written document that clearly defines what each side will provide will mitigate risks for both sides during contract performance.

Subcontractor Role in Request for Equitable Adjustment

If the situation merits an equitable adjustment, the subcontractor may put together its request for an equitable adjustment and provide it to the prime contractor. The prime contractor can then include the subcontractor's request with its own request for equitable adjustment.

Subcontract Closeout

The last phase of the subcontract relationship is subcontractor closeout. Part of terminating a prime contract is terminating all subcontracts. Contract termination can occur under normal circumstances—the contract is completed or the customer chooses not to exercise an option. Likewise, the contract may be terminated due to the default of the prime contractor or for the convenience of the government. In any of these instances, termination proceedings begin.

Subcontractor's Role

A subcontractor's role during subcontract closeout is as follows:

- Provide any outstanding deliverables
- Complete any outstanding contract work
- Return any government-furnished equipment or information
- Return any prime contractor-furnished equipment or information
- Resolve any open issues with the prime contractor
- Submit a final invoice for service rendered
- Submit any claims for equitable adjustment if the situation merits such requests

Resolving Subcontract Issues

Subcontract issues typically have a dollar effect. If the program team was good about resolving financial issues all along, there will probably be no surprises at the end of the contract. Otherwise, any money that the prime contractor owes to a subcontractor will need to come out of the prime contractor's current budget even though the problem may have occurred years ago. Similarly, if the subcontractor owes the prime contractor money, it too will pay from its current budget. Though this may present a potential windfall at the end, it is not a good idea to delay in resolving issues. Often, a subcontractor or the customer experiences personnel changes and the new employees are not familiar with the history of the issue and do not have any of the backup documentation for the claim. Additionally, the subcontractor may have merged with another company, been acquired, or have gone out of business by the time of contract closeout, thereby making resolution of issues even more complicated. For these reasons, it is best for the subcontractor and the prime contractor to resolve subcontract issues as they occur and not wait until the end of the contract.

Disputes

Disputes can arise in a subcontract relationship over any number of things:

- Perception that the subcontractor's products do not meet the contract requirements
- Failure to accept products or services
- Failure to pay for products or services
- Different products or services delivered than those ordered
- Schedule delays
- Changes in requirements
- Acting on a nonauthorized person's direction
- Related issues

How Disputes Get Resolved

Disputes can get resolved using proactive or reactive methods. Proactive methods, such as careful subcontract development, administration, and closeout, help prevent problems before they occur. Reactive methods, such as escalation management, contract-dispute process, arbitration, alternate disputes resolution, or litigation, all occur after a dispute has been raised and the two parties are trying to get it resolved.

Careful Subcontract Development

Many disputes can be resolved through careful subcontract development. For example, a subcontract that clearly delineates under what circumstances a product or service will be accepted will help resolve issues surrounding whether a subcontractor's product or service meets the specification. Warranty and maintenance terms that clearly state what is covered help to resolve issues surrounding broken components. Procedures for review and evaluation of purchase orders will help to ensure that what is ordered will meet the customer's requirements and not have to be shipped back. Formalized change process descriptions will help to keep the subcontract current between the two parties so that changes are not made on the fly and not documented.

Five methods help to ensure that all the relevant terms, conditions, and requirements are stated in the subcontract:

1. Review the prime contract to determine the requirements and clauses that should be flowed down to the subcontractor.

2. Review other subcontract documents, both internally and externally developed, that cover similar items to see if any terms and conditions are missing.

3. Conduct a team review with representatives from the technical, management, and business groups and other contracts people to review the subcontract to find any errors or omissions.

4. State topic areas once in the subcontract and put all relevant terms and conditions relating to that topic in one location. This will help to minimize inconsistencies between sections about the same topic.

5. Use an order of precedence clause to state which subcontract sections have precedence over other sections. By stating a hierarchy of sections of the subcontract, disputes can be quickly resolved because the contract already states which contract clauses should be used to resolve an issue.

Careful Subcontract Administration

Ensuring subcontracts are carefully administered goes a long way in minimizing disputes during contract performance. Careful subcontract administration means that:

- All issues are resolved at the time of subcontract signing

- Any changes made to the work being done, prices being charged, or terms and conditions being adhered to is documented through a formal contract modification process

- Telephone calls, correspondence, e-mails, and other conversations are recorded and kept in a subcontract file

- Issues, when they do arise, are quickly dealt with by the people who can resolve them

Contract Close Out

Going through the contract closeout process will help to ensure that both parties agree that work is completed, payment has been made, and there are no outstanding issues between the two parties. Contract closeout will help to minimize any problems occurring after contract work has been completed.

Escalation Management

Disputes or problems are resolved on a contract through an escalation process.

Functional-team resolution Typically on a contract, a technical team of the prime contractor works directly with a technical team of the subcontractor to accomplish the contract work. If the problem is tied to delivery of products or services, a purchasing team of the prime contractor works with a purchasing team of the subcontractor to order, deliver, and get shipped products to customers. When a problem occurs that cannot be resolved between the two parties, the problem is escalated to the functional area team manager.

Functional-area-team-manager resolution If a problem cannot be resolved by the functional team members, the problem is escalated up the management chain. Frequently, functional team members do not have the authority that the manager does to authorize changes that are outside the specific procedures. A prime contractor's functional area manager can get together with the subcontractor's functional area manager to resolve the problem. If these two individuals cannot resolve the problem, the problem gets sent to the program managers from each company.

Program managers As a final effort, from an operations perspective, to resolve an issue, the program managers from each company can work to come up with an agreeable solution. At this point, creative solutions are needed to keep work going and the relationship thriving. Program managers may make a subcontract modification; relax some of the terms, conditions or requirements; or may allow a delay in contract performance, all in an effort to resolve the issue. If the program managers cannot resolve the dispute, it is turned over to the contracts team for resolution.

Contract administrator   The contract administrator should be kept informed of the problem as it escalates and develop contingency plans in the event that the issue does not get resolved. The first course of action for the administrator is to follow the dispute resolution clauses outlined in the contract.

Contract Documented Disputes Process

Dispute resolution clauses are created and accepted by the prime contractor and the subcontractor at subcontract signing. The prime contractor's contract administrator contacts the subcontractor's administrator to notify him of the dispute and the procedures that are outlined in the contract. If the documented contract disputes process fails to bring resolution, the prime contractor's contract administrator may decide to enforce other subcontract clauses available for resolution, including arbitration, litigation, or termination.

Arbitration

Arbitration is a popular alternative to litigation because it tends to be less expensive for both parties. Arbitration is agreed to in the original subcontract or is agreed to after a dispute has begun. In arbitration, both parties agree to present their respective cases to an outside, unbiased person, known as an *arbitrator,* and to accept the final decision. Typically, an outside arbitration company or industry group is used to supply an arbitrator. Both sides present their cases and the arbitrator makes a decision based on the merits of each case, the facts, contract performance, subcontract, and reasonable person contract interpretation. The arbitrator renders a decision and both parties carry out his or her decision. The matter remains private between the two parties and no one else has privy to the settlement unless one of the parties shares information about the settlement.

Litigation

A less popular, but sometimes necessary, approach to contract dispute resolution is litigation. Obtaining and retaining legal counsel is time consuming and expensive. It should only be used when the amount to be won or lost is great.

Contract Termination

When the dollar value and time commitment does not merit litigation, the two companies can terminate the contract. Contract termination is the final recourse between the two companies and is where the relationship and all future business transactions cease. Contracts typically have clauses delineating how contract terminations will work, what each party is entitled to, and under what conditions terminations will occur. At this point, communication between the two parties have broken down and the prime contractor is busy trying to find a replacement company to provide similar products or services so it can meet its prime contract requirements. In such situations, the two companies will seldom work together as prime contractor and subcontractor because the level of trust has disintegrated.

Because reactive methods can escalate to the point of relationship deterioration, the prime contractor and the subcontractor are better off establishing proactive methods, such as subcontract development, administration, and closeout.

Contract Interpretation

When a dispute goes before arbitration or litigation, the arbitrator or judge will review the contract to determine how it should be interpreted to resolve the dispute. John Cibinic, Jr. and Ralph Nash discuss in their book, *Administration of Government Contracts*, several key areas for how contracts are interpreted.

- *Contracts are usually interpreted to avoid rendering terms meaningless*—Someone looking at the contract tries to look at the contract as a whole. He assumes that none of the portions of the contract language are meaningless, useless, ineffective, or superfluous. A contract interpretation rendered by one of the parties that ignores part of the contractual language will tend to be rejected.

- *Contracts are interpreted to avoid conflict*—Another aspect of contract interpretation, which is tied to the first aspect, is that when a contract is read as a whole, the provisions should, if possible, be interpreted so as to be in harmony with each other.

- *Interpret to fulfill principal*—A contract that has omissions will be interpreted to include the missing contractual language so that the purpose of the contract is fulfilled.

- *Order of precedence*—As discussed earlier, order of precedence is normally stated in the contract. If it is not, specific provisions take precedence over general provisions.

Prime Contractor Considerations

Solicitation Issues

In government contracts, a company acting as a prime contractor (unless they are SBs or SDBs) is required to conduct solicitations so that they can provide the government with the best solution at the best price. In fact, in order to pass a contractor purchasing system review (CPSR), the company must prove how it conducted each step of the solicitation process. (For an explanation of CPSR, see the section titled Government Considerations.) CPSRs do not apply to commercial customer contracts. In commercial contracts, companies acting as prime contractors may conduct solicitations so that they get a competitive price on products and services to meet the customer's requirements.

If a company intends to conduct a solicitation, it must be prepared to invest the time needed to conduct a fair competition. Careful work needs to go into planning an unbiased RFP document, source selection plan, and proposal evaluation. In addition, seldom does a company award on initial offers. More typically, a BAFO is required to secure the best prices from the competing companies.

One final note on the solicitation process: when the company acting as prime contractor conducts solicitations for companies to provide products and services to the government, the company opens itself up to potential protests from losing companies. A protesting company will either lodge the protest against the prime-contractor company directly to the company or to the customer's governmental agency. The agency will typically conduct some type of investigation into the procurement process and award selection to see if the protest has any merit. If it does, the government could order the prime-contractor company to either re-solicit, re-evaluate, or re-award the contract. In the commercial-customer environment, a company cannot protest formally.

Drive the Processes

Although a lot of the collaborative work occurs between the prime contractor and the subcontractor throughout this book, it is the prime contractor the must drive all of the processes for the work. Strategic planning, marketing, proposal development, after-submission activities, subcontract development, and, eventually, contract start up, performance, and shut down are all ultimately the responsibility of the prime contractor. A prime contractor must drive the process for several reasons:

- The prime contractor, more often than not, has the experience to act as a prime contractor. This means that it understands the entire program, not just a small piece of it. In addition, the prime contractor understands how all the parts need to fit together, where the areas of risk are, and how to pull many organizations to meet a customer's program objectives.

- The team needs one individual from one company to be in charge. The program manager from the prime-contract organization is that person. When more than one person is running the show, chaos typically ensues. The person who will work as the program manager needs the best talents from all the team members to make the program a success. The manager will ask for advice from the team members, but ultimately, the program manager makes the final decisions.

- The prime contractor has a greater potential for risk and must, therefore, ensure that all the contract details and processes are managed to mitigate those risks. By driving the processes, the prime contractor can help to ensure that it identifies the problem areas early and then figures out creative ways to solve the problems.

- Finally, the subcontractor will be looking to the prime contractor to lead the effort. A subcontractor has chosen, by its very nature of being a subcontractor, to support a prime contractor; not to lead the charge. The subcontractor may have chosen because of a lack of overall program understanding, desire to only take on part of the contract risk, or because it does not have the capability (or desire) to manage the entire program. As such, the subcontractor expects the prime contractor to take on the leader role.

Subcontractor May Have Its Own Agreement

When a company issues a subcontract that it designed based on the flow-down clauses from the prime contract, and the subcontractor ignores the subcontract and sends back instead a copy of its own agreement, the two parties are starting off at divergent points. Every company has an agreement that it wants to follow. The agreement probably has all the terms and conditions that are favorable to the company that developed it and protects that company from every possible contingency. Such an agreement may work just fine when the company sells its products or services directly to a customer.

However, such an agreement doesn't work when a prime contractor has certain contractual obligations that it must meet with the customer and the contractor needs the subcontractor's support to meet the obligations. Also, a prime contractor will not be willing to sign a agreement that is too heavily supportive of the subcontractor that designed it. By doing so, the prime contractor would open itself up to even more risk.

Unfortunately, either through contract administrator naiveté, corporate machismo, or a desire to avoid the negotiation process, some companies don't want to give up their agreement that they use with all their other customers. When this situation exists, a prime contractor must surmise very early on in the process what its negotiable points are or those terms, conditions, or requirements that it is willing to support without the support of the subcontractor. In addition, it must determine its non-negotiable points (i.e., those terms, conditions, or requirements that it must have subcontractor buy-in on otherwise the relationship cannot work). It must obtain subcontractor support of those terms, conditions, or requirements either on its own developed subcontract or on the subcontractor's master agreement before the relationship can continue. The prime contractor does not want to find itself in a position in which it has submitted a proposal to the customer and does not have the support of its subcontractor to share the burden of meeting the contractual requirements.

Determine How Work Will Be Handled

A key decision that the prime contractor must make at the time of subcontract formation is how work will be handled on the contract. This decision has two components: how will work be divided between the prime contractor and subcontractor and how will work be divided among subcontractors that can provide similar products or services.

When a company decides to pursue a program, either as a prime contractor or a subcontractor, it tries to determine how much the deal will cost it to win versus the potential revenue to be gained if the program is won. This return on investment analysis feeds into the company's overall planning and budgeting processes, which drive investment, capital budgeting, and personnel forecasting decisions for the company. Because of the importance of these forecasts, a company likes to get a fairly accurate handle on how much of a deal it is likely to get. The prime contractor must do its part to accurately manage those expectations by deciding how the program will be implemented after award. For example, if two or more subcontractors can provide technical services on the contract and a delivery order comes in for technical work, the prime contractor must decide which company gets the work. The prime contractor is going to choose the company that has the lowest rates for technical services so that the prime contractor can preserve or enhance its own profit margin. A subcontractor has no control over which company the prime contractor selects unless the subcontractor's subcontract has terms and conditions built into it that guarantee the subcontractor a certain amount of work. A prime contractor might accept such terms and conditions on a firm, fixed contract, but the prime contractor would be foolish to do so in an indefinite delivery/ indefinite quantity type contract because it has received no guarantees from the customer itself. The problem has no easy answers, but it is one that the prime contractor needs to discuss with subcontractors so that, to the greatest extent possible, work can be divided among the subcontractors according to type or capability of the subcontractors. Or at a minimum, the subcontractors should have enough information to at least make a realistic return on investment analysis.

Draft Subcontract

Other issues related to the draft subcontract include the following areas.

Flow Downs from the Prime Contract

The prime contractor is responsible for everything in the prime contract. Any term, condition, or requirement that it cannot meet, the prime contractor flows down to a subcontractor. For example, the customer has a training requirement and the training has to commence within 30 days of a delivery order or the contractor will incur financial damages. The prime contractor subcontracted the training component and flowed down to the subcontract the requirement that training had to commence within 28 days (so the prime contractor gives itself some time to process the order) or the subcontractor would incur financial damages. The prime contractor flows down the training requirement to the subcontractor because the prime contractor is not providing the training on the contract and it does not have any control over when the subcontractor schedules the classes in response to the customer's requirement. By having the clause flowed down to the subcontract, the prime contractor now has some leverage against the subcontractor in the event that the subcontractor fails to perform in a timely manner. The leverage is that the prime contractor will recoup financial damages from the subcontractor, which it will need to pay the customer for the financial damages imposed by the prime contract for failed performance. If the prime contractor had not flowed down the clause, the prime contractor would have to pay financial damages to the customer if the subcontractor did not perform in a timely manner and the prime company would not recoup any money from the subcontractor.

Minimize Extra Terms and Conditions

On the flip side of this flow-down problem is the idea of trying to minimize extra terms and conditions. In contracting, additional requirements equals additional contract price, which means that the more requirements, terms, and conditions that a prime contractor has in the subcontract, the higher the contract price is likely to be. When a subcontractor reviews a subcontract, it looks at each clause and determines its likelihood for occurrence and the dollar effect to itself if that clause must be implemented. In addition, the subcontractor pads the risk slightly to protect itself even further, just in case. Therefore, the more requirements there are in a subcontract, the more a subcontractor is going to feel a need to pad its price to protect itself if those clauses have to be implemented. The subcontractor's higher prices are then padded with the prime contractor's loads and this whole process may make the proposal non-competitive and nobody wins.

For this reason, it is important for the prime contractor to decide the minimum terms, conditions, and requirements that it needs as support from the subcontractor to provide and pass only those items to the subcontractor in the subcontract. If the prime contractor believes an area is particularly risky, it can pad its price a little to cover the contingency plan. In this way, the prime contractor is accounting for risk once across the program, rather than the subcontractors each accounting for risk in their own areas.

Separate Subcontract for Each Type of Product or Service Provided

If the program is large and the prime contractor intends to bring on a lot of subcontractors, it may make sense for the prime contractor to develop generic subcontracts based on the type of product or service provided by a subcontractor. This approach helps the prime contractor to only glean those terms, conditions, or requirements from the prime contract that are relevant to the type of product or service the subcontractor is providing. For example, in an information technology program, a prime contractor may develop different generic subcontracts for hardware components, software components, maintenance, and services. For a hardware subcontract, the prime contractor would go through the RFP and pull out all the terms and conditions that would apply to hardware, such as performance standards, integration requirements, warranty, preventive maintenance, and user support. The prime contractor would then put those requirements in a hardware subcontract that would be the starting point for every subcontractor providing hardware on the contract. The contractor would then tailor the subcontract with the specific technical requirements for the components being supplied by the subcontractor. Once negotiations begin with a subcontractor supplying hardware components, the subcontract would be modified to reflect the actual relationship that is to occur between the prime contractor and that particular subcontractor.

A related concept to these generic subcontracts is bundling. If the same subcontractor is providing hardware and services, for example, the prime contractor would take all the hardware and services flowdown clauses and add the statements of work for both the hardware and services components to develop the subcontract.

Important to Keep Draft Subcontract in Sync with Current Statement of Work

If a subcontract is developed early in the process, for example, soon after the customer RFP is released, the prime contractor must keep the subcontract current by incorporating any changes that occur in the program. Changes occur as a result of demonstrations, customer questions, negotiations, BAFO, and customer amendments. There could be changes in terms, conditions, or requirements that should be passed down to the subcontract, unless the prime contractor is willing to accept the risk of handling the new requirement. The prime contractor also wants to ensure that the subcontract is current with all the latest developments so that the subcontractor gives accurate prices. If the prime contractor tries to add these requirements after contract award and subcontract signing, the subcontractor is not obligated to meet them. If the subcontractor chooses to meet them, it may charge the prime contractor a higher price.

One Subcontract per Contract or Company or Service Area

Subcontract formation does not have to be done to support the requirements of only one program. A company could develop a master agreement with a subcontractor that covers multiple programs. Similarly, the prime contractor could develop a master agreement that covers all similar type of work within a service area, for example, all software development efforts. In these situations, the prime contractor and the subcontractor negotiate a generic list of terms and conditions that are basic to all contracts. Then as each new program or additional service area is required, the prime contractor generates an amendment to the master agreement that covers the new products to be provided or work to be performed. Master agreements help develop a common operating environment between the two companies for how business will be conducted so that as each new negotiator on each side comes on board, they do not have to start from scratch. The prime contractor still minimizes its risk because the terms and conditions germane to this particular program are covered by the amendment that is negotiated and signed.

Subcontractor Considerations

Decide the Important of the Terms of Its Agreement

A subcontractor that, in response to the prime contractor's draft subcontract, submits its own agreement rather than negotiating from the draft subcontract risks losing the business. A prime contractor typically has a large amount of work to do to get the proposal to the customer and all subcontracts negotiated in a timely manner. A subcontractor's agreement that refuses to acknowledge the specific customer terms and conditions that the prime contractor must accept causes the prime contractor and subcontractor to start negotiations from two very different positions. It may be easier for the subcontractor if the prime contractor would just sign the agreement, but the prime contractor is looking out for its best interest, and the subcontractor's agreement does not cover the specifics of the particular program. The prime contractor may just not be willing to go through the effort and will, instead, find a subcontractor that is willing to negotiate from the draft subcontract.

Leverage

A subcontractor's leverage with a prime contractor increases or decreases depending on how valuable the subcontractor is to the prime contractor. If the subcontractor has a unique product or service, is wanted by the customer, enjoys a significant marketshare position, or in any other way improves the prime contractor's competitive position, the subcontractor will have greater leverage in negotiating terms, conditions, or requirements than if they do not have any of these characteristics. A subcontractor that can be easily replaced by another subcontractor of real or perceived equal value will be replaced if it does not strive to negotiate compatible terms between itself and the prime contractor.

Prime Contractor's Draft Subcontract

The prime contractor will draft a subcontract to use as a starting point for contract negotiations. Some prime contractors are particularly good at picking only the specific terms, conditions, and requirements that a subcontractor must meet in order to comply with program requirements. Other prime contractors do not do such a good job with this task and try to flow down every single requirement that they must accept in the prime contract whether or not the requirement makes sense for the subcontractor to accept. A subcontractor must carefully review the subcontract and, through the negotiation process, strive to remove any extraneous terms, conditions, or requirements from the subcontract before it signs the subcontract.

A second task for the subcontractor is to determine the level of risk associated with the contract terms and conditions and decide whether it is adequately protected in the event that something does not go according to plan. For example, a subcontractor receives functional requirements from the prime contractor and then is tasked to code a system based on those requirements. The subcontractor would not want to agree to a clause that states the code will be delivered to meet the customer's requirements because the subcontractor would suffer severe financial ramifications because the subcontractor has no control over the quality of the functional requirements delivered by the prime contractor.

Finally, it is important that the subcontractor negotiate the terms, conditions, and requirements before subcontract signing, because the subcontractor may not be able to get the clauses changed later.

Ensure the Subcontract Stays Current

Ensuring that the subcontract stays current is a prime contractor consideration, but keeping the subcontract current throughout its development and implementation is equally important as a subcontractor consideration. A prime contractor, because of the sheer number of tasks it is required accomplish to manage a contract, may overlook keeping a particular subcontract current. Keeping the sub-contract current becomes a secondary priority that the prime be-lieves it can handle later. However, such projects are often never done, and a subcontractor places itself in just as great a risk as the prime contractor does when the work it performs is not covered by a subcontract or a subsequent modification. In addition, keeping the subcontract current minimizes end-of-contract unresolved issues and additional expenses.

Don't Assume Anything

Every company operates differently and too often companies tend to assume things that are true in their company are true for other companies. For example, a company's product comes with a 90-day warranty and the prime contract states that the company has to provide on-site support during the warranty period. The company assumes that the on-site support lasts 90 days, however, the prime contractor uses the term warranty to mean that the warranty lasts for one year after purchase. To prevent this problem the subcontractor should document the definitions of some of commonly used words that could have different meanings to make sure everyone is using the same "definition."

Written Commitments

Equally important, *if a commitment is not in writing, it does not exist.* It might exist for a while if things are going fine between the subcon-tractor and the prime contractor, but the minute a problem develops the commitment will cease to exist because it is not in writing. It is important that any promises made or requirement relief made by the prime contractor is documented in either the subcontract or a subse-quent modification. No matter how many people on the prime con-tractor team tell you, "that's OK, we'll just keep this between us," the subcontractor places itself in unnecessary risk when it relies on commitments that are not in writing.

10 SUBCONTRACT ADMINISTRATION

This chapter focuses on two main topics with regard to subcontract administration. The first topic covers the basic tasks associated with thorough subcontract administration, such as the proper way to modify a contract, keep files current, and maintain good communication. These are tasks that subcontract administrators do as a matter of course to keep the subcontract function going. The second topic is risk management. Risk management includes specific strategies that contract administrators, their customers, and prime contractor teams or subcontractor teams can employ to define, manage, and mitigate the risk on the contract.

Process

Basic Subcontract Management Tasks

Modify the Contract

As was discussed in Chapter 9 and Chapter 7, the process for conducting a contract modification includes the following steps:

1. Prime contractor or subcontractor learns of a customer's need.
2. Prime contractor develops strategy with subcontractor's input.
3. Prime contractor goes to customer with strategy.
4. Customer either approves, requests a position paper, or denies strategy.
5. Prime contractor develops position paper, if needed.
6. Prime contractor conducts a solicitation, if necessary.
7. Prime contractor develops proposal with subcontractor input.
8. Customer completes review cycle to approve funding.
9. Prime contractor and customer negotiate prime contract modifications.
10. Prime contractor and subcontractor negotiate subcontract modifications.
11. New work begins based on contract and contract modifications.

Develop and Keep Current an Effective Subcontract

The first step to effective subcontract administration is a good subcontract. A good subcontract is one that accurately reflects the relationship between the two parties. If the subcontract has areas that are missing or if it does not reflect what is actually going on between the two parties, the subcontractor should modify the subcontract to include the missing or changed requirements, terms, or conditions.

Keep Track of the Process

A number of steps are involved in changing the prime contract and the subcontract. Part of effective contract management is keeping track of the change process to adequately protect all parties. Each of the steps listed earlier requires close coordination among the various prime contractor's teams (technical, business, management and contractual), the various teams of the subcontractor organization (same as the prime contractor's), and the customer. With so many people involved, communication problems are bound to occur if the process is not managed well. In addition, the contractor usually implements more than one change at a time. A prime contractor usually has multiple changes being evaluated by both the customer and the subcontractor.

Maintain Current Subcontract Files

The person responsible for maintaining subcontract files usually resides in either the contracts, subcontracts, or purchasing departments within the contractor's company. The company should designate this person early on in the procurement process so that he or she can maintain records from the beginning of a subcontractor relationship. The company should also set up standards for maintaining the subcontract files so the person assigned to that position will have proper guidelines. At a minimum, the files should contain:

- Telephone logs that track conversations occurring between the prime contractor and the subcontractor on substantive issues
- Correspondence to or from the subcontractor
- E-mail to or from the subcontractor
- Negotiation memorandum summarizing any negotiations between the two parties
- Subcontract, purchase orders, and any modifications

Ideally, the person should keep the information in chronological order and should include all communications between the two companies so that if a problem later arises, a contemporaneous record of its development exists.

Realistic Goal?

The problem with keeping all current subcontract files in one place is that typically more than one person within the company communicates with the subcontractor. At a minimum, the program manager, technical director, purchasing agent, and business manager discuss issues with the subcontractor on a daily basis. Getting all of these people to document their subcontracting files will be difficult because each is busy with other tasks. Additionally, each person believes that if a problem were to occur, the subcontract administrator would be brought in to solve it anyway.

However, the subcontract administrator needs proper and current documentation to solve problems. If the records are complete, detailed, and accurate, the subcontract administrator is more likely to come up with an equitable solution for the company. If the records are not kept or available, the subcontract administrator will have to rely on his or her own knowledge of the situation, oral history from team members, and oral history from the subcontractor to resolve the issue. This approach may not yield an equitable solution for the company.

Encourage Communication within the Company

It may seem redundant to continually stress good communication throughout this book, but its importance cannot be overlooked. A company gets into a great deal of contractual trouble and business risk when it does not have a process for the technical, management, business and contractual teams to coordinate their efforts. Frequently, problems occur when people make decisions outside of his or her area of expertise; for example, when a technical person starts making decisions that should be made by the business manager.

When the teams do not work together, they cannot develop a mutually satisfying solution for all functional areas. Some issues result in a better solution when they are developed by a team whose members represent each of the key contract areas. Such a team can develop a solution with full knowledge and support of each team member's department or function.

Encourage Communication between the Two Companies

Unfortunately, some people take a we-they approach to business transactions and automatically assume that both parties are competitors working against each other to win. Another approach that does not foster a cooperative business relationship is a win-lose mentality. In this case, one party believes that if it wins, the other party loses or if the other party wins, it loses. Both approaches are detrimental to open and honest business relationships between the two parties and do not result in mutually satisfying solutions.

If the contractor knows that a party practices either of these techniques, the contractor should not deal with the party, particularly if it has proven itself not to be trustworthy in the past. However, most contractors know the value of good partnership relationships and try to maintain a trustworthy reputation.

A useful technique for effective subcontractor management is to encourage open communication with the other company. This will help build a trusting relationship; one that is built on facts not rumors and one that will serve both parties well in the long term.

Facilitate Strategy Sessions to Help Reach a Negotiated Agreement

The negotiation process can drag on if the contractor does not have a plan to organize the issues needing resolution. A technique that is particularly useful is to get a complete list of open issues from both parties and schedule a facilitated strategy session. The contractor team needs to ensure that decision-makers from both companies are available for the session so that the two teams can leave the session with a negotiated agreement. Sometimes it is useful to review all the issues initially at the meeting so that the two teams can make some strategy decisions that will affect the negotiations. By making these overall decisions initially, the teams may be able to resolve the remaining issues quickly.

Get the Facts

During the negotiations process and during contract performance, problems will occur. Once they do, tempers may flare, rash behavior may reign, and overall ineffective activity may occur because of missed deadlines and minimized customer satisfaction. The contracts team will need to intervene quickly and get the facts so it can solve the problem. It is a simple strategy, but one that helps both parties not jump to unfounded conclusions that can harm the relationship for the long term.

Know the Subcontract

Another technique that is useful in subcontract management is to know the subcontract. The subcontract will change during the negotiation process with the prime contractor. The subcontract administrator cannot make any assumptions about what is or what is not in the subcontract. He or she must know what is actually in the subcontract. The administrator must review the terms and conditions whenever new products and services are added to the subcontract to ensure that the new products and services come with equivalent warranties, maintenance terms, and so on.

Ensure the Operations/Program Team Is Adhering to the Subcontract

The subcontract administrator must ensure that the operations or program team accepts only the products and services from the subcontractor that actually meet the subcontract's requirements, terms, and conditions. If the program or operations team is changing the acceptance terms, technical requirements, or any part of the subcontract, the team should alert the contracts team so it can update the subcontract. This helps to ensure that everyone working on the prime contract knows about the issues with the subcontractor.

Understand and Communicate to the Management Team the Risks Associated with the Decisions under Consideration by the Company

Each company team is expected to accomplish certain tasks on a contract. Technical people ensure that the solutions proposed and provided by the subcontractor meet the customer's requirements. Business people ensure that the solutions provided by the subcontractor are accepted by the customer so that payment can be made. Management people ensure that the overall program objectives are met by utilizing the subcontractor to the maximum extent possible. Finally, contracts people ensure that the company does not take on any unnecessary risk in dealing with subcontractor.

Problems can occur on a contract when people make decisions affecting their particular functional area without understanding the risk it puts the company in other areas of the contract. For example, a program manager decides to utilize a subcontractor product that has more features than the one currently on the contract, the manager does not have the price for the new product from the subcontractor. The manager uses the new product and later learns that the subcontractor's price is so high that the company loses money by offering the product to the customer. Another problem that may occur is that the new product may not meet the customer's technical requirements, in which case the customer could terminate the contract. Finally, the contracts person may have a problem because the subcontractor is providing a product under the prime contract that is not protected by the terms and condition of the subcontract. For all of these reasons, it is important that teams work together on a contract.

Contracts as the Second Level of Escalation for Resolving Contractual Issues

As was discussed in Chapter 9 on developing subcontracts, subcontract administrators are the second level of escalation for resolving contractual issues. The first line is operations; they deal with subcontractors on a daily basis as they work to meet program objectives. If operations cannot resolve the problem through their chain of command, the problem is sent to the subcontracts or purchasing group. If the problem is not resolved at this level, the group decides if the issue should be turned over to either internal or external legal counsel. The subcontract administrator assigned to a particular subcontract should be made aware of any problem arising out of that subcontract. The subcontract administrator is the person who is responsible for ensuring that the problem gets resolved one way or another no matter what level of escalation it takes. For this reason, the subcontract administrator should be kept in the loop of any subcontract problem situation.

Manage Contract Risk

Avoiding Contract Changes through Program and Contract Risk Management

The successful implementation of any program is due to successful risk management. Risks are inherent in any program and on any contract. Examples of risk include cost overruns, program delays, scheduling conflicts, and poor performance. There is a direct relationship between program risks and contract risks. *Contract risks* can jeopardize program success; for example, contracts that are not modified to reflect changing program requirements can cause the contractor to provide the incorrect product. Similarly, *program risks* can jeopardize a solid contractual relationship; for example, when a subcontractor cannot perform program requirements, the prime contractor must enforce contractual remedies.

Many risks can be anticipated and mitigated before they occur; other risks cannot be anticipated and require handling when they are discovered. The challenge of the program management team and the contract team is to understand the complexities of the program and to develop strategies for risk mitigation. Team members should consider critical program areas, anticipate possible problems, and develop contingency plans. This type of proactive planning will help to ensure program success.

Contract risks concern the customer, the prime contractor and the subcontractor teams. This section discusses the more common risks that occur for the teams and the strategies they can use to mitigate their risks. Keep in mind the various levels of relationships as we go through this information: the term *customer* in this section can apply to the prime contractor's customer or to the prime contractor in the subcontract relationship. Similarly, the term *contractor* can refer to either the prime contractor or the subcontractor.

Risk Areas for the Customer

The customer establishes programs to help meet a particular company or agency mission. If a program fails, it could mean that the company's ability to perform its core business or an agency's ability to meet its mission is in jeopardy. The customer's program manager, working with the contracts person, must effectively use both the internal resources and the external contractor resources to ensure program success.

The risk management areas that concern the customer's internal resources include the following.

Insufficient Resources

The age-old problem of not having the appropriate resources, such as people, equipment, funding, or facilities, available at the critical points in the program can lead to substantial program risk. If internal resources are not available, or if contractual vehicles are not in place to secure contracted resources, the program could be delayed. If the resources that are not available are critical to the program's success, the program could fail.

Ineffective Service Level Agreements

When the customer determines it is more efficient to use internal resources for certain tasks than using external resources, the challenge becomes locating the resources within the organization. If the contractor locates the resources in another agency (government contract) or in another department (commercial contract), the two parties may enter into a *service level agreement* (SLA), which is an internal document outlining what resources each party will provide. The challenge for the customer becomes drafting an SLA that accurately depicts what each party must contribute to the relationship. If the SLA is not drafted carefully, the customer runs into the same types of performance problems that it does with poorly drafted contracts. Performance problems can be a significant risk factor to program success. An SLA affects program changes because work that would have been previously contracted out may now be performed by internal customer personnel.

Funding Cuts

In today's environment of declining budgets, governmental programs typically face the risk that funding will be diverted to another program, delayed, or eliminated. Funding cuts can happen before the program is contracted out or during contract performance.

Customer Reorganization

Reorganization is common in today's streamlining initiatives. Although streamlining and reorganization may be beneficial in the long run, during the transition period, most organizations experience instability, particularly if the reorganization is due to a merger or an acquisition. This instability can result in a lack of decision making or resource expending until things "calm down." The instability stems from inertia before the reorganization and a shake up after the reorganization. Either of these situations can cause program risk because priorities may shift and personnel may be transitioned.

Schedule Slippages

Schedules need to be carefully planned and executed for successful program implementation. But if the original schedule is not realistic, or if any problems occur, schedule slippage may occur and result in delayed program implementation. The secret to managing schedules is to establish a realistic schedule up front and then to develop contingency plans for alternative scenarios.

Protest Delays

Contractor-initiated protests may delay a government program. The government needs time and resources to assess the protest, conduct research, determine if the protest has any merit, conduct a hearing, and determine an equitable solution if the situation warrants.

The risk management areas that concern the customer's external resources include the following:

Contractor-Induced Program Delays

Contractors may cause program delays by providing poor performance or providing unacceptable products. Inexperienced contractors (including those unfamiliar with a particular governmental agency) may overestimate their abilities to win the program. If the customer terminates the contractor for poor performance, the program will suffer: Legal proceedings and acquiring a new contractor do not happen quickly.

Contractor Overspending the Program Budget

Contractor inexperience or mismanagement can result in the customer overspending the program budget. The type of contract determines which party bears the majority of the risk for this excess. If the contractor overspends the budget in a firm, fixed-price contract, the contractor is at risk and pays any additional contract performance costs. In this situation, the customer is minimally at risk if the contractor goes bankrupt or cannot deliver and defaults on the contract. If the contractor overspends the budget in a cost-plus contract, the customer suffers the greater risk.

Inappropriate Contractor Behavior

If a contractor spends government funds inappropriately or commits any other criminal act, the regulated nature of federal procurements makes any inappropriate contractor behavior illegal, particularly if there is an intent to defraud, and subject to administrative, civil, and criminal sanctions. Although most government contractors are aware of the rules and regulations and perform well within them, some contractors think they can get away with something. If the contractor commits an illegal act, the government customer will begin administrative proceedings, which will result in the contractor's eventual suspension or debarment. In addition, civil and criminal proceedings can result in prison sentences, criminal penalties, lack of payment, or fines if found guilty (FAR 3.502, "Subcontractor Kickback"). Any of these situations can cause risk to a program.

Any of the contract risks discussed in this section can seriously affect a company's or an agency's ability to perform its mission within the allocated funds. This causes significant consternation for program managers, upper management, and, in the case of government business, taxpayers. For these reasons, it is imperative that the customer develop and use tools to minimize the potential risk areas.

What Can the Customer Do to Mitigate Risk?

The customer can do many things to mitigate the risks described in the previous section. Before awarding a contract, the customer should develop a clear solicitation to help minimize performance problems. During the proposal stage, the customer and contractor have opportunities to identify and resolve areas of misunderstanding (such as the statement of work, acceptance, and warranty). During contract performance, the customer can monitor the contractor's actions to ensure the contractor performs in accordance with the contract. The following paragraphs present some of the ways that the customer can mitigate many contractor-induced risks.

Know the Contract

The customer's contract person and program manager should be familiar with the contractual agreement. By knowing the document, the customer can quickly determine if the contractor's performance is consistent with the original contract terms and stop any minor deviations before they become significant problems.

Know the Contractor

A new contractor needs more direction and guidance than an incumbent contractor. The customer should understand the contractor's level of expertise and review the program's status more frequently if the situation merits it.

Ensure the Contractor Stays on Schedule and within Budget

Staying on schedule and within budget are two fundamental areas that can significantly affect program success. The customer can use life-cycle management techniques, work breakdown structures, critical path networks, and other similar tools to ensure that the contractor stays on schedule and within budget. If slight deviations occur, the customer should identify the potential problem as soon as the customer discovers it and work with the contractor to resolve the issue.

Know the Available Technology

Although the customer does not need as extensive a technical staff as contractors do, it behooves the customer to have at least a few people who understand the program's technical complexities. Some contractor suggestions may work in theory but will not work in the customer's environment. The customer's technical representative can verify the information and ensure the contractor does not cause technical problems in the program.

Risk Areas for the Contractor

Just as the customer must manage risk, so too must the contractor. The following section discusses risk areas that must be mitigated by the contractor.

Acting on Direction Other Than That from an Authorized Representative

On a government contract, the contracting officer is the only government representative authorized to bind the government. On a commercial contract, the prime contractor should find out ahead of time, if it is not stated in the contract, who the authorized decision makers are. If the need for a change arises and the contractor fails to get the change formally documented from the contracting officer or the authorized representative, the contractor is at risk for the work performed. Similarly, if the contractor fails to get an approved delivery before proceeding with the work, it is performing at risk. *At risk* means that the contractor is not performing in accordance with the contract and, therefore, may not receive payment for the goods and services provided and/or may be terminated for default.

Contract Overspending

The contractor typically experiences contract overspending problems in several specific areas. These areas include the following:

- Overspending on managing the program
- Poor or inexperienced subcontractor performance resulting in the need for replacement (often with higher-priced subcontractors)

- Contract mistakes, which may stem from the contractor not understanding the scope of work, that cause contract to over-run
- Unallowable costs that are not properly managed

Consequences of Terms and Conditions

If the contractor does not pay particular attention to contract clauses and their consequences before award, it runs the risk of losing a significant amount of money on the contract. Liquidated-damages and downtime-credit contract clauses are two examples of financial recourse clauses. The liquidated-damages clause allows the customer to charge the contractor a predetermined amount of money for any time lost by customer personnel when the contractor's products were not available for use. The downtime-credit clause allows the customer to receive a financial credit on the contractor invoice for any nonconforming products the contractor provides. The risk to the contractor increases when the contractor proposes products with unknown reliability. If these products belong to subcontractors, the prime contractor's risk increases if it has not flowed down the liquidated-damages and downtime-credit clauses to the subcontractor.

Poorly Drafted Contract

A contract filled with imprecise language will provide lots of problems for the contractor. It is in the best interest of both the customer and the contractor to ensure that unclear, contradictory, or ambiguous contract language is removed and resolved as soon as it is discovered. Otherwise, contractor performance may not meet the customer's expectations.

Poor Performance

If the prime contractor performs poorly, or if an inadequately performing subcontractor is not corrected by the prime contractor, the prime contractor has additional contract risk. Liquidated damages, downtime credits, consideration, award fee withdrawal, suspension, debarment, and termination are all options available to the government to rectify the situation.

Subcontractors

Many of the risks associated with the prime contractor are inherent in the prime contractor-subcontractor relationship as well. Subcontractors not meeting their subcontracts, poorly drafted subcontracts, subcontractor refusal to accept flow down clauses, and poor subcontractor performance can cause risk for the prime contractor.

What Can the Contractor Do to Mitigate Risk?

The contractor can do many things to mitigate risk on a contract. The good news is that many of these techniques are just good business practices and management practices that a contractor should be using as a normal matter of course.

Identify Risk Areas and Develop Contingency Plans to Mitigate Those Risks

Although it is not feasible for the contractor to have contingency plans in place for every conceivable outcome, understanding the critical components of the program and establishing alternative plans for those areas makes good business sense. Having additional suppliers, back up facilities, or additional subject matter experts are all methods to mitigate risks in critical component areas.

Know Your Customer

A contractor must understand the customer environment in which it operates. For example, if the customer usually waits until the last minute to issue a delivery order and then expects the contractor to quickly provide the goods or services to meet the program schedule, the contractor should start program reviews or status reports that highlight upcoming program activities and identify the party responsible for each activity. This technique may allow the contractor to reduce its operating risks. In the case of government business, the contractor must understand the process, regulations, and operating environment that the government must operate within in order to be successful.

Keep Communications Channels Open

Both sides benefit by keeping the communication channels open. Open communication minimizes risks for both parties because the customer can inform the contractor of changes in program direction or milestones and the contractor can inform the customer of potential problem areas. Together they can work on an acceptable solution.

Know the Contract

The contractor should understand that the original proposal sets baseline expectations for contract performance. When the contractor needs to modify the contract, the contractor should understand how potential solutions will affect the rest of the contract. The contractor should discuss any changes it wishes to make after contract award with the customer before implementing the change. By having the change approved and the contract modified before implementing the change, the contractor reduces contractor risk because the contractor keeps the customer apprised of any changes. If the contractor implements the change before it receives customer approval, the customer can corrective actions when a contractor's performance does not match contract requirements.

Know the Technology and Industry

As technology advances, industry determines better ways to accomplish its goals to improve productivity and to minimize costs. The contractor can become a more valuable team member by determining how the advances might be implemented on the contract and by suggesting improvements to the customer. The customer is under no obligation to use any of these suggestions, but contractors may be able to help the customer solve its problems by recommending the correct application of new technology. Providing accurate and useful technology information reduces contractor risk because it keeps the contractor as a viable member of the partnership, one to which the customer can go for assistance.

Know Your Subcontracts

The prime contractor must understand the specific terms and conditions negotiated with each subcontractor. Equipped with this information, the prime contractor can quickly determine if a problem area exists and work with the subcontractor to resolve the problem. Careful subcontractor management and work inspection reduces the prime contractor's risk because it allows the contractor to catch any operational problems and take corrective action before the problems reach the customer's attention.

Manage All Aspects of the Contract

No one area of the contract can be overlooked. Understanding how all the pieces of the contract fit together to make the whole helps to determine when particular components are not performing as needed so that potential problems can be isolated and resolved. In this manner, the prime contractor can maintain a proactive rather than a reactive approach to problem solving. Tools such as program reviews and status reports help the customer and contractor review the program as a whole to identify problem areas.

Ensure All Changes Are Formally Documented from the Contracting Officer or the Authorized Representative

The contracting officer is the only person authorized to issue contract modifications on government contracts. In commercial contracts, someone is designated with the responsibility to approve all contract changes. Having one person responsible for contract changes protects the customer and the contractor. Formally documenting changes protects the customer because it is assured of getting products that the contractor knows meet the customer's requirements as per the contract. (If the products do not meet the customer's requirements, a nonconformance issue exists.) Formally documenting changes protects the contractor because the contractor is liable for default if it is not providing goods and services in accordance with the stated contract.

Tools Available to Minimize Risks

Every company and every customer has its own tools for managing projects to mitigate risks. Internally developed software products, well-established project management tools, or skilled personnel are standard tools that have helped managers manage risk in programs for years. A traditional tool for managing risk is the contract type. The customer can manage risk by the contract type it uses for the program. A stable program with known risks may best be suited for a firm, fixed-price contract. Research and development efforts may merit a cost-plus contract. Additional tools to minimize and mitigate risk are discussed in this section.

Tools Used by the Customer and the Contractor

Plans with Established Objectives, Milestones, and Budgets

The first way to minimize risks to a program is to conduct a planning process to identify the critical areas of the program and to determine alternative methods of achieving the goals. The customer regularly undergoes a planning process for funding justification for the program. The contractor also has a planning process for proposal development to assess bidding risks. Both the customer and the contractor continue to refine their plans throughout the program life cycle.

Various planning methodologies are available. Many customers and companies have their own methodology for program planning. The basic steps of a planning process include:

1. Understand the goals of the program.
2. Review the environment within which the program will be conducted—both from an internal and external perspective.
3. Determine the constraints or risks in each area of the program and the ways to mitigate those risks.
4. Develop the objectives for the program and the milestone for each objective.
5. Determine the strategies for meeting those objectives.
6. Develop the schedule.
7. Assess the internal and external resources required for meeting the program objectives.
8. Develop the operating budget for the program.
9. Determine whether the current organization will support the program objectives.

Planning helps the customer and the contractor reduce program risk by anticipating potential problem areas before they occur and analyzing contingent solutions for dealing with the problem.

Work Breakdown Structure (WBS)

Some customers require a contractor to use a WBS. If it is required, the contractor must submit a WBS in its proposal. The winning contractor must report against the WBS throughout the life of the program. A WBS is a hierarchical approach to program planning and management. To develop a WBS, the contractor must:

1. Identify the major components of program implementation (e.g., engineering, development, production, distribution, and user training).
2. For each major program component, identify the subcomponents (e.g., in user training, three different types of training must be provided: formal classroom, computer-based, and on-the-job).

3. Continue the process of taking each component and breaking it down into its subparts to the lowest process level (typically five to seven levels).
4. Assign budgets and schedules for each subpart.
5. Add budgets together to determine how much it costs to perform a function (e.g., adding the costs for formal classroom, computer-based, and on-the-job training will yield the total cost for providing user training on the contract).
6. Assign a price to each cost component of the contract.
7. Based on the WBS, the customer develops an estimate of the contractor's program operating costs.
8. During contract performance, the government determines at what WBS level it wishes the contractor to report progress and expenditures.

WBS helps the contractor identify the costs necessary for running a program. Equipped with this knowledge, the contractor can reduce its program risk by using the schedule to develop a true estimate of the operating expenses the program will require after award. This tool also helps the government determine the expenditures for each component of the program. Armed with this information, the customer may quickly identify any areas of the program that are experiencing budget overruns.

Automated Tools

A series of software applications can be used on a contract to automate portions of the management function and minimize risks for the customer and the contractor. These tools may be developed or purchased. Several of the functions that these tools might perform are described in the following paragraphs. Some contractors and customers combine several of these functions into one tool so as to not duplicate data; others only automate one or two of these functions and keep each function as a separate system. The customer and the contractor may share the data contained in their respective systems.

Configuration Management

Configuration management is a tool that originated in large-weapon systems and data-processing programs. Configuration management is now used to track individual items on a contract. For example, configuration management can be used to:

- Track the current contract baseline and previous iterations.
- Track specific manufacturer product numbers that are offered on the contract.
- Track when changes to a product have occurred.
- Track when and where specific components were delivered to the customer.
- Track specific serial numbers of products that were sent to customer sites.
- Track warranty or maintenance issues.

Configuration management helps the customer and contractor reduce program risk because it helps to ensure that the contractor delivers and the customer receives the products on the current and approved contract baseline.

Planning/Scheduling Tools

Planning and scheduling tools have been used for a long time to reduce risk on programs by allowing the management team to determine the milestones for each project, identify the resources required for each project, and depict the relationship between projects. Program Evaluation and Review Technique (PERT), Critical Path Method (CPM), and other network schedulers have been part of the project manager's tool kit for decades. These tools basically require the user to define all tasks required for the project. The next step is to define the relationships between the tasks and the resources required for the tasks. These relationships help to establish a priority for certain tasks to be accomplished; failure to accomplish these particular tasks on time may delay program implementation. These tools are useful only if the contractor continually updates the program it is using to reflect additional information as it becomes known. These tools help the customer and contractor determine when projects are falling behind schedule, determine when resource conflicts exist, and identify cost overruns, which allow them to take corrective action to minimize their risks.

Customer and Contractor Conferences (Program Reviews)

Customer and contractor conferences provide a forum to discuss program status, new directions, and problem areas. The conferences can be scheduled or held on an as-needed basis. The conferences reduce program risk for the customer because during the meeting the customer learns about the contractor's status so that it can take corrective action if deemed necessary. The conferences reduce the program risk for the contractor by giving the contractor the opportunity to discuss particular problem areas and to work with the customer to reach a mutually agreeable resolution.

Other Control Systems

With increased emphasis on improving quality, both the customer and the contractor are developing new *metrics*, or methods to assess performance. Metrics can be developed for any part of a program. Because of the commercial and the federal customer's increased emphasis on a contractor's past performance, the customer uses metrics to determine if quality levels have improved. Contractors have long used metrics to make improvements in performance to remain competitive. Now customers require contractors to step up to new performance measures for improvement on contracts. Working to get things right the first time helps both the customer and the contractor reduce program risk.

Cost/Price Tracking

On government contracts, cost tracking is done by the contractor. The contractor tracks the direct costs, or the amount of expenses, that a contractor actually incurs (or expects to incur) for providing the goods and services to the government. To that direct cost, the contractor adds overhead, general and administrative (G&A), fee (or profit), and other applicable expenses that are part of its rate structure. The resulting number becomes the government's price on the contract. The contractor must contain its internal costs to successful. Cost tracking tools help the contractor determine if it is within budget for each contract component. The types of information contained in this tracking tool include:

- Items and prices on the contract
- Total quantities remaining on the contract for each component (if applicable)
- Items being purchased from subcontractors (prices based on negotiated subcontracts)
- Labor rates on the contract
- Labor costs
- Actual rates used on the contract (as disclosed to DCAA)

Cost tracking helps the contractor reduce risk because the tool alerts the contractor of the components that are costing more to provide to the government than originally budgeted. Depending on the cause of this problem, the contractor may be able to take steps to fix it and improve operating profit margins.

Price tracking is conducted by the government. Price tracking allows the government to measure the contractor's level of performance in relation to the amount of contract dollars spent to determine if the contractor is on schedule and within budget. The government may use several types of tools to conduct this analysis: work breakdown structures, contractor reporting, expenses incurred to date reports, and outside analyses.

Price tracking helps the government reduce risk by alerting the government of the components that are costing more to provide than originally budgeted. Armed with this information, the government can take corrective action with the contractor and reduce its program operating risk. This corrective action may include withholding payment (until the contractor is on schedule), withholding award fee (if applicable), or other contractual remedies.

Tools Used by the Contractor for the Customer

Problem Management System

Some contractors have an automated problem management system. This is a tool that provides the customer with one central place to report problems. It also helps the contractor identify particular problem areas that the customer is experiencing with the contractor's products. The contractor can then prioritize and fix those particular problems to maintain customer satisfaction. The tool reduces contractor risk by allowing the contractor to identify recurring problems and to identify fixes proactively before the customer is forced to take recourse.

Delivery Order Tracking

If the contract contains many products, or if many delivery orders are anticipated, the contractor can use a delivery order tracking tool to monitor what has been ordered and delivered to the customer. The tool can also be used to track the following types of information:

- Long lead-time items on the contract that must be ordered from subcontractors

- Terms and conditions of the subcontracts, such as payment discounts
- Contract requirements
- Customer ordering date
- Date each component was ordered from a subcontractor
- Date products are delivered to the government

By tracking delivery orders, the contractor can ensure the appropriate goods and services are ordered and delivered within the time frames allotted by the contract. The contractor can use this tool to reduce risk by delivering all products and services on time to the customer and, therefore, not incurring downtime credits, liquidated damages, or any other contractual remedy the government can use for late order delivery.

Tools Used by the Customer with Input from the Contractor

Eighty Percent Reporting

The government often requires the contractor to notify the government when the contractor has expended 80 percent of the allotted funds for a project (FAR 32.705-2, "Clauses for Limitation of Cost or Funds"; FAR 32, "Contract Financing,"; FAR 32.5, "Progress Payments Based on Cost"). If the contractor is behind schedule for the amount of funds expended, the government may take corrective actions. In this manner the government can reduce its risk by focusing on problems slightly earlier than the end of the project and determine methods to mitigate its risk.

Contract Deliverables

The customer uses contract deliverables as a method of assessing contractor performance. Contract deliverables are usually written documents or reports provided to the customer on a predetermined schedule. The customer may require whatever deliverables it believes is necessary to evaluate the contractor's performance. The deliverables are identified in the solicitation so that contractor may price the effort. Sometimes, the contractor will require a draft deliverable that the customer reviews and comments on before the actual deliverable is evaluated. The number of drafts and revisions should be specified in advance. Deliverables provide the contractor with interim evaluation points throughout the course of a program so that if a problem exists, the contractor can make the necessary improvements. The interim nature of contract deliverables, and the contractor improvements that result from customer feedback, reduces program risks for both the customer and the contractor.

Tool Used by the Contractor

Cost Recovery

Cost containment is only part of a contractor's profit picture. The other key to contract success is *cost recovery*—making sure that the contractor receives timely payment for goods and services provided to the customer. The contractor uses a cost recovery tool to ensure the customer is paying the appropriate amount for goods and services being rendered. The contractor may tie this tool into its corporate accounts receivable system. The cost-recovery system collects the following types of delivery order information:

- Number of orders placed
- Total value
- Date issued
- Date filled
- Date accepted
- Date invoiced
- Date paid
- Cost allocation (e.g., independent research and development or bid and proposal)

Cost recovery helps the contractor reduce contract risk by ensuring the customer pays the amount owed for goods and services based on the prime contract. The contractor reduces contract risk by ensuring the customer pays for goods and services on time (thereby managing cash flow) and pays the price that the government and contractor have previously negotiated (thereby making the preestablished amount of profit on each contract component).

The other component to cost recovery is ensuring that the prime contractor pays the subcontractors according to the subcontract's negotiated terms and conditions. The prime contractor must understand and manage the acceptance criteria, delivery schedules, performance standards, and early payment discounts stated in each subcontract. By ensuring the subcontractor delivers quality products that meet the government's acceptance on time and for the negotiated price, the prime contractor can effectively manage program cash flow.

Monitor Subcontractor Performance

Just as the customer uses deliverables to assess prime contractor performance, prime contractors use similar tools to assess subcontractor performance. Status reports, progress meetings, product evaluation, review of performance data, and inspections are all tools that a prime contractor can use to evaluate the subcontractor's performance. Listening to the subcontractor's problems and helping it obtain mutually satisfying solutions benefits both the prime contractor and the subcontractor by reducing program risk.

Prime Contractor Considerations

Separate People Handling Various Components of Subcontract Administration

The prime contractor has multiple people handling each component of contract administration. For example:

- The prime-contract administrator is responsible for reviewing and negotiating the prime contract, which could affect subcontracts.
- The subcontract administrator is responsible for developing, reviewing changes, and negotiating the various subcontracts used to support a prime contract.
- The operations people work with the subcontractors on a daily basis to meet the requirements of the customer.
- The purchasing people determine which subcontractor's products and services are necessary to meet the customer's requirements.
- The business people work with subcontractors to develop proposals to get new products and services on the contract.
- The managers may be working on new aspects of the contract.
- Executive level personnel may be working on strategic alliances between the two companies.
- Lawyers litigate issues between the prime contractor and customer or the prime contractor and subcontractor, should the need arise.

Ideally, subcontract administration is more carefully handled when each of the teams working with the subcontractor to fulfill the requirements of the prime contract talk to each other and share their goals with one another. However, due to the proprietary nature of some business transactions, or a focus on just one functional area, or a desire not to share information, subcontract administration can get complicated when each of the teams works alone. The subcontract administrator cannot develop integrated solutions if he or she lacks information about what is being pursued within the other areas. This is why it is important to emphasize information sharing across functional areas within a company.

Subcontracts Can Be Managed by Subcontractor, Service Area, or Prime Contract Program

The prime contractor can organize its subcontracts in whatever manner supports it best. Some companies assign all subcontracts related to a particular subcontractor to one person regardless of the number of prime contracts the subcontractor is supporting. Other organizations establish subcontracts by the service area and have one subcontract administrator responsible for all labor or hardware subcontracts. Another popular way of organizing subcontracts is by the prime contract they support. For example, one person would be responsible for all subcontracts related to one particular program.

The prime contractor should decide how to organize the subcontracts by using the following criteria:

- Number of subcontracts managed within an organization
- Number of prime contracts in the pipeline that will drive future subcontractor requirements
- Number of people in the subcontract organization
- Strategic nature of the subcontractor
- Amount of business being done in each service area

Sharing Information Across Organization

Due to the various methods of managing subcontracts, the subcontract administrator must share information with other employees working on the contract. The administrator would want to share the following information:

- Strategies employed in one service area that can be applied in another service area

- Negotiation techniques used with a subcontractor to support one prime contract can be shared with other administrators negotiating with the same company to support a different prime contract
- Clauses used in prime contracts can be shared with administrators negotiating subcontracts
- Methods to resolve problems can be shared across organizational boundaries

Subcontractor Considerations

Subcontracts Can Be Managed by Prime Contractor or by Service Area

Just as a prime contractor can organize its subcontracts in whatever way supports the contractor best, a subcontractor can do the same. The subcontractor can have one administrator handle all the subcontracts related to one prime contractor or all subcontracts within a service area. The subcontractor can decide how to best organize the prime contracts by using the same criteria that a prime contractor uses.

Obtain Acceptance or a Receipt on Delivered Product/ Services

The subcontractor should obtain the prime contractor's acceptance on products delivered or services provided. The contractor's acceptance can be indicated by payment, however, the subcontractor may experience times when it must complete a great deal of work before it receives payment. In these situations, the subcontractor would want to have some sort of sign off from the prime contractor that it approves of the subcontractor's work it has done to date. By getting the prime contractor's acceptance, the subcontractor has a record of solid performance. This approach also helps when the two companies are closing out the subcontract. By having a contemporaneous audit trail of products and services delivered and accepted, the companies will have an easier time closing out the contract.

Government Considerations

Regulations Are Evolving

In the government marketplace, there is a great impetus of streamlining the acquisition process, doing more with less, and taking advantage of lessons learned in the commercial marketplace. These forces are shaping regulations with untraditional speed. The National Performance Review, the Federal Acquisition Streamlining Act (FASA), the Federal Acquisition Reform Act (FARA) and the subsequent executive orders, and Federal Acquisition Regulation (FAR) updates have shaped and continue to shape the federal procurement process.

In addition to all of these enterprise-wide changes, government personnel are experiencing a kind of freedom that they never really had in federal procurement. They currently have the freedom to act as a prudent business people rather than relying on volumes of federal regulations to govern their every decision. This freedom has manifested itself in innovative approaches to problem solving, partnerships between government and industry, and pilot programs to test new ways of conducting business.

It is an exciting time, but just as federal personnel cannot rely on the "way we've always done things," prime contractors or subcontractors cannot either. This makes almost every procurement unique. Guiding principles are still in place, but methodologies used to meet the principles are as diverse as the people doing the procurement.

Contracting Officer Decides How Prime Contract Will Operate

Regardless of the way procurements can now be conducted, the final decision maker in each procurement is the contracting officer. Some contracting officers have embraced change; others are rebelling against it; and still others do not have the training needed to do things a different way. Regardless of how many stories about successful contracts are contained in *Contract Management* magazine or stories about changes that have worked to reduce cost, time, and effort on government procurements that are in *Federal Computer Week*, it is still up to the contracting officer who will drive how innovative the approaches can be to solve contractual issues.

Strict Conformance Doctrine

Chapter 1 discussed the government's strict conformance to doctrine. This has not gone away as a result of all the recent procurement changes. The prime contractor and the subcontractor that are working on federal programs must realize that there is a distinct difference in doing business with the government; they have to provide what they said they would provide. If the prime contractor fails to do this by either being negligent themselves or accepting substandard performance from its subcontractor runs the risk of contract termination, fines, suspension, or debarment in addition to lower profit margins.

Sponsorship of Subcontractor Claims

The concept of privity has been discussed in this book and how a contract is developed between two parties and protects only those two parties. When a claim is made to appeal adverse decisions by a contracting officer, the government gives the subcontractor the right to bring forth that claim with the sponsorship of the prime contractor. This still protects the privity of contract between the prime contractor and the government and that between the prime contractor and the subcontractor, but it gives the subcontractor a method to obtain satisfactory results in a dispute situation. When the prime contractor sponsors a subcontractor, it means that the subcontractor's attorneys can litigate the claim directly with the government but it must file all paperwork *in the name of the prime contractor.*

Severin Doctrine

The Severin Doctrine is a legal rule that prevents contractors from recovering damages on behalf of subcontractors (as described earlier in Sponsorship of Subcontractor Claims) for a contract breach if the contractor has no liability to the subcontractor. For example, if a subcontract contains a clause that exculpates (or removes) a contractor from liability, the subcontractor does not have the right to go back to the government and try to recover damages because the subcontractor has no legal liability to the subcontractor. In the original case, *Severin v. United States,* 99 Ct.Cl. 435 (1943), the courts held that the contractor was barred from bringing a claim against the government on behalf of the subcontractor because the contractor could not prove it had suffered any damages even though the subcontractor had.

11 ETHICS

Golden Rule

A great deal has been written on business ethics. There are schools of thought, interpretations, and value identification, all of which have great philosophical and practical merit. For purposes of this book, I'd like to keep it simple and rely on the Golden Rule:

Do unto others as you would have them do unto you.

I believe this works for several reasons:

1. Solid companies are around for a long time, which means that they hope to establish business relationships with other companies for the long term. If a contractor treats a company poorly on a program, the company will do its best to reciprocate on the next program opportunity and treat the contractor poorly. Which the contractor then feels the need to continue the trend on the next program, and so on, and so on, and so on. This assumes that the two companies will work together in the future.

2. As companies streamline, downsize, and get back to providing only their core competencies, they start to form new relationships that they may have never thought possible. A company with a solid, honest reputation in the marketplace can land opportunities that never seemed possible.

3. The world is small and what goes around comes around. If a contractor treats another company poorly, word will get out about the contractor, which may limit the contractor's future opportunities.

4. When it comes right down to it, ethics are not about one company versus another company; they are about people. If you mistreat a person, you not only have to deal with the person's dissatisfaction, but your own as well.

5. The world economy is great, and companies do better by working out strategic alliances in which all parties win because there is more than enough opportunities to go around.

6. Employees take pride and satisfaction in working for a company that has a solid, ethical position in the marketplace.

7. With solid ethics, you would feel proud if your child said, "I want to work where you work one day," and encourage them to do so.

8. With solid ethics, a company will be able to recruit top notch individuals because the company's reputation speaks for itself.

9. Solid ethics help save the company time, embarrassment, and expense of being found out later particularly in the government marketplace if it makes an illegal act.

The Practical Side

In order for a company's ethics policy to work, the management team should keep the following in mind:

- Ethics that are beautifully worded and placed on a plaque don't work.

- Ethics that are only paid lip service to don't work.

- Employees who see managers act unethically or tolerate unethical behavior from their subordinates don't work.

- Ethics that are discussed at an employee orientation and are never seen again don't work.

- Ethics aren't the latest high-paid consultant's work product; they are a way of life at the company.

- Employees need a method to communicate violations of their company's ethics policy and not be ostracized for doing so.

- Swift action must come to those who choose not to adhere to the ethics policy if it is to be taken seriously by the other employees.

A friend of mine changed jobs and went to work for another company. Within two weeks, she had been asked to tell everything she knew about her former company, had seen competitor information stolen and the act approved of by the superiors, and had seen bid tampering. The basic way of life at that company wore against her very nature so much that she left a short time after. She returned to her former company and told the people there, "I didn't realize how much our ethics meant until I went to a company without them."

Internal vs. External Sources

One final introductory note: Realize that ethics violations can occur through internal or external sources or a combination of the two. Ethics violations also range in terms of severity and can occur at any level of the organization. For example, internal violations committed by people working for the company include:

- Taking office supplies (e.g., notepads, pens, pencils, or copy paper) for personal use
- Using computer, the Internet, copy machines, and telephones for personal use
- Lying about time worked on time cards
- Breaking into corporate computer systems or managers' offices to obtain sensitive information
- Sharing competitive information about the company with people outside of the company
- Insider trading
- Embezzling money
- Violating procurement integrity laws and jeopardizing future government business for the company
- Conspiracies between two or more members working from different organizations to orchestrate ethics violations

In addition, the company can commit internal ethics violations against its own people or people joining the company by:

- Pay inequity based on gender, race, creed, or sexual preference
- Using different standards to evaluate people's performance
- Unmerited preferential treatment to a person or group
- Unfair hiring practices

External violations occur when a member of another company seeks to harm the other company by, for example:

- Breaking into computer systems or facilities to obtain competitive information
- Using information obtained unethically to cripple the other company's position

Internal and external violations occur when members of another company work with the company's own people to harm the company or a competitor. Examples include:

- Hiring people away from companies in order to exploit the other company's knowledge about the company
- Hiring people away from companies in order to strengthen the other company's own competitive position while crippling the company
- Sharing competitive information inappropriately to give one company an unfair advantage over another in a solicitation
- Not evaluating proposals equitably across all competitors

Process

Establish the Policy

Establishing an ethics policy can be difficult. The most ideal situation is for the company to gather ethics policies from other companies to formulate its own. Many companies send their ethics policies to new subcontractors so that the subcontractors are aware of how the company operates. This helps to avoid ethics violations before they occur.

A second approach is for the company to gather a team of employees from within the company to determine the types of situations that should be covered. The employees can rely on situations that they have seen in the past and update the policy as new situations occur and are resolved.

Why Establish a Policy?

Why should the company go through all the effort to develop a policy when it can just tell everyone to treat companies fairly? Well, unfortunately, this approach doesn't go far enough and is not visible enough. The company's ethics must be outlined and shared with all employees involved in buying decisions. The policy must become ingrained and a way of life for the employees in order for the company to establish and maintain its reputation as an ethical company. As the company hires new employees, it must educate them on its ethics policy and be willing to accept the responsibility of maintaining its policy when employees act on behalf of the company. By having a written policy, the company accomplishes these objectives.

Scope

Items to be included in an ethics policy or coordinated with the ethics policy include guidelines for the following:

- Marketing
- Procurement
- Hiring
- Interviewing
- Compensation
- Appraisal
- Competitor information gathering
- Financial controls
- Legal controls
- Source selection
- Gift giving/receiving
- Information release
- Public relations
- Government business
- Subcontractor management

Educate Employees on the Policy

Once the company has formerly documented and agreed on its ethics policy, the company should used it in the training materials for employees. At a minimum, the company should use its policy during the following training situations:

- New employee orientation
- Purchasing training sessions
- As part of the government's procurement integrity training
- Yearly letters to employees re-stating the company's ethics policy to serve as a reminder of the behavior the company expects
- Introductory letters to subcontractors so that they are aware of the policy at the beginning of the business relationship

Develop Systems That Support the Policy

A key step before implementing an ethics policy is ensuring that the corporate systems support the objectives of the policy. For example, requiring a sign off on new business proposals from representatives from operations, business, contracts, and management help to ensure that adequate reviews and controls are in place to ensure that projects are known about and agreed on before the projects are submitted to a customer.

Follow the Policy

Following the ethics policy has three different components:

1. *Corporate atmosphere of following the policy*—Perhaps the most important component to achieving success with a corporate ethics policy is the overall feeling in the company about how important the ethics policy is to the company. Employees know when policies are truly believed in and used within the company and those that are just paid lip service to.

2. *Methods used to correct ethics violations*—If ethics violations are ignored or approved of within the company, employees will know that ethics are not taken seriously. If the company has repeat offenders and no action is taken against them, the company may experience a growth in the number of offenders. It will become increasingly difficult to get rid of these people as well because precedence has been set and tolerated.

3. Attitude toward whistle blowers—The term *whistle blower* conjures up images of someone disturbing the peace, but if the company expects its ethics policy to be taken seriously, employees who follow the rules and report employees who do not follow the policy should be encouraged to report them. These employees should be rewarded not quieted, dismissed, or ignored.

Review and Update the Policy Periodically to Determine Applicability

Ideally, the ethics policy should be developed at a company's inception. Unfortunately, when a company begins business, it tends to focus on other things rather than ethics. If the company did not develop an ethics policy in the beginning, it should develop a corporate ethics policy right away. However, establishing a policy is not enough. An ethics policy that is never reviewed tends to fall short of meeting the challenges of today's business world. The company needs to make sure it has a policy that covers contemporary problems. For example, does the company's policy cover situations in which an employee gathers information illegally by breaking into a competitor's computer system? How does the company handle business abroad in countries where bribes are an acceptable part of a business transaction. Will the company use the Internet to publicize upcoming procurements and related data so that multiple companies may bid on them? These are just a few examples of places that antiquated ethics policies fall short of meeting the challenges of today's market economy.

Prime Contractor Considerations

An ethics policy basically translates into the following tenets for prime contractors:

- If the contractor is going to run competitions, keep them fair by sharing the same information with all the parties involved and do not keep competitive information from certain companies.
- Be honest with the competitors by telling them the real requirements, the company's best guess at the business case, and when the company has selected an apparent winner to provide the products and services on the contract.
- Limit competitive information to that information which the company gains through open channels. If the company is securing the information in a way that it would not want stated in the *Washington Post*, the company's method is probably unethical.
- Do not try to lure subcontractors by promising them things the company does not have control over, such as customer buying patterns, budgets, or effects of regulations.
- Document information and changes between the company and the subcontractor so that there is a record of what promises have been made.
- Do not accept or allow the employees to accept gifts from subcontractors pursuing business with the company.
- Do not change source selection plans to favor one company over another.
- Provide relevant information to subcontractors on a timely basis so that they can plan accordingly.

Subcontractor Considerations

Following are similar suggestions for subcontractors:

- Do not bribe the prime contractor or the contractor's customers in order to gain future business.
- Do not offer a low price at initial proposal submission and then raise it at BAFO when the prime contractor is counting on working with you.
- Do not wait to fix problems with the subcontract until after contract award.
- Do not have or give the perception of improper conduct with the prime contractor's buyers.
- Tell the prime contractor immediately if you no longer wish to participate in the procurement process so that the contractor is not counting on a proposal, solution, or BAFO from you and so the contractor can make other plans accordingly.
- If you are behind schedule or do something wrong, let the prime contractor know immediately so that it can try to fix any problems with the customer.
- Do whatever you can at whatever cost to you to fix a problem that you created.
- Stand behind the products and services that you sell and help the prime contractor support your products and services with the customer.
- If you agree to work with a prime contractor, do whatever you can to make the team successful.
- Be aware of your company's limitations in respect to time, money, and resources and plan your business deals accordingly.
- If the subcontractor has employees working on multiple prime contractor teams for different programs, you should ensure that information about each prime contractor team is only shared with those members from your company working on that prime contractor solution.

Government Considerations

The government takes ethics very seriously and strives to keep things fair among all competitors. Some of its initiatives are discussed in this section.

Contractor Purchasing System Review (CPSR)

The FAR (Part 44.3) states "The objective of a CPSR is to evaluate the efficiency and effectiveness with which the contractor spends Government funds and complies with Government policy when subcontracting." The government is trying to accomplish two things with this audit: (1) It wants to make sure that the prime contractor, when it is buying goods on behalf of the government, buys the products and services that represent the best value for the government and, consequently, the American taxpayers. (2) The government wants to ensure that the prime contractor is doing whatever it can to help the government meet its socioeconomic objectives by buying products and services from small and small and disadvantaged businesses. The government conducts CPSRs at least every three years, and if the contractor passes, the contractor does not have to get an administrative contracting officer (ACO) approval to purchase items on behalf of the government. All of the contractor's direct purchases made during an audit period are subject to review.

To conduct a CPSR, the government decides if a prime contractor will be selling the government more than $25 million of products or services within a given year. If the answer is yes, the Defense Contractor Audit Agency (DCAA) will send a letter to the contractor requesting preliminary information, such as:

- Number of employees
- Organizational chart
- Office locations
- Sales volumes for major customers
- Subcontract activity for current and previous years
- Types of subcontracts issued by the prime contractor (e.g., fixed price, cost-reimbursable, competitive, negotiated, letter, or blanket purchase orders)
- Company's purchasing guidelines

If the auditor decides an audit is warranted, it will request that the contractor provide a list of the purchases made in each of the following categories:

- Those greater than $100,000
- Those between $25,000 to $100,000
- Those between $10,000 to $25,000
- Those between $2,500 to $10,000

The auditor will then arrive on site to review a sample of the purchases the contractor made in each of the categories to determine if the company has been following its own purchasing guidelines. When the government auditor conducts a CPSR, he or she reviews the following information:

- Purchase request
- Solicitation
- Government supplier letter
- Representations and certifications
- Subcontracting plan
- Proposal
- Evaluation/source selection
- Non-selection of SB/SDB
- Cost or pricing data exemption
- Cost or pricing analysis
- EEO clearance for subcontractors
- Flow-down clauses
- Negotiation memorandum
- Other requirements

After completing the audit, the auditor summarizes his or her findings and provides a report to the DCAA office and the contract administrator. If the contractor passes the review, the DCAA will probably not schedule another review for three years. If the contractor does not pass the review, the DCAA will issue a letter outlining the problem areas and requiring the contractor to submit its plan for correcting the deficiencies within 15 days. Once the government reviews and approves the plan, it follows up with the contractor much more frequently to ensure that the contractor is abiding by the new approaches. If the contractor fails to make the required modifications or if the government decides that the contractor's system is too deficient, the government will withdraw the contractor's approved purchasing system certification. This withdrawal means that the contractor is no longer authorized to buy products and services on behalf of the government in support of its contracts. The contractor must notify all existing and potential future government customers that the customer is not able to carry out government purchasing requirements on the customers' contracts without securing contracting officer approval on each and every purchase. This extra responsibility of having to get a contracting officer's approval tends to encourage prospective customers to not select the contractor for future business until its purchasing system is reapproved.

Government Policies in Prime Contracts

The government also has developed policies that contractors are required to follow. For example, the government has an Equal Employment Opportunity requirement that states that prime contractors must not prejudice their hiring decisions on factors such as race, creed, color, or sexual preference. Other examples are discussed in this section.

Procurement Integrity Act

Public Law #100-679; 41 USC 423 is the Procurement Integrity Act. By the Act, the government considers it unlawful for a contractor to receive source selection information, offer a job to a government procurement official involved in a program, or offer a bribe to a source selection official. Likewise, it is unlawful for a government official to provide source selection information, ask for or accept a job offer from a contractor involved in a procurement, or ask for or accept a bribe from a contractor. The law is written so that both sides are equally responsible for reporting people who violate procurement integrity. For example, if a government procurement official asks for a job in exchange for a positive award decision to a particular company, the company must report that request otherwise it is just as guilty as the government official.

Following are the several components to procurement integrity:

- *Prime contractor certification*—The prime contractor must certify when it submits its proposal that it is not aware of any procurement integrity violations that occurred while it pursued the program.

- *Subcontractor certification*—The prime contractor typically requires its subcontractors to sign similar certifications before the contractor makes its prime contractor certification because the prime contractor certification covers the entire team submitting the bid.

- *Employee training*—To ensure that employees are aware of the implications of procurement integrity, companies typically require employees to go through a training session so that people understand the Act and can ask questions and gain knowledge about the Act.

- *Employee certification*—Some companies require their employees to sign certifications stating that they understand the Act and promise not to violate procurement integrity while working on the program.

- *Follow-up notices*—Managers will typically send out letters to their employees working on federal contracts on a yearly basis restating the company's position on procurement integrity and ethical behavior to serve as a reminder of how the company expects its employees to operate on a daily basis.

Requirement for SBs and SDBs

The government requires the prime contractor to support the government's small business and small and disadvantaged business goals by subcontracting part of the work done under the prime contract to these types of companies. The policies that establish the government's goal help to ensure that small companies are not overlooked in the procurement arena.

Conclusion

Developing an ethics policy that is coordinated with other initiatives throughout the company must be well thought out, documented, integrated, communicated, and practiced. An ethics policy is not something that the company can establish in a 2 to 3 hour session on one afternoon. The policy requires a great deal of thought, practical application, risk analysis, and desire to do the right thing.

The positive side of all of this is that by implementing the ethics policy, the company has a much greater chance of avoiding the trouble, expense, time, resources, and wasted energies necessary to reconstruct how violations occurred . The company should not delay in establishing and implementing an ethics policy. An ethics policy takes a lot of up-front work and even more work to ensure that the employees adhere to it on a daily basis, but the benefits of improved employee morale, loyal customers, trusting subcontractors, and a positive image in the marketplace are all worth the effort.

REFERENCES

1994 Advisory Panel to Congress on Procurement Reform, Section 800, Commercial Items, Recommendations to Simplify DOD Acquisitions

Adelson, Dennis, "The New Bid Protest Procedures," *Contract Management,* June 1996

Agreement on Government Procurement, P.L. #96-39

Applegate, Jane. *Jane Applegate's Strategies for Small Business Success.* New York: Penguin, 1995

Armed Services Procurement Act of 1931

Black, Henry Campbell. *Black's Law Dictionary.* 5 ed. St. Paul, MN: West Publishing Company, 1979

Burns, Anthony P., "Internet Construction Solicitations," *Contract Management,* March 1998

Churchill, Gilbert A. Jr. *Marketing Research Methodological Foundations.* New York: Dryden Press Harcourt Brace College Publishers, 1995

Cibinic, John Jr and Ralph C. Nash. *Administration of Government Contracts.* 2 ed. Washington, DC: The George Washington University, 1986

Coates, Elinor Sue. *The Subcontract Management Manual.* Pacifica, CA: Coates and Company, 1994

Competition in Contracting Act (CICA), P.L. #98-369

Corbin, Lisa, "Procurement and Contracting: 10 Hot Issues," *Government Executive,* May 1993, p. 68

Datapro Publications

Defense Management Report Decision (DMRD) 941: Mandated the implementation of electronic data interchange (EDI)

Department of Defense FAR Supplement, "Policies and Procedures for the DoD Pilot Mentor-Protégé Program," DAC 91-10, February 1996

Deputy Secretary of Defense William Perry, Policy Memorandum on Use of Commercial Products, October 1, 1993

"DoD Information Technology Solicitations and Contract Compliance for Year 2000 Requirements," DoD IG Report Number 98-065, February 6, 1998

Dunn and Bradstreet Reports

Edwards, Paul and Sarah. *Making It on Your Own.* New York: Putnam, 1991

Edwards, Paul and Sarah, and Douglas, Laura. *Getting Business to Come to You.* New York: Putnam, 1991

Edwin C. Cassidy and Judith E. Payne, "Implementing the Department of Defense's Standard Approach to Electronic Commerce in Procurement," *Contract Management,* June 1992

Executive Order promoting procurement with small, disadvantaged businesses (SDBs) owned and controlled by socially and economically disadvantaged individuals, historically black colleges and universities (HBCUs), and minority institutions (MIs), William J. Clinton, September 16, 1994

Federal Acquisition circular 97-04, *Federal Register,* February 23, 1998

Federal Acquisition Regulation. Chicago: Commerce Clearing House, 1991.

Federal Acquisition Regulation (FAR) 1.101 Purpose of the Federal Acquisition Regulations System

FAR 2.1 Definitions

FAR 4.101 Contracting Officer's Signature

FAR 4.804 Closing Out Contract Files

FAR 5.1 Dissemination of Information

FAR 5.101 Methods of Disseminating Information

FAR 5.102 Availability of Solicitations

FAR 5.4 Release of Information

FAR 6.203 Set-Asides for Small Business Concerns

FAR 6.204 Section 8(a) Competition

FAR 6.302 Circumstances Permitting Other than Full and Open Competition

FAR 6.4 Sealed Bidding and Competitive Proposals

FAR 6.5 Competition Advocates

FAR 13

FAR 15.1002 Notification to Successful Offeror

FAR 15.405 Solicitations for Information or Planning Purposes

FAR 15.406-1 Uniform Contract Format

FAR 15.409 Pre-Proposal Conferences

FAR 15.410 Amendment of Solicitations Before Closing Date

FAR 15.6 Source Selection

FAR 15.601 Definitions

FAR 15.606 Changes in Government Requirements

FAR 15.610 Written or Oral Discussion

FAR 15.611 Best and Final Offers

FAR 30 Cost Accounting Standards

FAR 31 Contract Cost Principles and Procedures

FAR 33.2 Disputes and Appeals

FAR 42 Contract Administration

FAR 42.4 Correspondence and Visits

FAR 43 Contract Modifications

FAR 43.2 Change Orders

FAR 43.5 Post-Award Orientation

FAR 44 Subcontracting Policies and Procedures

FAR 44.2 Consent to Subcontracts

FAR 44.3 Contractors' Purchasing Systems Reviews

FAR 46 Quality Assurance

FAR 49 Termination of Contracts

Federal Acquisition Streamlining Act (FASA), P.L. #103-355

FASA Title 1, Subpart B: Planning, Solicitation, Evaluation, and Award Secs. 1011–1016

FASA Title VIII Commercial Items

FASA Title IX Federal Acquisition Computer Network

Federal Computer Week

The Federal Tort Claims Act of 1946

Federal Workforce Restructuring Act of 1993

Fisher, Brian T. "Winning on FAFOs: A Proposal Manager's Tailoring Techniques" (*Contract Management*, May 1997), page 15.

Gartner Group Publications

Garrett, Gregory A. *World Class Contracting*. Arlington, VA: ESI International, 1997

Government Computer News

Government Electronics and Information Technology Association (GEIA) 10th Annual Five-Year Federal Information Systems Opportunities (FYs 1998-2002) Proceedings, Electronics Industries Association Government Division, Arlington, VA, 1998

Hernandez, Richard J., "An Improved Model for Best Value Contracting," *Topics in Procurement Series*, National Contract Management Association, Vol. 5, No. 5

Johnson, Mary M. Dickens. "International Contract Law: the U.N.'s CISG," *Contract Management*, December 1998, p. 4

Kellman, Steven, OFPP Administrator, pledge signing address to improve government-industry communication, December 1994

King, Jan B. *Business Plans to Game Plans*. Santa Monica, CA: Merritt, 1994

Lesko, Matthew. *Getting Yours: The Complete Guide to Government Money*. New York: Penguin, 1987

Levinson, Jay Conrad. *Guerrilla Marketing*. New York: Houghton Mifflin, 1993

Nash, Ralph C. Jr. and Steven L. Schooner. *The Government Contracts Reference Book.* Washington, DC: The George Washington University, 1992

Office of Federal Procurement Policy Act of 1974

OMB Circular A-130, Government's Policy on Management of Federal Information

"Policy and Procedures for the DOD Pilot Mentor-Protégé Program," DAC 91-10, issued as part of the Department of Defense FAR Supplement, February 1996

Procurement Integrity, P.L. #100-679; 41 USC 423

Rosen, William M., "Considerations When Deciding Whether to Challenge Federal Procurements," *Contract Management,* June 1996

Small Business Administration's 8(a) Program

Software Engineering Institute Capability Maturity Model Version 1.1, February 1993

Treacy, Michael, and Wiersena, Fred. *The Discipline of Market Leaders.* Reading, MA: Addison-Wesley, 1995

Truth in Negotiations Act

U.S. Army Communications-Electronics Command, Performance Risk Assessment Group (PRAG), May 1994

U.S. Small Business Administration pamphlet, "The Most Frequently Asked Questions About the 8(a) Program," Office of Minority Small Business and Capital Ownership Development, 409 3rd St. S.W., Washington, DC 20416

Whay, H. Todd, "Corporate Risk Management: The Year 2000 Threat" *Contract Management,* April 1998, p. 4

Wilson, Hugh H. (Hamp), "RFPs—Let's Make Them Better" *Contract Management,* September 1996, p. 18

Appendix

Proposal Team Positions

Though companies vary in how they organize their proposal efforts, there are some standard functions that must be completed on every proposal effort. Below is a list of the functions that must be performed on most *federal* proposal efforts and the title most companies give to the person performing that function.

Program Manager

The program manager has overall responsibility for the proposal effort and may stay with the program after it is won as the account manager. Additionally, the program manager:

- Manages all relationships outside of proposal team (e.g., upper management, teaming partners, and the customer)
- Directs overall program planning
- Chairs kickoff meeting
- Approves proposal process schedule
- Organizes total proposal review
- Monitors proposal budget
- Allocates personnel

Salesperson

The salesperson has tracked the program since its early stages and understands the customer's needs and requirements. Additionally, the salesperson:

- Makes customer visits to gain an understanding of the customer's environment
- Tracks the program by attending governmental agency briefings, reading Web page announcements, and reviewing the *Commerce Business Daily* (CBD)
- Identifies potential teaming partners and subcontractors for the program
- Gains internal management support for the program
- Assists in developing win themes, discriminators, and benefits the customer derives from the solution

Proposal Management Team

The proposal management team consists of the program manager and his/her direct reports. These direct reports include the technical manager, proposal manager, management volume manager, live test demonstration manager (if needed), and the business manager. The proposal management team also includes representatives from the support organizations, such as marketing, contracts, engineering, and purchasing.

Proposal Production Team

The proposal production team is managed by the proposal manager and consists of an editor, production coordinator, system administrator, word processing specialist, documentation specialist, and graphics specialist. The proposal management team's responsibility is to produce a compliant proposal that addresses customer requirements and presents the company in the best manner possible.

Proposal Manager

The proposal manager leads the proposal team on a daily basis and completes the following tasks:

- Guides the development of customer issues and discriminators
- Assists in solicitation process for products to be bid in the proposal
- Monitors the development of detailed outlines
- Integrates the tasks of the various functional areas
- Develops a compliant, responsive proposal that reflects the company's offering to the government requirements
- Provides logistics support by coordinating information flow with suppliers and remote-site personnel
- Manages the production team to produce the proposal
- Develops and manages the proposal schedule
- Manages writing assignments from team members
- Conducts proposal review sessions
- Educates team members on the proposal process
- Reviews draft text and graphics

Editor

The editor works with the proposal team and:

- Ensures that the proposal is written in a clear and concise manner
- Develops a list of standards that will be used throughout the proposal
- Edits and proofs text for grammar, style, content, and theme
- Ensures writing styles and formats are consistent throughout the proposal

Production Coordinator

The production coordinator has overall responsibility for producing the proposal and completes the following tasks:

- Sets up tracking procedures for text and graphics
- Works as a liaison between the graphics, word processing, and writing teams
- Ensures the proposal meets quality assurance standards
- Schedules and oversees the production process
- Coordinates proposal packing and delivery

System Administrator

The system administrator ensures the writers' PCs and local area network, if used, stay operational throughout the proposal process. The system admistrator:

- Creates proposal directories
- Provides system access to authorized users
- Archives backups
- Creates file and drive naming standards
- Creates electronic copies for submission
- Manages proposal version control

Word-Processing Specialist

The word-processing specialist is responsible for producing the text portion of the proposal. To do this, the word-processing specialist:

- Recommends a word-processing package to use that meets the government's requirements
- Trains writers in the use of the word-processing package, if necessary
- Works with the graphics specialists to merge text and graphics files to produce the proposal
- Types in data from writers or formats files received from writers
- Ensures proposal meets government's format requirements

Documentation Specialist

The documentation specialist handles all the user and system documentation required by the RFP to substantiate the claims made in the contractor's proposal. In this capacity, the documentation specialist:

- Works with the technical team to determine the names of vendors and corresponding products
- Orders and obtains requisite copies of documentation from the vendors
- Ensures documentation meets required government standards
- Conducts inventory to ensure all documentation has been received from the vendors
- Labels, binds, and packs documentation for shipment

Graphics Specialist

The graphics specialist is responsible for the graphics that will be used throughout the proposal. To accomplish this task, the graphics specialist:

- Recommends a graphics package to use that meets the government's requirements
- Trains proposal team members in the use of the graphics package, if necessary
- Works with the word processing specialists to merge text and graphics files to produce the proposal
- Works with writers to produce graphics
- Incorporates graphics into the final proposal

Technical Team

The technical team comprises the technical manager and technical experts knowledgeable in each area of the solution. The technical team is responsible for developing a technically compliant solution and documenting the solution in the technical volume. If a live test demonstration is required, many of the technical team members will assume positions on the LTD team. The technical team also works with other proposal teams, such as the business or contracts team, to provide the most cost-effective solution to the government. The technical team conducts the following tasks for each solution component:

- Reviews the government's requirements and develops a preliminary solution based on the draft RFP
- Determines suppliers for each component and evaluates proposals from potential vendors to assess technical compliance
- Develops the technical solution that best meets the customer's requirements
- Develops technical section outlines and writes about the technical solution in the proposal
- Determines if all the components of the technical solution will work together
- Incorporates comments of the review team as appropriate
- Works with the business team to ensure technical solution is properly costed
- Works with the contracts and management teams to assess potential risks
- Helps identify components of the competitors' solutions
- Helps prepare for management and government briefings or demonstrations
- Answers any clarification or deficiency reports the government may issue on a section
- Makes technical changes to the proposal, if deemed appropriate
- Assists in vendor negotiations for any product or service relevant to technical area
- Assists in developing strategies to reduce costs for the technical solution at the time of best and final offer

Live Test Demonstration Team

The live test demonstration (LTD) team is made up of the LTD manager, demonstration developers, presenters, and support personnel.

LTD Manager

The LTD manager may be the same person who was selected as the technical manager or may be a different person. The technical manager, having the responsibility to develop and document the solution, is in the best position to assume the LTD manager function of demonstrating a compliant technical solution. However, depending on the due dates for the technical proposal and the LTD, the technical manager may be unable to accomplish both tasks, so a LTD manager would need to be added to the team. The LTD manager:

- Manages the LTD team
- Understands the technical solution being offered by the team
- Understands the government requirements for the technical solution and the LTD
- Prepares any LTD plans required by the RFP
- Conducts any solution demonstrations or benchmarks
- Secures equipment, software, and resources to illustrate solution features

Demonstration Developers

The demonstration developers conduct all the preparation work for the LTD. Specifically, the demonstration developers:

- Understand how each component of the solution meets the RFP requirements
- Determine what components of the solution should be demonstrated
- Prepare the solution for presentation
- Ensure all solution components are integrated

Demonstration Presenters

The demonstration presenters include many of the demonstration developers who will present the actual solution and others who will make presentations at the demonstration, such as corporate executives or technologists who may give overview presentations. The demonstration presenters:

- Understand the solution that is being proposed
- Understand the solution features and benefits
- Develop scripts for the presentation
- Develop any handouts or materials that will be provided to the evaluators
- Present their portion of the LTD and are prepared to answer any questions from the evaluators

Business Team

The business team comprises the business manager and cost/price analysts. The business team works with vendors to secure best available pricing and develops the price volume of the proposal. Specifically, the business team:

- Develops the cost proposal
- Works with the business manager to collect and document costs
- Builds financial models based on costs provided from vendors to get an accurate total life-cycle cost for each CLIN
- Ensures that quotes from vendors are for the same things so that accurate comparisons are made
- Evaluates cost proposals from potential vendors
- Assists in management reviews and incorporates comments, as appropriate
- Ensures cost-estimating techniques are applied in a consistent fashion for each price proposal component
- Finalizes business solution, including pricing strategies
- Ensures vendor products used in the technical solution are costed in the business solution
- Ensures vendor quotes match what is in the cost model
- Works with the legal and management teams to assess potential risks and attribute a potential dollar value to that risk
- Manages changes to the cost proposal and answers any clarification or deficiency reports the government may issue on the cost section

- Assists in vendor negotiations
- Assists in developing strategies to reduce costs for BAFO
- Manages the bid and proposal (B&P) budget
- Develops financial outlook to determine when the contract will become profitable
- Documents pricing assumptions and relevant data for audits

Management Team

The management team comprises the management volume manager and other analysts. The team develops and documents the program management solution. The type of people needed for the management volume depends on the specific RFP requirements. For example, if the RFP requires a description of the training approach, the team will need a training specialist to develop the section. The management team:

- Reviews the government's requirements
- Reviews existing management approaches to determine if they are applicable to the current RFP requirements
- Develops the approach of how the contract will run after award and ensures the solution meets the government requirements and program cost objectives
- Determines suppliers for each management solution component and evaluates proposals from potential vendors to assess compliance
- Develops any necessary procedures or processes needed for managing the contract after award, such as user training, order processing, or management reporting
- Determines corporate experience citations that demonstrate the company's capabilities
- Determines people to meet personnel requirements and provides resumes, if necessary
- Develops management section outlines and writes about each functional area in the proposal
- Incorporates review team comments, as appropriate
- Finalizes management solution
- Ensures products used in the management solution will work, as required

- Determines if all the components of the management and technical solutions will work together
- Works with the business team to ensure management solution is properly costed
- Works with legal and management teams to assess potential risks by understanding the RFP clauses
- Helps determine what each competitor's solution will be for the management section
- Helps prepare for management and government briefings or demonstrations
- Answers any clarification or deficiency reports the government may issue
- Assists in vendor negotiations for any product or service required in the management volume
- Assists in developing strategies to reduce costs for the management volume at the time of best and final offer

Contracts, Audit, and Purchasing Team

This team contains several different functional areas (audit, contracts, and purchasing) that must work closely together to ensure the company protects itself contractually in its relationship with the government, passes government audits, and enters into mutually agreeable subcontracts with suppliers. This team is also responsible for developing the contracts volume.

Government Regulation Compliance Representative

The government regulation compliance representative or audit representative helps to ensure that the company passes any government-initiated audit. Because the audits are varied, this person:

- Helps ensure Contractor Purchasing System Review (CPSR) requirements are addressed
- Validates that the proposal team is doing everything according to regulation
- Helps the proposal team prepare for audits
- Insists on getting dated, written quotes from vendors
- Drives the solicitation process
- Drives the CPSR and other audit documentation efforts

Contracts Representative

The contracts representative is primarily responsible for developing the contracts volume of the proposal. In addition, the contracts representative:

- Interfaces with the government CO to resolve contractual issues
- Works with the proposal team to develop solutions for issues
- Reviews the government's requirements
- Acts as the subject expert for contractual issues arising during contract pursuit and performance
- Develops the approach for how the contract will run after award with regard to contractual issues
- Ensures the solution meets the specific government requirements
- Develops solicitation package components
- Evaluates vendor proposals to assess risk areas
- Collects representations and certifications from vendors
- Reviews proposal to determine effect of commitments made
- Works with the business team to ensure management solution is properly costed according to government regulations
- Works with proposal management to assess potential risks
- Attends all government conferences, visits, and demonstrations
- Answers any clarification or deficiency reports the government may issue on the contract volume
- Ensures that changes to technical requirements or price-affecting terms are sent to vendors
- Assists in developing strategies to reduce costs at the time of best and final offer
- Negotiates the prime contract with the government
- Negotiates subcontracts with vendors/partners
- Understands licensing requirements, maintenance options, and other requirements that affect costs

Purchasing Representative

The purchasing representative helps the team identify suppliers for the goods and services required on the contract. Specifically, the purchasing representative:

- Helps ensure adequate competition for components being provided by outside vendors
- Maintains vendor contacts
- Helps identify product sources
- Assists in solicitation process
- Helps document the purchasing process for CPSR purposes

Sample Source Selection Plan

[Date]

I. Objective

The objective of this source selection plan is to procure (a) [product/service] to satisfy the [name of customer's] requirement for [what customer wants to obtain] for the [name of contract] contract.

II. Type of Procurement

[Name of buyer] intends to run a [type of procurement] for the required [product or service]. [Name of buyer] intends to make (an) award(s) to the responsive, responsible seller(s) whose proposal is deemed to be in the best interest of [name of buyer] and its customer based on the factors described in this document.

The RFP package includes the technical specifications, mandatory terms and conditions, the subcontract, the current installation schedule, price proposal format, and other miscellaneous information. Sellers will be requested to provide the technical proposal, a subcontract with any exceptions marked, and a price proposal.

Sellers [may/may not] submit alternative proposals.

III. Requirement

[This section contains a description of how the requirement was developed. For example, it will let you know if the requirement was due to a customer request, replacement of an existing product, or upgrade of an existing product. The technical requirements are also briefly summarized. The actual technical requirements provided to the sellers along with the rest of the RFP is included as an attachment to the source selection plan.]

IV. Minimum Acceptable Requirements

Proposals will be reviewed and evaluated against the technical requirements stated in the RFP document and found in the Appendix.

[The buyer can either state that the failure to meet all the technical requirements will result in the elimination of a seller from the competitive range or allow the seller to propose the best available solution. Minimum acceptable requirements are described in this section.]

V. Clause Authorizing Change

[This section describes the prime contract clause that allows the change to take place. Examples include substituting a product or a service because it was discontinued, adding a customer requested product or service, providing a new capability under the contract, upgrading technology, or revised requirements.]

VI. Competitive Range Determination

[This section lists the terms and conditions of the contract. If the seller fails to meet any of the following terms and conditions, it will be eliminated from the competitive range. Sample terms and conditions include:

- Failure to propose correct contract type
- Compatibility with other equipment
- Failure to perform at contract location
- Failure to meet delivery schedule
- Maintenance response time
- Performance or reliability history provided on products
- Environmental issues
- Technical risk
- Cost risk
- Inability to perform]

VII. Implementation Schedule

The planned implementation schedule is as follows:

[Event Date]

[Sample schedule follows:]

- RFP sent to sellers 5/18
- Questions due 5/25
- Proposals due 6/4
- Technical evaluation 6/18
- Subcontract negotiations 6/4–6/18
- Price evaluation 6/18
- Source selection 6/21

- Proposal to the customer 7/8
- Award 7/30

VIII. Evaluation Team

The following individuals will participate on the evaluation team:

[Sample team follows:]

- Mary Smith, Business Manager
- Ted Jones, Marketing
- Susan Bell, Pricing
- Beth Howard, Technical
- Harry Dean, Contracts

The team shall evaluate the proposals submitted in response to the RFP, prepare a written report identifying the major strengths and weaknesses of the various proposals, and recommend to the program manager, if appropriate, the award of one or more subcontracts.

IX. Evaluation Criteria

- Attachment 1: RFP Document

Sample Letter Proposal

Date
[Company to which proposal is being made]
[Company address]
Attention:
Subject:

Reference Documents:

Dear _____,

As requested, attached are the upgrade prices for [name of contract]. This proposal is made in accordance with the terms and conditions of the referenced subcontract.

Below is a description of the technical merits of this upgrade:

- [list technical merits]
-
-
-

The proposed prices are valid through [date].

Please feel free to contact [company representative] at [phone number].

Sincerely,

[Company Representative]

[Title]

Enclosures:

Technical Description

Prices

Sample Subcontract

[**Note:** This sample subcontract illustrates the parts of a subcontract. Your subcontract will vary based on the terms and conditions of your particular prime contract.]

Witnesseth

This agreement, including all attached appendices, is entered into on [Date in which the subcontract was signed] between [Company A], a [State in which Company A is incorporated in] corporation, and [Company B], a [State in which Company B is incorporated in] corporation. [Company A] is the seller and [Company B] is the buyer.

Whereas, Buyer has been awarded one or more [type of contract] with [Customer]; and

Whereas, Buyer desires to have the right to purchase products and services from the Seller for resale to these customers; and

Whereas, Seller is willing to provide products and services to Buyer according to the terms and conditions set forth in this Subcontract;

Therefore, in consideration of these promises, and other good and valuable consideration received and to be received, Seller and Buyer hereby agree to the following terms and conditions:

Article 1. Definitions, Agreement, and Term

1.1 *Definitions.* Definitions that apply to this Subcontract are listed in Appendix 2 and are hereby incorporated by reference.

1.2 *Agreement.* This agreement shall apply to Seller's provisions of products and services to Buyer for resale to the customer.

1.3 *Term.* The term shall commence on the effective date and end when the selling and/or maintenance and warranty periods of the contract cited in the appendices to this subcontract have all expired, all purchase orders in support of this customer contract have been processed, and products included in those purchase orders have been shipped and accepted.

Article 2. Purchase Orders

2.1 *Issuance and Acceptance of Purchase Orders.* The following terms and conditions govern issuance and acceptance of purchase orders under this subcontract.

2.1.a Buyer may issue to Seller written purchase orders that identify products and services Buyer desires to obtain from Seller at the prices specified in the appendices to this agreement.

2.1.b Seller shall accept purchase orders that do no establish new or conflicting terms and conditions from those set forth in this subcontract by providing Buyer acceptance or by beginning performance related to the purchase orders. Seller may only reject a purchase order within three (3) days of purchase order receipt.

2.1.c Buyer shall have no responsibility or liability for products or services provided without a purchase order.

2.2 *Cancellation of Purchase Orders.* Buyer may cancel any purchase order, or any portion thereof, without charge or penalty up to fifteen (15) days prior to shipping date of the products, or at any time prior to commencement of Seller's performance of services specified on the purchase order.

Article 3. Provision of Products and Services

3.1 *Transportation of Products.* Seller shall coordinate delivery of products to Buyer on the required delivery date set forth in a purchase order. Buyer may use its approved shippers for transportation. If Buyer shippers are not used, Buyer shall reimburse Seller for reasonable charges for transportation of the products including insurance but not including surcharges or additional expenses due to Seller's failure to allow sufficient time for transportation. Buyer shall also pay required unpacking or placement charges. Seller agrees to work with Buyer to minimize transportation costs for products shipped under the provisions of this section.

3.2 *Title and Risk of Loss.* Title to products delivered to Buyer, for re-sale/transfer to end users, shall pass to Buyer upon delivery. Supplier agrees to concurrently assist Buyer to process claims for such loss or damage and to expedite replacement of lost or damaged products.

3.3 *Right to Cancel for Delays.* If delivery of products or performance of services is unreasonably delayed and not excused by Buyer, Buyer may cancel all or any portion of products and services for which delivery has been so delayed. Buyer shall receive a full refund of any payments made to Seller for

such canceled or returned products and services within thirty
(30) days of cancellation or return.

3.4 *Product Deferral.* Buyer has the right to defer product shipment for no more than thirty (30) days from the scheduled
shipping date, provided written notice is received by Server
at least fifteen (15) days before the originally scheduled shipping date.

Article 4. Product Provisions

4.1 *Acceptance.* Buyer will accept the products upon visual inspection that all components have been delivered.

4.2 *Non-Conforming Products.* If the products do not perform in
accordance with Appendix 3, Statement of Work, Buyer will
either request new products or terminate contract.

4.3 *Documentation.* Seller shall ship with each product, at no
additional charge, one set of documentation describing how
to install the product and troubleshoot potential problem
areas.

Article 5. Maintenance Provisions

5.1 Seller shall provide Buyer with detailed instructions on how
the product should be maintained to prevent possible mis-
use.

5.2 If Buyer decides to procure maintenance services from Seller,
Buyer will assume transportation costs associated with delivering product back to the Seller for repair. Seller shall either
satisfactorily fix the product or replace the product. Seller
will assume transportation costs associated with returning
product back to the Buyer.

Article 6. Payments to Seller

6.1 *Payment.* Any undisputed sum due to the Seller under this
subcontract shall be payable within thirty (30) days after
shipment from the supplier. Amounts due will be calculated
based on the prices stipulated in Appendix 4.

6.2 *Invoice.* An invoice must contain the following information:
Seller's name, invoice date, purchase order number, description and price of product delivered or service rendered, credits applicable, name and address of person to whom payment
should be sent, and any supporting documentation.

Article 7. Product/System Changes

7.1   *Changes to Product.* Seller shall notify Buyer of any discontinuance or desired change, substitution, or addition to products a minimum of [number of days] before the effective date of such discontinuance or change. Notification shall be made to contract administrator of Seller organization at the mailing address, fax number, or e-mail address listed in this subcontract under the "Notices" section. Seller will deliver a discontinued product to Buyer for a period of [number of days] after the effective date of such discontinuance or change.

7.2   *Product Upgrades.* Seller shall submit proposals for upgrades to products to Buyer at a commercially reasonable period after commercial availability. Upgrades must be addressed in a proposal.

7.3   *Competitiveness.* Seller understands that maintaining competitiveness, in both technology and price, of its products and services with those of its competitors' products and services that are of the same type is necessary for Buyer to continue purchasing these products and services to support its customer.

7.4   *Standards Compliance.* Seller warrants that products will be in compliance with applicable specifications as listed in Appendix 3.

Article 8. Warranties, Indemnities, and Liabilities

8.1   *Warranty.* Seller warrants that products purchased under this subcontract will be free from defects in material and workmanship for a period of [number of days] from shipping date. During the warranty period, Seller will make all necessary adjustments and repairs and replace parts free of charge provided Buyer has given Seller immediate written notice of such defect within the warranty period and that the product is returned to the Seller in a manner described in this subcontract.

8.2   *Return Product Authorization.* In all cases where a product is returned to Seller, Buyer shall call and obtain an authorization number from the Seller. Seller agrees to send replacement part(s) or product(s) that same business day for requests received by Seller prior to [time].

8.3 *General Indemnification.* Buyer agrees to indemnify, defend, and save harmless Seller, its officers, agents, and employees from any and all claims and losses of personal injury, including death, and damage to tangible personal property resulting from negligent acts or omissions of Buyer, its employees, or agents during the performance of this subcontract.

Seller agrees to indemnify, defend, and save harmless Buyer, its officers, agents, and employees from any and all claims and losses of personal injury, including death, and damage to tangible personal property resulting from negligent acts or omissions of Seller, its employees, or agents during the performance of this subcontract.

Article 9. Limitation of Liability

9.4 *Limitation of Liability.* Notwithstanding anything else herein, all liability of Seller under this agreement or otherwise shall be limited to the money paid to the Seller under this agreement during the [length of time] preceding the event or circumstances giving rise to such liability or [amount of money], whichever is greater.

9.5 *Survivability.* The provisions of this article shall survive the term or termination of this subcontract for any agreement.

Article 10. Consequential Damages

10.1 *Consequential Damages.* Neither Buyer nor Seller shall be liable for any incidental or consequential damages, lost profits, or lost data, or any other indirect damages, even if supplier has been informed of the possibility thereof.

Article 11. Termination

11.1 *Termination of Customer Contract.* Notwithstanding any other provision of this subcontract to the contrary, this subcontract may be terminated in whole or in part by the Buyer in the event of termination, expiration, or non-renewal of the customer contract for whatever reason. Notification to Seller of such termination shall be made by telephone and confirmed in writing in accordance with the section of this subcontract entitled "Notices."

11.2 *Termination for Cause.* Buyer may, by written notice, terminate the whole or any part of this subcontract for cause in the following circumstances: (1) if Seller fails to deliver the products or to perform the services required by the subcontract within the time specified herein or any extension mutually agreed to in writing between the two parties, or (2) if Seller materially breaches any of the covenants or terms and conditions set forth in this subcontract, fails to perform any of the other provisions of this agreement, or so fails to make progress as to endanger performance of this subcontract in accordance with its terms, and in any of the circumstances under (3) does not cure such breach or failure to Buyer's reasonable satisfaction within a period of [number of days], or as otherwise specified by Buyer, after receipt of notices from Buyer specifying such breach or failure.

11.3 *Reprocurement.* In the event Seller defaults on this subcontract in whole or in part as stated above, Buyer may procure, upon such terms and in such manner as Buyer may deem appropriate, products and services similar to those so terminated.

Article 12. Disputes

12.1 *Initial Resolution by Parties.* Any claim, controversy, or dispute concerning questions of fact or law arising out of or relating to this subcontract; or to the performance by either party; or to the threatened, alleged, or actual breach thereof by either party, which is not disposed of by mutual agreement within a period of [number of days] after one party has provided written notice of the dispute to the other, shall be subject to executive-level review by the Buyer and Seller.

12.2 *Agreement Dispute.* In the event of any agreement dispute, the parties shall attempt to reach a negotiated resolution. If such a dispute remains unresolved for a period of [number of days] after one party has provided written notice of the dispute to the other, then the officers conducting the executive legal review to resolve the dispute shall be granted an additional reasonable period of time, but in no event more than [number of days] to achieve resolution. This procedure must be followed prior to the institution of any legal action.

12.3 *Attorneys' Fees.* In the event of a breach of this subcontract, the breaching party shall pay to the other party any reasonable attorneys' fees and other costs and expenses incurred by the non-breaching party in connection with the enforcement of any provisions of this subcontract. In no event will the breaching party be required to pay costs and expenses exceeding [amount of money].

Article 13. Miscellaneous

13.1 *Binding Nature, Assignment, and Subcontracting.* This subcontract shall be binding on the parties and their respective successors in interest and assigns, but neither party shall have the power to assign this agreement nor to subcontract or delegate any of its duties or obligations to be performed as set forth in this subcontract, other than monies due to become due, to any third party without the prior written consent of the other party, which consent shall not be unreasonably withheld. Consent to an assignment or a subcontract shall not relieve the assigning party of full responsibility for complete performance of all of its obligations set forth in this subcontract or in such purchase orders and such assigning party shall remain responsible for any assignee's or subcontractor's compliance with the non-disclosure and confidentiality provisions set forth in this agreement.

13.2 *Notices.* All notices, orders, directives, or other written communications required or permitted to be given or sent pursuant to this subcontract shall be deemed issued if mailed first class, sent by fax, or e-mailed, and if addressed as follows:

In case of Buyer: [Contact information]

In case of Seller: [Contact information]

Either party may, by a notice given in accordance with the above, change its address or designated recipient for notices. Any notice given as aforesaid shall be deemed to have been received on the date of the overnight mail receipt, on the date imprinted by the fax machine or on the date that the electronic message was sent, or [number of days] after deposit in the mail, whichever is applicable, unless the addressee party is able to establish conclusively that such notice was not received by it.

13.3 *Severability.* If, but only to the extent that, any provision of this subcontract is declared or found illegal, unenforceable, or void, then both parties shall be relieved of all obligations arising under such provision, it being the intent and agreement of the parties that this subcontract shall be deemed amended by modifying such provision to the extent necessary to make it legal and enforceable while preserving its intent. If that is not possible, another provision that is legal and enforceable and achieve the same objective shall be substituted. If the remainder of this subcontract is not affected by such declaration or finding and is capable of substantial performance, then the remainder shall be enforced to the extent permitted by law.

13.4 *Entire Agreement.* This subcontract, including any appendices and each purchase order, each of which is incorporated herein, constitutes the entire and exclusive statement of the agreement between the parties with respect to its subject matter, and there are no oral or written representations, understandings, or agreements relating to this subcontract which are not fully expressed herein.

13.5 *Governing Law.* This subcontract shall be construed in accordance with the laws of the State of [State].

In witness whereof, [name of Buyer] and [name of Seller] have each caused this subcontract to be signed and delivered by its duly authorized officer or representative as of the effective date.

[Name of Buyer]

[Authorized Representative, Signature]

[Authorized Representative, Printed Name]

[Title]

[Date]

[Name of Seller]

[Authorized Representative, Signature]

[Authorized Representative, Printed Name]

[Title]

[Date]

List of Appendices

Appendix 1: Business Code of Conduct

Appendix 2: List of Definitions

Appendix 3: Statement of Work

Appendix 4: List of Prices

INDEX

HARCOURT BRACE SOFTWARE LICENSE AGREEMENT

READ THE TERMS AND CONDITIONS OF THIS LICENSE AGREEMENT CAREFULLY BEFORE INSTALLING THE SOFTWARE (THE "PROGRAM") TO ACCOMPANY THE 2000 SUBCONTRACT MANAGEMENT MANUAL (THE "BOOK"). THE PROGRAM IS COPYRIGHTED AND LICENSED (NOT SOLD). BY INSTALLING THE PROGRAM, YOU ARE ACCEPTING AND AGREEING TO THE TERMS OF THIS LICENSE AGREEMENT. IF YOU ARE NOT WILLING TO BE BOUND BY THE TERMS OF THIS LICENSE AGREEMENT, YOU SHOULD PROMPTLY RETURN THE PACKAGE IN RESELLABLE CONDITION AND YOU WILL RECEIVE A REFUND OF YOUR MONEY. THIS LICENSE AGREEMENT REPRESENTS THE ENTIRE AGREEMENT CONCERNING THE PROGRAM BETWEEN YOU AND HARCOURT BRACE & COMPANY (REFERRED TO AS "LICENSOR"), AND IT SUPERSEDES ANY PRIOR PROPOSAL, REPRESENTATION, OR UNDERSTANDING BETWEEN THE PARTIES.

1. License Grant. Licensor hereby grants to you, and you accept, a nonexclusive license to use the Program CD-ROM and the computer programs contained therein in machine-readable, object code form only (collectively referred to as the "Software"), and the accompanying User Documentation, only as authorized in this License Agreement. The Software may be used only on a single computer owned, leased, or otherwise controlled by you; or in the event of the inoperability of that computer, on a backup computer selected by you. Neither concurrent use on two or more computers nor use in a local area network or other network is permitted without separate authorization and the possible payment of other license fees. You agree that you will not assign, sublease, transfer, pledge, lease, rent, or share your rights under the License Agreement. You agree that you may not reverse engineer, decompile dissemble, or otherwise adapt, modify, or translate the Software.

Upon loading the Software into your computer, you may retain the Program CD-ROM for backup purposes. In addition, you may make one copy of the Software on a set of diskettes (or other storage medium) for the purpose of backup in the event the Program Diskettes are damaged or destroyed. You may make one copy of any additional User Documentation (such as the README.TXT file or the "About the Computer Disc" section of the Book) for backup purposes. Any such copies of the Software or the User Documentation shall include Licensor's copyright and other proprietary notices. Except as authorized under this paragraph, no copies of the program or any portions thereof may be made by you or any person under your authority or control.

2. Licensor's Rights. You acknowledge and agree that the Software and the User Documentation are proprietary products of Licensor protected under U.S. copyright law. You further acknowledge and agree that all right, title, and interest in and to the Program, including associated intellectual property rights, are and shall remain with Licensor. This License Agreement does not convey to you an interest in or to the Program, including associated intellectual property rights, are and shall remain with Licensor. This License Agreement does not convey to you an interest in or to the Program, but only a limited right of use revocable in accordance with the terms of the License Agreement.

3. License Fees. The license fees paid by you are paid in consideration of the licenses granted under this License Agreement.

4. Term. This License Agreement is effective upon your installing this software and shall continue until terminated. You may terminate this License Agreement at any time by returning the Program and all copies thereof and extracts therefrom to Licensor. Licensor may terminate this License Agreement upon the breach by you of any term hereof. Upon such termination by Licensor, you agree to return to Licensor the Program and all copies and portions thereof.

5. Limited Warranty. Licensor warrants, for our benefit alone, for a period of 90 days from the date of commencement of this License Agreement (referred to as the "Warranty Period") that the Program CD-ROM in which the Software is contained is free from defects in material and workmanship. If during the Warranty Period, a defect appears in the Program diskettes, you may return the Program to Licensor for either replacement or, at Licensor's option, refund of amounts paid by you under this License Agreement. You agree that the foregoing constitutes your sole and exclusive remedy for breach by Licensor of any warranties made under this Agreement. EXCEPT FOR THE WARRANTIES SET FORTH ABOVE, THE PROGRAM, AND THE SOFTWARE CONTAINED THEREIN, ARE LICENSED "AS IS," AND LICENSOR DISCLAIMS ANY AND ALL OTHER WARRANTIES, WHETHER EXPRESS OR IMPLIED, INCLUDING, WITHOUT LIMITATION, ANY IMPLIED WARRANTIES OF MERCHANTABILITY OR FITNESS FOR A PARTICULAR PURPOSE.

6. Limitation of Liability. Licensor's cumulative liability to you or any other party for any loss or damages resulting from any claims, demands, or actions arising out of or relating to this Agreement shall not exceed the license free paid to Licensor for the use of the Program. IN NO EVENT SHALL LICENSOR BE LIABLE FOR ANY INDIRECT, INCIDENTAL, CONSEQUENTIAL, SPECIAL, OR EXEMPLARY DAMAGES (INCLUDING, BUT NOT LIMITED TO, LOSS OF DATA, BUSINESS INTERRUPTION, OR LOST PROFITS) EVEN IF LICENSOR HAS BEEN ADVISED OF THE POSSIBILITY OF SUCH DAMAGES.

7. Miscellaneous. This License Agreement shall be construed and governed in accordance with the laws of the State of California. Should any term of this License Agreement be declared void or unenforceable by any court of competent jurisdiction, such declaration shall have no effect on the remaining terms hereof. The failure of either party to enforce any rights granted hereunder or to take action against the other party in the event of any breach hereunder shall not be deemed a waiver by that party as to subsequent enforcement of rights or subsequent actions in the event of future breaches.